Franz Kafka

THE OFFICE WRITINGS

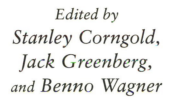

Edited by
Stanley Corngold,
Jack Greenberg,
and Benno Wagner

Translations by
Eric Patton with
Ruth Hein

PRINCETON UNIVERSITY PRESS

PRINCETON AND OXFORD

Library of Congress Cataloging-in-Publication Data

Kafka, Franz, 1883–1924.

[Selections. English. 2009]

Franz Kafka : the office writings / edited by Stanley Corngold, Jack Greenberg, and Benno Wagner ; translations by Eric Patton with Ruth Hein.

p.   cm.

Includes bibliographical references and index.

ISBN 978-0-691-12680-7 (cloth : alk. paper)

1. Kafka, Franz,1883–1924—Translations into English.   2. Kafka, Franz, 1883–1924—Career in insurance.   3. Kafka, Franz, 1883–1924—Knowledge—Law. I. Corngold, Stanley.   II. Greenberg, Jack.   III. Wagner, Benno, 1958–   IV. Title.

PT2621.A26A2 2009

838'.91208—dc22   2008025192

British Library Cataloging-in-Publication Data is available

This book has been composed in Sabon

Printed on acid-free paper. ∞

press.princeton.edu

Printed in the United States of America

1 3 5 7 9 10 8 6 4 2

CONTENTS

PREFACE

In the years 1908–1922 Franz Kafka, a Doctor of Laws, rose to a high-ranking position (*Obersekretär*) at the Workmen's Accident Insurance Institute for the Kingdom of Bohemia in Prague (called, after 1918, the Workmen's Accident Insurance Institute for the Czech Lands). During the war years he was its virtual CEO. Kafka was not a "little clerk," as were Italo Svevo and Fernando Pessoa.[1] He was a significant innovator of modern social and legal reform in the Crown Land of Bohemia, "the Manchester of the Empire"—one of the most highly developed industrial areas of continental Europe. Much of Kafka's greatness as an analyst of modern life—of the fusion of bureaucracy and technology as its governing principle—is owed to his office job. Kafka worked at the turbulent intersection of the new legal, social, political, technical, and publicistic developments that constitute industrial modernity.[2]

The Prague Workmen's Accident Insurance Institute was one of seven Austro-Hungarian Imperial institutes with wide geographical responsibilities. That meant, according to the un-German logic of the Austrian system of workmen's compensation, that Kafka was responsible, with his staff and his superiors, for setting and obtaining the premiums for every sort of industrial enterprise in the whole of this provincial sector—including, for example, farms, quarries, toy manufacturers, automobiles (thought of as "firms"), and boarding-house proprietors who had installed elevators. Time after time, this brilliant young lawyer was called upon to defend his institute against the subterfuges of employers who resisted their assigned risk classification. At the same time, he was charged with bringing about improvements in accident prevention, with public relations (speech writing, journal articles), and then, during the war, with propaganda campaigns for the improved medical treatment of wounded veterans. All these efforts had to be achieved under adverse conditions: the unwritten law of the time restricted the public-service careers of Jewish citizens of the Empire. Kafka's letters to the directors of his institute indicate how much his responsibilities exceeded his rank and pay.

Considering the range of his functions, Kafka was no Bartleby the Scrivener, no put-upon office furniture. In certain respects, he was more like the American poet Wallace Stevens, also a lawyer and high-ranking officer of a large accident and indemnity agency.[3] This point matters enormously for our sense of the conditions under which Kafka accomplished his nocturnal writing. He wrote his prose poetry, not after a day's restful-restive finger exercises at an anonymous office but typically after writing or dictating briefs of considerable intricacy and social importance.[4] Many lives and livelihoods depended on Kafka's success in introducing such safety measures as *cylindrical* lathe shafts less inclined to chop off workers' fingers and prohibiting brandy drinking and pipe smoking in the immediate vicinity of dynamite sheds in quarries, let alone continuing to bring in accident insurance premiums from recalcitrant and chicaning employers. It is well known, for example, that the ending of Kafka's most famous story, *The Metamorphosis,* was, to his mind, ruined by the "business trip" he had to take while in the throes of composition. Less well known is the fact that the purpose of this business trip was to present a complex legal defense, which he won, obtaining a solid judgment for the Institute (LF 69).[5]

Kafka often complained about his immersion in the phantasmagoric hell of office life. In 1913, he wrote to his fiancée, Felice Bauer, that "writing and office cannot be reconciled, since writing has its center of gravity in depth, whereas the office is on the surface of life. So it goes up and down, and one is bound to be torn asunder in the process" (LF 279). But without meaning to downplay the tension involved—at his two different desks, Kafka was responding to different demands—we propose to see his literary work as striving to accomplish their "reconciliation." Kafka's office writings are an integral part of his literary oeuvre. His later writings especially point to a growing awareness of his debt to the office as a conduit of contemporary experience—and hence as an indispensable basis for the dreamlike transmutations of his art. Not every basis would have served, not every day's residue would have produced dream images with the power to rouse us a century later. Kafka's daily job routine provided him with a trove of themes and images—and something more fundamental: *a mode of being.* Late in life he noted the "*Steigerungen* [the taking of things to a higher level] of which the bureaucracy is capable, the necessary, inevitable *Steigerungen* [also: enhancements, 'evolutions'], springing straight out of the origins of human nature, to which, measured by my case, the bureaucracy is closer than any other social institution" (L 328–29).[6] And so, despite his protracted clamoring about the office as a dreadful obstacle to his creativity ("the office is a horror," LF 21), the impact of his office writings on his stories and novels should not be underestimated. Kafka's insurance and publicistic documents reveal that Kafka the author borrowed strategies from Kafka the legal secretary, just as Kafka the legal secretary borrowed strategies from Kafka the author.

Here, in a concrete, material sense, we see Kafka "before the law," to cite the title of his most famous and most austere parable, "Before the

Law," which reappears in the penultimate chapter of *The Trial*. There, the protagonist, one Joseph K—a high-ranking bank official—feels obliged to produce the correct interpretation of the parable so titled and cannot; it is the last test in his trial, in which the proceedings (including his own conduct) pass imperceptibly into the verdict. K fails the test and is then stabbed to death on a loose stone in a quarry. This is the rather fraught mood of our project, as we struggle to redeem Kafka's Imperial Austrian legal and publicistic documents as so many parables.

Kafka "*Before* the Law": the philosopher Jacques Derrida has developed this "before" in a predictably original way.[7] The preposition "before" can suggest both a spatial position—standing in front of (and not passing through) the gates of the law—as well as a temporal hiatus: we always come *before* the law, we are not yet ready for the law, the law will come (to mind or body) only when we are done for. But for the editors of this volume, "before" can also mean "confronted by," and in Kafka's case, it refers to the fact that for these crucial fifteen years, including the years of world war, he was confronted daily by the demands of an ever-changing, ever-adapting Austro-Hungarian Imperial Insurance law. (Kafka had sought to enlist, presumably preferring to be exploded at the front rather than suffering a brain explosion behind the lines: he thought he was going mad from the office; from the struggle for and against Felice Bauer, his fiancée; and from the demands of his real fate—literature. He was accepted for service but deferred on grounds of his indispensability to the home front, to the Institute.) On Czeslaw Miloscz's example, Kafka is "the secretary of the invisible." That is true, but for us he is just as centrally the Chief Legal Secretary of the Workmen's Accident Insurance Institute for the Kingdom of Bohemia in Prague.

This volume of Kafka's office writings includes the first translations in any language of Kafka's more interesting legal briefs, together with commentaries that aim to situate these papers in the history of Austrian workmen's compensation insurance at the beginning of the new twentieth-century technology-saturated state. But as a literary study that means to be exemplary, there is something more at stake. We want to highlight themes, images, and ideas as they flow back and forth between the documents and Kafka's fiction; in doing so, however, we are confronted with the question of method—of the rightness of carrying over pieces of the socioeconomic base of a writer's life into his literary constructions. But in this case, the "base" consists of *texts written* by Franz Kafka. Stanley Corngold's introductory essay deals closely with this question of method. But this matter would not have arisen if it were not for a certain cadence of thought in the office writings that immediately urged us to begin the exercise: you cannot fail to hear Kafkaesque overtones.

Themes and topics from his office writings are audible in Kafka's novels and stories. The somewhat arbitrary-seeming profession of the hero of *The Castle* (1922)—he is a (self-appointed) land surveyor—repeats the profession of land surveyor that appears in Kafka's early writings on the industrial hazards of farm machinery, where precise findings as to acreage are as crucial as they are elusive. Material *associations* (not *repetitions*) are abundant in topics based on partial resemblance or contiguity: the habitat of the badgerlike animal of "The Burrow" can be associated with the trenches of the combatants in the World War—a resemblance that can have entered Kafka's mind through his broodings, as an advocate of psychiatric hospitals, on the traumas suffered by wounded veterans.[8] (Few know that Kafka was a vigorous advocate of such hospitals and saw the ideal site for one, bemusingly, in the provincial Bohemian city of Frankenstein). But more interesting are recurrent types of logic and rhetoric.

Open a document, such as one of Kafka's more accessible newspaper essays in the *Tetschen-Bodenbacher Zeitung* of 1911 titled "Workmen's Insurance and the Employers," almost at random. Keeping in mind that Kafka's institute taxed companies for back premiums for workmen's insurance, you will hear Kafkaesque echoes in this disclaimer:

> Of course, at the same time we must make certain that the honest endeavor toward redress and reorganization does not turn into pure budgetary concerns and oppressive taxation. In short, industry can welcome and promote the efforts of the Prague Institute only as long as these are aimed at forcing the dishonest employers to fulfill their obligations in order to relieve all honest employers. Any effort beyond that aimed at depriving industries of capital only to amass it sterilely in the Institute's coffers would have to be resisted with all our might.

This is a very subtle and pleasant display of consideration for the employer, the more powerful partner—the *Herren*, so to speak, in this Castle world, where incontestable power is concentrated in the hands of a class of high administrators. Kafka can argue all sides. He shifts the looming class war into a contest between *honest* employers (readers of the article will know who they are) and . . . the others. . . .

In the sequel to this article, we read:

> Now we gladly admit that until 1909, the annual reports of the Institute, with their figures documenting a deficit that seemed to spread almost like a living organism, offered little encouragement to feel excitement. Instead, these reports succeeded in damping all the Institute's hopes for the future; the Institute seemed simply to be a corpse, whose only living element was its growing deficit.

One commentator refers to the tone of gallows humor found in many of these briefs.[9] Is it unreasonable to think here of the wound in the side of the moribund boy in "A Country Doctor," that wound being—quote—"his only endowment"?

Again:

> We do not overlook and did not overlook in our earlier article [. . .] the fact that the psychological blame for the large supplementary contributions must be laid at the door of the Institute's previously completely inadequate inspections (since opportunity is the author of the evasion of contributions, as one industrialist replied in response to our first article); but the actual blame is that of the employers, and if the Institute is currently engaged in putting a stop to the earlier shortcomings, then it is the concern of the interested parties to support its efforts.

These are distinctions that would be right at home in *The Trial*. Admittedly, it is a good thing that we have read *The Trial* first; it would not be easy otherwise to draw lines directly from Kafka's newspaper essay to a virtual *Trial*, to project and construct the novel if it were not already at hand. What we are stressing now is that arguments about the passage from Kafka's office writing to literature need to be very dialectical; this passage is certainly not a matter of transposition, of Kafka's "writing up" his office thoughts, or the opposite, Kafka's willful erasure of his experience, his wings away from the harsh facts of his empirical life. In a word, we do not see Kafka's fiction as chiefly *repeating* or as *avoiding* but as transforming, creating anew with an agility and intellectual magic that emerges all the more distinctly when there is concrete evidence of what recalcitrant things, the stuff of litigation, are at its basis.

Proceeding now—dialectically—from the fiction to the office writings, consider these passages from the most politically philosophical of his works, "Building the Great Wall of China." The first passage concerns the right to question the edicts of the High Command; it is spoken by the embodied narrator, who is an administrator of very much the same rank as Kafka. The narrator discusses the intuitively odd decision by the leadership to build the Great Wall in only partial segments:

> And therefore to any unprejudiced observer the idea will be unacceptable that the leaders, if they had seriously wanted to, could not have overcome the difficulties that stood in the way of a continuous Wall construction. And so the only remaining conclusion is that the leaders purposely chose partial construction. But partial construction was only a makeshift and unsuited to its purpose. The conclusion that remains is that the leaders wanted something unsuited to their purpose. An odd conclusion, certainly. And yet in another respect there is a good deal of justification for it.

Nowadays, it may be safe to discuss such matters. In those days the secret principle held by many, even the best, was: Try with all your might to understand the decrees of the leaders, but only up to a certain point; then stop thinking about the subject. A very reasonable principle, which was further elaborated into an often repeated parable. Stop thinking about it, not because it could harm you, since it is not at all certain that it will harm you. What we have here is neither a matter of doing nor not doing harm. You will be as the river in spring. It rises, becomes more powerful, nourishes more richly the land bordering its long banks, keeps its own essence intact as it runs into the sea, and becomes more nearly equal and more welcome to the sea. Think this far about the decrees of the leadership. But then the river overflows its banks, loses its outline and its shape, slows in its downward course, tries to run counter to its destiny by forming little inland seas, damages the fields, and yet, since it cannot continue spreading itself so thin, instead runs back into its banks and in the hot season that follows even dries out dismally. Do not think this far about the decrees of the leadership. (KSS 117)

This is Kafka pulling in his revolutionary horns. Here, as in his office writings, he is a negotiator, a balancer of forces.

Here is another delectable legal-political passage from this work: the narrator comments on the inability of the citizens in the remote provinces of empire to conceive of anything like Peking and the seat of the Emperor and hence on their active skepticism about the existence of any such center:

I am on guard against generalizations, and I do not maintain that things are the same in all ten thousand villages of our province or, indeed, in all five hundred provinces of China. But still, on the basis of the many texts I have read on this subject, as well as my own observations—the building of the Wall in particular, with its wealth of human material, gave anyone of sensibility the opportunity to journey through the soul of almost all the provinces [We might characterize the enterprise of building the Wall for protection from the horse-backed tribes as "nomad insurance"—Eds.]—on the basis of all this I may perhaps be permitted to say that the dominant attitude toward the emperor again and again and everywhere exhibits certain features in common with the attitude in my homeland. Now, I have no intention of accepting this attitude as a virtue, on the contrary. And while it is mainly the fault of the regime, which in this most ancient empire on earth has always been unable, perhaps through neglect of this concern for other matters, to develop the institution of empire with such clarity that it would exercise its influence immediately and incessantly as far as the realm's most distant frontiers. On the other hand, this attitude also exhibits a weakness of imagination or conviction among the people, who are unable to embrace the empire obediently, in all its liveliness and presence, raising it from its submersion in Peking; and yet the subjects wish nothing more than just for once to feel this connection and drown in it.

Thus this attitude is unlikely to be a virtue. It is all the more striking that precisely this weakness appears to be one of the most important means of unifying our people; indeed, if one may be so forward as to employ such an expression, it is the very ground on which we live. To supply detailed reasons for a reproach here would not mean assaulting our conscience but, what is far worse, assaulting our legs.[10] And for this reason I will for the moment go no further into the investigation of this question. (KSS 122–23)

A signal, perhaps, to end this preface, but let us note how wonderfully perceptive this passage is on Kafka's part: universal skepticism concerning superior authority is the very ground of moral life. But we dare not overflow the banks of this argument.

Instead, we conclude with a final summary and elaboration of our program. In our view, the world of Kafka's writing, both literary and official, is a single institution, in which the factor of bureaucracy is ever present, for this world is informed by a continual flux of written signs—signs that circulate incessantly and are ultimately untraceable. Modern theories of bureaucracy characteristically speak of this institution as marked by a multiplication of offices (ultimately defined by their files) and of the absorption of the individual into hierarchies he does not see for the pursuit of goals he cannot know. Texts that factor in delays in the communicative loop take the place of an immediate application of main force. We are accustomed to encountering such bureaucracies in Kafka's novels and stories, *The Castle* being a prime example. Less apparent, though to our mind equally striking, is the likeness of this sort of (legal) bureaucracy to Kafka's own inner world of writing, to his sense of being an author, for which he coined the word "Schriftstellersein" (literally: "the being of a writer"; and, indeed, Kafka wrote that he was without "literary interests," being instead "made of literature") (Br 384; LF 304). This inner world is marked by the ceaseless circulation of signs arriving with more or less self-evident authority from hidden sources and possessing force, signs that are quite capable of "tearing him apart" (LF 279).

Kafka ceaselessly imagined the "house" in which this being-a-writer might be at home. The figure of the right habitation haunts his work: the search of many of his characters for personal and artistic fulfillment is depicted as the entry into an appropriate house—for example, the Gate of the Law, the Castle, the Court, a secure Burrow. It would not be wrong to grasp the kind of house that he needed for his inner world of writing as a transfigured body, a being that Kafka's continually imagined interlocutor Nietzsche called "a new and improved Nature."[11] Here we have an imaginary structure of flesh and blood corresponding to the architectonic structures of earth and stone that house real bureaucracies, but this new flesh and blood is supplied with a dimension that makes the analogy more convincing. Kafka imagined, as in the story *In the Penal Colony* and in diaries, flesh that would serve as a kind of paper, on which, in blood, crucial, life-defining sentences would be inscribed. This trope, this turn of the imagination, can have been inspired by the sort of event that daily crossed his desk and with which he would have sympathized: bodies mutilated in industrial accidents, which he was required to redeem in the form of legal decisions. Such redemptive sentences might be performed in the "house of art," which Kafka often figures as a creative body—wound and womb—and also in the house of the bureaucracy—"natural" originator of sublime "enhancements" (supra, p. x).

A plainer way of putting this relation would be to identify (a) the transfigured body, (b) literary writing, and (c) bureaucracy as neighboring modes of information management. We will be chiefly addressing the latter two. In detailed ways, certainly, the habitus of the writer differs from that of the bureaucrat. But we believe in the likeness of these worlds, owing to the permeability of the membrane between them, through which pass cogent images, strategies of (legal) argument, and Kafka's never abandoned passionate concern for justice. It is again wonderful to think of the many things that may have been in Kafka's mind when he wrote to Felice Bauer, "If there is a higher power that wishes to use me, or does use me, then I am at its mercy, if no more than as a well-prepared instrument" (LF 21).

What follows are two detailed introductory essays. The first, by Stanley Corngold, is titled "The Ministry of Writing"; it aims to create a rationale for passing from Kafka's office writings to a deeper understanding of his fictional work. It builds on the unaccustomed idea that Kafka's conception of bureaucracy in his office, confessional, and imaginative writings might shape his literary enterprise as a whole. Especially in Kafka's late masterpiece *The Castle*, we find a full literary work-up of Kafka's bureaucratic experience. Hence, the title of this introduction refers to Kafka's fate as a writer as his employment in a "ministry of writing."

The second introductory essay is by Benno Wagner and is titled "Kafka's Office Writings: Historical Background and Institutional Setting." It outlines the origin and history of real insurance law in Imperial Austria and the involvement of Kafka's institute, and Kafka himself, in this practice. It attends to individual documents as well, in order to highlight techniques of legal argument as part of the organization of knowledge within the institution or "discourse" of accident insurance: these tech-niques in turn inform Kafka's fictional work.

These introductory essays follow a wide arc of reflection, which, when read back to front, begins with the point of real intersection be-tween Kafka the lawyer and "industrialization, mechanization, and bu-reaucracy, as well as with the struggle between capital and labor . . . ," and ends with Kafka's early story " 'You,' I said . . . ," a first step in Kafka's elegant transformation of this cultural stock.

In an important "wraparound," found at the back of this volume, ti-tled "From Kafka to Kafkaesque," Jack Greenberg explores the grounds for the eye-catching frequency with which the word "Kafkaesque" is used in contemporary legal practice. To the extent that it is used with understanding, it may have its roots in the issues that Kafka encoun-tered at the workplace and their bearing on his "literary weltanschau-ung." These issues, as Greenberg shows, in crucial ways resemble many recent and contemporary social problems, especially those bearing on the fair treatment of persons of color.

Readers are invited to roam through these three introductory and summary parts of this volume in whatever sequence they might find most interesting.

Principles of Selection and Organization

The core of this book consists of a selection of Kafka's office writings. All the documents that can be attributed to him with reasonable cer-tainty can be found in a volume titled *Amtliche Schriften* (Office writ-ings) in the German Critical Edition of Kafka's works.[12] In our book, we confine ourselves to those writings that, in our view, most vividly reveal aspects of Kafka's craft as an insurance lawyer—articles and briefs with literary value that are at the same time relevant to his literary work. A short introduction to each document states reasons for its inclusion; the longer commentary following each document supplies evidence of Kaf-ka's authorship. With one exception these writings are organized by timeline. We did consider grouping the documents under rubrics (for example, documents from Kafka's personal file; newspaper and journal articles; legal briefs) but realized that there would be too many catego-ries for the relatively few documents selected. The one break in chronol-ogy occurs at the beginning, with Kafka's 1909 speech on the occasion of Dr. Robert Marschner's assuming the directorship of the Prague In-stitute. It is a brief, elegant, relaxed text. Yet this talk is *followed* by a text that Kafka wrote in *1908* on on-site insurance in the building trades. Why have we chosen this sequence?

We were concerned that readers might be put off the legal writings by the 1908 document as an augury of things to come. This document is Kafka's very first brief and seems designed to establish his credentials: it is intricate and erudite beyond telling. Of all the documents in the book, it calls for the most stringent intellectual attention. With an advance summary, various strategic cuts, and an ample commentary, we have tried to ease the difficulty and reveal straightaway many of the document's riches: it contains *in nuce* elements of Kafka's legal philosophy, which is bent on rigor and authenticity and also pragmatic success. But we still thought it best if the entrance to the book could be simplified.

The astute reader will identify another chronological mishap on finding Kafka's letters dated 1912–15 in between legal documents dated 1912 and 1913. But note that the latter text consists of a series of letters telling a single story—of Kafka's tireless efforts to earn a salary commensurate with his abilities and usefulness to the Institute. We think of them as one story, one history, one argument. It would do the story no justice to scatter parts of it throughout the volume.

A basically chronological arrangement brings to the fore the ongoing developments in Kafka's professional field, which, as we will see, bear sharply on Kafka's biography as a writer. In this light, we decided not to include documents from Kafka's last years on the job (1918–22). During that time, his tuberculosis forced him to take long leaves, and the Insurance Institute was reorganized within the new Czechoslovakian state. Traces of his professional contribution are too fragmentary and uncertain to furnish the sort of vivid connections that we want to profile.

ABBREVIATIONS FOR KAFKA CITATIONS

A   *Amerika (The Man Who Disappeared)*, trans. Michael Hofmann. New York: New Directions, 2002

BF   *Briefe an Felice*, ed. Erich Heller and Jürgen Born. Frankfurt a.M.: Fischer, 1967. See LF

Br   *Briefe, 1902–1924*, ed. Max Brod. Frankfurt a.M.: Fischer, 1958. See L

C   *The Castle*, trans. Mark Harman. New York: Schocken, 1998

CS   *Franz Kafka: The Complete Stories*, ed. Nahum N. Glatzer. New York: Schocken, 1971

DF   *Dearest Father*, trans. Ernest Kaiser and Eithne Wilkins. New York: Schocken, 1954

D1   *The Diaries of Franz Kafka, 1910–1913*, trans. Joseph Kresh. New York: Schocken, 1948

D2   *The Diaries of Franz Kafka, 1914–1923*, trans. Martin Greenberg (with the assistance of Hannah Arendt). New York: Schocken, 1949

GrW   *The Great Wall of China*, trans. Willa and Edwin Muir. New York: Schocken, 1960

H   *Hochzeitsvorbereitungen auf dem Lande und andere Prosa aus dem Nachlaß*, ed. Max Brod. Frankfurt a.M.: Fischer, 1953

KKA   *Schriften. Tagebücher. Briefe. Kritische Ausgabe der Werke von Franz Kafka*, eds. Gerhard Neumann, Jost Schillemeit, Malcolm Pasley, and Gerhard Kurz. Frankfurt a. M.: Fischer, 1982ff

KKAB 1   *Briefe 1900–1912*, ed. Hans-Gerd Koch, 1999

KKAB 2   *Briefe 1913–März 1914*, ed. Hans-Gerd Koch, 1999

KKAB 3   *Briefe April 1914–1917*, ed. Hans-Gerd Koch, 2005

KKAN 1   *Nachgelassene Schriften und Fragmente 1*, ed. Malcolm Pasley, 1990

KKAN2   *Nachgelassene Schriften und Fragmente 2*, ed. Jost Schillemeit, 1992

KSS   *Kafka's Selected Stories*, Norton Critical Edition, ed. and trans. Stanley Corngold. New York: Norton, 2007

L   *Letters to Friends, Family, and Editors*, trans. Richard and Clara Winston. New York: Schocken, 1977. See Br

LF   *Letters to Felice*, trans. James Stern and Elizabeth Duckworth. New York: Schocken, 1973. See BF

M   *The Metamorphosis*, trans. and ed. Stanley Corngold. New York: Norton, 1996

Pp   *Der Proceß, in der Fassung der Handschrift*, ed. Malcolm Pasley. Frankfurt a.M.: Fischer, 1990

T   *The Trial*, trans. Breon Mitchell. New York: Schocken, 1998

V   *Der Verschollene*, ed. Jost Schillemeit. Frankfurt a.M: Fischer, 1983

KAFKA AND THE MINISTRY OF WRITING

STANLEY CORNGOLD

∾

> For everything comes from the castle.
> —Kafka, *The Castle*

Toward the end of his life, in a tormented letter to his friend and editor Max Brod, Kafka described his writing as the product of a state of being, for which he coined the expression "Schriftsteller-sein" ("the being of a writer") (Br 384, L 333). The sense of this term unfolds from the word *sein*, which means, as Kafka wrote, "being" and also "belonging to him."[1] Kafka felt *possessed* by the being that craved to write.

This deeply rooted second nature could never become a familiar presence. It haunted Kafka as a possibility of his actual person—an inherent strangeness, stirring longing and anxiety. To come to grips with this strangeness was to come to grips with the writer in him, but what would it mean to "come to grips" with writing when writing is a "monstrosity"?

> What is it about? What is that—literature? Where does it come from? What use is it? What questionable things! Add to this questionableness the further questionableness of what you say [about it], and a monstrosity [*ein Ungeheuer*] arises. (A loose page from Kafka's notebooks, October/November 1922, KSS 212)[2]

To "deal" with this monstrosity would be to cope with the mandate that it laid on him—to write well at some unheard-of degree of proficiency or else be lost. "I can still get fleeting satisfaction from works like 'Country Doctor,' " he wrote in 1917. "But happiness only in case I can raise the world into purity, truth, immutability" (KSS 205). The stakes were as serious from the very beginning. In 1903, when he was twenty, Kafka wrote to his friend Oskar Pollak, "God doesn't want me to write, but I—I must" (L 10). To write is to consent to a pact more than merely monstrous, for this antiself—literature—can also figure as a stranger-god, an opponent god. To be bent on writing is to consent to "service to the devil" (KSS 211). Kafka rarely wavered as to the gravity of his mission, describing himself, in 1922, toward the end of his life, as

> a son incapable of marriage, who produces no carriers of the name; pensioned at 39; occupied only with an eccentric writing that aims at nothing else than the salvation or damnation of his own soul. (KSS 212)

Justifying this relation and its costs defined Kafka's sense of the ethical life.

The lure of this otherness, *Schriftstellersein*, literary being, is constitutive for Kafka: "I have no literary interests; something else: I am made of [*bestehe aus*] literature" (LF 304, BrF 444), but there is no constancy to this *Bestand*—this stock: Kafka's sense of it is complex and changing.

It is easier to say how it cannot be understood. It cannot be conceived of in relation to one sort of self-identical entity called the empirical ego, for, as Kafka writes, "What do I have in common with Jews? I have hardly anything in common with myself. . . ." (D1 11). Nor can it be conceived of in relation to a stable, self-identical otherness that could figure as the object of intellectual curiosity. For this other term "insists" in the empirical subject, though not as a guest. As an *Ungeheuer* (a monster), it is literally "infamiliaris," having no place at the family hearth. It is inside as a thing forever out(sid)ing him, exposing him as a subject while it remains inconsistent with itself, a fact that its monstrosity suggests. The writing self has *various* agencies, *various* "departments," *various* laws.[3] In Kafka's late epic *The Castle*, the figure of Klamm, the pilgrim-hero's target bureaucrat, is never seen as self-identical:

> They say he looks completely different when he comes into the village and different when he leaves it, different before he has had a beer, different afterwards, different awake, different asleep, different alone, different in a conversation, and, quite understandably after all this, almost utterly different up there at the castle. (C 176)

Klamm is the allegory of such instability.

Kafka's sense of strangeness to self is continuously displayed in various fictional appearances—in the bachelor; "the Russian friend" of *The Judgment*; the unholy, monstrous insect body; an outlandish homeland, America; the court; the burrow; "the false hands" that led him astray; the "spirits" that twist his words (KSS 212f). What threads these modalities together is the "eccentricity" of the writer's being.[4] The trajectory of Kafka's works is a history of approaches, more or less effective, to the elusive otherness of writing.

In this book about Kafka's work as a lawyer and bureaucrat, we are concerned with the way in which Kafka's sense of his fate as a writer is implicated in his work life—the way in which his *Beamtensein*, his "official" being, is involved in his *Schriftstellersein*, his writerly being. At first glance, this association could seem a poor idea—as an adversary relation, yes, but scarcely a fraternal one or one based on resemblance. The comparison suggests a demeaning of writing by its likeness to work that is merely rulebound, calling for ordinary skills of application when not inspired by a philistine detestation of intelligence.[5] And indeed, thinking so would tally with many of Kafka's complaints in his letters to his fiancée Felice Bauer and elsewhere.[6] In 1912 he wrote in his diary, "My development is now complete and, so far as I can see, there is nothing left to sacrifice; I need only throw my work in the office out of this complex in order to begin my real life" (D1 211). And yet we propose to see Kafka's fiction, and most especially his *Castle* novel, as moving toward the reconciliation of these separate activities.

A certain reconciliation is already in play in Kafka's choice of the term *Schriftstellersein* over the other words available to him: *Dichtersein* or *Autorsein*. It is quite in line with modern professional life that Kafka chooses a word whose general connotations—and certainly its etymology—lend it a disenchanted, merely technical flavor. He is not a "poet" and not an "author," both of which names are laden with an archaic, untimely authority (the poet) or autonomy (the author). The *Schriftsteller* is one who is assigned the function of setting down script in producing "literature."

We intend to show that Kafka's legal and publicistic activity shares *a mode of being* with his fictional activity, allowing him to represent the destiny of a writer in the metaphor of bureaucratic social organization. Since this figure of bureaucracy is consistent in shape and aura with the Workmen's Accident Insurance Institute for the Kingdom of Bohemia, we may, as a result, relate quite concrete skeins of thought and imagery from Kafka's legal briefs and articles to his writer's notebooks. Here we are approaching the otherness of Kafka's fictional writing through one quite particular set of Kafka's texts—the "official" set. It is a little like following the tracks that Kafka's "vice-exister," the pilgrim K, takes to the castle, which is rightly seen as a representative of the being of the writer.[7]

This attempt to enter into relation with this otherness-to-self is a solicitation of "authenticity," a word (*authentisch*) that Kafka uses in such contexts. This approach is the recurrent motive of his work. This "plot" is found at the beginning and at the end—a career that might be defined by the markers " 'You,' I said . . . ," a text of 1910, and *The Castle* of 1922.

"'You,' I said . . ." is a "story" collated by Max Brod, Kafka's editor and friend, from early diary fragments written at the time of the composition of *Description of a Struggle*. Here, a striver, a would-be bourgeois, describes his attempt to enter into personal relation with a monstrous other called, at various times, "the bachelor" (KSS 193, D1 24), "no better than some sort of vermin" (D1 23). The strangeness of this creature is pronounced: "Whether I lie here in the gutter and stow away the rainwater or drink champagne with the same lips up there under the chandelier makes no difference to me" (D1 23). In a powerful aria spoken by the "I," whose voice, at the end, coalesces with that of the bachelor:

> The bachelor has nothing ahead of him and therefore nothing behind him either. In the moment there is no difference, but the bachelor has only the moment. At that time—which no one can know today, for nothing can be so annihilated as that time—at that time he missed the mark when he constantly felt the ground of his being, the way one suddenly notices an ulcer on one's body that until that moment was the slightest thing on one's body—yes, less than the slightest, for it did not even seem to exist, and now it is more than everything else that our body has possessed since birth. If until this time our entire being was directed to the work of our hands, to whatever was seen by our eyes, heard by our ears, down to the steps of our feet, now we suddenly turn completely in the opposite direction, like a weathervane in the mountains. Now, instead of having run away at that moment, even in this latter direction—for only running away could have kept him on the tips of his toes, and only the tips of his toes could have kept him on the earth—instead of that, he lay down, as children now and then lie down in the snow in winter so as to freeze to death. (KSS 193–94)

This passage is remarkable: no details of milieu are given; no distinctions as to what went before or after "that time." An "I"-and-"he" story suddenly becomes a "we" story, involving "our entire being." What remains of a seemingly realistic narrative is only the bare bones of an idea, a structure of relationships. The bachelor has been given the exceptional opportunity of making contact with his depth, his basis (*Grund*); he can realize or fail to realize what Heidegger calls "the existential possibilities of a *Befindlichkeit*," a moodfully attuned state of mind.[8] The moment occurs as a scene of primal energy—a reorientation away from the world of perception, of experience, toward what could very well be the space-time of a burgeoning literary imagination. It would seem desirable in principle to make contact with one's basis so as to take the direction opened up by it. But the bachelor misses his chance; his "ulcer" forecasts the deformation of his opportunity.

The outcome is his ruin: the bachelor "misses the mark" by dint of "lying down." (Throughout his notebooks, Kafka scatters such myths about the origin of his writing that invariably place a negative mark on it: the movement proceeding from the origin is contaminated by a wrong motive or another's hostility, forcing the narrator to err, to turn away).

This creature who has failed to secure his "basis" figures in Kafka's early mythology of literature as a deficient mode of the writer. He is marked by a "Russian" coldness, a Russian "indifference" (D2 115)—attributes that we can begin to project toward the world of *The Castle*. The bachelor is present at the scene of the birth of a literary destiny ("we suddenly turn completely in the opposite direction") but misses this turning. And now, what amounts to a second turning takes the story onto an eccentric path. It narrates a reorientation toward a quite different dimension—that of the *higher social organization*. The new goal of the narrator is to join a society, a *Gesellschaft*, that promises a critical "organization" (*Organisierung*) of his powers—a "society" that I will mark now as the protobureaucratic social institution figuring as an object of desire:[9]

> Certainly, I stood here obstinately in front of the house but just as obstinately I hesitated to go up . . . [D1 61]. I want to leave, want to mount the steps, if necessary, by turning somersaults. From that company [*Gesellschaft*] I promise myself everything that I lack, the organization of my powers, above all, for which the sort of intensification [critical heightening: *Zuspitzung*] that is the only possibility for this bachelor on the street is insufficient. (D1 24)

Here we can again look ahead to the figure of *The Castle*'s K, who contains both these clusters of identity elements; he is the provincial, bent on acquiring possessions—a wife, a home; and he is also the frozen bachelor, cuckolded almost immediately. He too promises himself that the Castle society will provide everything he lacks, above all, the organization of his powers.[10] The bachelor's failure to run in the direction opened to him, which I have taken to represent the poetic imagination, reappears in his bourgeois double as *his* lack, requiring a fulfillment that only a "society" can supply.

The bourgeois speaker looks for refuge from the horror conveyed by "the bachelor," "some sort of a vermin," by seeking entry into a "society" lodged in a grand house among whom, one can suppose, there are high officials of a ministry in a light, celebratory mood. We encounter such persons in *The Castle*—in the figure of Momus, for one, Klamm's village secretary, "a young gentleman, extremely good-looking, pale and reddish, but very serious" (C 104), who radiates a ministerial smoothness, and, above all, in K's dream of conquest from the depths of his sleep at Bürgel's bedside when "it seemed to him as though . . . he had achieved a great victory and a society or party of persons (*Gesellschaft*) was already there to celebrate it and he or someone else was raising a champagne glass in honor of the victory" (C 264). Because, in " 'You,' I said . . . ," the speaker has the extraordinary idea that such a group will heighten and organize his talents and faculties, we must attribute to this society an unusual measure of interpersonal power, in which light it amounts to a *political* agency, if by "political" we understand institutions that, by appealing to custom and law, wear a mask of interpersonal concern, with the aim of producing, storing, and transmitting power. Crucially, however, this narrator does not go up these stairs; along with the bachelor he "freezes." So one will feel the element of menace in this higher society too: the little town palazzo rays out in equal measure both fascination and rejection. In this fragment of Kafka's deepest imagination, the figures of (1) writerly being and (2) participation in a social-political organization are brother phantasms of fear and desire, tangled together at the beginning in a poetological dream navel. At the outset of Kafka's writing career, we find the deep mutual involvement of the radically solitary, monstrous other and the sought-after protobureaucratic ministry as figures of writing.[11] And indeed, we might push back this entanglement to the earliest days, to the letter that Kafka wrote, at age twenty, to Oskar Pollak, because there the full context of Kafka's ambition reads:

> God does not want me to write—but I, I must. And so it is an eternal up and down, in the end God is the stronger party. . . . There are so many powers in me tied to a post, which might perhaps become a green tree while they are liberated and become useful to me and *to the state*. (L10, emphasis added)

In the matter of bureaucracy, Kafka may be said to know on his living body those factors profiled in part 3, chapter 6, of Max Weber's *Wirtschaft und Gesellschaft* (Economy and Society). "The management of the modern office," writes Weber,

> is based upon written documents ("the files"), which are preserved in their original or draught form. There is, therefore, a staff of subaltern officials and scribes of all sorts. The body of officials actively engaged in a "public" office, along with the respective apparatus of material implements and the

files, make up a "bureau." In private enterprise, "the bureau" is often called the "office". . . . [12]

In modern capitalist society, the institution of the office, for Weber and most decisively for Kafka, is ubiquitous and uncanny, "the admired adversary, spreading inexorably into every department of life."[13] We are at a stage, as Cornelius Castoriadis notes, where "bureaucratization (i.e. the management of activity by hierarchized apparatuses) becomes the very logic of society, its response to everything."[14] The omnipresence of files arises from a continuous amassing of data—rules, procedures, matters of fact—in the service of instrumental logic. But the cold rationality of its procedure is a mask, a trope that Kafka the artist was among the first to see and exploit. On the face of it, the bureaucratic principle leaves no place, in Weber's scheme, for charisma. For him, as John Guillory observes, "Truly bureaucratic authority dissolves charisma and replaces it with a cathexis of the office rather than the person." Thus Weber:

> It is decisive for the specific nature of modern loyalty to an office that, in its pure type, it does not establish a relationship to a person, like the vassal's or disciple's faith in feudal or patrimonial relations of authority. Modern loyalty is devoted to impersonal and functional purposes.[15]

But here Weber misses the reality of affect and interest at work in the hierarchies of power, failing to account for the "affective attachment to superior office*holders*." The superior is never in fact anonymous or impersonal; the affect that binds one to the office cannot be readily distinguished from the affect that binds one to the officeholder.[16]

Guillory's analysis of the two faces of bureaucracy is perfectly apt to Kafka's relation to his *other* office. Features of the personal and impersonal faces of bureaucracy are indistinguishable from the masks of "writerly being." On the impersonality of his "office cathexis," we recall Kafka's description of his fate as a writer:

> There is nothing to me that . . . one could call superfluous, superfluous in the sense of overflowing. If there is a higher power that wishes to use me, or does use me, then I am at its mercy, if no more than as a well-prepared instrument. If not, I am nothing, and will suddenly be abandoned in a dreadful void. (LF 21)

This early picture of Kafka's writing destiny consorts with the impersonal face of bureaucracy. But his office machine is also animate and charismatically charged. In an extraordinary letter to Milena Jesenská at the end of his life, Kafka describes the office as "a living human being, who looks at me . . . with its innocent eyes . . . a being with whom I have been united in a manner unknown to me" all the while it remains "alien."[17] The office Kafka is speaking of here is the Workmen's Accident Insurance Institute for the Czech Lands in Prague! And what agency, one might ask, is Kafka speaking of when he writes of "the false hands that reach out to you in the midst of writing"?[18] These are not the demons of the bureau but archons employed by the "office" of literature: here Kafka is referring to the nightly combat that writing forced on him. Conversely, during the day, he dealt with legal objects (business) who would have considered Dr. Franz Kafka, the adversarial institute lawyer, as precisely one of these wicked archons.

The sociologist Claude Lefort has explored Marx's insight that bureaucracy is capable of translating "all social relations into a diction of formal relations between offices and ranks."[19] Kafka was the skilled bureaucrat able to translate into such diction his relation to the alien god of writing. Lefort points up the absurdity that this "translation" betrays: "Behind the mask of rules and impersonal relations lies the proliferation of unproductive functions, the play of personal contacts and the madness of authority."[20] This is the ludic function drawn out in Kafka's fiction but by no means absent from his bureaucratic life. Hartmut Binder identifies the ludic dimension in Kafka's daily practice: "He could play with considerable success on the apparatus of 'instances.'"[21] How poorly, then, is Kafka's relation to bureaucracy captured in the standard view that the aim of his fictional representation of bureaucracy is to pillory its crimes against the hapless supplicant.

Given the two faces of bureaucracy evenly profiled, Kafka's fiction turns bureaucracy into a political grotesque—a grotesquerie that is "abysmally" comic.[22] We have this rather cheerful account in Joseph Vogl's essay on Kafka's "political comedy":

> From the terror of secret scenes of torture to childish officials, from the filth of the bureaucratic order to atavistic rituals of power runs a track of comedy that forever indicates the absence of reason, the element of the arbitrary in the execution of power and rule. However, this element of the grotesque does not merely unmask and denounce. It refers—as Foucault once pointed out—to the inevitability, the inescapability of precisely the grotesque, ridiculous, loony, or abject sides of power. Kafka's "political grotesque" displays an unsystematic arbitrariness, which belongs to the functions of the apparatus itself. There is really no real reason why [in *The Trial*] an exhausted court official at the end of the working day should occupy himself for an hour with tossing lawyers down the stairs. . . . Kafka's

comedy turns against a diagnosis of the modernization of political power as a "rationalization process."[23]

Vogl refers to the Court bureaucracy in *The Trial*; Kafka's *Castle* is even richer in comic-grotesque effects. The world of the castle is marked by a traffic in script that circles around higher authority at an immeasurable distance. Precisely this *Spielraum* encourages mad play in both the writer and his persona, K. In the anonymity of the office, the official in the castle world descends into a dreamlike trance of writing, sending, sorting, and storing messages as opportunities to exert power. Although these messages may concern matters on which he has no overview, he belabors them as an arm of the authority he does not know. Words in such hands take on demonically uncertain proportions, and they can be performatives that coerce subaltern behaviors in men and women. They can and do produce powerful literary effects.

In another section of part 3 chapter 6 of *Wirtschaft und Gesellschaft,* Weber writes:

> In principle, the modern organization of the civil service separates the bureau from the private domicile of the official, and, in general, bureaucracy segregates official activity as something distinct from the sphere of private life.[24]

This point, however, is problematic for Kafka. In general, for him, family has at least a family relation to the larger social-political organization Kafka calls *the office* and which, under the conditions of modernity, displays the features of bureaucracy. Paramount here is the splendid formulation:

> He does not live for his personal life; he does not think for his personal thoughts. It seems to him that he lives and thinks under the compulsion of a family, which is surely itself overabundant in the power of life and thought, but for which he signifies, in accordance with some law unknown to him, a formal necessity. [For this unknown family and these unknown laws, he cannot be released (dismissed, *entlassen*).] (KSS 207)

The semantic variant "dismissed "—along with other terms belonging to the lexicon of modern political organization, viz. compulsion, law, formal necessity, and, perhaps, thought—suggests the *official* character of this family.

Kafka's sense of the "normal" connection of family with higher organization is further spelled out in his exquisite account of relationships within the family, via Jonathan Swift, whom Kafka explicitly identifies:

> The family, then, is an organism, but an extremely complex and unbalanced one, and like every organism it continually strives for equilibrium. . . .

In humanity every individual has his place or at least the possibility of being destroyed in his own fashion. In the family, clutched in the tight embrace of the parents, there is room only for certain kinds of people who conform to certain kinds of requirements and moreover have to meet the deadlines dictated by the parents. If they do not conform, they are not expelled—that would be very fine, but it is impossible, for we are dealing with an organism here—but accursed or consumed or both. The consuming does not take place on the physical plane, as in the archetype of Greek mythology (Kronos, the most honest of fathers, who devoured his sons; but perhaps Kronos preferred this to the usual methods out of pity for his children). (L 294–95)

Note that each member of the organism has his super- or subordinate place and that the actions of the parents can be readily attributed to the top official of a bureaucratic organization: like him, they "dictate deadlines." Compare this picture with Bürgel's comment in *The Castle* that speaks of the castle as "a great living organization" (C 267). This remark tends to confirm K's observation in a particular case: "Nowhere else had K ever seen one's office and one's life so intertwined as they were here, so intertwined that it sometimes seemed as though office and life had changed places" (C 58).

The special horror of chapter 2 of *The Metamorphosis*, in which Herr Samsa hurls into the verminous body of the "writerly" son the hurtful pieces of family language that are very likely the allusive sense of the small, hard apples he has stored in his pockets, is not trivially owed to the uncanny mingling of his official authority—for he sports the uniform of the bank employee—with his authority as family father (M 28–29).[25]

In undoing the distinction between family life and bureaucracy, Kafka's account radicalizes Weber's. Kafka's vision marks a departure from Weber—and a huge prophetic advance. For Kafka, the spirit of an ever-spreading bureaucracy is the circulation of ultimately unintelligible script of one sort or another, whether office or family language (as, for example, "In the next room . . . they are talking about vermin" "[KSS 196]).[26] He has forecast the multiplication of the opportunities for unintelligibility in what is called the media.

Some books act like a key
to strange rooms in one's own castle. (L 10)

There is a wonderful precedent in the English literary canon for the poetic imagination that conceives of its activity as administered by an office. It is found at the beginning of Wordsworth's autobiographical poem *The Prelude* (1805), a work exemplary within an English Romantic tradition not unknown to Kafka.[27] The example I have in mind turns on the term *ministry*—a word found in book 1, where it compresses a doublet of ideas: it defines poetic existence as a passionate reading of signs and connects it, in a certain atmosphere of anxiety, to a powerful social-political agency—indeed, considers poetic existence literally as cooperation with this social-political agency. The narrator addresses

> Ye Presences of Nature in the sky
> And on the earth! Ye Visions of the hills!
> And Souls of lonely places! can I think
> A vulgar hope was yours when ye employed
> Such ministry, when ye, through many a year
> Haunting me thus among my boyish sports,
> Impressed, upon all forms, the characters
> Of danger or desire; and thus did make
> The surface of the universal earth,
> With triumph and delight, with hope and fear,
> Work like a sea?[28]

Note the fragments of the discourse of work and employment even in this pristine natural scene of reading. Here the word "ministry" chiefly adverts to the idea of precapitalist agencies benevolently—but also threateningly—"administering" lessons through signs made manifest by the cooperation of psychic "faculties." In his 1943 novel *The Ministry of Fear*, Graham Greene restores to Wordsworth's "ministry" its menacing, bureaucratic sense; this antipoem, like Kafka's *The Trial*, concerns a hunted man pursued by shadowy killers. Vogl's discussion of Kafka's political grotesque is apt to Wordsworth here: Kafka's work is "less a disenchantment of the world than a bureaucratization of the heavens."[29]

The main feature of Wordsworth's Nature, in one important respect not unlike the world of *The Castle*, is its profusion of signs ("characters of danger or desire") offering themselves to interpretation. My late colleague Charles Bernheimer discussed this dimension of the castle world with great finesse.[30] The difference between the relation of ministry and sign in *The Prelude* and in *The Castle* illuminates this latter world. Bernheimer begins with Kafka's great parable:

> Everything submitted to him for the construction. Foreign workers brought the marble stones trimmed and fitted to one another. The stones lifted and placed themselves according to the measuring movements of his fingers. No construction ever came into being as easily as did this

temple—or rather, this temple came into being in true temple-fashion. Except that on every stone—from what quarry had they come?—was scratched, with instruments obviously of a marvelous sharpness, the clumsy scribblings of senseless child-hands, or rather the inscriptions [better: entries, *Eintragungen*] of barbaric mountain dwellers, in order to spite, or to desecrate, or to destroy completely, for an eternity outlasting the temple. (DF 205)

The "ministry" of such "Presences" is barbaric—not benevolent—seemingly archaic but, from the standpoint of the "aeon," uncannily modern: like *Schreibtischmörder*, bureaucrats who issue death notices from their desks (the castle presences are more nearly aggressive philanderers), they, too, do not fail to accompany their violence with "entries": *Eintragungen*. The standard translation "inscriptions" misses the crucial bureaucratic nuance. At the inside of the mask of the barbarian is the official sworn to duty.

Bernheimer's master text, throughout his discussion of the castle world of fleeting signs, is Walter Benjamin's *Origin of the German Mourning Play*. In its light, Bernheimer identifies, with reference to the castle world, a profusion of signs in circulation, signs of and among ruins, signs that represent only things that have become irretrievable.

> K is a land-surveyor in a quicksand of shifting signs. The castle refuses to confront him on his own terms, refuses to be conjured into presence. [Cf. Wordsworth's "Presences," SC]. Instead it insists on the purely allusive nature of its textuality. [Such] allegorical sign-scripts or script-images do not solicit belief: they solicit contemplation and interpretation.[31]

And yet such a thing as victorious interpretation can hardly be imagined *actualiter*, since there remains always the dizzying task of distinguishing "official meaning" from "private meaning" (which is anything but negligible). Indeed, it is "usually greater than any official meaning could ever be" (C 73). Nonetheless, K pursues a sense of "victory" by attempting to grasp the intentions of the castle toward him. We saw this desire for hermeneutic mastery in " 'You,' I said . . ." when the narrator addresses the bachelor's writing self: "If only I knew for certain that you were being truthful [*aufrichtig*] with me" (D1 24). Cognitive mastery (by the "well-prepared instrument") might be one approach to the otherness ("a higher power that wishes to use me"), whose deep sense is literature. But this relation is more than an affair of correct interpretation; it is a practical matter, involving an entire reorientation. Recall from " 'You,' I said . . .":

> If until this time our entire being was directed to the work of our hands, to whatever was seen by our eyes, heard by our ears, down to the steps of our

feet, now we suddenly turn completely in the opposite direction, like a weathervane in the mountains. (KSS 194)

The final reference of cognitive mastery is an action, a "turning" that Kafka must make into his text "in order," while wearing the mask of K, "to keep himself upright in this [castle] world" (Cf. DI 26).

K's concerns in *The Castle* may be taken as an essential refraction of Kafka's concerns—even, and especially, K's ruthless side. At times, K appears as an aggressive, worldly agent, an unscrupulous manipulator of persons, but then, after all, the stake for Kafka is similarly great in his resistance to "the spirits" (KSS 212), to "the false hands that reach out to you in the midst of writing."[32] If we conceive of K's relentless march toward the castle as a reflection of Kafka's relentless march toward *The Castle*—that is, as the writer's relentless search for entry into his work, proceeding ruthlessly, as is his wont, since "sometimes in his arrogance, he is more afraid for the world than for himself" (KSS 206–7)—then K's raw directness precisely characterizes Kafka's drive. As K forcibly seeks to find his way aright in this castle world, so Kafka forcibly seeks to find himself aright in the castle world of his imagining.[33]

And yet we see K pursuing "victory" through correct cognition—a matter of what one can *know* of the other and not how one must *act* toward the other. His choice of an assumed profession projects success along these lines, relating to this foreign construction—the castle—as its *Landvermesser*, a word that means "land surveyor." Professionally armed, as a delineator of boundaries, K means to take the measure of his adversary. But the title he gives himself also suggests conceptual activity gone awry: "Landvermesser" can also mean "materialist *mis-measurer*."

Since the castle to which K seeks entry by acts of conceptual mastery is humanly inhabited, the relation of knower to known is inevitably cast in the imagery of interpersonal *acknowledgment*. Where the act of knowing is successful, the knower is *acknowledged* by the known: "entry" is an affair of reciprocal recognition.

Here is K at the outset, aggressively pursuing his goal of entry. The first note is menacing.

> So the castle had appointed him land surveyor. On the one hand, this was unfavorable, for it showed that the castle had all necessary information about him, had assessed the opposing forces, and was taking up the struggle with a smile. (C 5)

In terms of the metaphor of cognition, we have the failure of the pitifully human truth seeker on approximately this Faustian model: All you know of the object is what you take it to mean: "Du gleichst dem Geist,

den Du begreifst, / Nicht mir!" ("You are like the spirit whom you com-
prehend/Not me" [*Faust*, ll. 512–13]). The truth of the castle conde-
scends to be known not as it is in itself but in a manner defined by the
capacities of the subject, a manner that does not allow it to be pene-
trated. Truth can be known by the human subject only as what that
truth is not.

But here, for one moment, the discouraging condescension of the adversary appears as only one side of K's relation of the castle: his stubborn,
mensurative mind seeks a balance of powers. "On the other hand, it was
favorable," he thinks of the readiness of the castle to take up the gage,

> for it proved to his mind that they underestimated him and that he would
> enjoy greater freedom than he could have hoped for at the beginning. And
> if they thought they could keep him terrified all the time simply by ac-
> knowledging his surveyorship—though this was certainly a superior move
> on their part—then they were mistaken, for he felt only a slight shudder,
> that was all. (C 5)

There is a Promethean, an altogether usurpatory feeling, to such parables of mastery in their independence of custom and law.[34] What is here
called "Promethean" could equally be called, following Benjamin, a
"primordial satanic promise: what is alluring: the semblance of freedom
in the fathoming of what is forbidden."[35] Yet, all in all, the tonality of
this act of apparent hermeneutic mastery over the castle is a much men-
aced, merely dusky and delusory occasion of the "triumph and delight,
hope and fear" that Wordsworth celebrated. Indeed, later in the novel,
Olga alleges, with remarkable penetration, apropos the letters that K
has received from Klamm, the fallibility of all such interpretation:

> And staying in the middle between the exaggerations, that is, weighing the
> letters correctly is impossible, their value keeps changing, the thoughts that
> they prompt are endless and the point at which one happens to stop is de-
> termined only by accident and so the opinion one arrives at is just as acci-
> dental. (C 231)

This observation says a great deal about the random character of the
signs, forms, and impressions administered in the modern period.

The moment of K's putative victory remains significant for the wider
logic of the novel: it represents the impersonal struggle with the other as a
cognitive relation and then by degrees as an intersubjective relation. But
what is finally at stake is a mode of practical being, something to *do* with
the truth.[36] The possibility, however, of *action* in the castle world remains
inhibited by a general uncertainty of orientation—about what would constitute the true direction to what is genuinely opposed. This world is shot
through with bewildering administrative directions, interrupted both lit-

erally and figuratively by a traffic in signs requiring K's attention. No part of this world escapes this circulation (ridiculed as "chatter [*Geschwätz*]"); even the straightforward identity of the emitter of signs is compromised, for the village is indistinguishable from the castle ("had one not known that this was a castle, one could have taken it for a small town" [C 8]); even the village inhabitants are indistinguishable from the castle ("there is no difference between the peasants and the castle" [C 9]). The castle and its environs are a single bureaucratic institution, marked by the ubiquity of its written signs and the untraceableness of their circulation: it is chiefly in this sense that the castle is a figure for the "house" of writerly being, *Schriftstellersein.* The word "bureaucratic," above, should point to a maximum of detail and complication, of mediation that has lost the knowledge of the straight way and has turned in upon itself. This point is made in *The Castle* with delicious irony: "Should it [the file] ever lose its way, the excellence of the organization is such that the file must zealously seek the wrong way, for otherwise it won't find it, and then it does indeed take a long time" (C 63). One recalls throughout Kafka's drama of writing, the many instances where the simple inverse of this point occurs, and writing falls effortlessly "in the shameful lowlands of writing" (D1 276). The comedic castle version would liberate Kafka from the anguish of writing that has lost its way.

We have insisted, somewhat monomaniacally, on the aptness of the bureaucratic castle world to "writerly being," yet isn't this identification finally rather restrictive? To be sure, *The Castle* is encyclopedic, comprising forms of life that invite study through the lens of political philosophy (we have the story of an individual seeking citizenship and the rights that pertain to it in modern societies having democratic and liberal features);[37] through linguistic philosophy (the novel's notions of transgression, collaborative hermeneutics, and textually modeled culture tie it into the work of the Prague School);[38] through stereotypical *fin de siècle* gender politics (the woman appears as pawn, as whore, as ascetic priestess) . . . this list of applications can be broadly extended. Accordingly, Hartmut Binder had uncovered a wide range of empirical references serving as raw material for Kafka's fictive constructions.[39] But here, along with every reader's debt to Binder's findings, one cannot but recall Kafka's poetological advertisement invoking "the freedom of authentic description . . . that releases one's foot from lived experience" (D1 100). Binder's massive study presents plausible models for the likes of Frieda and Klamm and does not fail to see Kafka himself the writer underpinning the representation of Momus, Klamm's secretary. The association is cogent—and witty: Momus takes down evidence, of course, and moreover, alights in the castle world from a Greek mythological cloud; from Hesiod on, he is the small god of carping criticism.[40] There is no question but that this chapter 9, "Struggle Against a Hearing," is full of parodic resonances with Kafka's own writing practices. The difference, however, between Binder's thesis and my own is that I see *no* essential feature of the action of *The Castle* that does not resonate with Kafka's sense of his fate as a writer.

Furthermore, it would be understandable if one were to object, But surely the bureaucratic world, for Kafka, the drear of office life, is constitutive only *by negation* of the writer's world. It is this other life that literature dramatizes as its enemy, as the continual threat of its undoing—a counterliterature, for "*real hell is there in the office, no other can hold any terror for me*" (LF 238). But bureaucracy is at the same time a leading, a capacious metaphor of the a priori otherness of Kafka to himself—his second nature—as he himself noted more than once. He wrote of himself as "I—or the deep-seated bureaucrat inside me—which is the same thing" (L 134) and of "the born-and-bred (*großgezogen*) official inside me" (LF 462).[41] Until now we have seen Kafka define the sense of his strange, deep-seated, second nature through the metaphor of writerly being. Now we see him defining this strangeness to self through the metaphor of "bureaucratic being," but it should come as no surprise, since both metaphors have in common the fact that they are uncentered writing agencies.

The specter of bureaucracy haunts Kafka day and night in every corner of his writing life. I use the word "specter" advisedly. In the letter to Milena earlier cited, Kafka described the office as "not dumb but phantasmal [*phantastisch*]." At the end of a day in 1911, having written nothing, Kafka noted in his diaries, "How do I excuse my not yet having written anything today? In no way [*mit nichts*]. . . . I have continually an invocation in my ear: 'If you would come, invisible court [*Gericht*]!' " (KSS 194). It is wonderful to reflect on whether the court is literature itself (and that might be a good thing or a bad thing—writing come to save him or writing come in an angry mood to chide him). Or else, the court might constitute an extraliterary ethical agency, as in *The Trial*, alert to punish him for dereliction of duty. But in each case, writing appears as an institution or as the concern of an institution and, as a court in the modern age, necessarily a bureaucracy. So there was scarcely a day or night in which Kafka did not write something for the bureaucracy—the objective form of which he knew daily, outside in, as Chief Legal Secretary of the Workmen's Accident Insurance Institute. In this light, in its proximity to his writing, Kafka's office life cannot be summed up as pure waste, pure suffering. Aside from its ludic dimension, in the matter of its supplying Kafka with theme and substance—our starting point—the English Germanist Jeremy Adler observes:

Although Kafka constantly stresses the conflict between his writing and his profession, this perceived dualism . . . provides the premise for his authorship, enabling him to write about modernity and its discontents from the inside. . . . His job brought him into direct contact with industrialization, mechanization, and bureaucracy, as well as with the struggle between capital and labor, and his official writings antedate his literary breakthrough.[42]

There is a relevant irony in the workings of this negative, this "hell": it is not the *opposite* of writerly being; it shares its territory, it is an insistent and provocative double; and even as "hell," and hence the outcome of "service to the devil," it is, once again, like writing itself. Kafka imagined that he needed only to throw his duties at the office out of the "complex" of writing to be free,[43] but his confessional writings show time and again that, though on leave from the office, he accomplished little. It is a hook into the real, and hence a "brother *adversary*," but purely adversarial only in the sense that it is an empirical distraction. True, his office work could never, by itself, under the real conditions of its operations as a governmental insurance agency, be a source of justification. Yet in its aspect as script—as the impersonal circulation of signs—it held for him a baffling fraternal likeness to the movement of writing: its "laws" are beyond ego, uncontrollable, self-involved: "Our fumbling interpretations," we recall, "are powerless to deal with the 'evolutions'/enhancements/climaxes [*Steigerungen*] of which the bureaucracy is capable" (L 328–29).[44] In the pages that follow, we hope to illustrate the writerly elegance of many of the documents that Kafka produced at work. The office was a world of signs on the surface of paper—in the purest sense, in Benjamin's phrase, "the sign-script of transience."[45] And since transience is another name for the everyday, for the contents of lived experience under the conditions of modernity, then, in its processing of industrial "cases"—of accidents to which Kafka the bourgeois would not have had access—the office supplied him with a subject matter to consume. It is not these "real things" that are vivid in *The Castle*: the novel does not do the history of land surveying or the telephone or the fire department, though these modern entities make a fleeting appearance. It is the spiraling self-involvement of office-generated signs—of letters and files, of interpretations gone mad amid the rumor of laws—that captivates Kafka. In *The Castle*, by a bold creative act of fusion, the bureaucracy becomes the house of an ideal in which writing is at home: Kafka shelters the terrible-sacred, the numinous, of the writing destiny in the profane hell of office life.

The mood of gaiety, of sly good humor, that glances off the pages of *The Castle* would be Kafka's bliss in joining, at the order of this fiction, his two alien worlds: the being of the writerly life, the being of bureau-cracy. What a happy thing to make the hell of bureaucracy redound to the benefit of his fiction. It is finally the only happiness Kafka could know: linking, fusing together in literature, contesting parts of the structure of his desire, "the tremendous/monstrous [*ungeheure*] world I have in my head" (D1 288). There is a frightening strangeness in the substance of the myth—this bureaucratic castle world—but a giddy bliss, too, in playing the trick of fictive mastery over it.

KAFKA'S OFFICE WRITINGS: HISTORICAL BACKGROUND AND INSTITUTIONAL SETTING

Benno Wagner

At a street corner Karl saw a poster with the following announcement: 'The Oklahoma Theater will be hiring for its company today at Clayton racetrack from six o'clock in the morning until midnight [. . .]. Everyone welcome! If you want to be an artiste, join our company! Our theater can find employment for everyone, a place for everyone' " (A 202, translation modified).

In the summer of 1907, when the young insurance lawyer Franz Kafka was lamenting his eight-hour workday as a major obstacle to his literary ambitions, he may have come across a poster displayed at Prague's street corners. The Austrian Workmen's Insurance Institute was offering free vocational training for secondary-school graduates and public servants. Like the seemingly fantastic Nature Theater in the final chapter of Kafka's "America novel" *Der Verschollene* (*The Man Who Disappeared*, translated under the title *Amerika*), this new branch of public insurance promised a place for everyone, in the status of either client or staff. Like the Nature Theater, its propaganda apparatus was also "continually on the move," "recruit[ing] in every major city" (A 206).[1] While the Nature Theater displayed certain higher features—it was "the greatest theater in the world" and there were "almost no limits to it"—it was material and worldly, "an old theater, but being extended all the time" (A 205–6).

The parallel with the Austrian Workmen's Insurance Institute is wonderful. Ever since Emperor Franz Joseph had proclaimed workmen's insurance in 1885, it too had been all-encompassing (according to imperial rhetoric) and continuously extended through piecemeal legislation. At once complete and under permanent construction, its actual existence was just as questionable as that of the Theater.[2] Draft workmen's-insurance legislation to realize the Emperor's proclamation was proposed in 1903 but was still under discussion in 1915, when Kafka wrote the chapter on the Nature Theater. As for the Prague secondary-school graduate Karl Rossmann, Kafka's protagonist in *Amerika*, the chief inducement for Kafka was that, according to the recruitment posters, "everyone [was] welcome," whether artiste, engineer, or even industrial employee.

In February 1908, Kafka began attending evening lectures on workmen's insurance at the Prague Commercial College, and eventually, like all the other students in the program, he passed the final examination. On June 30, he submitted his job application to the Workmen's Accident Insurance Institute; it was accepted; and on July 30, 1908, Kafka entered the Institute's new office buildings at Na poříčí for his first day of work.

As the implicit autobiography of Kafka's first novel suggests, the connection between his professions is closer and deeper than mere chronological overlap. As in his imagined America, the jobs of artiste, engineer, and industrial employee have an intrinsic fit. They belong to the same life project, at times seeming to merge into one unique, hybrid profession. We find an early trace in a confession the young writer-to-be and insurance tyro sent to a young woman in Vienna in October 1907, while he was still suffering in his first job: "I am in the Assicurazioni Generali and have some hopes of someday sitting in chairs in faraway countries, looking out of the office windows at fields of sugar or Mohammedan cemeteries; and the whole world of insurance itself interests me greatly, though my present work is dreary" (L 35).[3]

"The whole world of insurance itself interests me greatly"; for many decades, this remarkable confession has been ignored by Kafka scholarship. This oversight is stunning when we consider that on entering the new office building, Kafka was also passing through a newly opened entryway to the law—the revolutionary finding of a statistical constant in occupational injury.

As François Ewald has shown in his seminal book on the insurance state, industrial-accident statistics had, by this time, confronted the liberal legal norm of responsibility[4] with an unheard-of phenomenon, a "regular evil" that was not connected to human fault but, on the contrary, was irrevocably connected to the benefits of industrial progress.[5] Ewald describes the emergence of a new "juridical landscape," a "rule of judgment" that replaces the principle of guilt by the principle of risk and replaces retroactive punishment of the individual with the precautionary collection of fees, or premiums, from a multitude. Like Kafka's providential Nature Theater, this new economy of injury and compensation comprises society as a whole, including, without exception, the entire population. It is, moreover, the scene of a curious alliance between the industrial worker and the *actor*. Just as in the new, statistics-based law of social insurance, the judge is replaced by the expert who refers the damage suffered by an individual to a table of compensatory payments, the worker assumes the role of "speculator on [. . .] his own misery."[6] His success depends on his ability to lay out convincingly his damages and his claim to compensation before a board of experts—a scenic constellation Kafka obsessionally varies throughout his literary work.

Since Kafka was so much interested in the "whole world of insurance," we are obliged to go beyond a few easily uncovered analogies between his work life and his writing. Before passing through this exciting new entrance to his literary world, we will take a circuitous route to his office to describe the historical framework of his profession.

Public Accident Insurance in Austria

In distinctive ways, Austria varies from Ewald's account of the insurance state and its theoretical framework; the latter relies on Michel Foucault's analysis of "biopolitics" and the emergence of the nation-state.

In Foucault's history, the discourse of the biased and violent conflict between two groups divided by ethnicity, language, and in some cases, space—what Foucault, adopting a historical term, calls the "struggle of races"—continued beneath the surface of society. Their conflict spurred a "counterhistory," a narrative that rewrites the *grand récit* of the nation-state as the sovereign pacifier of all internal conflict. In the "long" nineteenth century (1789–1914), the story of this ethnic struggle undergoes a double transformation. It is replaced by the rational discourse of revolutionary class struggle. And at the same time we see an *anti*revolutionary revision of all such *dialectical* accounts of ethnic struggle: the political-historical dimension is suppressed by a biological-medical one. Parallel to the historical dialectic of the class struggle, there emerges the biopolitics of the welfare state. The "struggle in the warlike sense" is now replaced with the "struggle in the biological sense" for the selection and survival of the fittest: "The state [. . .] becomes the protector of the integrity, superiority, and purity of the race," while the nation, the pivotal point of violent counterhistory in the eighteenth century, becomes the "active, constituent core of the state."[7]

Foucault's genealogy certainly allows for new insights into the emergence of "complex nationalities," especially in England and France, but it does not altogether fit the situation of "compound nationalities," such as Austria in the eighteenth and nineteenth centuries.[8] Here, "the struggle of races" smoldered in the form of a conflict between ethnicities over their legal status under the Hapsburg crown. This struggle generated an often barbaric discourse with proliferating archaic images; in this instance, "the nation" functions, not as the creative nucleus of the state, but as its deadly virus. At the same time, Austrian social insurance remained closely connected to the most advanced system of its kind at the time—the Bismarckian welfare state of the German Reich. This contradictory involvement in the most archaic and the most advanced sectors of knowledge is of great significance for the genealogy of the Hapsburg state and, as I shall show, for the world view of the poet-clerk Franz Kafka.

We find in at least one fictive Kafkaesque scenario, *In the Penal Colony*, a staging of the popular image of animal training—"the carrot and the stick" (in German, "sugar bread and the whip"). This figure helps to explain the origin of both German and Austrian social legislation. The takeover of the defeated French capital by rioting workers in the spring of 1871 gave rise to the rule of the Paris Commune. Troops shed blood, igniting concerns in neighboring monarchies about managing the class conflict. In the late summer of that year, German and Austrian imperial chancellors Prince Otto von Bismarck and Count Friedrich Ferdinand Beust met in the Austrian spa of Bad Gastein to discuss ways to combat the dangers of the Socialist International. They agreed that a strategy grounded merely in police and military power—in the vein of the Karlsbad resolutions of 1819—was no longer timely. Instead, the two noblemen decided to consider the question "from the higher standpoint of public welfare"—in other words, join the stick of repression with the carrot of biopolitical regulation.

In that same late summer of 1871, however, Count Beust was facing a far more complex political challenge than that confronting Prince von Bismarck. In 1867, Beust had been the Austrian spokesman in negotiations to create a dual constitution for the Austro-Hungarian monarchy. In the Austrian, or Cisleithanian, part of the Empire, this so-called Compromise (*Ausgleich*) secured German national hegemony, while the Czechs, who had aspired to equal status with Hungary in a constitutional triad, were "left out in the cold."[9] The Czechs responded with boycotts of parliamentary proceedings and displays of distrust toward the Germans—a feeling that increased when the German victory in the Franco-Prussian War revitalized Greater German sentiments in Austria. In February 1871, Emperor Franz Joseph, in an attempt to secure a viable compromise for the Cisleithanian situation, appointed Count Siegmund Hohenwart, a conservative and more federally minded Austro-German aristocrat, as prime minister. After protracted negotiations with leaders of the Old Czech Party, Hohenwart's cabinet presented several bills, known as the Fundamental Articles. This equivalent of the Austro-Hungarian Compromise provided for far-reaching political and administrative autonomy for the three lands of the Bohemian crown (Bohemia, Moravia, and Silesia). Against this loosening of the Empire's constitutional ties, a binding element was sought in new social legislation. Compulsory social insurance, developed within an advanced theoretical framework by Hohenwart's minister of trade and agriculture, the Swabian professor of economics Albert Schaeffle, was meant to serve as a "clamp" on the centrifugal thrust of the nationalities.[10] A biopolitical solution would pacify an ethnopolitical struggle.

While the actual regime of Hohenwart and Schaeffle lasted barely nine months (February 5–October 30, 1871), in retrospect, their policies appear as an avatar of future (and eventually fatal) political developments. When the Liberals split near the end of the decade over the issue of nationalities, an alliance—the so-called Iron Ring—was formed between German conservative workers, Czechs, and Poles, led by Count Eduard von Taaffe, a conservative supported by the Emperor.

The Taaffe alliance was to remain in power for fourteen years, the longest period of continuous government between 1848 and the end of the Empire. From the beginning, in the spirit of Hohenwart and Schaeffle, the Taaffe government identified the constitutional principle of the equality of all nationalities and the social question as the double focus of its concern. In political practice, this legislation was connected to another core image in Kafka's fictional world, "a message from the emperor."

In the Reich, Prince von Bismarck delivered his First Imperial Message on the Social Question on November 17, 1881, followed by a second such message and a number of speeches from the throne, throughout the 1880s. Starting October 8, 1879, the Austrian Emperor delivered a corresponding set of speeches, proclaiming, on September 26, 1885, extensive plans for social insurance.[11]

The Austrian Workmen's Accident Insurance Law of 1887

When the Emperor eventually proclaimed a Workmen's Accident Insurance Law for Austria on December 28, 1887, it consisted of sixty-four paragraphs and covered twenty pages in the *Amtliche Nachrichten* (the Official Intelligencer of the Ministry of the Interior). This legislation was "partly modeled on the German pattern and partly self-styled and original."[12] It is mainly the latter set of features that was to affect Kafka's professional profile and the very particular atmosphere of his workplace.

- The most far-reaching among the "self-styled" features of the law concerned the pattern of *administrative organization*. In the German model, workmen's accident insurance was organized by trade associations, along the modern pattern of *functional* differentiation by industrial branches. Language variety and the political demands of Taaffe's federalist course called for a *territorial* organization—that is, a premodern plan of spatial mapping. Each of the seven regional institutes (see below) was designed to deal with a full variety of industrial branches and technologies, a sort of transverse mapping of vocational or professional knowledge that favored the production of dilettantes rather than specialized experts.

- The promise of social security connected to workmen's insurance was fulfilled in a highly selective manner. Since §1 of the new law restricted compulsory insurance to machine-operated businesses and to businesses using explosives (such as quarries), only one million workers out of a total workforce of seven million were initially subject to compulsory insurance. Most workers in small-scale businesses, agriculture, and forestry were excluded. Although step-by-step extension was copied from the German model, the process proceeded much more slowly and left many more sectors of production uninsured than in the Reich. Thus, even after the passing of the Extension Law (*Ausdehnungsgesetz*) of 1894, most workers remained uninsured, and many others were trapped in a legal limbo. Kafka's first long juridical essay for the Prague Institute (in 1908) dealt with the resulting problems (doc. 2).

- A further difference with far-reaching consequences concerned the *financial system of accident insurance*. Here, Austria chose to follow the level-premium system successfully applied in England, instead of the allocation procedure used in Germany. The German system aimed at short-term coverage of expenses, starting from a lower level of premiums, with a steady progression of premiums in future years. The more advanced English system anticipated future costs and thus began with a higher premium level that offered fairly stable and calculable premium increases. The success of the English system, however, depended largely on reliable accident statistics for all branches of industry and a subsequent correlation between premiums and statistical results.

- But when workmen's accident insurance was established, Austria lacked reliable *statistical evidence on industrial accident risks*. A contemporary commentator pointed out this lack very clearly: "§14 of the Accident Insurance Law specifies that the risk classification of the firms liable to insurance shall 'be based on the results of accident statistics.' That is certainly extraordinary. For [a record of] accident statistics does not exist, nor is it under construction at the present time."[13] Eventually, the earliest risk classifications were based partly on statistical data "borrowed" from the German Reich and partly on plain and simple estimates. The result was a practice of calculating with dubious figures—a practice of the sort that Kafka fought against and that has come to be called Kafkaesque. In two long articles for the Northern Bohemian *Tetschen-Bodenbacher Zeitung* in 1911 (doc. 8), Kafka publicly discussed the legal and economic consequences of that specifically Austrian way of calculating risk.

- Finally, a uniquely Austrian feature of the legal framework of workmen's accident insurance was the central supervisory body and court of appeals for public insurance, the Reichsversicherungsamt; it was provided for only in the third draft of the German law. As the Austrian law was based on the second draft of the German law, which did not mention such an institution, a superior court for public insurance was never established in Austria, despite numerous claims and proposals. Instead, a decentralized network of arbitrary courts consisting of employers and employees issued verdicts without a possibility of appeal; this legal setting anticipates basic features of the mysterious attic courts in Kafka's novel, *The Trial.*

The following sections treat in detail the institutional framework and the administrative and legal context of Austrian accident insurance, which were the basic settings of Kafka's professional environment.

The Territorial Institutes

With the significant exception of railroad employees who, owing to the transterritorial nature of their work, organized their insurance as a trade association, Austrian workers' accident insurance followed a territorial pattern. In 1889, the Ministry of the Interior established seven institutes—in Vienna (for Lower Austria), in Salzburg (for Upper Austria, Tyrol, and Vorarlberg), in Graz (for Steiermark and Kärnten), in Trieste (for the Coastland), in Lemberg (for Galicia and Bukovina), in Prague (for Bohemia), and in Brno (for Moravia and Silesia). These were autonomous public bodies based on the principle of mutuality; their membership consisted of business owners subjected to compulsory insurance and the workers they employed.

An eighteen-member board of trustees consisting of an equal number of employers, employees, and industrial experts appointed by the Ministry of the Interior was set up to supervise each institute. From their membership, the trustees elected the institute's president and his deputy. The trustees also elected the board of managers and a director responsible for each institute's business operations. These territorial institutes constituted autonomous bodies under public law but operated under state supervision.

Administrative Background

The emergence of these institutes—Kafka's future workplace—marks a turbulent intersection of the history of administration, the history of the state, and the history of the Hapsburg Empire.

At the time of the Schmerling Constitution of 1861, two parallel systems of administration existed in Austria. After the 1848 Revolution, the young Emperor Franz Joseph introduced a principle of "ruthless bureaucratic centralization," following the French model. The Emperor appointed all ministers; and even though they were also formally responsible to the parliament, the result was a "government by administration" that, to a great extent, excluded parliamentary influence. In the three decades following the Revolution, a traditionally German class of legally educated public servants administered a regime following the eighteenth-century ideal of "good police" in the service of a supreme ruler. This regime maintained a strict top-down organization, extending from the Vienna ministries over the provincial governments or offices of the governor (*Statthaltereien*) down to the local level of the district authorities (*Bezirkshauptmannschaften*).[14]

To balance this rigid centralism, the 1861 constitution provided for provincial constitutions and provincial diets in each crownland. Provincial boards, elected freely by their parliaments, were also given limited powers of self-government. This system of local self-rule arose from an eventually fatal misunderstanding between the Germans and the Slavs, an agreement that soon proved to be more apparent than real. While the German Liberals had it in mind

> to secure a definitely "State-free" atmosphere in local administration that would liberate the individual and the community as such from the omnipotence of the Central Government and its bureaucracy [. . .], Poles and Czechs sought a constitutional autonomy [. . .] as a first step toward a future federal reconstruction of the entire State.[15]

Thus, the "delays and overloading of the administration," in the ongoing process of "yoking together" the two systems of central government and self-government from the 1880s on, turned the Austrian administration into a battleground between two conflicting concepts of freedom—national autonomy versus individual freedom.

In the same decade, social legislation entered this constitutional scenario as a third power and brought with it a historically new type of administration. Under the paternalistic regime of imperial and royal political officers, a new type of public servant emerged—the professional expert on all aspects of insurance (industrial technology, medicine, statistics, social law), who replaced the traditional regime of "good police" with modern biopolitics. In practice, however, this new class of social engineers had to struggle to defend its technical solutions against the aspirations of civic and ethnic groups (regional self-government) on the one hand and the rigid procedures of the imperial and royal bureaucracy (central government) on the other. We find a precise diagram of such a bureaucratic constellation in Kafka's last novel, *The Castle*. Here the protagonist struggles for acknowledgment of his presumed appointment as the new land surveyor while two hopelessly entangled corrupt bureaucracies—the village authorities (the local government) and the castle authorities (the central government)—attempt to settle the issue of the newly arrived foreigner's status and usefulness. At the same time, the figure of the land surveyor brings a rich philosophical and literary genealogy, stretching from Plato's *Politeia* to Ferdinand Kürnberger's novel *Der Amerikamüde*.[16] These vivid analogies between the setting of *The Castle* and young Kafka's campaign for a land survey enabling fixed-rate insurance on Bohemian farms (doc. 3 and commentary) are some of the most striking evidence we have of a fusion of official and literary writing. Clerk and poet define the two genealogical lines of the land surveyor.[17]

Legal Background

In Austria, the legal framework of public accident insurance was established even more uncompromisingly than it was in the German Reich, increasing the tension between traditional and modern forces. Owing to the slow development of social legislation between 1848 and 1879, Austria skipped French-style and German-style attempts to adapt the categories of Roman law to the phenomenon of industrial accidents (France and Germany, for example, sought to introduce employers' liability). Instead, Austria "immediately passed from Roman Law into the stage of accident insurance."[18] This circumstance led to a disconnect between civil and criminal law on the one hand and insurance law on the other.

To regulate conflicts over compensation payments to injured workers, a court of arbitration was established at the headquarters of each institute. These lay courts consisted of a professional judge and four assessors—two technical experts, one employer, and one worker. The Ministry of the Interior appointed the judge and the two technical experts, while the employer and worker were elected by their respective representative bodies. Since no central court for public insurance existed in Austria, no appeal was possible against the rulings of the arbitration courts. These courts were compelled to handle a considerable workload. In 1901 alone, 6,063 compensation claims were filed throughout Austria, or approximately one in every four insured accidents. Of these appeals, around 2,000 were fully or partially successful, a further 3,000 were turned down, and the rest were rejected either because the courts had no jurisdiction or because of technicalities.

On the other side of the agenda, no provisions were made for special adjudication of the less frequent conflicts between the insured business owners and the insurance institutes. Appeals could be lodged only with the responsible district authorities. This procedure was based on the right of every Austrian citizen to file a legal complaint against the decisions of state authorities. The provincial governor—that is, the midlevel central bureaucracy—was to decide each individual case after hearing statements from the relevant insurance institute and often from the local concerned trade inspector as well. Both sides could—and often did—call for a review of the governor's decision by the Ministry of the Interior. And even his decisions were, under certain conditions, open to appeal at the Administrative Court, a body established in 1875 as the highest authority in the growing number of conflicts resulting from an ever growing administration.

This legal setting, too, was to take its place in Kafka's literary universe. The protagonist of his 1915 novel, *The Trial*, is arrested by a mysterious court on the basis of an unspecified accusation. Although Joseph K, on his way to his first court hearing, is looking for a characteristic building—indicated, perhaps, by some public traffic around the entry—he in fact ends up in a working-class tenement block. K's interrogation by the judge is accompanied by the hissing and applause of a crowd that seems to consist of two opposing groups, corresponding to the lay-court structure of Austrian arbitration courts. After the hearing, however, K discovers that under their long beards, the members of the crowd wear badges of different sizes and colors that identify them as members of the court rather than as representatives of the public. Like the injured Austrian worker, who in fact faced a court that consisted, in the final analysis, of social bureaucrats, Joseph K looks in vain for a supreme court to which he can submit his appeal against the procedures of those outlandish "attic courts."

Crisis

At the time Kafka decided to join the profession, workmen's accident insurance had a very bad press. A contemporary observer summarized the situation in drastic terms:

> It is a remarkable phenomenon that the operation of the Accident Insurance Law over fifteen years has not succeeded in making the law popular,

nor has it proved satisfactory for a single group of those affected by it. [. . .] Instead of leveling social differences, the law has indeed unleashed the dogs of war among the groups involved. . . . The insurance institutions— through no fault of their own—stand at the center of these attacks and are publicly labeled the "most hated institutions."[19]

Public opinion was confirmed by economic performance. At the end of 1908, the budgetary deficit of all Austrian institutes amounted to K80 million, among which the Prague institute's deficit of K39 million was unrivaled. Experts agreed that, economically speaking, this institute was beyond repair.

This situation is even more "remarkable" considering that the period between the introduction of workers' accident insurance in Austria and the First World War was one of almost uninterrupted economic growth. This calamity was caused by an array of factors, many of them reaching beyond the wide scope of the economy.

Rampant Bureaucracy

The basic cause was a bureaucracy run rampant, a trend triggered by its new branch of social administration. We find a graphic description of this expansion in the history of the Prague insurance institute: "In the first period of its activity, the Institute rented rooms in an apartment house (the k. k. Hofbräuhaus, Stephansgasse 625/II) and used them as its offices. By and by the rental contract was expanded to the second and third and parts of the fourth floor. [. . .] However, the location eventually proved unsuitable for the purposes of the Institute as only residential apartments were available in that building."[20] We do not know if Kafka, who had widely contributed to the report quoted here, was the author of this specific passage. We have, once again, a strikingly realistic blueprint of the seemingly surreal attic-court bureaucracy Joseph K faces in *The Trial*. As opposed to the court of the novel, however, the Institute did not spread its offices over the whole city but moved into a newly built office complex conveniently located between Prague's two major railway stations.

"There's a great deal of writing here," remarks another K protagonist, on observing the enigmatic castle bureaucracy's proliferation into the living rooms of the village in *The Castle* (C, chapt. 9). In fact, the Prague Institute's new office building was more a symptom of the underlying problem than a solution to it: "Ever since social legislation was introduced in the 1880s," the governor of Lower Austria wrote in a widely read series of lectures advocating administrative reform published in 1906, "paperwork has been growing constantly."[21] By 1900, incoming forms and files at the level of the district authorities had increased by a factor of four, and Austrian bureaucracy was on the verge of "being suffocated by files and drowning in ink."[22] Since the administrative rules of procedure had not changed for half a century (they dated from 1855), the time-honored practice of copying whole chains of arguments from the files of earlier cases into new files led to an abundance of superfluous administrative paper that could not keep pace with the latest developments in technology and legislation. Moreover, the official idiom (*Amtsstil*) was increasingly alienated from the spoken language and professional discourse, to the point that the administration and the populace were "speaking two different languages."[23] This problem of inefficient communication was aggravated by a problem of memory. Owing to an ever-expanding administration, the reference systems for shelved files proliferated accordingly and produced "the most incredible catchwords." (Thus, more and more frequently, files simply went missing, only to emerge on unexpected occasions years later as the booty of so-called "raids," retrieved by sifting through all the desks, closets, and shelves of a specific department.)[24]

Social Conflict

"Dissatisfaction with workmen's insurance is endemic to it," the Austrian Association of Workmen's Accident Insurance Institutes wrote in a 1907 memorandum. A survey of the opinions stated and the claims made in the prewar debates about social insurance in Austria indicates that the institutes were, in fact, trapped in a no-win situation. Owing to the weak statistical foundation of risk classification during the early years, workmen's accident insurance soon became the object of intense lobbying and social-political bartering.

The employers who were responsible for contributing 90 percent of the premiums attacked all three pillars of accident insurance. First, their associations criticized the system of *risk classification*—the essential basis of the entire insurance plan—as too bureaucratic, inflexible, and unjust because it allegedly made all industries pay for the underinsured risk of a few critical branches. The second pillar, *accident prevention*, was criticized in the same vein. The state-controlled premium system did not, allegedly, offer sufficient incentives to business owners to improve their safety measures. Furthermore, it was an undisputed fact that accident prevention in the German Reich had developed to a much higher level, employing more detailed and binding prescriptions and exercising more efficient control. This fact was used to support demands to replace the state-controlled territorial system with the German model of a self-administered organization subdivided by branches and completely in the hands of industrialist associations. A third point of attack was the *system of financial coverage of damages*. The employers urged the abandonment of the allegedly inflexible procedure setting premium levels, which set insurance fees according to *statistically probable* future damages, and its replacement with a more flexible but, in fact, far less reliable allocation procedure that aimed to cover only the *actual damages* on a year-to-year basis (doc. 8 and commentary). The strategic goal of these attacks was a complete takeover of the state-controlled institutes. The employers flatly denied the autonomous status of the institutes, likening them to state authorities: "The members [insured employers] are not granted any overview of the institutes' management. Their administration is veiled in darkness,"[25] the Committee of the Chambers of Commerce and the Association of Industrialists in Austria complained in a 1906 memorandum. Accordingly, these bodies argued, the most efficient way to get industrial accident insurance back on track would be to hand it over to the employers, restricting the participation of workers to issues concerned with establishing accident pensions.[26] On the other hand, the diagnosis of the Social Democrats, the main political voice of the workers (as well as all social democrats), presented a mirror image of the picture painted by the employers. The workers, too, considered the issue of accident pensions to be pivotal. However, they saw the insurance institutes as capitalist tools of exploitation, describing the associated courts of arbitration as "pension squeezers" (*Rentenquetschen*). They, too, criticized centralized bureaucratic government supervision; they did so, however, not because of its strength but because of its weakness.

In 1911, in what could serve as a blueprint for Kafka's description of bureaucratic centralism in China in his story "Building the Great Wall of China," the leading Social Democrat expert in social insurance, Leo Verkauf, stated that in the Austrian governmental bureaucracy, "the influence of local interests is stronger than that of the central authorities. Crownland governments and district authorities are much less concerned with the wishes and instructions of the superior authorities in Vienna than they are with the dictates of the political powers in their crownland. They can indulge in this practice with impunity. What originally was contrary to the regulations has gradually developed into common law."[27] Verkauf analyzes this semilegal zone of public life as the "sociopolitical milieu" of a given region and develops a whole typology of fraudulent behavior among employers and lack of social conscience among workers. In Verkauf's account, ethnic and regional factors add to the complexity of a given milieu, as in his vivid picture of manners in Galicia: "The majority of tailors in Lemberg are Jews. Barely fifty of them are among the 500–600 members of the local health-insurance plan." In such a milieu, health-insurance companies cannot help but "dispatch controllers to literally hunt for members among the places of business. [. . .] When, for example, such a checker shows his face anywhere in Lemberg, there is universal panicky flight. Someone, at some street corner or other, will signal his arrival and in no time, all workshops and stores are deserted [. . .]. People hide in kitchens, in living rooms, behind the counters, etc."[28] According to most Social Democrats, then, the crisis of workers' insurance was not caused by centralized control but, on the contrary, by the absence or weakness of government supervision. This weakness, Verkauf argues, created the greatest obstacle to efficient accident prevention. Only the strong hand of the law could balance employers' "natural inclination" not to spend money on workplace security. As for the institutes' high annual deficits, the law should allow taking employers who withhold premium payments to criminal court—criminalizing social-insurance fraud. Most of the blame, however, lay with accident-insurance bureaucrats, who, like "shy" colleagues in Kafka's Castle bureaucracy, "had a true horror of exerting power." Hence Verkauf, too, eventually demands the reorganization of the institutes. This time, of course, they should meet the needs of the workers who, "as the legitimate agents of social-political morals, must be granted the influence they deserve."[29]

The workmen's accident insurance institutes did not silently accept the role of scapegoat. In a 1907 memorandum, they countered attempts to "sidetrack the institutes" with their own analysis. They maintained that insufficient statistical data in the first years of Austrian accident insurance, "severe shortcomings" of the principal law of 1887, and a flawed application of the law by the state authorities and the courts had caused the institutes' disastrous financial performance.[30] They complained that the system of state supervision denied the institutes all executive power, making them dependent on the decisions of incompetent central authorities; and they complained that they were denied the right to conduct technical inspections of the insured firms. But they also claimed severe losses owing to employers' premium fraud. They lobbied for a law that would force employers to keep workers' wage lists as a sound basis for setting premiums. They also pointed to the steep increase in compensation claims. This situation could not be sufficiently explained by the increasing speed of industrial production, with a consequent increase in accident rates. A general suspicion of insurance fraud by the workers—in the form of simulated injuries and of malingering—was raised in careful diction: "In not a small number of cases, doubts need to be cleared up as to whether an actually existing ailment had in fact been caused by the accident in question, or whether subjective symptoms in the absence of objective evidence merit consideration."[31]

National Conflict

A century later, Western readers will recognize such opinions and arguments. As it developed, however, the Austrian welfare state differed significantly from that prevailing in Western Europe and Germany. The distinctive difference—the conflict of nations that was cutting across the battle lines of class conflict in Austria—remained remarkably absent in sociopolitical debates. In Verkauf's three-hundred-page monograph, we find only one rather cryptic paragraph on the issue. Abandoned to their local environment by the central government, the institutes had to implement their agenda alone.

Austria's national struggle was played out in its most industrialized area—Bohemia; language politics would continue to obstruct the creation of an efficient administration. The "rebirth" of the Czech nation during the Enlightenment period had been closely linked to a restoration (better, a reinvention) of the Czech language as a language of high culture (*Kultursprache*). The challenge to German to become the unquestioned administrative language of the Hapsburg Empire became a reality in 1848–49, when the constitution established the legal equality of all languages of the Empire. For three more decades, this norm had few practical consequences. In 1880, the federally minded government of Count Taaffe required that administrative actions be taken "in the language in which they were initiated by an individual party, with interpreter service provided for the other party, if necessary."[32] In Bohemia, the emerging Czech middle class produced a rapidly growing group of bilingual public officials. Their mostly monolingual German colleagues now feared for their careers. They began to call for the administrative segregation of districts by nationality and language. The conflict escalated in the mid-1880s, when social legislation created a new job market in public service. Taaffe's electoral reform of 1885 brought more than two million new voters to the polls, mainly from the lower middle class, giving rise to nationalist and racist political parties and dealing a death blow to German and Czech liberals. The struggle of nations for equal acknowledgment *by* the state turned into the "struggle of nations *for* the state," as the Social Democrat leader Karl Renner put it. "[F]rom the outset," Joseph Redlich added, in retrospect, "the prize was the state organization."[33]

The road to destruction was taken by Taaffe's predecessor, Count Kasimir Felix Badeni who, in the spring of 1897, issued two ordinances providing for the equal treatment of German and Czech, not only as "external languages" but also as "internal languages," within and between all Bohemian public authorities. Accordingly, all public officials would have to prove a sufficient command of both languages within three years or lose their jobs. German nationalists filibustered in parliament; their electorate rioted in the streets of Bohemia's German towns. That fall, Badeni bowed to pressure from the masses and resigned, leading to new riots, this time by the Czechs. A state of emergency was declared. In the fall of 1899, the Badeni ordinances were rescinded; parliamentary procedures were obstructed almost continuously until the end of the Empire. Even the sophisticated Social Democrats, the explicitly international party in the supranational Empire,[34] were infected by the nationalist rage. Eventually, Czech separatists (calling themselves "Centralists") founded their own Czech Social Democratic Party at the Brno Convention in May 1911. Similar divisions cut across workers' and even public servants' organizations (doc. 11 and commentary).

Stifled Legislation

While in Foucault's genealogy of biopower, the nation was the "active, constituent core"[35] for the emergence of the state, it was a lethal virus in the multinational Hapsburg Empire. For all the furor the national conflict raised on the "classical" stages of politics—the parliament and the street—it existed as a silent infection within the system of social insurance. Sociopolitical discourse had no words for the ethnopolitical issue, and the risks of ethnic conflict could not be covered by accident insurance. Instead, ethnic conflict fatally fused with class conflict with far-reaching consequences, not only for the economic performance of accident insurance but also for overall social legislation. In the two decades following the end of the Taaffe era (1879–93), no less than eight different cabinets, sometimes interrupted by provisional ministries, struggled to transform the Empire into a modern welfare state. In the first year of his term as prime minister (1900–4), the social visionary Ernest von Koerber submitted the draft of a law on the use of administrative language in Bohemia; it postulated a compromise, introducing Czech as the second "internal language" of public authorities while granting authorities in German districts the right to use German only. Since each side bluntly rejected the concessions made to the other, another promising attempt to settle the issue failed. Once again, all political hopes rested on social insurance as a means of decreasing national tensions. In 1904, Koerber submitted a comprehensive "Program for the Reform and Development of Workers' Insurance" that aimed to introduce disability and old-age insurance as well as unite all branches of workers' insurance under a single piece of legislation. In December 1904, however, the national conflict, together with attacks from clerical circles, forced him to step down, leaving all his providential projects unfinished. His draft was under discussion until the summer of 1908, when, at last, the insurance department of the Ministry of the Interior issued an official draft for the new law. It was submitted to the House of Representatives in November (while parliament was paralyzed by the political furor in the wake of the Balkan crisis) and, without a first reading, passed for further debate to a special committee of fifty-two experts. A year later, this group resubmitted the draft unchanged. The Social Democrats then successfully called for establishing a permanent committee on social insurance, which had almost finished its work on the draft when, in the summer of 1911, nationalist obstruction once again dissolved parliament. Count Karl von Stürgkh, the last prime minister appointed before World War I, and his so-called ministry of bureaucrats (*Beamtenministerium*) were unable to deal efficiently with the national and social issues. In March 1914, Stürgkh adjourned parliament, once again in response to nationalist obstruction. When the Empire collapsed at the end of World War I, the promises of comprehensive social security that Emperor Franz Joseph had made in two speeches from the throne in 1907 and 1911 remained unfulfilled.

Kafka's "Office"

The Trainee Clerk as Special Agent

When, in the summer of 1908, Kafka began his career in social insurance as an assistant secretary (*Aushilfsbeamter*), the Prague Institute employed more than two hundred mathematicians, lawyers, engineers, doctors, clerks, typists, and office assistants, a number that had been increasing annually. Kafka was not entirely unknown to his new employers as he entered his bustling new workplace. Since, in pre-World War I Austria, access to careers in public service was widely restricted for Jews, it would not have been enough for him merely to have passed the exam at the Commercial College. Ewald Příbram, a former classmate at the Prague German secondary school, was the son of the Institute's president, Otto Příbram; surely he helped open the door for Kafka.[36] The elder Příbram, a former lawyer and president of one of the Institute's biggest clients, Prager Maschinenbau AG, had been elected to the Institute's Board of Trustees by the influential association of mining and metal-work industries in 1893 and in 1897 was elected president of the Institute. This mildly reform-minded liberal German industrialist had apparently been able to integrate, at least symbolically, the class and ethnic tensions cutting across the Institute's agenda at the time. He must have represented the old spirit of the monarchy within this new branch of social administration in so suggestive a manner that Kafka, on the formal occasion of his own promotion, was seized by protracted fits of laughter in his presence.[37] On a more professional level, Kafka had already met a number of other key persons at the institute during his vocational course at the Commercial College. Among them were Siegmund Fleischmann, later head of the Institute's legal-affairs department, who, in the summer of 1911, tried to anticipate his dismissal from that position in a letter depicting the overflowing workload of his unit,[38] and Eugen Pfohl, a former lower-ranking army officer without a secondary-school diploma or any other sort of academic degree, who had joined the Institute in 1889, the year it was founded. An indefatigable worker, by 1908 Pfohl headed the actuarial (*versicherungstechnische*) department, the Institute's core unit entrusted with processing the statistical data of the insured firms and their work force, as well as accidents and risk classifications. At the College, Kafka had also listened to lectures by Dr. Robert Marschner, the new director-designate of the Institute. Marschner, a lawyer and renowned social thinker, whose articles on social insurance were widely published, had joined the Prague Institute in 1894. Three years later, he accompanied his predecessor as director, Jacob Haubner, on a trip to Germany to study the organization of Bismarckian social insurance. A Goethe scholar and an elegant writer, Marschner was certainly the most impressive figure when the young law clerk and writer Franz Kafka entered his new workplace. Marschner took over as the Institute's managing director in 1909, with the firm intention of rescuing the Institute from its almost hopeless situation by means of radical reorganization.

In his first two years, Kafka trained in every aspect of the Institute's agenda. Pfohl began by introducing him to the actuarial department and taking him along on business trips, mostly to industrial towns in Northern Bohemia with a predominantly German population. In April 1909, reassigned to the accident department, Kafka confronted the dark side—the raw reality of wounded, crippled, and killed workers and the business of compensating the harm done to them according to a calculus that estimated the impact of their injury on their potential earning capacity. In September 1909, Kafka returned to the actuarial department as a trainee (*Anstaltspraktikant*), and there he began to focus on his two future fields of responsibility: accident prevention and risk classification.

During this period, Kafka's activities went well beyond the routine itinerary of a new clerk. In fact, the first four documents of our selection indicate the beginning of a most remarkable professional career. Kafka was not only entrusted with the task of writing the speech for Marschner's inaugural ceremony (doc. 1), but as docs. 2, 3, and 4 show, the new trainee was asked to deal with a number of strategic issues in the overall framework of Marschner's reforms. A key document is Kafka's long and intricate essay on workshop insurance in the construction trade (doc. 2)—a remarkable piece of work for a clerk four months on the job! There are a number of external reasons for this rapid rise. In November 1908, the leading position in the legal-affairs department was vacant, only to be filled by the unlucky Fleischmann in June 1909. Eugen Pfohl, as head of the actuarial department, was another potential candidate to write this major section of the annual report for 1907, but he was not a lawyer and, as a few samples of his writing show, his literary skills fell far short. Marschner, in turn, was anxiously awaiting his election, scheduled for January 22, 1909, as the new director and, being under fire from conservative opponents,[39] would, at that point, have been well advised to avoid unnecessary exposure. So the newly matriculated Charles University Doctor of Jurisprudence and published writer[40] Kafka became the obvious candidate, despite his junior status, to produce the complex argument of the annual report.

Meanwhile, the particular shape of these initial assignments was more than a matter of circumstance. As our commentaries show in detail, all of Kafka's major assignments in 1908 and 1909—comprising such different subjects of insurance as workshops, small farms, and even automobiles—were part of a comprehensive strategy, aimed at advancing the Institute's struggle for greater autonomy—autonomy vis-à-vis the Vienna bureaucracy and its regional and local subdivisions and autonomy in forging more direct relations between the Institute and its clients. This struggle is grounded in two forms of administrative communication. On the one hand we find the established system of bureaucratic state control, where almost every move of the Institute depended on the permission of the political authorities, the latter usually consisting of nonexperts who made their decisions on the basis of insufficient legislation and under the influence of powerful lobbies. On the other hand, the Institute struggled to detach its agenda from the governance of political authorities and to connect it more closely to the will of its clients, the insured employers and workers. And so we see Kafka mastering the Institute's new agenda: correlating statistical data, industrial surveys, and opinion polls to establish a series of new deals between the Institute and its clients (owners of construction firms, small farmers, automobile owners, and drivers).

"The Greatest Expert on Power"

In March 1910, Marschner's reforms brought about far-reaching changes in the Institute's organization. He fused the actuarial, controls, and finance departments into one huge unit, the business department (*Betriebsabteilung*). He introduced an appeals division to reduce the increasing workload of the legal-affairs department. While injured workers could turn to an arbitration court to claim higher compensation, the procedure for employers dissatisfied with the risk classification—that is, the premium level—of their firm was, as we have seen, more complex. In the Austrian classification schedule (see figure 1), the percentage of insurance premiums to be paid per K 100 of wages was determined by the firm's *risk level*. For each individual firm, this figure was established by three criteria: first, the type of business, which defined the overall risk class of a firm, although risk levels within that class would vary according to safety performance over the previous five years; second, the actual amount of compensation for damages paid by the Institute to workers of that firm in relation to the fees it had received; third, the technical safety standard of the firm's machinery. Since the statistical performance of a firm had to be accepted as an unquestionable fact, most appeals referred to the third criterion, and a much smaller number to the first (doc. 5). Employers had to file their appeal with their local district authority; once correctly submitted, it would be passed on to the office of the governor, initiating the usually protracted procedure described above.

In April 1910, Kafka obtained a permanent position as *Concipist* (a law clerk who wrote drafts for official statements, commentaries, and petitions), whereupon he was promptly installed as head of the new appeals department. Just at this time, the Institute notified Bohemian employers of their reclassification for the period 1910–14. Within a few weeks, employers filed no fewer than 3,100 appeals. For the next two years, Kafka's main task, assisted by the statistician Alois Gütling, was to deal legally with this flood of protests. He spent his work days delegating the statements on routine cases and attending to the more complicated cases himself (docs. 5, 9, 10). At the same time, he observed and assessed the procedure as a whole, writing a critical memorandum to the Vienna Ministry (doc. 7) concerning the role of industrial inspectors within the process of risk classification and classification appeals. Furthermore, he was entrusted with exemplary legal cases even beyond the agenda of risk classification. In the spring of 1913, for example, he represented his Institute in an unsuccessful criminal charge against the orchard and quarry owner Josef Renelt, a stubborn northern Bohemian villager who did not care in the least about risk percentages but simply declared his quarry workers to be orchard workers so as to be able to exempt their wages from insurance fees (doc. 12).

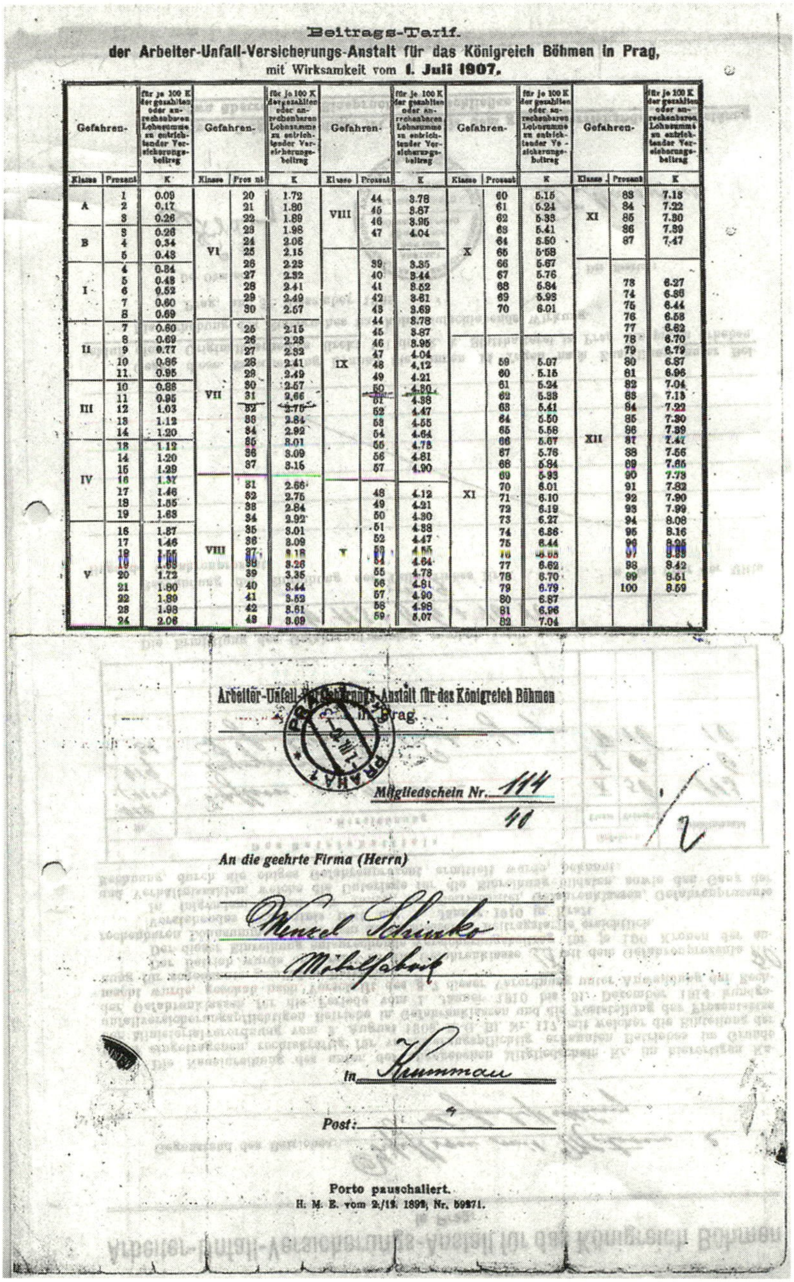

Beitrags-Tarif.
der Arbeiter-Unfall-Versicherungs-Anstalt für das Königreich Böhmen in Prag,
mit Wirksamkeit vom 1. Juli 1907.

Arbeiter-Unfall-Versicherungs-Anstalt für das Königreich Böhmen
in Prag.

Mitgliedschein Nr. 114

An die geehrte Firma (Herrn)

Wenzel Schinko
Möbelfabrik

in Krummau

Post:

Porto pauschaliert.
H. M. E. vom 2/11. 1899, Nr. 59971.

Figure 1. Austrian Risk Classification Schedule

Kafka's second area of responsibility was accident prevention—not with the statistical conversion of accidents into probabilities and liabilities, but with mechanical and physical circumstances. Risk classification addresses the legal dimension of technology: firms are classified within a schedule of fees based on statistically probable risk. The focus of accident prevention, on the other hand, is the mechanical dimension of technology, the interaction of machines and humans. Here, too, Kafka was engaged in pioneer work, struggling to close the gaps in legislation on workplace safety. In 1910, he displayed stunning technological precision in promoting new safety devices in wood-planing machines, including meticulous drawings for the first time in one of the Institute's annual reports (doc. 6). In another publishing innovation, he introduced photographs to accompany an exemplary analysis of the sources of danger in quarries (doc. 14). At the same time, he helped to organize exhibitions on workplace safety and public screenings of the films on accident prevention that Marschner borrowed from the Allgemeine-Elektricitäts-Gesellschaft (General Electricity Company) and from the permanent exhibition on workers' welfare in Berlin (doc. 8; doc. 15). It comes as no surprise, then, that Kafka, the unlikely Jewish official and the special agent for Marschner's reform projects, would act as ghostwriter for his superiors (Marschner and Pfohl) when, on the occasion of the Second International Congress for Rescue Service and Accident Prevention in Vienna, they lectured on Bohemian and Austrian accident prevention to an international public (doc. 13).

According to Foucault, the origin of modern state power—the power to normalize individuals and populations—is located at the intersection of the "norm of discipline" (directed at the individual body) and the "norm of regulation" (directed at whole populations).[41] Kafka's job profile places him exactly at this junction. While accident prevention aims to optimize the interaction between bodies and machines, risk classification calculates accident probabilities for different industrial branches. By establishing various risk percentages within each risk class, it encourages employers to maintain workplace discipline and technical safety standards. But while such well-meant incentives had more effect on the technological fantasies of business owners (doc. 9) than on their will to technological innovation, a 1916 article by Alois Gütling demonstrates the full potential of the normalizing power, of which Foucault speaks, at the intersection of industrial discipline and regulation. Three years after Frederick W. Taylor's pathbreaking work, *The Principles of Scientific Management*, had appeared in German, Kafka's colleague and close collaborator Gütling discussed the equally pathbreaking idea of combining Taylorism, accident statistics, and accident prevention in a new regimen of industrial control:

> In each factory, the entire process of production can be broken down into stages, phases, activities, and finally, separate manipulations and motions. And just as it is theoretically possible to establish such subdivisions, it is equally possible, in theory, to establish the accident risk of each separate motion. The great American statistician Frederick Winslow Taylor, hon. PhD, Honorary President of the American Society of Mechanical Engineers, has proven, even if for a different purpose, that such a procedure can be introduced in practice.[42]

Obviously, such statistical control—no longer of whole industrial branches or even individual factories but of each single motion a worker makes—would have been much superior to the nineteenth-century workplace morale Kafka ironically refers to in "Marschner's" speech on accident prevention at the Vienna conference.[43]

Elias Canetti's well-known remark, "Of all writers, Kafka is the greatest expert on power,"[44] holds true far beyond the symbolic frameworks of family, religion, and higher law. In fact, Kafka's office profile connects him to yet another emergent dimension of state power: mass-media-based publicity. Thanks to his literary skills, it was Kafka who on several occasions was assigned public campaigns for workmen's accident insurance (docs. 8, 13, and the wartime writings discussed below).

Despite these high-profile responsibilities at the Institute, Kafka's career seems to confirm a pattern of anti-Jewish discrimination at work within the Institute. His long letter requesting a raise of December 1912 (doc. 11C) was written on behalf of his whole professional group (the legal clerks or *Concipisten*); in fact, it led to his somewhat belated promotion to the rank of a Vice-Secretary in March 1913. At the same time, he makes it very clear in January 1915 (doc. 11D) that a "disparity exist[ed] between his earnings and those of both the secretaries on the one hand and his less-experienced colleagues on the other—a disparity based neither on the number of years of employment nor the type of work performed," without, however, suggesting a reason.

Kafka's War

It is generally held that Kafka owed his literary "breakthrough" in the fall of 1912 to his heightened awareness of Jewishness and the tension of his epistolary relationship with Felice Bauer. His feverish activity in high-profile professional writing undoubtedly added to the pressure.

With his "birth"[45] as an author, Kafka's correspondence with Felice registers this conflict on a new note of extremity. In a frequently cited passage from the spring of 1913, Kafka calls his office work a "dreadful impediment to my life," deploring at the same time his "incapacity to carry out my work, which at times has been tremendous." By March 1914, he was determined to resign from the Institute and move to Berlin, "to get my foot in on the lowest rung of journalism."[46]

With the beginning of World War I, a heroic option is added to the range of Kafka's professional decisions. In June 1915, the Institute had Kafka exempted from military service on the grounds of his indispensability "in matters of public interest."[47] On Christmas Eve of that same year, Kafka has a confidential discussion with Pfohl to examine three options for escape from the office: first, handing in his resignation; second, taking an unpaid leave; and third, revoking his exemption from military service and reporting for active duty. In a letter to Felice of May 14, 1916, Kafka gives an account of a similar discussion with Marschner. During this whole period, however, Kafka is more deeply involved in his office work than ever before. Staff reductions as the result of military service increased the workload of the remaining staff; furthermore, the war economy had a severe impact on industrial production, posing new challenges to workplace security and accident prevention (doc. 16). Ironically, in the fall of 1914, when industrialized mass killing exposed the "thanatopolitical"[48] reverse of biopolitics, Kafka was busy writing major portions of a report to be published on the occasion of the twenty-fifth anniversary of workmen's accident insurance in Austria (doc. 15). But the impact of war on Kafka's office work went far beyond workmen's accident insurance.

A few months later, the war arrived in full force at the gates of Kafka's office. During the winter of 1914–15, the ever rising flood of wounded veterans returning from the front could no longer be handled by local initiatives. The Ministry of the Interior centralized the scattered welfare institutions by establishing Public Crownland Agencies for Returning Veterans in all the crownlands of the Empire. On February 23, 1915, the ministry ruled that the operation of the Bohemian Agency was to be entrusted to the Workmen's Accident Insurance Institute. On May 26, the Bohemian Agency was officially constituted, with Robert Marschner as its managing director. Under the roof of the Prague Workmen's Accident Insurance Institute, the new Agency united the work of the previously existing State Commission for Disabled Veterans and the Welfare for Blind Veterans with a new, comprehensive program to fight the tuberculosis epidemic spreading among soldiers and civilians. The Agency established special subcommittees to develop treatments for wounded soldiers, vocational training for those unable to return to their former jobs, job placement, and publicity and fund-raising. At the same time, the Agency administered a fund to support disabled veterans, which led to a depressing reunion of soldiers and the civilian work force: "As more and more wounded soldiers were appearing, they were made to wait in the lower part of the hallway and in two waiting rooms, adding to the usual number of people pushing and shoving outside the offices. For it has to be kept in mind that the building of the Institute already faces a daily stream of visitors consisting of injured workers receiving a pension. When they present themselves for medical examination, they are often accompanied by members of their families."[49]

Kafka was assigned to the treatment-development committee and, not surprisingly, became involved in various publicity campaigns. His main project was to prepare and organize the establishment of a psychiatric hospital for shell-shocked war veterans. His writings for this purpose (docs. 17, 18) follow a specific line of argument: they underline the continuity between "peaceful" industrialism and industrialized war, and they convert the rhetoric of heroism from an agenda of mass sacrifice into a code of protection of individual life (doc. 18). In a letter to Felice Bauer of October 30, 1916, Kafka remarks, regarding the public appeal he wrote for the German Society for the Foundation and Maintenance of a Soldiers' and Psychiatric Hospital (doc. 17B): "You will find my name among the signatories; originally I was meant to be high up on the organizing committee, but then, indeed without too much effort, my name slipped into the larger group" (LF 531). In truth, new findings in the Czech State Archive confirm Kafka's deeper involvement in this project. He was a member of a committee set up to select a suitable location for such a hospital. In the first stage of this project, a selection committee circulated a questionnaire to all spas and clinics of Bohemia in order to identify potentially suitable sites. As the holdings of the Bohemian Crownland Committee in the Czech State Archive show, the response was hardly overwhelming. As the burden of the war bore heavily on many small spas and private clinics in particular, their owners obviously welcomed the opportunity to sell them to the state at a price probably above market value. Figure 2 proves Kafka's involvement in the rejection of a particularly impertinent offer. In Sangerberg, a small town near the "world spa" of Marienberg, one Leonhart Sabathil owned an "inexpensive and pleasant spa for public servants, teachers, and small businessmen," as was advertised on a flyer. In fact, it was a rooming house surrounded by a forest, with a nearby mineral spring providing Sabathil with so-called "therapeutic baths." In two lengthy letters to the Crownland Committee, Sabathil argued that his place would be ideal for the treatment of shell-shocked soldiers who would not only regain their nervous equilibrium but also contribute to the cost of their therapy by chopping wood and selling mineral water from the natural source. As the selection committee's secretary, Kafka signed the committee's negative, if diplomatically worded, judgment on Sabathil's offer (see figure 2).

Although in October 1916, Kafka's article in the *Rumburger Zeitung* (doc. 17A) seems to mention Geltschbad—a northern Bohemian summer spa located close to Aussig (Ustí)—as a possible location, we may assume that the eventual choice—the sanatorium at Rumburg-Frankenstein—had been placed on the agenda earlier. Because this sanatorium was recognized for its advanced use of electricity for the treatment of neurological disorders as early as the prewar period, the boom in electrotherapy in the treatment of war-induced trauma favored the choice of Frankenstein. Kafka would have come to this sanatorium, where he stayed from July 20 to August 1, 1915, less as a patient than as the explorer-traveler of his *Penal Colony*, to whom the local officer, explaining the battery-driven torture machine for disobedient soldiers, remarks, "You will have seen similar machines in sanatoriums" (KSS 39). Eventually, on May 15, 1917, the Public Agency bought the Frankenstein sanatorium from the German industrialist Carl Dittrich at a "patriotic" price, with public donations collected by, among others, Franz Kafka. By mid-October, when the hospital was reopened with a new function, Kafka finally achieved his long-desired long leave from the office—not as a journalist and not as a soldier but as a wounded veteran of sorts: a tuberculosis patient with but a poor chance of full recovery. In October 1918, the Public Agency nominated Kafka for a "decoration for his merits in the field of Veterans Welfare."[50] A few weeks later, the addressee of this message, the Hapsburg Empire, no longer existed.

Epilogue

On August 12 and 13, 1917, Kafka suffered two pulmonary hemorrhages, which his doctor later connected to apical tuberculosis. On September 12, he was on his way to his sister Ottla's farm in the northwestern Bohemian village of Zürau, where he was to spend his first long sick leave. When he returned to his office in May 1918, the situation had changed. Two days before Kafka left for the countryside, the Institute's president, Otto Příbram, had passed away. On December 1, Vice President Albert Hošek had called a meeting of the Board of Trustees to elect a new president, but the meeting had ended without a decision. When Czech board members, now holding the majority, proposed

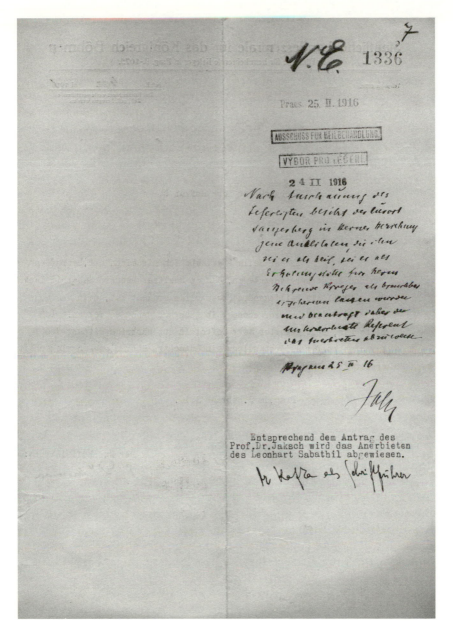

Figure 2. Autograph. Veterans' Welfare: "Dr. Kafka als Schriftführer (Secretary)"

Therapy Development Committee

(*Handwriting*):

In the view of the undersigned, the Sangerberg spa in no way possesses the qualities—whether as a convalescence center or a recreation center for returning veterans—that would make it appear suitable, and therefore the undersigned advisor moves to reject the proposal.

Prague, February 25, 1916

(*Signature*) Jaksch

(*Typewritten*):

In accordance with the motion of Prof. Dr. Jaksch, the proposal of Leonhart Sabathil is rejected.

(*Signature*) Dr Kafka as Secretary

electing a Czech to the presidency, German members boycotted subsequent meetings. On January 25, the Ministry of the Interior installed two officials from the office of the governor as provisional heads of the Institute. They remained in charge until the Czech Republic was proclaimed, on October 28, 1918.

The Imperial Royal Workmen's Accident Insurance Institute for the Kingdom of Bohemia in Prague became the Workmen's Accident Insurance for the Czech Lands, in Prague, operating under the control of the Czechoslovakian Ministry of Social Welfare. On December 24, 1918, the Ministry nominated a twenty-member administrative commission, presided over by Albert Hošek. From this time on, Czech was the language of all internal administrative communication. On March 14, 1919, the new administrative commission sent Director Marschner and his two deputies into early retirement and elected Bedřich Odstrčil, until then a secretary of the Institute, its new director. A few weeks later, Eugen Pfohl died and was replaced by his deputy, Jindřich Valenta. Pfohl therefore was spared reading the Czech newspapers in which, in October 1919, Marschner was described as the "chief schemer" for the Germans and Pfohl his "evil spirit," who had "perpetrated many a crime."[51] Both were held responsible for signing K82,000,000 of Austrian war loans and for having concluded illegal deals with German employers in the matter of risk classification. Remarkably, Kafka was never mentioned in such allegations, which were raised in a number of Czech newspapers.

In October 1918, Kafka contracted a severe case of influenza, probably the fatal turning point in the course of his disease. From this time to his retirement in the summer of 1922, he spent no more than eighteen months at his daytime desk. In all other respects, his transition to the new Republic went smoothly. He was on good terms with his new boss, Jindřich Valenta, and his Czech was no doubt better than that of most of his German colleagues.[52] On December 19, 1919, he was promoted to the rank of Secretary, and beginning in January 1920, he headed a newly created drafts department, a four-member unit serving the larger units of the Institute, which had been reorganized once more. As the superior of three legal clerks and a German native speaker, his actual production of documents written in Czech was, no doubt, restricted to a minimum. Instead, it was now he who had to approve and sign documents written by others (see figure 3); the Czech State Archive holds eight such documents signed by Kafka. Kafka's promotion to the rank of Chief Secretary on February 14, 1922, marked the peak of his career; at the same time, it was a measure taken to speed his early retirement, which occurred four-and-a-half months later. He was to live only two years longer. Kafka died on June 3, 1924, in the Kierling Sanatorium near Vienna.

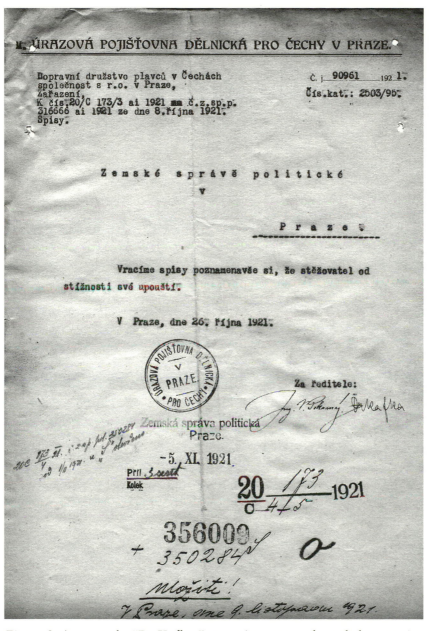

Figure 3. Autograph. "Dr Kafka," as cosignatory, acknowledges receipt of a letter stating that the Czech Bargemen's Association has withdrawn its appeal for a reclassification, 1921.

Acknowledgments

In the mid-1990s, the late Klaus Hermsdorf encouraged me to begin a comprehensive search for records of Kafka's legal work in the appeals department of the Workmen's Accident Insurance Institute for the Kingdom of Bohemia in Prague. Fortunately, many of these documents could be found in the holdings of the Office of the Governor of the Crown Land of Bohemia and the Ministry of the Interior of the former Austro-Hungarian Empire. In 1996 Dr. Jaromir Loužil generously provided me with key information on relevant holdings in the Czech State Archive. From 1999 to 2003, Dr Jindřich Schwippel organized and supported my study of Kafka's briefs and related material in various Czech archives and libraries. In Vienna, Ms. Annabell Lorenz, MA, was extremely helpful in my search for further historical background material. In addition to the persons named above, I would like to thank the staff of the Czech State Archive in Prague, the Austrian State Archive in Vienna, and the Austrian National Library in Vienna for their generous support of my work. I join my coeditors in expressing my gratitude to Professor Kim Scheppele of Princeton University and Professor John Witt of the Columbia Law School for the "new acquist of true experience" that came from every moment spent in conversation with them. And we are most grateful to Hanne Winarsky and Jill Harris of Princeton University Press, who have been unfailingly cordial, elegant, and efficient in their help.

DOCUMENTS

1

SPEECH ON THE OCCASION OF THE INAUGURATION OF THE INSTITUTE'S NEW DIRECTOR (1909)

❧

The text of the speech on the occasion of the inauguration of Dr. Robert Marschner as the new director of the Institute was written in Kafka's hand and preserved by his friend and editor Max Brod. Kafka's distinction as a writer is apparent. In the years to follow, Marschner would employ Kafka as his right-hand man in the comprehensive process of legal, economic, and even political reform that he pursued from his first day in office.

We heartily applaud this choice. It actually places a man in a position for which he is ideally suited, and the position gains the man it needs.

Dr. Marschner's unremitting capacity for work allows him to engage in such extensive and diversified activities that no one person can really do him justice, since no one person can grasp more than part of these activities. As the Institute's long-time Secretary, Dr. Marschner is all the more familiar with its workings as he used his previous position to participate in the improvements undertaken so far. He has always used his vast legal knowledge and skills in the Institute's best interests; he is well known and appreciated among experts as a meticulous writer; and his influence on recent social legislation (liability laws in particular) should never be underestimated. He has spoken at large international insurance congresses; and in the lecture halls of Prague we have also listened to his comments, always welcome, to the point, and informative, on insurance matters, of both general interest and topical. As a lecturer at the Technical Institute, he uses all his knowledge and experience, which serve to complement one another, to prepare our young students for the increasingly urgent problems social insurance is facing. At the Institute, he also established the course in actuarial practice—a subject particularly suited to him, since he is well versed in actuarial computation. His talents as a teacher—which he demonstrated last year to a wider audience when he taught the course on insurance at the Prague Commercial College—was publicly acknowledged with his appointment as a member of the civil-service examination board. To sum up: He is a man who has worked and continues to work with great usefulness and commitment in all areas of his field and who maintains active professional contact with all current colleagues.

Of course, all this is very important, casting Dr. Marschner as an expert in his field in such a light that hardly anyone in Bohemia could claim to be his equal—at least, let us add, without some temerity.

But given Dr. Marschner's new position—one that carries with it so much responsibility and visibility, one that places him at the head of such a complex operation—the human aspect of his academic and social influence truly takes on even greater importance.

He has been scrupulously objective in everything he has done in the past; he feels a need for openness in all his actions. Confident in himself—and in this he is particularly unique—he has sought no distinction other than that found in his work; his only ambition has been to attain that sphere of activity in which he is essential. His impartiality and fairness are unshakable, and the Institute's officials will presumably appreciate their good fortune in getting him of all people as their head. Those who are familiar with his writings, his professional work, and his personality are taken with his strong and keen sense for the situation of the working class, which has a devoted friend in him, but one who will always respect the limits to his efforts in this area dictated by the laws and by current economic conditions. He has never made any promises, leaving that to others (who are the sort to have such a need and who have the time for it). When it comes to actual work, he is the one who does it quietly, without deliberately creating a public outcry, unsparing only toward himself. And that may be why he has no rivals, except possibly in the area of scholarship; if he had, they would be sorry rivals indeed.

The Institute's board of directors was guided only by practical reasons, resisting diverse pressures, in arriving at this felicitous choice. For this it deserves the thanks of all: the government, the employers, the workers, and the Institute's officials.

Complaints against the Institute, both fair and unfair, have been lodged over the years, but one thing is now certain: the work that will be performed will be good, and everything that can be achieved in the way of necessary and advantageous reforms within the framework of the current laws will be done.

Commentary 1

∾

A copy of this speech, in Kafka's handwriting, was found among his posthumous papers and first published by Max Brod.[1] While there is no evidence that Kafka delivered it, this text demonstrates once again his rapidly achieved status as the public voice of the comprehensive reforms that Robert Marschner was to initiate as the Institute's new director.

This short laudatio suggests the importance of Kafka's professional work as a reservoir of poetic ideas. The constellations of individuals, machines, and institutions organizing most of his narratives are, in many instances, prefigured in his office writings. This inaugural speech, for example, contains a core model of the constellation Kafka constructs in *In the Penal Colony* of 1914. The New Commandant, who is trying to run the colony more rationally and efficiently than had the Old Commandant, occupies the position of Robert Marschner, who is taking pains, on a broad canvas, to change the old ways of his predecessor, Jacob Haubner. Egon Pfohl, head of the Institute's operations department and Kafka's immediate superior, who had begun his career in the Austrian army, resembles the officer trying to keep the machine—that is: the Institute—running as it used to, even while witnessing its disintegration in the years of World War I, when the story was written. Marschner's opponents, who existed as an unlikely possibility, anticipates that sorry lot of phantasmatic opponents of the New Commandant, who carry the officer's vain hopes for a return of the old regime. In fact, Pfohl probably introduced Kafka to the operations of the Institute in a manner like the officer's—an attitude of conservative resistance to Marschner's reforms. Read, now, against the background of Kafka's "Chinese" reflections on the organization of security and leadership in the spring of 1917 in "Building the Great Wall of China," Marschner appears to occupy the position of those higher-ranking leaders whose grasp of the building operations went well beyond the perception of the day laborers and even the leaders of lower rank—a position occupied by anyone trying to assess Marschner's overall performance of his wide range of responsibilities.

2

THE SCOPE OF COMPULSORY INSURANCE FOR
THE BUILDING TRADES (1908)

∼

Kafka was twenty-five when his first essay in jurisprudence was published in the Institute's annual report to the Ministry of the Interior in Vienna. This text deals with a legal and, in fact, political conflict of key importance. Between the lines of this reconstruction of recent developments in insurance law, Kafka negotiates a sphere of autonomy for the workmen's insurance institutes of the crownlands vis-à-vis the laws and regulations of the central government.

For background on this finely argued brief, it is well to keep in mind that Kafka believed in universal coverage on the strength of the original, "authentic" law and was chagrined by subsequent attempts to distort it in the direction of partial coverage. He welcomed the 1906 restoration of the original sense of the first law and was dismayed that it was watered down after 1906; but surprisingly enough, he was again distressed to think that the original sense might be restored by the Administrative Court. There is good reason for this paradox. At the time of the annual report, the Institute had already come to satisfactory accommodations with most of the insured employers on the basis of its inventive questionnaire campaign. At the same time, it fully expected that complete coverage would be introduced in the wake of new, comprehensive social legislation then under debate. To disrupt these arrangements in response to the administrative ruling before the passage of the new law would call for a pointless expense of time and effort. Unfortunately, the new law was never passed.

The most recent decisions of the Administrative Court regarding the scope of compulsory insurance for the building trades suggest that it may be of particular interest, especially in the current transitional phase, to provide an overview of this matter as it developed against the background of rapidly changing interpretations by the legal authorities.

It is surely understandable that the question of the scope of compulsory insurance for the building trades and its subsidiaries would meet with conflicting opinions from the outset. For among all construction firms, which constitute a large and very diverse group, what must be considered, along with the varied dangers of the individual operations that are characteristic of most work, is the distinction between two completely different types of accident risks, depending on the location of the respective workplaces. That is the distinction between potential dangers in the indoor workplace on the one hand and at the outdoor construction site on the other. In addition, there is the fact that workers within the same firm—and many such firms are small—are often exposed to one or the other area of risk in turn.

It is precisely because this question is so critical that the quickest, clearest, and most lasting solution possible would have been essential. For we should not have applied principles that were far from settled to a matter involving this group of interested parties, which is very large and riven by internal disagreements. Once done, however, not even proceeding with the greatest sensitivity could have prevented the idea of insurance from sustaining deep-seated and long-lasting harm among those concerned (even and especially among those with good will). This effect remains the same regardless of the particular principle actually applied in each case.

This is precisely what occurred, and in a way that was quite extraordinary, in the building trades and the subsidiary construction trades. In 1906 the original [restrictive] interpretation of the law, set out in ministries' ordinances, decrees, and decisions and in findings by the Administrative Court, was refuted in a finding by the Administrative Court that was constructed with acute logic. Nevertheless [in May 1908], the original interpretation is reinstated in new findings by that same court.[1]

The disputed passage in the law of December 28, 1887, [. . .] regarding workmen's accident insurance, § 1, paragraph 1 and the beginning of paragraph 2, on which the conflicting decisions are based, reads:

> All workers and managers employed in factories . . . as well as in all facilities belonging to these firms are insured against the consequences of accidents occurring at work according to the provisions of this law.
>
> The same provision applies to workers and managers employed in commercial firms whose operations include construction work or who are otherwise employed in construction. This provision shall not apply to workers whose sole work is the execution of occasional repairs in construction but who are not employed in a commercial firm of the designated kind.[2]

In the "comments" issued by the Ministry of the Interior (1888), this law is interpreted to mean that compulsory insurance is restricted to those workers who "are specifically occupied in construction." This restriction is additionally stressed by placing the emphasis on compulsory insurance for workers at construction sites—that is, in a workplace established for only a limited time and for only one specific project. The "Instructions to the Managing Directors of the Workmen's Accident Insurance Institutes" (1889) adopt this interpretation by explaining that whenever subsidiary construction trades are listed, those "enterprises whose workers are engaged in construction work, even if not on a permanent basis, are subject to insurance coverage for these workers for the length of such employment."

[...]

In spite of this situation, one workmen's accident insurance institute raised this question in an appeal before the Administrative Court and thereby brought about a decision on the principle [...]. The reasons given for this rejection were terse, probably in view of the preexisting ministerial pronouncements to the same effect, but were based on one section of the law that was nothing short of unassailable. The cited reasons begin by considering the obligation to insure occupations in general and express the view that occupations are subject to insurance, not because of the danger involved in the work itself but only because of the particular dangers incurred by the addition of special circumstances, such as the industrial nature of the firm, the use of motors, and the construction work being carried out.

The reasons next examine the passage in the law on "commercial firms whose business includes performing construction work" and attempt to prove through verbal interpretation ("performing" is not simply production; "construction work" can never be taken to mean work in the workshop; "includes" indicates activity beyond the usual scope of the occupation) that in this instance only those workers can be intended who carry out their activities at the construction site itself.

The same reason is explicitly used in the decision by the Administrative Court issued on April 6, 1894, [...] and implicitly in the ministerial decree of April 17, 1897, [...] and in the decision by the Administrative Court of March 26, 1898 [...].

The last two decisions already clearly express some ambiguity, since the circle of workers subject to compulsory insurance is drawn as widely as possible, even if only within the limits of the previously cited interpretation, so that watchmen, messengers, and transport workers also appear to be included. Furthermore, the cited decree contains the passage

that the law, in consideration of the particular dangers in commercial firms whose business includes performing construction work, has subjected all workers and supervisors employed in such businesses to compulsory insurance, based simply on the fact of their employment in the construction business and without consideration of its particular type.

However, this opinion stops short of drawing the necessary consequences.

To further justify this limited interpretation of the basic law, the new decisions also refer to the law of July 20, 1894, [. . .] concerning the extension of accident insurance.[3]

The practice we have described, which several of our previous annual reports have repeatedly shown to be quite unacceptable, remained in effect until 1906. The decision by the Administrative Court of April 19, 1906, put an end to this situation—once and for all, we hoped; and there was reason for such hope, because this finding constituted a lesson as much as a decision, in that it precisely justified legally imposing compulsory insurance for workshop labor without the need for any such requirement in the particular case (which involved compulsory insurance for the transportation work of a scaffolding supplier). This procedure must have been based on the consideration that in future, no insurance company would be seeking a decision from the Administrative Court regarding compulsory insurance for workshop labor.

The most important line of reasoning in the decision was the following:

According to the workmen's accident-insurance law, all firms named in § 1, other than the exceptions provided for agricultural and forestry enterprises, are insured entirely without regard to separate work procedures and the greater or lesser danger of each task for all workers and managers employed in the particular firm and with regard to any and all accidents occurring in the firm. The law expressly establishes the application of this principle to "commercial firms whose work includes construction" by linking the regulation applying to such firms, using the phrase "the same applies" to the first paragraph of § 1, in which the stated principle is described.

The assumption that the law for "commercial firms whose work includes construction" was intended to restrict compulsory insurance only to the performance of work directly on the building site or at a contractor's yard set up for a particular building project contradicts the regulation that workers who are not employed in a business of the aforementioned type are also subject to compulsory insurance "if they are employed in construction." Thus, while the law in general recognizes only one business insurance—that is, only one insurance resulting from employment in an insured business—it establishes here a compulsory insurance requirement merely in consequence of employment in construction. If the law had truly intended to establish a distinction between specific work procedures and to specify different treatment of workers according to the type and location of their respective employment when dealing with commercial firms, there would have been no need to begin by putting the emphasis on commercial firms and to list noncommercial construction workers in a separate category; in that case, however, the legislature would have chosen the following version, more directly applicable and preferable in its conciseness: "The same applies to all workers and supervisors employed in the execution of construction work—within or outside a commercial firm." It thus follows precisely from the fact that the legislator makes a distinction between commercial construction workers and individual noncommercial construction workers and contrasts the two that all commercial firms—as well as all other firms otherwise included under accident insurance—should be subject to accident insurance, without distinguishing among the various work procedures that make up the whole.

The conclusion to be drawn is that all commercial construction firms are subject to compulsory insurance, even if the reason for the inclusion of these firms is the specific risk entailed in work at construction sites, just as the risks involved in operating motors in other industries makes the entire firm subject to compulsory insurance.

This far-reaching change of direction of the law courts in the sense always striven for by the insurance institutes nevertheless presented these with a difficult task. For even if the immediate outcome of this crisis was beneficial and allowed hope for the future, it was still a crisis, and it became important to carry out the transition to compulsory workshop insurance as cautiously as possible [. . .].

The discussion joined by all insurance institutes on June 23, 1906, led, most importantly, to an agreement to proceed in the spirit of the Administrative Court's finding [. . .]. Its principles, which were universally accepted, were presented to the k.k. Ministry of the Interior and approved as stated in the decree of July 6, 1906 [. . .].

These measures insured that no particular difficulties arose when the new practice was introduced. Everything appeared to have adapted to the new situation. A further finding by the Administrative Court of March 20, 1908, also made use of the new interpretation by merely mentioning its decision of April 19, 1906, as a basis that needs no further investigation.

Two months later, the decision issued by the Administrative Court on May 22, 1908, was enacted as the beginning of a new practice and a return to the older [restrictive] interpretation of the principal law, though reached by a different route.

[Kafka now goes on to describe how the court returned to the old restrictive interpretation by using the wording of an extension law to show that the basic law originally intended only construction work proper to be subject to compulsory insurance. At this point, workshop labor in certain subsidiary building trades is insured but not in others.—Eds.]

If the insurance institutes were to hope for the continued existence of the decision of 1906, they had to fear that these [new restrictive] decisions would not be deviated from, for they are plenary resolutions that must be considered in the decision according to § 6 and § 8 of the rules of procedure of the k.k. Administrative Court, as long as the courts themselves or the legislation make no pronouncements to the contrary.

Yet another change [rescinding the new restrictive interpretation] by the Administrative Court would, admittedly, have had highly negative consequences, if for no other reason than that it would have introduced a new and dangerous confusion into the legal situation.

The new [restrictive] court findings forced the Ministry and the insurance institutes to implement the revised practices by establishing appropriate principles. This effort was all the more difficult, however, since very severe consequences had resulted from the earlier practices of the Administrative Court.

A ministerial decree sent to the crownland authorities on July 11, 1908, [. . .] declared that the Ministry of the Interior's legal practices would be conducted according to the Administrative Court's revised [restrictive] opinion.

[. . .]

[The above-mentioned decree assumes that the insurance institutes will return to the earlier condition (in which no extended coverage for workshops is necessary) and notes that employers are still free to purchase such extended insurance.—Eds.]

Even before the decree was issued, the Institute went beyond its requirements. In July 1908, it circulated an open letter to all employers in the building and subsidiary trades, primarily to report on the change in the Administrative Court's jurisdiction and the consequences for insurance law. The letter also stressed the possibility of voluntary insurance for workshop labor [. . .] and requested the employers to submit a reply by July 31, 1908, stating whether or not they wanted to maintain voluntary workshop insurance. [. . .]

As a consequence of the new situation, all the problems that existed before the decision of April 19 will reappear. We cannot even begin to encompass them in their current guise as long as we do not have the accident statistics of the corresponding years. And these problems will be further intensified by the sense that legal security is lacking.

[. . .]

The main factor to be considered here, however, is that the same worker in the same firm owned by the same employer is insured in one instance and not in another. If this circumstance has already repeatedly given rise to workers' complaints, of the kind that have frequently occupied the Institute's arbitration committee, the current restrictive interpretation of the law will only increase dissatisfaction. For a time, workers had felt reassured that insurance protected them from the consequences of every kind of industrial accident, but under the new provisions, that coverage will no longer always be the case. And if the workers—all of them as laymen, though the most concerned laymen—think about the issue, they can only conclude that it is chance rather than principle that governs insurance. For the work force, the facts that emerge are incomprehensible: The same worker performing the same work who was insured against accidents in the workshop until July 1, 1908, will no longer be insured after that date; in this case, then, the date determines the risk of accident. The same worker will be insured against accidents when he is employed in one employer's place of work, but when performing the same work for another employer, he is not; here, then, the employer's individual position determines whether there is insurance. Finally, following the Administrative Court's decisions, the locksmith, for example, who installs locks in the doors of a new building, is insured against accidents incurred at work, while the carpenter who has the extremely dangerous job of processing logs in the workshop is not insured against accidents. The paramount question then remains open: how will the various arbitration courts respond to changed practice? Whatever the outcome, however, the most widespread impact of the Administrative Court's latest ruling will be on the area of compensation practice. This impact is also the strongest and the most regrettable, the latter all the more so as the following discussion will show.

The principle of collective insurance (all persons employed in a particular firm are insured against the consequences of certain accidents, merely on the basis of their employment) dominates the entire law. [. . .]. Numerous decisions of the Administrative Court and ministries explicitly recognize this principle.

The Ministry of the Interior [. . .] responded with remarkable succinctness to the request of an association of china manufacturers that an exclusion from compulsory insurance be granted to certain groups of factory workers whose tasks do not expose them to the risk of accidents (e.g., painters, potter's wheel operators, etc.): "In contrast to individual insurance, in collective insurance it is absolutely necessary—as intended by the Workmen's Accident Insurance Law—to include all workers employed in any insured firm, regardless of the different levels of risk of accident to which individual workers are exposed." With this, the factories are denied something that the Administrative Court now grants to the building trades and their subsidiary trades.

The law addresses these latter trades, however, in paragraph 2 of § 1 immediately after dealing with factories, tying these two groups closely together with the phrase, "The same applies to . . ." The building and subsidiary trades are thereby inextricably linked to collective insurance.

The fact that the law places workers and managers in the forefront as insurance subjects rather than focusing on commercial firms, as it does in paragraphs 1 and 3, is due only to a stylistic reason: the second part of the second paragraph deals only with individuals not subject to compulsory insurance; therefore, for the sake of uniformity and greater clarity, the words "workers" and "managers" are from the outset given greater emphasis than is assigned to the word "firm."

In general this second paragraph strives for the greatest possible succinctness, as opposed to the prolixity of the first. The concise phrases, "the same applies" and "otherwise," as well as the word "employed"—used only once but forming the predicate in both coordinated sentences—serve this same purpose.

If we were to enrich the concise phrases, the first sentence of § 1, paragraph 2, would read as follows:

> All workers as well as managers employed in commercial firms whose operations include construction work, or who are otherwise employed in construction in noncommercial firms of the specified kind, as well as the workers and managers employed in facilities belonging to these firms, are insured against the consequences of accidents occurring at work according to the provisions of this law.

This sentence unconditionally includes workshop labor in the category of compulsory insurance.

If we proceed from the standpoint that this passage in the law strictly advocates compulsory insurance for workshop labor, we must rightly expect to recognize this intention clearly in the formulation of the passages that follow, given the succinct coordination of the individual provisions of this paragraph. Such is, in fact, the case, for the next passage reads:

> This provision shall not apply to workers whose sole job is merely the execution of occasional repairs in construction but who are not employed in a commercial firm of the designated kind.

If we were to assume that the first sentence of paragraph 2 determines that workshop labor is not subject to compulsory insurance, the next sentence would contain a striking provision that could not be brought into agreement with the previous sentence, as we have already emphasized above in citing the intent of the decision of the Administrative Court of April 19, 1906 [. . .].

The restriction of compulsory insurance in agricultural and forestry businesses to persons exposed to the risk associated with operating

machinery, as paragraph 3.2 and paragraph 4 of § 1 bring into conformity, also confirms the obligation to insure workshop labor. Paragraph
4 establishes an exception to the rule of collective insurance established
in paragraph 3.2 regarding agricultural and forestry businesses only in
cases in which a power tool that is part of the equipment of such businesses is operated in such a way as to expose only some workers and
managers to the risk associated with the general machine operation.

If we were further to assume that the law intended that insurance
cover only those persons employed in construction who are exposed to
exceptional dangers in construction or at the building site, it would be
incomprehensible why precisely the exception concerning mechanized
agriculture (which the law actually mentions only after discussing construction) is specifically emphasized in a separate paragraph in striking
detail, without the slightest reference to the preceding and more important exception concerning construction, which goes almost unnoticed in
half a subordinate clause.

Thus the passage in the law that requires the equal insurance of workshop labor in the building trades and their subsidiaries appears to be
secure in itself, and only further reinforced by the passages that follow.

[. . .]

Despite its reservations in principle about the new practices, however,
the Institute had officially to acknowledge the new basic findings of the
Administrative Court. Further, the Institute had to use its own resources
to adjust the scope of individual firms' insurance and premium obligations to the new practices, so as not to be caught in a welter of arguments.

When the time came for the Prague Institute to change its practices
according to the new legal findings beginning on July 1, 1908, it had to
choose between two implementation procedures.

For one, the Institute could stop at using the press to publish the relevant court findings with appropriate commentary and then, after a brief
wait, eliminating workshop labor from the insurance of all firms that
had not voluntarily requested it within the waiting period. At first
glance, this procedure appeared very simple and not very costly and able
to be concluded within a relatively short period.

However, realistic consideration showed that this approach was not
very appropriate, at least in our situation, for it depends on two assumptions that do not apply here.

The first is that in our country, publication in newspapers is far from
sufficient as a general announcement and as providing adequate information about specific insurance details. This is a lesson the Institute
learned quite thoroughly on earlier occasions, and there is a simple explanation of this phenomenon: either an employer thinks that the deci-

sion regarding insurance for his firm is proper, in which case he does not usually expect any concerns about possible questions that might arise; or the employer does not find the decision fair, in which case he takes matters into his own hands, sending out petitions or appeals, and looks to a resolution of his particular dispute. Therefore it often happens that the publication of decisions on legal principles is completely disregarded. But the question of workshop insurance was not to be exposed to this risk.

Second, given that once the new court decision was announced, the administrative machinery would immediately get to work, the Institute might well have assumed that the majority of employers would immediately decide to cancel workshop insurance ("Because that's so tempting," as a master locksmith wrote, though he agreed to voluntarily take out workshop insurance). But the Institute knew from experience that many employers have a very real understanding of what is best for their workers—and that means for their firm—and that others need only a calm and complete explanation to head them in the right direction.

For these reasons, the Institute chose another approach, which had one major advantage among others, namely, that the workers' interests could also be properly taken into consideration. Before undertaking any changes in the insurance register on its own initiative, the Institute sent the following letter, as previously noted, to all employers in the building and subsidiary trades:

The Administrative Court [. . .] has officially provided the authoritative interpretation of § 1, paragraph 2, of the Accident Insurance Law, to the effect that the legal obligation to carry insurance also applies to workshop labor in the building trade and its subsidiaries to the extent that they were not previously subject to compulsory insurance under the legal title concerning the use of motorized machinery.

With its decree of July 6, 1906, [. . .] the Ministry of the Interior, in explicit recognition of the legal opinion expressed in the Administrative Court's finding, approved the subsequent principles established by the workmen's accident insurance institutes for the inclusion of workshop labor. These principles were devised on the assumption that this finding would allow for consistent legal judgments and that the provisions of the law would receive the interpretation that appears to be the legislators' actual intention.

Sadly, the expectations of this legal finding, not only those held by our Institute but also the hopes of the workers and—we emphasize this especially—a large proportion of the employers, were not fulfilled. For most recently the Administrative Court has once again abandoned the legal opinion it pronounced in 1906 and has returned to the view that it had taken from the beginning, along with the opinion of the administrative commissioners even earlier. [. . .]

It would seem that as the natural result of the situation created by the courts, the Institute should immediately revise its earlier decisions about compulsory insurance for workshop and workplace labor without machinery, to the effect that in future such facilities would no longer be subject to compulsory insurance.

Such a move would, on the one hand, ignore the intentions of a number of employers who feel that it is important to insure all workers; on the other hand—and this may be the principal consideration—the workers' existing insurance would be canceled.

[. . .]

In view of these factors, our administrative committee has decided to leave it to your discretion whether or not you wish in future to maintain noncompulsory insurance for workers in the workshop and on the building site under the conditions described to you.

Should this not be your intention, please let us know at your earliest convenience; we would then reestablish the same status assigned to your firm at the time the decision of December 31, 1904, was issued.

The exclusion of workshop labor would become effective on June 30, 1908, assuming an immediate response to this letter; from this time forward, a higher classification for construction work might apply.

If we have not received a reply from you by July 30, 1908, we will assume that it is your intention to continue insuring all the employees in your firm. In that case, there would, of course, be no reason for further action on our part in one direction or the other.

Given the plan to limit the scope of compulsory insurance to the actual work done on buildings or at the construction site, the Institute leaves it to your own well-considered judgment whether or not you wish to declare workers employed in workshops or permanent workplaces to have forfeited insurance claims. In arriving at a decision, you must be aware that, should you decide to eliminate them from insurance coverage, your employees may bring a civil suit against you should they incur an accident. You may protect yourself against this eventuality by maintaining workers' insurance coverage.

Finally, we are pleased to announce that because of the revisions of the risk classifications currently under way, the classification of the building trade in general will find that the desired stabilization will set in at the beginning of the next risk-classification period, or January 1, 1910.

[. . .]

It turned out that when we decided on this course, we were doing the right thing, and the circular was successful beyond all expectation. The employers themselves clearly repudiated the new interpretation of § 1, paragraph 2, of the Workmen's Accident Insurance Law.

Out of 4,169 inquiries sent out by the Institute, only 963 came back with a strong statement of rejection. Moreover, 186 respondents sent in outspoken expressions of agreement, though the circular did not ask for a reply.

[. . .]

In addition to the above reasons, the Institute had still another motive in deciding to go beyond publication of the changed classification practice in newspapers. This move, however, met with only partial success.

It is obvious that an announcement on insurance matters made to an employer through the newspapers alone does not cause him to think as sharply about his own operation and its particular needs as he needs to, particularly under these circumstances. An announcement of this sort, intended for the general public and squeezed in between other announcements either of a general nature or promoting class politics in particular, has to be viewed from some general viewpoints.

The Institute's circular was also intended to mitigate this adverse effect. It was supposed to function as a personal negotiation with the employer about his own particular firm, free from outside influences.

And generally, the letter had this result, and very clearly so in some cases. It became apparent that the relationship between employers and the Institute is often one of great trust, since many of the replies took the Institute's financial well-being into account, and the Institute leaves it to the employers to come to their own decision, in the assumption that they will make the right choice.

In other cases, in contrast, even the open letter did not achieve its intended effect. Especially where it was a matter of exempting workshop insurance, the Institute wanted to hear from the employers, but in many instances, it was clear that particular organizations were speaking in the employers' voice, and unfortunately at times, the voice was that of an organization without the mediation of the employers.

In these instances, the response to the Institute's initiative met, not with the thoughtful decision of each individual employer dealing with the particular situation of his firm, but with retorts from organizations and trade associations. In these cases, the question of workshop insurance frequently and understandably fell into the hands of those who had no personal connection to the subject, did not have the necessary understanding of it, could not grasp its technical aspects, and thus, given the number of conflicting interests that they have to represent, chose the solution that was theoretically the most immediately comfortable and that thus appeared to be the most plausible.

Naturally, these respondents had every advantage over the Institute.

The Institute had to expect more work from those employers who might want to keep workshop insurance than from those who did not; therefore the Institute required employers to reflect on their decision.

The organizations, on the other hand, usually responded by advocating only what the majority of employers thought on first hearing about the most recent form of this issue. The organizations could go from employer to employer and arouse their concern. Not only had these organizations already been in touch with these employers on insurance matters; their interest now required no thought on the part of the employers, and they provided printed forms, written statements, and printed complaints to the Ministry of the Interior, which the employers need only sign.

Their success was therefore preordained.

And so we have also received many printed statements that reject the plan as well as many, often lengthy, handwritten statements using exactly the same wording; in addition, 116 printed petitions were sent to the Ministry of the Interior, almost all of them from master carpenters.

One reply recently received from a master carpenter shows that these organizations also had very concrete goals in mind. He canceled the insurance for the workshop labor of his firm with the explanation that he had insured his employees with an association of master carpenters named in the letter. It is easy to see that a private insurance company is behind this association, as may well be true in other cases in which the originator is not so readily identified.

[...]

The intensity of the agitation for eliminating workshop insurance is shown by the peculiar fact that in the professional association of master carpenters, where the organizations enjoyed the greatest success in persuasion, the same employer sent in two contradictory statements even before the Institute had arrived at any kind of decision. One statement, on a printed form, declared firmly that master carpenters were placed in a category that was much too high, and for this reason the workshop and building site insurance could not be kept. A second statement, which the Institute received a few days later, requested that the full insurance be kept in force; this missive was equally unambiguous and declared the first statement void. It appears that two different organizations exerted opposite influences in this case; they are the Association of Master Carpenters of the Kingdom of Bohemia and a union of building-trade professionals allied with the Reichenberg Chamber of Commerce.

One employer who had submitted a printed rejection statement declared after receiving the Institute's notification that he wanted to provide workshop insurance for his workers after all, for the difference in the premiums for the two types of insurance was negligible.

Having received the Institute's letter, one master metalworker wrote that, after careful consideration, he had come to the conclusion that keeping accident insurance as it existed before July 1, 1908, seemed more expedient after all. Similarly, a master housepainter revoked his cancellation of workshop insurance.

The organizations' methods of persuasion often went further than the Institute's initiative: it affected firms that had no stake whatever in this matter and thus had not been circularized by the Institute. The Institute thus received many statements of rejection from firms whose workshop labor had never been insured and from others whose workshop labor had been excluded from insurance long ago in consequence of appeals. Similarly, statements of rejection came from firms whose workshops were subject to compulsory insurance under another legal title (mechanical operations).

When the Institute sent its notification to one employer from whom it received a form statement of rejection and a form complaint to the Ministry of the Interior, he answered that he desired the full range of the insurance and that he had signed neither a statement of rejection nor a complaint.

The harmful rabble-rousing in this matter was by no means new, however; at the time workshop labor was included in the compulsory-insurance rules, the appeals process was altered through similar initiatives. Happily, however, the Institute can now declare that our proposal met with more than opposition; it also received applause and support from various other trade associations. Since opposition, as we have noted, has been unable to prove that workshop insurance is unnecessary, agreement must be a very strong argument for it. There was little need to cite convincing arguments against workshop insurance in practice, for this position was based on a first, superficial view of the matter, but arguments are certainly needed to overcome that opinion. But just such persuasion is what must have taken place in many trade associations.

The above-mentioned union of building-trade professionals from the Reichenberg Chamber of Commerce considered the choice with particular objectivity; and as best we can determine, we have their influence to thank for 52 statements from master builders and 10 from master bricklayers agreeing to continue with workshop insurance. In this case, the union took a further positive step than did the Institute; we generally do not assume that bricklayers are employed in workshop and on the site. Additionally, there were 7 statements from master carpenters and 1 from a master glazier.

The association of varnishers in one of our largest towns had previously introduced a far-reaching measure against including workshop labor in compulsory insurance. But now, the chairman of this association writes that he recognizes the advantage of workshop insurance and will keep all his workers insured. However, he believes that there must be a fair adjustment of the premium rate, stating that the current rate of K 1.37 is the top limit of what he can support. Should there be an increase, he would have to revoke the workshop insurance.

The Institute can cite a relatively large number of additional employers' statements of agreement that are at least equally important as indicators of the general opinion as those just mentioned, because many employers used the statements as an opportunity to pass on to the Institute their particular requests. This allowed them to articulate their views on the implementation of obligatory insurance more precisely.

[Kafka goes on to explain that the antiworkshop-insurance agitation used two main catchphrases in its campaign: the supposed lack of risk of workshop labor and the expediency of the new court ruling. He counters the first catchphrase by quoting statements from employers to the opposite effect and then declares that "the catchphrase of the expediency of the new situation is incomparably more dangerous. One needs only to examine the circumstances impartially with open eyes to see that here there is no expediency whatsoever."—Eds.]

In conclusion, the Institute can state the following: The kind of answer that the public gave to the Administrative Court's new ruling might be expected; the only surprise was that such an impressive majority of employers gave the same positive answer on the one hand and that the voice of the workers was entirely absent on the other.

And yet workers' vital interests were at stake; they could not know what decision their employers would make, and if the workers had made their voices heard, the outcome would surely have been even more favorable, especially during the transition period. But the workers showed only indifference. (Only one employer responded to the Institute's letter by writing that he would have to keep workshop insurance after all because all his workers demanded it.) Perhaps the reason for the workers' silence is that we are, for the most part, dealing with rather small firms, whose workers are not well organized, while larger firms kept the full range of insurance from the beginning.

If we consider everything we have discussed, we can present a broad overview of the situation as follows:

The forces working against workshop insurance are: a stubborn adherence to received forms that is not consistent enough; a trend among some employers motivated by agitation and general prejudices; and finally, in rare instances, a complete lack of understanding of the social needs, and this is something that can be remedied, not by persuasion, but only by legal means.

The arguments in favor of workshop insurance are: the law interpreted in its intention, its history, its text, and its context; theoretical and practical reasons of practicality; and the wishes of the overwhelming majority—not only in number but also in importance—of employers.

And as every specific question of social insurance, if only we think it all the way through, must incontestably lead to the common center of all these questions, where all find a satisfactory solution, so it is with this question: only the broadest possible generalization of insurance can satisfy the intention of the legislature (to grant the benefit of insurance to as many segments of the working population as possible) and the interests of those most closely affected—the workers, the employers, and the Institute. We must add one reservation, however: actually only two interests apply here, those of the workers and of the employers, because the Institute has no other interest but theirs. If the interests of the workers (protection for as many workers and compensation for as many accidents as possible) and the interests of the employers (premiums as low as possible through fair distribution to as many employers as possible) are satisfied, the interests of the Institute will be satisfied as well. At that time, the Institute will no longer meet with open and covert hostility from both sides, as unfortunately so often happens today, since people have become accustomed to viewing the Institute as the originator of all shortcomings in accident insurance, while it is only the guiltless representative of a law that is perhaps inadequate, and in this case, inadequately interpreted as well.

In the particular matter of workshop insurance, order can be restored only by a genuine legal interpretation or by a process of reform; the latter can occur only by rising above the voices of those who have advised the total exclusion of workshop labor in any reform of insurance matters. These are the potential consequences that must inevitably result from the situation we have described. We present our account to the authorities chosen to settle these questions.

Commentary 2

❧

Kafka was proud of this brief, his first essay in jurisprudence. Shortly after meeting his fiancée, Felice Bauer, in 1912, he mentioned his "article on workshop insurance" as one of the "pleasures" he was keeping "in store" for her. However ironically slanted, the remark confirms the dignity with which he approached his legal writing. The text displays many of the features that distinguish the best of his essays, including:

- precise, detailed knowledge of the issues;
- the ability to perceive and describe a dispute from all possible points of view and to create a document containing this conflict of voices;
- a heightened sensitivity to the discursive aspects of language: its power to produce subject positions and influence attitudes, behaviors, and opinions;
- a method of settling disputes, not by force of precedent or other legal authority, but by mediating the desires and convictions of the parties.

The question at stake in Kafka's juridical essay of 1907 was of paramount importance for the system of accident insurance as a whole. Unlike health insurance, accident insurance covered, not individuals, but business firms and entire branches of industry. Hence, extending compulsory insurance across all sectors of production was of crucial importance to the worker's sense of security. In many cases, workers were insured against accidents only in some sites of their daily work routine and not in others. As Kafka's essay shows, this spatial dimension of workmen's insecurity was compounded by a temporal factor. Courts had recently reached different decisions at different times. The basic law of 1889 governing workmen's insurance had left open to interpretation whether workshop labor was covered by insurance. A 1906 decision of the Administrative Court in Vienna seemed to settle this matter for good in favor of workmen's security across the board. But in May 1908, industrial lobbies urged this same Administrative Court to revoke its former decision. Then, in early November 1908, a few weeks before the publication date of the Institute's annual report for 1907, a special parliamentary committee of experts submitted to the Reichsrat (the legislative body of the Austrian part of the Empire) the draft of a new piece of comprehensive social legislation aiming to close all previously identified gaps in the insurance law and to provide complete legal security for Austria's working class.[1]

The director of the Institute, Robert Marschner, decided not to lose any time in publishing the position of the Prague Institute concerning these recent developments, and he sought to include a commentary on them as early as the annual report for 1907. The fact that Kafka was assigned to write the commentary on this complex and momentous matter indicates the high prestige he must have enjoyed after barely half a year of service at the Institute.

The line of argument Kafka takes is a key to understanding many of the intricate views on social relations he was to dramatize in his literary works. As the public (and anonymous) voice of his Institute, Kafka by no means speaks out as an advocate of the working class. While in the great mass of social and political literature of his day, social insurance was conceived of as a medium of balancing the opposing interests of employers and employees, and hence of incessant bargaining, Kafka's contributions to the public debate (see the following documents, esp. docs. 7 and 8) are informed by the original idea of integrating these interests by *risk calculation* in order to dissolve the conflict between capital and labor. In other words, the essay in question follows the model of a risk community rather than the model of bargaining and compromise. So, while in this report Kafka's precise linguistic analysis of the law succeeds in showing that its authors had intended from the beginning to include workshop labor in compulsory accident insurance, his proposals for the future indicate that the popular myth depicting him as an ardent spokesman for the working classes is exaggerated. In view of the latest legislative drafting, Kafka, in fact, urges the Vienna court *not* to abandon its May 1908 decision to exclude workshops from compulsory insurance, "because a repeated modification of the interpretation would only entail another dangerous confusion of legal relationships." Although Kafka's commentary seems to side with the workers at one point and employers at another, its goal is not political in the sense of being partisan. It expresses a jurisprudential choice at once political and cultural: the calculability and reliability of the law, the report tells us, is of greater value than the question of its correct or incorrect interpretation by adjudication. In other words, vacillation in the law is a greater danger to society than its possible misinterpretation.

We see in the report a new contradiction of crucial significance for Kafka's literary universe as well, between a "top-down" bureaucracy based on centralized power and a "bottom-up" model based on the voices of individuals. In the political and cultural environment of his time, the young Jewish clerk Franz Kafka displayed considerable courage in bluntly asserting that the Administrative Court's exercise of power "was neither in accordance with the spirit of the law nor with its wording." He charged the Court with the responsibility for a power vacuum that forced the Prague Institute to break the rule of "state-controlled" administration and to take over the management of the new legal situation created by the decision of May 1908.

Kafka offers in its place the questionnaire, which aimed to discover employers' and workers' preferences without interference from lobbies and unions. The poll that the Institute had conducted among employers in its territory established that they were, by and large, in favor of including workshop labor in workmen's insurance. By November 1908, the Institute had already responded accordingly, supplementing the May 1908 decision of the Administrative Court with a variety of individual contracts made with employers. Kafka's procedure presents, for all its limitation of scope, a model for balancing the forces of centralism and federalism in a multiethnic state. The key is, once again, not narrowly political. It is based, not on such ideological values as "freedom" or "autonomy," but on a calculated response to the great fact of modern industrial production: increasing differentiation and specialization of function. The problems of social insurance can be solved only by specialized professional expertise, not by the authority emanating from the top position in the hierarchy of a centralized administration.

At a time when the Austro-Hungarian Empire was struggling for a political organization to make it fit for the twentieth century, Kafka's essay develops a micro model of such a political future. Nine years later, in the spring of 1917, Kafka reenacted the questions of power raised in 1908 in his fragmentary novella, "Building the Great Wall of China." Here, a Chinese construction engineer announces the completion of the Great Wall; he then immediately revokes this statement by stressing the piecemeal construction of the Wall, which complicates the Empire's goal of securing its lands against attacks from the unpredictable nomads. This contradiction leads the narrator to reflect on the intentions of the Chinese government (the "leadership") and its way of relating to and communicating with the people. The piece ends with his plea for a loose administrative organization as a crucial means of national integration. What in one respect is a weakness (a mere fiction) is in another the very foundation of the country's existence.[2]

By replacing the problem of security in the building trades with the problem of security based on building the Great Wall of China as a protective device, Kafka the writer maintains close pragmatic relations with Kafka the clerk. At the same time, his poetic imagery extends these relations to a variety of discourses built on the symbolic structure of architecture, such as religion, the philosophy of history, nationalism ("nation building"), Zionism, psychoanalysis, aesthetics, and the like, and thereby creates a unique kind of diagnosis of his age in a moment of extreme danger to the cultural order of his day (the "age of the bourgeoisie," said to have vanished in and after 1917). If we compare Kafka's essay on workshop insurance with "Building the Great Wall of China," we witness the return of specific problems of Austrian accident insurance as ciphers for the description of general, overarching cultural problems, to wit:

- the system of piecemeal construction and the only questionable security resulting from it;
- the narrator's investigation of the aims pursued by the leadership through a seemingly inexpedient system of construction—that is, the gap between expert knowledge and political knowledge; the decision to look for an answer to these questions, not in the center of political power, but in the people;
- the phantasmal status of a successful communication between the government and the people, as implied in the formal act of a "message from the Emperor." This can be likened to the original "message" from the German parliament (Reichstag) that set social insurance only partly on its way in 1883; or the *Thronrede* of the Hapsburg Emperor Franz Josef in 1885.[3]
- the twofold and contradictory conclusion praising the weakness of central power while exposing the catastrophic consequences of a power vacuum.[4]

Finally, it should be noted that Kafka's Chinese narrator is a precise encryption of Kafka the clerk: as a "subordinate supervisor" in a project of national security, he had finished his education at a time when many young men had been enlisted for that national task, and he had been entrusted with only a fragment of the task, which effectively sustained his professional ambition. We will witness more than once in this collection of official documents how the narrative voices of Kafka the clerk and Kafka the writer intersect or, indeed, merge.

3

FIXED-RATE INSURANCE PREMIUMS FOR SMALL FARMS USING MACHINERY (1909)

∿

An exploration of the world of small farmers in Bohemia, this document concludes by stating the difficulty—indeed, the impossibility—of surveying individual farms for the purpose of insuring them as well as by remarking the ignorance of the central administration in Vienna in regard to such local problems. This text makes suggestive reading for every lover of Kafka's great novel, The Castle, *whose hero, a supposed land surveyor, succeeds in surveying nothing.*

T he supplementary law concerning accident and health insurance provided a legal basis for resolving the question of fixed-rate insurance premiums for small farms using machinery, a topic that has been the subject of long-drawn-out discussions for some years. Thus the matter could be brought close to the definitive conclusion, so long aspired to, this year.

Allow us to add the following comments to the pertinent debate.

[. . .]

The essential preliminary steps in the process of setting a fixed rate have already been taken. We began by sending questionnaires to all the local authorities, so as to ascertain reliably the total number of farmers eligible for the fixed rate. A subsequent letter to the local authorities laid out in detail the reasons that absolutely necessitate fixed insurance premiums for small farmers and the principles that guided the Institute in implementing this decision. Finally, the prospective approach for setting the fixed premiums was communicated to the local authorities, and the farm owners—who unconditionally agree to the fixed rate—were made aware of the favorable treatment the Institute intends to grant them, even apart from the advantages inherent in the fixed rate itself. In order to be able to take the net earnings of the individual farms into the proper consideration in setting the fixed rates, we intend further to establish the particulars pertaining to the extent of the fields and pastures as well as of the net income.

Even while we were working on all these preliminary consultations and drafts, the law of February 8, 1909, [. . .] was enacted; this is a significant element in establishing the fixed rate. It was not until this law took effect that the Institute was provided with a legal foundation for agreeing on annual fixed rates instead of calculating premiums. It was characteristic of the urgency of this entire matter that the government saw the necessity of bringing this question among others to a solution before engaging on the far-reaching reform of social security as a whole.

The fact that even among the large landowners—who were, admittedly, excluded from the fixed rate—there are many who openly state that they, too, would find such a reform in premiums a benefit demonstrates how urgent and necessary the fixed rate has already become and the recognition granted the advantages connected with this reform.

The Institute views this fact, as well as the sincere support for our preliminary work from appointed representatives of agricultural interests, as a favorable sign for the success of the entire measure; the project will be carried out, not without great effort, but with equally strong hopes and expectations. We believe that not only will there be an end to the enormous losses our Institute has been forced to show from year to year for this professional group, but that there will be a reduction in the labor of calculating premiums as well—an advantage, both for the farmers and for us, that should not be underestimated. In addition, there is the fact that a desire of the farmers, long held but previously thwarted, is now proceeding toward fulfillment: namely, that the farm owner and his wife themselves be insured against professional risks as well. Finally, this rate reform is expected to achieve no less than a reduction in the actual insurance premiums. We can say with absolute certainty that the precise calculation of total payrolls, to which the fixed rate is related, will inevitably lead to this goal, as will the inclusion, without exception, of all farm owners subject to compulsory accident insurance. Of course, the advantage of insurance for the farmer and his wife and all other prospective benefits can be granted only to farmers who display good will and do not make any difficulties or otherwise create obstacles to the flat rate, which is intended to serve the interests of the farmers themselves just as much as those of the Institute. Any farm owner who does not accept the fixed rate, in contrast, becomes subject to the provisions of § 21 of the Accident Insurance Law. According to this regulation, each farmer in this situation will have to calculate his own premiums; since the Institute will not, in such cases, be preparing the appropriate forms at all, the farm owners will have to procure these printed forms themselves and at their own expense. Timely submission of the completed forms will be strictly enforced, and proceedings according to § 52 of the law will be brought against anyone who fails to file by the deadline. The submitted forms will be checked by accountants, the applicable premiums will be determined, and collection will be made by the authorities. If the farm owner does not fulfill his obligation to submit them, the authorities will also determine the amount.

Now that the Institute can be confident that the plan to introduce the fixed rate will be crowned with complete success, we also wish to thank the corporate bodies and associations that have promoted this difficult but promising work with a zeal that is worthy of appreciation. It was these organizations that, relying on the high esteem they enjoy in agricultural circles, knew how to rouse the farmers' trust in our project and helped the farmers to understand that the flat rate would benefit them. It was these corporate bodies and associations, too, that, in honestly representing the farmers' interests in the negotiations, brought about the far-reaching advantages that the Institute decided to grant those farmers who agree to the fixed rate. The rural press also deserves our thanks and appreciation, for in publishing articles on this matter it informed the farming population and deepened their understanding of this significant issue.

Finally, let us express the hope that the affected farmers will properly appreciate the fact that the intentions that guided the Institute in establishing the fixed rate are in their own best interests, so that the matter can come to a fruitful conclusion that will benefit both the Institute and the farmers.

Commentary 3

∿

We know from Kafka's job résumé that he had written a section of a report on the assignment of group insurance fees for small farms operating machinery and that he had conducted the correspondence with the farmers and authorities.

Kafka was entrusted with an assignment in a trouble zone of workmen's accident insurance. Small farms had long been a problem child for the Institute. Influential agrarian lobbies argued that the traditional solidarity of rural communities made accident insurance unnecessary.

Agrarian insurance created many anomalies for a system that had been devised for industrial production: a preindustrial wage base (a large part of wages consisted of food, housing, and clothing); seasonal variations in labor; a high rate of temporary employment and a low level of training among the work force; and finally, the uncertain status of small farms. They might be considered as independent firms or as subcontractors to a wholesaler, and the farmer's family might be considered self-employed or paid labor.

The situation was currently managed by a law restricting compulsory insurance to farm workers who actually operated machinery, the most dangerous part of farm labor. Given this partial coverage, insurance fees never covered the Institute's costs of reimbursing damages resulting from the accidents caused by such machinery. The industrialist associations, which feared a general increase in insurance fees if only the "bad"—that is, the most costly—agricultural risks were insured, resisted the partial accident insurance of small farms, demanding that they be either completely subjected to compulsory insurance or else be entirely excluded.

When the 1908 draft of new social legislation (see doc. 2) left this unsatisfactory legal situation unchanged, the Prague Institute, as it had done in the case of the building trades, decided to find a solution of its own. In negotiations with the agricultural council of Bohemia, it proposed offering small farmers flat insurance rates, simply related to acreage and the kind and number of machines in operation. While these arrangements are described in the first part of the report, most probably written by Kafka's head of department, Eugen Pfohl, Kafka described the technical basis of the flat-rate solution, a fact confirmed by a stylistic analysis of the report. Hardly anywhere else in the Institute's records is the gap between ordinary Austrian official language and the official documents written by Kafka so visible as in this report by two authors. The gap is not simply a matter of the switch from Pfohl's clumsy German to Kafka's elegant command of the language. In a striking way, Kafka introduces elements of narrative into a seemingly endless enumeration of facts and events. The introduction of a law that enforced wage lists in all Bohemian firms by February 1909 appears as a dramatic turning point, endowing the Institute's Bohemian arrangement with the authority of governmental legislation. And, like the essay on the insurance of building trades (doc. 2), this report subtly analyzes the motivations and aspirations of the acting personae and balances all points of view, while insisting that social insurance be, not the object of conflicting interests, but their solution.

Here, as in many other cases, Kafka the clerk repays Kafka the writer for his support. At least two aspects of this case create a close connection between accident insurance for small farms and the very heart of Kafka's oeuvre, his last novel, *The Castle*. In his report for 1908, Kafka writes that a prerequisite for flat-rate insurance is "to establish the particulars pertaining to the extent of the fields and pastures as well as of the net income" of the individual farms. But a note of protest from the Institute to the Ministry of the Interior in 1911, which was probably written by Kafka, maintained that this project was foundering on the issue of competent land surveying. The Ministry of Finance refused to make the necessary data available to the Institute. But with the help of the district authorities, at least the acreages could be established. Nonetheless, many small farmers complained about the flat-rate calculations, arguing that, owing to the mountainous nature of their land, the surveys were invalid. Lacking reliable data, the Institute's note concludes, the Institute would have to operate in "complete darkness" until new legislation for comprehensive insurance was passed.

Here the insurance institute offers us a real-life prototype of the strategic situation of *The Castle*. Like Kafka the clerk, K, the hero of *The Castle*, tries to mediate between the world of the Castle (one thinks of the Ministry in Vienna)—a higher authority, emanating messages that K has to interpret—and the world of the village. But he soon finds himself trapped between them. And indeed, the main opposition within this triangle does not lie between the castle and the village but between the two of them and the newly arrived stranger, who receives an early warning from the village teacher that here "there is no difference between the peasants and the castle."

Obviously, the lessons that the engineers of the new social technique of accident insurance had to learn while interacting with the traditional Austrian bureaucracy and the local communities were not restricted to the case of small farm insurance. If it is true that the new discourse of social insurance was just as alien to the Austrian bureaucracy and to business people as the new voice of Kafka's literature has been to readers in the fields of deconstruction and reconstruction, then a late diary entry may be referred to the practitioner of both of Kafka's professions: "A connoisseur, an expert, someone who knows his field, knowledge, to be sure, that cannot be imparted but that fortunately no one seems to stand in need of" (D1 395).

4

INCLUSION OF PRIVATE AUTOMOBILE "FIRMS"
IN THE COMPULSORY
INSURANCE PROGRAM (1909)

⌘

An anecdote in the history of accident insurance, this document shows how, owing to the inadequacies of Austrian liability law, the private ownership of an automobile came to be defined as a "firm" and the owner as a "proprietor." Using statistics and insurance law, Kafka describes the emergence of a new kind of risk and once again exposes the ineffectuality of a centralized administration in the face of novel and increasingly complex kinds of social and technical information. The statistical passages of the document also point to the phantasmal scenes of automobile traffic in Kafka's America novel, The Man Who Disappeared.

The law of August 9, 1908, [. . .] regarding liability for damages incurred in the operation of motor vehicles, which in § 11, paragraph 1, requires compulsory automobile insurance for anyone "operating motor vehicles in the performance of their contractual employment," presented the Institute with a new, difficult task.

[Assumption or redemption of private automobile insurance contracts under § 61 of the Accident Insurance Law.]

§ 11 states:

Persons operating motor vehicles in the performance of contractual employment, insofar as the laws of December 28, 1887, [. . .] and July 20, 1894, do not already apply to them, are insured according to the requirements of the earlier law.

Employees covered by the provisions of § 4 of the law of December 28, 1887, [. . .] are exempt from compulsory insurance.

Accidents incurred during races or preparation for races (training) shall not be considered to be occupational accidents within the provisions of the automobile-insurance law.

With regard to insurance, the owner of the motor vehicle shall always be considered the proprietor of the firm subject to compulsory insurance.

The Ministry of the Interior shall determine the deadline by which the existing motor-vehicle firms newly subject to insurance must file a declaration according to § 18 of the Accident Insurance Law, as well as the time when their policy shall become effective. In private insurance contracts as specified in § 61, paragraph 2, of the Accident Insurance Law, the insurance institute will be liable in accordance with § 61, paragraphs 2 and 3, of this law, if the contracts were entered into before December 1, 1907.

Thus, on the basis of this law, a new class of persons was introduced into the group subject to compulsory auto insurance; and though this new class differs markedly in terms of its businesses and occupations from those previously insured, it should nevertheless be given more or less the same treatment. Previously, the class of persons carrying compulsory occupational accident insurance was engaged in manufacturing and commercial enterprises, and the proprietor's personal affairs were not covered. Motor vehicles constituted an object of accident coverage regarding insurance, employer status, premiums, and compensation only insofar as they constitute an element of the commercial firm subject to compulsory insurance or served independently to transport persons or freight. Now, not only the automobiles set aside for the personal use of the proprietor of a firm subject to compulsory insurance but also the automobiles of others who are not proprietors by any definition come under the definition of a commercial "firm." Nor do these new "firms" fall under the usual terms of collective insurance; rather, the circumstances approach those of individual insurance, since the automobile firms generally are ones with only one insured person (though without providing the institute with the advantages of individual insurance), so that each firm represents an individual risk, without any possibility of an internal counterbalance within the firm.

It was especially critical that the new legislation—[. . .] which brought to the Institute a class of persons subject to insurance that seemed at first glance a far cry from the groups covered in the structure the Institute had previously maintained—was not systemically appended to the original law or its extension concerning accident insurance. Rather, the compulsory insurance of the affected persons was regulated only incidentally in a law that primarily contains civil-law liability provisions. This legislation thus lacks the necessary specificity and forcefulness, so that it leaves more opportunity for loose interpretation than is helpful in a matter followed keenly by so many interested parties, while it offers too few points of reference to allow for adequate interpretation, given its overly brief treatment of the complicated subject.

As a result, the Institute's task consisted not in simply carrying out the regulations of § 11 of the cited law but in further developing the intention upon which the law is based. For this purpose, therefore, all the regional institutes set about preparing a uniform approach. The institutes were excluded from any collaboration in the preliminary work for this new law, especially from the formulation of § 11, and they were presented only with the final legal formulation. It became apparent that numerous questions regarding compulsory insurance and its scope were left unresolved until the institutes were asked to consult on the draft of the ordinance based on the law for assigning automobile firms to risk categories. The ordinance issued by the office of the governor on August 7, 1908, [...] gave the Institute an early opportunity to express itself about the edict of the Ministry of the Interior of July 29, 1908 [...], specifically, about the question of the legal validity of introducing compulsory accident insurance through a liability law and, further, about the legally unclear sphere of activities and persons subject to compulsory insurance (work done in garages, purifying automobile oil, etc.), and finally, about the lack of statistical material except among the automobile firms previously compulsorily insured—firms that are already heavily overburdened.

Immediately after the law and the executive order were issued on October 23, 1908, [...] the Institute set about to acquire as rapidly as possible an informed overview of the number, type, and distribution of the motor-vehicle firms in Bohemia whose employees were insured with the Institute after November 1, 1908, according to § 1 of the executive order. The Institute, however, became aware of the decree of October 27, 1908, [...] "regarding the division into risk classes of the motor vehicle firms included under accident insurance by § 11 of the law of August 9, 1908 [...]" only in mid-December.

The Institute gained the essential overview of the automobile firms within its district by circulating a letter to the district authorities who [...] keep a running account of the motor-vehicle firms in their areas; the letter requested them to send in summaries of their lists as of November 1, 1908. These collected lists showed that on November 1, 1908, over 800 automobiles were registered at 91 district offices, while 11 districts had no records of automobiles. However, not all of these 800 automobiles could be considered as subject to compulsory insurance; the number was diminished by the commercial automobile firms already subject to insurance, as well as by firms that did not employ anyone subject to insurance; finally, firms exempt from compulsory insurance according to § 11, paragraph 2, of the applicable law had to be subtracted from the total. The number was further decreased by subtracting those firms that contained several automobiles and those firms that had shut down after November 1, 1908. The last group that had to be excluded consisted of individually owned firms that were insured by miners' insurance associations. On the other hand, there were also additions, since various motorcycle firms employ persons subject to insurance (which separate lists the Institute was not able to obtain from all districts) and since a number of new firms have been established since November 1, 1908.

A final discussion about the classification of motor-vehicle firms was held, as indicated above, on November 9, 1908, in the Ministry of the Interior. Representatives of all the institutes and the interested parties, including our Institute, took part. The discussion centered on a draft of a classification decree the Ministry of the Interior had drawn up after listening to interested parties from among the employers. If this draft is compared with the present classification decree issued by the Ministry of the Interior on November 27, 1908 [. . .], it becomes clear that the institutes needed to advocate much more meticulous attention to individual differences within the various categories as compared to the draft. This intention was also expressed in Title 1 of the decree, since, unlike the draft, this document did not include all motor vehicles used to transport people in risk category X but instead divided them into the following three subgroups:

Motor vehicles used to transport people:

With power of

a. up to and including 8 hp: risk category IX

b. up to and including 40 hp: risk category X

c. more than 40 hp: risk category XI.

That discussion initiated the process of bringing a degree of clarity to those questions the law did not answer but whose clarification was essential in practice. This was done by asking government representatives to provide an accurate account of the relevant points. To the extent that these principles were feasible and acceptable to the institutes, these principles were resolved at the institutes' association's meeting on January 4, 1909, after a number of revisions.

Only after these points were established could the Institute feel sure enough to begin classifying the insured firms and issuing invoices for premiums. Until this time, the Institute could communicate the most important legal instructions on compulsory accident and health insurance to the firms in question only by sending out circulars and urging the recipients to fill out the general questions on the registration forms; at most, the Institute could use these forms to gain information about the firms' obligations though not about the risk factor.

The Institute next sent out a questionnaire to motor-vehicle firms on the pattern of the questionnaires the Institute had issued for all firms; these questionnaires had generally proved to be extremely useful in providing statistics and facilitating practical evaluation of the various firms. With its 35 questions, some of which go into great detail, the questionnaire is intended to provide a precise and verifiable description of the firms, since only such a description would allow for the fair classification of a firm.

Incidentally, Question 32—"Does the automobile carry first-aid equipment for accidents to persons, and if so, of what does this equipment consist?"—proved useful right from the start, since in a number of cases first-aid kits and the like were installed only in response to this suggestion, as was explicitly admitted.

The question of taking over private insurance contracts as required by the cited § 11, paragraph 6, presented special difficulties, however. This problem, almost entirely overlooked in the beginning, becomes important as the process unfolds, because in bringing the interests of the proprietors into line with those of the Institute, particular problems in interpretation arise from the different character of compulsory and private insurance.

For § 11 of the cited law states that—once certain technical conditions have been met—the institute's obligation to assume private insurance contracts in accordance with § 61, paragraph 2, of the Accident Insurance Law applies only to such contracts "as were concluded between a private insurance institute and the proprietor of one of the firms subject to compulsory insurance under this law, regarding the insurance against occupational accidents of the persons employed in this firm." Now among all of the policies the Institute received for assumption, only two met the legal requirements, while all others covered not only occupational accidents but also a great number of accidents occurring in everyday life and even in other occupations. This circumstance released the Institute from any legal obligation to assume such policies and forced the parties concerned to maintain two insurance policies for the present.

Not even consideration of the relevant report by the parliamentary judicial committee was able to remedy the lack of clarity and practical use implicit in the legal provisions. The report makes only brief mention of this passage, as follows: "The addendum regarding the accident insurance institute's entering on private insurance contracts is a necessary interim regulation."

For a time, a possible solution was seen, by the government as well, in expressing the risks of everyday life as a certain percentage of the private insurance contracts and reducing the premiums accordingly. Apart from the question of whether such a procedure would have been in accordance with the law, it proved to be impossible to implement mathematically.

Although the Institute would have had the legal right to reject any request for assumption of the stated contracts with reference to § 11, it did not exercise this right but offered to redeem the various contracts with the companies for an appropriate settlement. After lengthy negotiations, this attempt was successful. In this effort the Institute was guided by the following considerations: There could be no doubt that the law was intended to protect the proprietors from paying two insurance premiums. This intention was realized by redeeming the certificates. Given that such redemptions would impose costs on the Institute, it can be pointed out that the law also intended to impose costs on the Institute, for the assumption planned by the law would have entailed considerable costs—though distributed over years—and long-lasting inconvenience (considering merely settlements for firms' cancellations, compensation, payment of awards, and the like).

But the Institute itself was eager to avoid double insurance contracts. In no case were premiums to appear as an excessive burden. Had the Institute not enacted the redemption, the drivers would certainly have felt the doubled insurance in their pay envelopes, generally without gaining any benefit. In addition, the doubled insurance would have done a disservice to precisely those proprietors who had acknowledged the necessity of compulsory insurance of motor-vehicle firms before it was introduced.

Redemption was specifically carried out as follows:

Overall, the Institute entered into negotiations with seven different insurance companies for the purpose of redeeming the accident-insurance contracts concluded with drivers. In all, 45 cases resulted in redemption; 24 of these were with a single company, 12 with another, 3 with a third, 2 cases each with two more companies, and 1 case each for another two. In 43 cases the contracts applied not only to occupational accidents but also to accidents of everyday life. These were redeemed for a 16 percent sum of all gross premiums that had not yet fallen due.

[. . .]

With the conclusion of these redemptions, the new set of firms was incorporated in the original group of companies subject to compulsory insurance, the new group being given as much protection as possible for the present without disrupting the whole. The implementation of legal insurance had thus begun for a group of drivers exposed to danger arising from an activity in the personal interest of their employers—an example of the flexibility and capability of the organization of the Institute, though it was originally established for different purposes.

As occurred in the case of pension insurance for workers in private firms, in this area, too, Austria has taken a step ahead of the German Reich, since the German law of May 3, 1909, [. . .] does not grant even the liability claims that are uniformly applied to persons occupied in operating motor vehicles. For this reason, it is only now that the draft of the insurance regulations for the German Reich lists these people as persons to be covered by compulsory accident insurance.

Commentary 4

❧

Kafka's job résumé identifies him as the author of this article in the Institute's annual report.

The issue of compulsory insurance for vehicle owners highlights the close nexus between technological progress and legal development that Kafka's work addresses. In 1901, citizens of the Hapsburg Empire were offered private vehicle insurance by the German Mannheimer Versicherungsgesellschaft; but Austria jumped ahead by introducing compulsory automobile insurance in August 1908—even before the German Reich. We can, then, observe here the full cycle of the construction of a new insurance risk: from data collection with the help of forms and circulars, via the differentiation of risk classes, to the fixed contractual regulation of the new insurance deal.

In those days, most cars were operated by a chauffeur employed by the vehicle's owner. Consider, now, that in Austria, compulsory accident insurance was related not to individuals but to firms and their owners. In order to use categories that existed within the regulations of the Workmen's Accident Insurance law of 1887, therefore, insurance institutes needed to conceive of the relation between vehicle owner and chauffeur as a fiction, according to which each individual vehicle was a firm, each vehicle owner the owner of a firm, and each chauffeur his employee.

The issue of automobile insurance created a problem that contrasted with the Institute's usual struggle to furnish legal security to Bohemian workers. In this instance, social insurance was being overstretched, extended to risks politically and technically beyond its realm—politically, as automobiles belonged to the private households of their owners; technically, as these "one-man-firms" were not fit subjects for actuarial calculation over time. Here, again, in its annual report to the Vienna Ministry, the Institute used Kafka's legal and literary skills to oppose the drafting of legislation without seeking advice of the other crownland institutes and their experts in social insurance (doc. 2 and commentary).

This marginal contribution to Austrian workmen's accident insurance made its way into Kafka's fiction. A vivid passage from his America novel, *The Man Who Disappeared*, will also seem to disappear if we read it without knowledge and understanding of the annual report.

Having violated the elevator regulations (doc. 10 and commentary), Karl Rossmann, the hero of the novel, runs away from the Hotel Occidental, whereupon his flight is interrupted.

> [I]t was impossible to get to the street, where an uninterrupted line of automobiles moved haltingly past the main entrance. So as to reach their masters as quickly as possible, these automobiles had practically driven into each other, each nudged forward by the one at its rear. Though some pedestrians, who were in a special hurry to cross the street, occasionally climbed through the separate automobiles as if they were public roadways, and they did not seem to care whether the people sitting in these automobiles were merely the driver and servants or members of the highest nobility. Karl felt that such behavior was really extreme; surely these people must be very familiar with these conditions to take such chances, how easy it would be for one of them to find his way into a car whose passengers would be outraged, would throw him down, and cause a scandal, and that was surely the worst that an escaped hotel employee who was under suspicion and in his shirtsleeves had to fear.

The reader acquainted with the historical background of automobile insurance could see in this facet of Kafka's fantasy of America a grandiose parody of the legal realities of Old Europe. The cars' eagerness to get to their owners may very well allude to the strange legal ties between vehicles and their "owners" when the latter have become the economic and legal subjects of their "firms." Equally, the behavior of the pedestrians reads like another grandiose parody of the firm on wheels, at once static and nomadic, territorial and vectorial. In a word, Kafka's realism is relentless precisely in those passages that appear most phantasmal at first glance (doc. 10 and commentary).

The advent of the automobile forced legal systems elsewhere to create other fictions to deal with new problems in terms of existing legal categories. United States law, for one, was poorly equipped to deal with injuries inflicted in one state by an automobile from another. A New York resident, for example, injured in New York by a car and driver from California, could sue the California driver in New York only by serving the driver with a summons in New York—a holdover from ancient doctrine that linked jurisdiction with territoriality. Otherwise, the injured party, to obtain relief, would have to go to the driver's state, perhaps thousands of miles away. But New York (and other states) passed a law that constituted driving in New York consent to the jurisdiction of the New York courts and service of summons by mail by the New York Secretary of State. So the New York resident could sue the California driver in New York, even though, in truth, the California driver never consented. The United States Supreme Court dealt with a defendant's objection as follows: "The defendant may protest to high heaven his unwillingness to be sued and it avails him not. The liability rests on the inroad which the automobile has made on the [pre-existing doctrine] as it has on so many aspects of our social scene. [. . .] We have held that this is a fair rule of law as between a resident injured party [. . .] and a non-resident motorist [. . .]. But to conclude from this holding that the motorist, who never consented to anything [. . .] has actually agreed to be sued [. . .] is surely to move in the world of Alice in Wonderland" (Olberding v. Illinois Central Ry. Co., 346 U.S. 338, 341, 1953).

APPEAL AGAINST RISK CLASSIFICATION OF CHRISTIAN GEIPEL & SOHN, MECHANICAL WEAVING MILL IN ASCH (1910)

This text is one of the first appeals to which Kafka had to respond in his capacity, from 1910 on, as head of the appeals department, the Institute's unit responsible for dealing with employers' protests against the assigned risk classification of their workplaces. Kafka's particular concern was "translating" or mediating between the average, everyday conception of danger according to the industrialists and its formal and statistical definition according to law. The Geipel case is typical in the way it turns on the gap between the meaning of identical words in the sphere of industrial production on the one hand and of insurance regulations on the other. Owing to this obviously well-educated claimant's awareness of the linguistic issues at stake in this legal dispute over the technical characterization of his machinery, he wins his case against the Institute.

Unlike most of his official writings, this brief shows Kafka with very little leeway to deviate from the letter of the law and statistical tables in this "exact" subfield of accident insurance. Furthermore, this case is exceptional in that the decisive repudiation of the claim is written entirely in Kafka's hand.

A. Geipel & Sohn to the Office of the Governor: Appeal against Reclassification for the Period 1910–1915 (02/02/1910)

To the esteemed k. k. Office of the Governor:

Re: The decision of the Workmen's Accident Insurance Institute for Bohemia in Prague, of December 31, 1909, regarding the reclassification of our mechanical textile weaving and sizing mill in Asch. We herewith lodge an appeal, because we consider ourselves placed in a position of hardship, since the above-named firm has been classified in risk category II, with a risk factor of 7 percent.

First and foremost, we consider ourselves aggrieved at having been classified under Title 323, Weaving Mill for Cotton Goods (Textile Sizing), in risk category II. In our description of the firm of July 31, 1909, we designated it as a "mechanical weaving and sizing mill," manufacturing fabric for women's clothing and processing cotton, wool, and silk. We work almost exclusively with worsted yarn, compared to which the small quantities of cotton (thread only) and silk in small quantities are hardly worth mentioning.

Accordingly, our firm should have been classified under Title 303, Weaving Mill for Sheep's-Wool Goods Using Machines, in risk category I—the category to which, by the way, it was assigned in the past. The partial processing of cotton thread does not change the situation. If we were to argue that under the circumstances there is an increased risk of accidents because weaving mills for cotton goods are classified in risk category II, such an increase would certainly appear to be offset by the simultaneous processing of silk in our mill, and this fact would indicate a decrease in risk, because silk-weaving mills are classified in the lower risk category B. With this explanation we believe we have given sufficient reason for our request that our firm be classified under risk category I.

Inclusion in the risk-factor category I must now proceed according to paragraph 14 of the law of December 18, 1887, [. . .] based on the risk of accidents in individual firms and with regard to the individual safety measures for accident prevention. In this context we must pay particular attention to the nature of the physical facilities and operational equipment; further heed must be given to the arrangements made to prevent accidents and to the technical management of all functions (this latter caution also with a view to the workers' qualifications for their specific tasks, insofar as these factors allow us to arrive at conclusions about the risk of such accidents as are constantly present within the mill); finally the evaluation must include the insurance institute's record in previously insuring the firm in question.

We are convinced that if these factors, which are specified by law, are taken into consideration when assessing the risk factors in classifying our firm, only the lowest level of risk factors in risk category I can be applied.

The esteemed k. k. Office of the Governor also responded to our objection to our classification for the past period in the 5 percent level of risk category I when it rendered its decision on October 2, 1905, to the effect that the firm was classified in the 5 percent group of risk factors. The reasons are expressly stated in the aforementioned decision:

[B]ecause with regard to the opinion of the trade inspector, which appears to certify that good safety measures exist in the business and that the mill employs relatively few juveniles, classification below the mean in risk factor of 5 percent appears justified.

In providing further reasons for our request for reclassification in the risk factor of 4 percent in risk category I, we must note here that since the previous classification, we have made a large number of safety-related arrangements, some quite expensive, regarding both construction and our operating equipment. We thus expressly request that this matter be communicated to the k. k. trade inspectorate in Karlsbad, which undertook an audit of our firm on the same day the classification decision under appeal was delivered, namely on January 21, 1910.

The accident expenses of our firm will further indicate that only the smallest possible operating risk in the category is feasible. Our appeal against the classification for the past period listed the relevant figures for the past 15 years to demonstrate the glaring disparity between the amount of damages and the amount of the premiums we are assessed; today, we will mention only that there has been no change whatsoever in this regard.

Thus, in accordance with paragraph 18 of the law of December 28, 1887, we request that the Workmen's Accident Insurance Institute for Bohemia study this appeal, inform us of any response, and finally revise the decision under appeal to the effect that our mill be classified in risk category I, risk factor of 4 percent, with an insurance premium of 0.34 kreuzer for every 100.00 kreuzer paid out in applicable wages.

Asch, February 2, 1910
(signed) Chr. Geipel Son

B. Workmen's Accident Insurance Institute to the Office of the Governor: Statement on the Reclassification of the Company Geipel & Sohn (04/26/1910)

Subject: Appeal by the Company Christian Geipel & Sohn against the decision by the Institute on 12/31/1909 regarding the risk category revision for the period 1910–1914, involving the insured firm of a mechanized cotton-weaving and sizing mill.

Reasons for Reclassification

The firm was described by the trade inspector as a cotton and linsey-woolsey-weaving mill. One factor described as increasing the mill's risk was a large textile-sizing department, while the presence of equipment only periodically used for weaving sheep's wool was noted

Arbeiter-Unfall-Versicherungs-Anstalt
für das Königreich Böhmen
——— in PRAG. ———

Betriebs-Titel: **323**

Gewerbeinspektorat: *Karlsbad*

Politischer Bezirk: *Asch*

N. E. 26068 17125

M. No. 31/1

Hochlöbliche

k. k. Statthalterei

in PRAG!

Äußerung zur Zahl 30 471 / 58 429 *vom* 17. II. / 12. III. 1910.

Gegenstand: Einspruch der *Fa. Chr. Geipel & Sohn*

in   gegen den Anstaltsbescheid

vom 31. XII. 1909, bezüglich Revision der Gefahrenklasseneinreihung

auf Grund der Verordnung vom 2. August 1909, R.-G.-Bl. No. 117,

für die Klassifikationsperiode 1910—1914, rücksichtlich des ver-

sicherten Betriebes:

Mech. Baumwollweberei u. Appretur

Beilagen: 2 *Einsprüch* 1 *Kuvert,* 1 *Bescheid in* Original/Kopie *, 1 Fragebogen* 2 Abschriften

Einreihung bis 31. XII. 1909: Titel 323 *, Gef. Klasse* I *, Gef. %* 5

Einreihung ab 1. I. 1910: Titel 323 *, Gef. Klasse* II *, Gef. %* 7

Begründung der Neueinreihung:

Der Betrieb wurde vom Gewerbeinspektor als Baumwoll-
und Halbwollweberei beschrieben, als gefahrerhöhendes
Merkmal Vorhandensein einer umfangreichen Appretur
als gefahrverringerndes Merkmal Vorhandensein
einer teilweisen Schafwollweberei konstatiert im übri-
gen jedoch normale Betriebsverhältnisse festgestellt.
Trotz des Ausgleiches des erwähnten gefahrverringern-
den und gefahrerhöhenden Momentes wurde mit
Rücksicht auf die Höhe der Unfallsbelastung der Betrieb

nach Titel 323 in die Gef. Kl. II andrerseits in das niedrigste Gef. % 7 dieser Klasse eingereiht.

Äußerung in formeller Hinsicht: *Der angefochtene Bescheid wurde am* 20 . I 10 *hierorts expediert und dem Unternehmer direkt mittelst einfacher Postsendung zugestellt. Der Einspruch ist am* 4. II 10 *überreicht, daher* ——— *innerhalb der gesetzlichen Frist eingebracht worden.*

Äußerung in meritorischer Hinsicht:

ad I Nach dem Gutachten des Gewerbeinspektors, den Angaben des Fragebogens und ebenso den Angaben des Einsprechers stellt sich der vorliegende Betrieb als eine Baumwoll- und Halbwollweberei dar (im Fragebogen ist sogar reine Baumwolle unter den verarbeiteten Halbfabrikaten an erster Stelle genannt) als solche aber gehört der Betrieb gerade unter den in der angefochtenen Einreihung gewählten Titel 323 denn wenn auch im Wortlaut des Titels selbst Halbwollwarenwebereien nicht erwähnt sind, so sind doch durch die Überschrift dieser Subgruppe IX. d) "Baumwolle und Halbwolle" alle Betriebe der Halbwolltextilindustrie den einzelnen Titeln dieser Subgruppe zugewiesen. Neben dieser Baumwoll- und Halbwollweberei ist wohl auch teilweise Schafwollweberei und Seidenweberei vorhanden, doch steht diesem

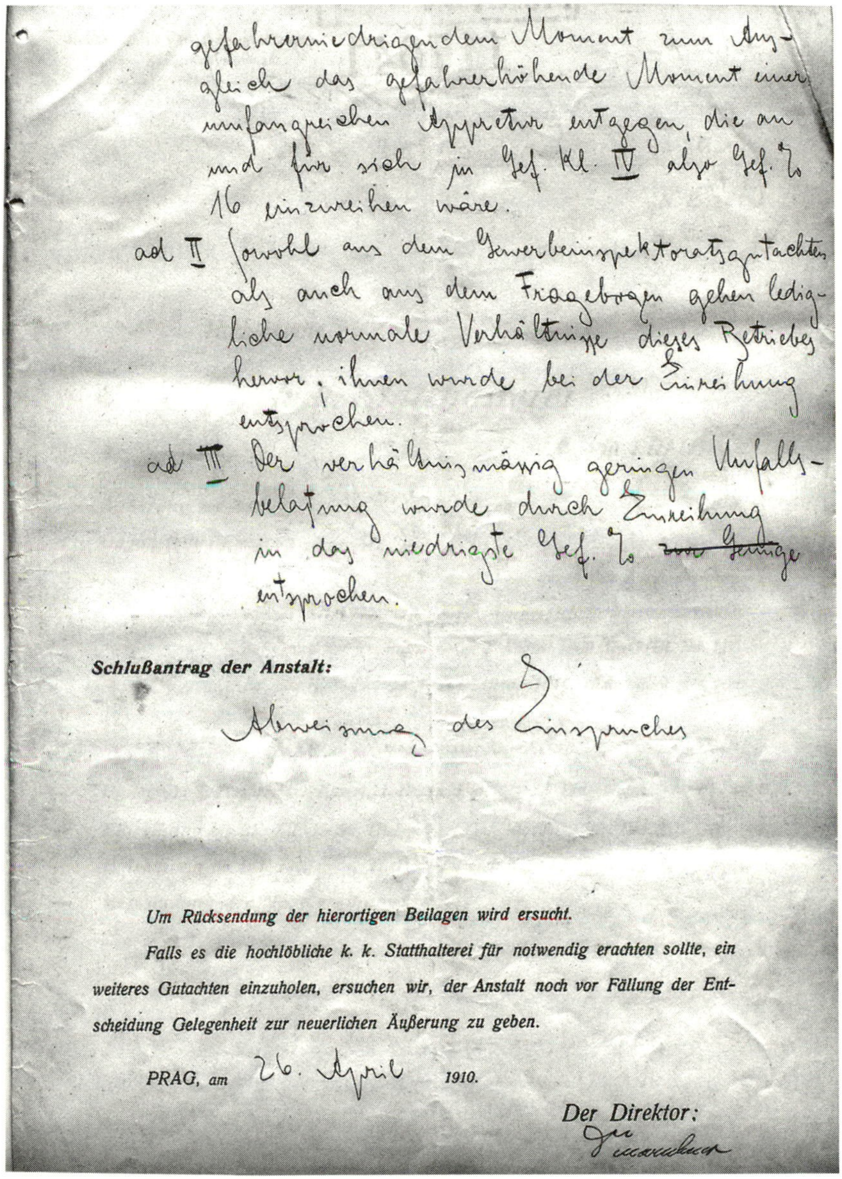

gefahrvermindernden Moment zum Ausgleich das gefahrerhöhende Moment einer
umfangreichen Appretur entgegen, die an
und für sich in Gef. Kl. IV also Gef. %
16 einzureihen wäre.

ad II sowohl aus dem Gewerbeinspektoratsgutachten
als auch aus dem Fragebogen gehen ledig-
liche normale Verhältnisse dieses Betriebes
hervor; ihnen wurde bei der Einreihung
entsprochen.

ad III Der verhältnismäßig geringen Unfallsbelastung wurde durch Einreihung
in den niedrigste Gef. % ~~geringe~~
entsprochen.

Schlußantrag der Anstalt:

Abweisung des Einspruches

Um Rücksendung der hierortigen Beilagen wird ersucht.

Falls es die hochlöbliche k. k. Statthalterei für notwendig erachten sollte, ein

weiteres Gutachten einzuholen, ersuchen wir, der Anstalt noch vor Fällung der Ent-

scheidung Gelegenheit zur neuerlichen Äußerung zu geben.

PRAG, am 26. April 1910.

Der Direktor:

Figures 4a, b. c. Report form for the appeals procedure in risk classification, in Kafka's handwriting.

as a factor decreasing overall risk. In all other respects, however, normal operating conditions were found. In spite of the factors that increased and decreased risk, which balanced each other out, the firm was classified in accordance with the amount of accident expenses under Title 323 in risk category II but in the lowest risk percentage of this category.

Statement of Formal Compliance

The contested decision was submitted on 01/20/1910 and was thus entered within the terms of the legal period.

Statement of the Merits of the Case

I

Taking into account the trade inspector's expert opinion, the information provided by the questionnaire, and the statements in the appeal, the firm in question can be characterized only as a cotton- and linsey-woolsey-weaving mill (the questionnaire even places pure cotton first among the semifinished textiles the mill processes). As such, the firm fits absolutely in Title 323, to which it was assigned in the contested classification, because even if linsey-woolsey-weaving mills are not specifically included in the rubric, the title of this subgroup IX, "Cotton and Linsey-Woolsey," means that all firms in the linsey-woolsey textile industry are allocated to the various items in this subgroup. The weaving of sheep's wool and silk is also included with cotton and linsey-woolsey, but this risk-reducing factor is balanced by the risk-increasing factor of a large textile-sizing department, which in and of itself should be classified in risk category IV—that is, risk factor of 16 percent.

II

Both the opinion of the trade inspectorate and the answers on the questionnaire indicate entirely normal conditions in this firm; the classification was decided accordingly. [. . .]

III

The relatively low accident expenses were acknowledged by classifying the firm in the lowest risk factor of the category.

Final Motion of the Institute

Rejection of the appeal.

Prague, April 26, 1910
The Director
Dr. Marschner

C. Trade Inspectorate in Karlsbad to the Office of the Governor: Expert Opinion on the Operations of the Company Geipel & Sohn (06/20/1910)

Karlsbad, June 20, 1910.

Re. Appeal, Chr. Geipel & Sohn
Mech. Textile Weaving and Sizing Mill in Asch

To the k. k. Office of the Governor in Prague:
The following statement is made regarding the assignment of May 11, 1910, [. . .] following a recent inspection of the above-named company in Asch:
The company Chr. Geipel & Sohn operates a mechanized weaving mill in Asch as well as sizing the produced textiles. The textiles for women's clothing here manufactured include worsted, cotton, sheep's wool, and silk.
Approximately 850 workers are employed in the weaving mill and approximately 50 in the sizing department.
The company is equipped with very good safety facilities, its workrooms are high-ceilinged, light, and very well ventilated, and the mill has always promptly complied with all instructions from the authorities regarding safety measures. However, we are dealing here, not with a pure sheep's-wool-weaving mill that does not include spinning and sizing facilities with motors as specified by Title 303, but rather a mechanized weaving mill that processes cotton and linsey-woolsey along with sheep's wool. It is therefore our opinion that classification under Title 323, or Mill for Weaving Cotton Goods with the Use of Machinery, is justified. This classification is all the more applicable as the very good safety facilities were acknowledged by classifying the firm as a whole in the lowest percentage of risk category II in spite of the presence of textile sizing, a circumstance that in itself would have indicated an increase in the percentage of risk factors.

We further note that, even with the lowest possible classification of the firm—since the weaving departments and the sizing facilities are in different spaces and the workers in the mill are not employed in sizing—no more favorable percentage of risk factors can be achieved; Title 323, Mill for Weaving Cotton Goods With the Use of Machinery, risk category II, 7 percent, for approx. 850 workers, and Title 330, Textile Sizing Facility Using Machinery, risk category IV, 13 percent, for approx. 50 workers, would have to be considered in arriving at a classification, taking into account as well the very good safety record in both classes and therefore assessing the lowest risk percentage. In our opinion, therefore, the appeal should thus not be approved. We are also informing the company of this opinion.

k. k. Trade Inspector
Jordan (by proxy)

D. Geipel & Sohn to the District Authority in Asch:
Counterstatement (07/15/1910)

Re: Chr. Geipel & Sohn in Asch
Risk Classification of the Mechanized Textile Weaving and Sizing Mill in Asch
under Title 323

Esteemed k. k. District Commissioner's Office, Asch:

Counterstatement by the company Chr. Geipel & Sohn in response to the statements of the Workmen's Accident Insurance Institute of April 26, 1910, and of the trade inspectorate of June 20, 1910.

After all other matters have been sufficiently discussed, the emphasis of the choice between risk category II at 7 percent, as the Insurance Institute would have it, and risk category I at 4 percent, as the undersigned firm proposes, must be placed on the following:
In question 6 of the questionnaire we described the materials we work with as cotton, wool, and silk, and in question 4 we identified the nature of our firm as a mechanized textile weaving and sizing mill.
In its statement on April 26, 1910, the Workmen's Accident Insurance Institute describes the firm as a MECHANIZED COTTON-WEAVING and sizing mill and remarks in its statement that our firm represents itself as

a *cotton* and linsey-woolsey weaving mill, further noting expressly that the answer to point 6 of the questionnaire lists PURE cotton first among the semifinished products we process.

The statement of the k. k. trade inspectorate followed these descriptions by the Workmen's Accident Insurance Institute, calling our firm a weaving mill for cotton goods.

The statements of both the Workmen's Accident Insurance Institute and the k. k. trade inspectorate are not based on the correct facts, and we request that what follows be thoroughly studied and found persuasive.

1. By its nature, our firm is not a weaving mill for cotton goods but essentially a wool-weaving mill. We use woolen yarn almost exclusively—for the most part cotton and silk come into play only as so-called decorative thread; only very occasionally is cotton thread used across an entire warp. Cotton and silk represent only a very small percentage of the total volume processed.

The fact that cotton was named first in the answer to question 6 of the questionnaire is purely accidental and meaningless for the actual reality, which is that we use woolen yarn for the most part and that cotton and silk, as we have already stated, comprise only a very small percentage of the material we process. The designation of our firm as a weaving mill for cotton goods and its classification in this group, even if under the rubric "Weaving Mills for Linsey-Woolsey Goods," is thus completely incorrect.

2. The further and most important issue in determining the question in dispute is the following:

The factor that increases risk in cotton-weaving-mills as compared to wool-weaving mills lies, not in the material itself, but in the looms used in the different mills. The looms used in cotton weaving are narrower than those used for wool and thus run faster than the broader ones used for wool weaving. This difference increases the risk run in operating cotton looms over the risk associated with wool weaving.

All of our machines are meant only for wool weaving, however, and are thus the same machines used in other wool-weaving mills. Our mill does not operate even one narrow loom of the kind that must be used when weaving cotton. [. . .] The small quantities of other, nonwoolen materials we process are also worked on the looms meant exclusively for processing woolen yarn.

The actual conditions stressed in points 1 and 2 above, along with the facts already presented by us and officially filed, justify the full scope of the request in our appeal.

Asch, July 15, 1910
(Signed) Chr. Geipel Son

E. Workmen's Accident Insurance Institute to the Office of the Governor: Statement on the Appeal of Geipel & Sohn (09/30/1910)

Classification Appeal of Christian Geipel & Sohn in Asch
16 attachments
To the esteemed k. k. Office of the Governor in Prague:
Statement Regarding No. 192095 of August 2, 1910

In the case under review, the Institute must observe the regulations of the statute, which specifically determine, under the rubric "On Business Group IX d," that companies processing cotton and linsey-woolsey are to be combined in this group, in contrast to Subgroup B, in which only sheep's wool and other animal hair are specifically named.

We freely admit that the type of loom can be an element in the level of risk within a weaving mill, but this fact does not allow us to sidestep the official regulations so lightly.

We are enclosing herewith the ministerial decision of June 18, 1906 [. . .] for your perusal; you will note that it approved the classification as a cotton-weaving mill in this case for the period of the past five years.

The request for the rejection of the appeal is thus renewed.

Prague, September 30, 1910.
The Director
(Signed) Dr. Marschner

F. Geipel & Sohn to the Ministry of the Interior: Appeal against the Decision of the Office of the Governor (11/11/1910)

Esteemed k. k. Ministry of the Interior:
Against the decision by the honorable k. k. Office of the Governor for the Kingdom of Bohemia of October 12, 1910 [. . .], by which our appeal against the decision by the Workmen's Accident Insurance Institute in Prague of December 31, 1909 [. . .] was rejected, we submit the following appeal:

Both the legal question and the question of fact have now been clearly stated in the material on file, and we may therefore be brief:

The legal question is whether the law should treat our company as a cotton-weaving and sizing mill or as a wool-weaving and sizing mill.

This legal question is closely connected to a question of fact, which in turn is also easily answered by recourse to the material on file:

It is undisputed and indisputable that we operate a wool-weaving mill and that our firm must be designated as a wool-weaving mill from the standpoint of the manufacturer and from the standpoint of the expert in the field.

Since the law has established no separate definitions in the designation of the industries but instead has followed general usage or the general designation of experts, there is no doubt that our company must be treated in law as a wool-weaving mill. The fact that we also use cotton and, as will be made clear below, silk, and both in extremely small quantities relatively speaking, does not turn our wool-weaving mill into either a cotton-weaving mill or a silk-weaving mill.

The fundamental reason must be sought in the following circumstance, which we have previously stressed. The looms used in cotton weaving are incontestably narrower than those employed in wool weaving. The consequence is that these narrower looms operate more rapidly than the wider looms used in wool weaving. This faster operation of the looms means that there is a greater danger of accidents compared to the incidence of accidents connected with the slower looms, and this is the fundamental and exclusive reason why the law has set a higher risk class for cotton-weaving mills than for wool-weaving mills.

Since our firm uses only the wider looms for wool weaving, it is clear that according to the law there is no fundamental reason whatsoever to treat our firm as a cotton-weaving mill and thus to classify it under risk category II.

We must further point out that until 1909, wool- and cotton-weaving mills were classified in the same risk category I; only the new ordinance separated cotton-weaving mills and classified them in risk category II.

We have just explained the reason why this change was made: narrower looms are used in cotton-weaving mills than in wool weaving-mills, and as a consequence, the operation of cotton-weaving mills was determined to be more risky.

In order to demonstrate the injustice of the contested decision still further, we might mention that because we also use silk, we could have made a claim to be classified in the lower risk category B.

It would be quite appropriate to respond to such a claim by pointing out that our looms are set up for wool weaving and that any expert opinion would have to determine that we are a wool-weaving mill.

What is reasonable in the latter case must be fair in the former, and a wool-weaving mill remains a wool-weaving mill, even if, as the work requires, extremely small amounts of cotton or silk are used in extremely small measure.

Every law must be interpreted according to its purpose, and every law exists to achieve a particular purpose; the purpose of the ordinance that classifies cotton- and wool-weaving mills differently is to point out the difference in risk factors between cotton- and wool-weaving mills according to the looms in use in each.

In consideration of these observations, we hold our complaint to be well-founded; accordingly, we should be treated as a wool-weaving mill and be classified in risk category I.

Up to the present time, this classification in risk category I was evaluated with a risk factor of 5 percent.

Classification at 5 percent instead of 4 percent was justified by the fact that our firm also includes a textile-sizing facility. Thus the risk factor of 5 percent acknowledges the increased risk factor, eliminating any reason to classify us in risk category II.

So that the high k. k. Ministry will understand that we do not lodge a complaint about every minor matter but only when we suffer an obvious injustice, we wish to emphasize in conclusion that we are willing to accept being assigned to the risk percentage of 5 percent in risk category I, which corresponds to the prior classification.

We thus petition for a remedy of the contested decision and for upholding our appeal by granting classification in risk category I with a risk factor of 5 percent.

Asch, November 11, 1910
(Signed) Christian Geipel & Sohn

G. Karlsbad Trade Inspectorate to the Office of the Governor: Statement concerning the Operations of the Company Geipel & Sohn (05/12/1911)

Karlsbad, May 12, 1911
To the k. k. Office of the Governor

The following statement is rendered in response to the assignment, overleaf:

The operations of the stated company in Asch consist of a mechanized textile-weaving and sizing mill. The company produces cloth for women's garments, along with fabric of various kinds. Sheep's wool is the principal yarn used to manufacture these products, along with cotton and silk.

Production is carried out on wide, slow-moving looms (in contrast to the rapid-moving, narrow looms used in weaving cotton).

It is not possible to ascertain the percentages of wool and cotton used in the mill, since the proportion of these yarns varies with the different quality of the article to be produced; in every case, however, the amount of sheep's wool is greater than that of the cotton with which it is admixed.

k. k. Trade Inspector
(Signed) M. Schutt

H. Ministry of the Interior to the Office of the Governor: Decision in the Appeal of Geipel & Sohn (12/04/1911)

Letterhead: K. K. MINISTRY OF THE INTERIOR

Vienna, December 4, 1911

After questioning experts from among the employers and workers according to section 10 of the ministerial ordinance of August 2, 1909, [. . .] the Ministry of the Interior upholds the appeal of Chr. Geipel & Sohn in Asch against the decision of this authority on October 12, 1910, [. . .] regarding the reclassification of the firm as "Mechanized Textile Weaving and Sizing Mill" under risk category II, with a risk factor of 7 percent. In amendment of the contested decision of this authority and the underlying report by the Institute on December 31, 1909, [. . .] the Ministry further finds in favor of the classification of the company at a risk factor of 5 percent in risk category I, as provided in the cited ordinance for Title 303, "Weaving Mills for Sheep's Wool Goods (Firm Without Textile Spinning and Sizing Mills): Firms Using Motorized Machinery." The grounds for this decision are that the company weaves primarily sheep's wool and that the firm must therefore be considered as a weaving mill for sheep's-wool goods; the circumstance that cotton is also woven in the mill can be grounds neither for classification under Title 323 nor for an increased risk percentage within risk category I, since cotton and silk are also woven upon the wide, slow-moving looms associated with the lower risk of accidents in weaving mills for sheep's-wool goods. The incorporation of textile sizing in the otherwise very favorably equipped weaving mill argues against classification under the lowest risk factor of 4 percent. The files of the hearing will follow by return mail.

On behalf of the k. k. Minister of the Interior
(Signed) Wolf
(Stamp)

Commentary 5

❧

The claim of Christian Geipel & Sohn against the risk classification of its machine-weaving operation is revealing in several respects. We have the Institute's first statement, written in Kafka's own hand, to tell us that he was employed in the claims process. This particular dispute is also one of the very few cases of a successful claim by a business owner, revealing a blind spot in the classification procedure that Kafka treats in detail in doc. 7. This blind spot, in turn, can be seen as the source of the light shed by the Geipel case on the bureaucracies we encounter in Kafka's novels and stories.

To grasp the logic of the protracted procedures of this case, we should note that the claimant fits the pattern neither of the desperate producer of wooden articles in the Erzgebirge nor the sly and inventive juggler of paragraphs in the cases "Hochsieder" (doc. 10) and "Renelt" (doc. 12). Geipel & Sohn was a renowned firm with 900 employees and branches in Vienna and Prague. In 1873, the Emperor had awarded Christian Geipel an honorary charter for his role in making the regional textile industry competitive with that of the German Reich.

In January 1910, however, after businesses had been reclassified for the period from 1910 to 1914, Geipel's son learned of an increase in insurance fees by no less than 40 percent—without this increase having been accompanied by any change in the actual machinery of production in place. But what is more, the documents of the case prove that until its final stage, none of the parties was fully aware of the factors that caused this considerable increase in the stated danger in Geipel's textile business. These factors were a matter, not of wool or mechanics, but of paper; their origin was not the technology of the textile production in Asch, but a slight modification of the Prague Institute's classification system. While, until 1909, weaving mills for sheep's wool and for cotton wool were classified in the same risk category, the invention of narrower, faster, but also more dangerous looms for cotton wool led to a reclassification of these mills and to a corresponding increase in their insurance rates. Now, even while Geipel & Sohn had been chiefly processing sheep's wool along with only small amounts of cotton wool, the firm had from the outset been classified as a manufacturer of cotton wool. But since sheep's wool and cotton wool were equivalent terms in the old classification, officials obviously never paid much attention to this terminological inaccuracy. In January 1910, therefore, in the first weeks of Kafka's new position as the head of the claims department, the scene was set for a truly Kafkaesque ordeal. Geipel, who was obviously ignorant of the bureaucratic mode of perceiving reality, simply saw a "gross disproportion" between the statistics pertaining to accidents in his business and the newly fixed insurance fees. He claimed that the unchanged use of his technical equipment should guarantee the continuity of his fees; in fact, based on improvements in workplace safety, he was entitled to a slight decrease. The Prague claims department, in turn, had no choice but to apply the infallible logic of the classification system, a logic that was hardly ever based on first-hand knowledge of the individual firm, relying instead on forms filled in by the firm's owners along with the expert reports submitted by the trade inspectors (doc. 7). At this point, we encounter what the philosopher Jean-François Lyotard calls a *différend*: the clash of two discourses based on incompatible sets of assumptions. Kafka, who had identified the three major arguments of the claim by numbering them with the roman numerals I, II, and III by hand in the margin of Geipel's note of protest, now stated—in fact, correctly—that the business had been classified as a cotton-wool mill (argument I), thus laying the foundation against which Geipel's recourse to technical standards and statistics was futile. Kafka's form was backed up by a report from the responsible trade inspector. Obviously, this report, too, was based on previously gathered written evidence, thus confirming the Institute's judgment: Geipel was running a cotton-wool mill and was therefore subject to the higher fees.

Upon receiving these two documents from the district authority, Geipel wrote a counterstatement. Here the *différend*, the difference between the machinery of wool production and the machinery of file production, comes to the fore when Geipel argues:

> The fact that cotton was named first in the answer to question 6 of the questionnaire is purely accidental and meaningless for the actual reality, which is that we use woolen yarn for the most part and that cotton and silk, as we have already stated, comprise only a very small percentage of the material we process.

And then, for the first time, "the actual reality" is, in fact, named: it is the difference between narrow, fast, more dangerous looms and wide-bodied, slow, less dangerous ones.

Eight weeks later, when this counterstatement was answered by the Prague Institute, Kafka was out of the office, away on a business trip to Gablonz, trying in vain to convince local business owners of the advantages of accident insurance. The Institute's response is the more revealing in that it was written in the clumsy officialese, probably of Kafka's superior, Eugen Pfohl. He wrote (in a slightly smoothed-out translation):

> In the case under review, the Institute must observe the regulations of the statute [. . .]. We freely admit that the type of loom can be an element in the level of risk within a weaving mill, but this fact does not allow us to sidestep the official regulations so lightly.

At this point, the bureaucratic vehicle gathered speed: only four days later, the Office of the Governor decided to reject Geipel's claim.

Geipel, however, was not deterred. His claim to the Minister of Interior in Vienna (F) is among the most remarkable documents in the flood of complaints Kafka's department had to contend with. Geipel's is neither the voice of a legal professional trying to adapt the paragraphs of the law to his case nor the desperate outcry of a semieducated small business owner on the verge of economic ruin. Geipel speaks as a cultured citizen, quite capable of stepping back and observing the operations of the law from a certain distance. And by now, he appears to be fully conscious of the cause of his trouble. Right from the start, therefore, he takes a metajuridical position, distinguishing a question of law, *Rechtsfrage*, from a question of fact, *Tatfrage*, arguing from the realism of industrial practice against the nominalism of the bureaucratic classification system; insisting that the law should employ the language of experts in the field; pointing up the misclassification of his firm in 1909; and ending on a triumphant note:

> Every law must be interpreted according to its purpose, and every law exists to achieve a particular purpose; the purpose of the ordinance that classifies cotton- and wool-weaving mills differently is to point out the difference in risk factors between cotton- and wool-weaving mills according to the looms in use in each.

This case illustrates the basic conflict that produced most of the appeals against risk classification: the difference between the pragmatism of the employer and the probabilism of the risk-classification system. In a typical shift of perspective from official to literary text, Kafka shows the potential excesses of the power of definition that accrues to the questionnaire and its author in such instances. In the fragment of his America novel, *The Man Who Disappeared*, composed in October 1914, the protagonist, Karl Rossmann, seeks to become a member in the Nature Theater of Oklahoma, but he cannot produce identity papers.

> It was true that the record showed his identity papers were missing, and the office director called it an incomprehensible piece of negligence. But the clerk, who had the upper hand here, dismissed the fact lightly, and after the

director had asked a few insignificant questions and was gearing up to posing a weightier one, the clerk declared that Karl was hired. The director, mouth agape, turned to the clerk but the clerk gestured as if to put an end to all argument; he said "Hired," and at once he entered the decision in the book.

Then, when Rossmann is asked his name and only gives the nickname he had used in his previous job, the truth of the dictation system once again asserts itself against the truth of appearances:

"Negro?" asked the director, turning his head and making a face as if to indicate that Karl had arrived at the height of implausibility. The clerk also looked Karl up and down for a while, but then he repeated, "Negro," and entered the name in his book. "You didn't put down 'Negro,' did you?" the director snapped. "Yes, 'Negro,'" the clerk replied calmly, gesturing as though it were now up to the director to take all further steps. The director controlled himself, stood up, and said, "On behalf of the Theater of Oklahoma, you are now—." But he got no further, for he could not go against his conscience; he sat back down and said only, "His name is not 'Negro.'" The clerk raised his eyebrows, stood up in his turn, and said: "Then I will be the one to inform you that you have been accepted into the company of the Theater of Oklahoma, and now you will be introduced to our leader."

6

MEASURES FOR PREVENTING ACCIDENTS FROM WOOD-PLANING MACHINES (1910)

This brief has gained considerable prominence in Kafka scholarship. Kafka attended a special course at the Institute of Technology in Prague to acquire the requisite technical knowledge. For the first time in the two decades of its existence, the annual report includes illustrations—technical drawings of wood-planing machines and the injuries they could inflict on workers' hands. The imagery of this essay, as well as its genre—the technical protocol—are taken up in Kafka's great story In the Penal Colony. *Equally remarkable is Kafka's use of technological arguments to resolve the corporate tension between employers and employees. This is a concrete instance of Kafka's impulse, vivid in his literary work, to subvert the stereotypical oppositions informing the discourse of his time on issues of class, race, gender, politics, and the like.*

The Institute respectfully submits the following remarks on the activities outlined in last year's report regarding the introduction of cylindrical safety shafts and regarding equipping square shafts with metal flaps in wood-planing machines.

The introduction of the cylindrical safety shafts in wood-planing machines is finally progressing well, as is attested in the edict circulated by the k. k. Office of the Governor to the k.k. district authorities regarding the introduction of the safety shafts; the same opinion is expressed by the k. k. trade inspectors, who are pressing us with increasing urgency to use these shafts. Finally, there is the fact that a considerable number of employers are already working with such shafts and have spoken very favorably, not only about the important safety feature of the cylindrical shafts—which was never in question—but also about their practical usefulness. There is thus a well-founded hope that in the near future the cylindrical shafts will have won such widespread acceptance that any business that does not use them will have to be classified as indicative of above-average risk. We can only wish that the technical journals would devote greater attention to the cylindrical shafts, for judging by the current situation, it appears that the only thing now needed to make the cylindrical shafts quickly and universally accepted equipment is a final detailed discussion that would reach all circles involved. The reason for this is primarily that the cylindrical shafts occupy a very special position in the area of safety equipment, since apart from their protective effect—which is, in fact, absolute—they combine a number of other advantages, being basically cheaper than the square shafts and functioning both more cheaply and more efficiently. Thus their adoption does not call on employers' sociopolitical judgment but is clearly advisable as a practical matter.

I. The cylindrical safety shaft provides perfect protection.

Our illustrations show the difference between the square and the cylindrical shafts from the perspective of safety. The blades of the square shaft (figure 1) are screwed directly to the shaft, and their exposed cutting edges spin at 3800–4000 revolutions per minute.

The danger that arises for the worker from the large gap between the blades on the shaft and the surface of the table are obvious. These shafts would therefore have to be used either out of ignorance of the danger, which may become even greater as a result, or in full awareness of constant and unavoidable danger. An extremely cautious worker might well take care that as he works guiding the piece of wood over the planing blade, no part of his fingers protrudes beyond the wood, but the primary danger makes a mockery of all caution. The hand of even the most careful worker would inevitably slide into the blade slot in case of a slip, or when the piece of wood to be planed is pitched backward—a mishap that is not infrequent—as he presses it down on the table with one hand and guides it toward the blade with the other. This act of raising and pitching back of the wood can never be either predicted or prevented,

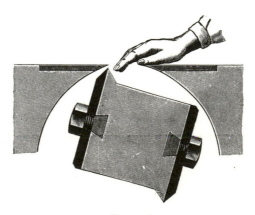

Figure 1.

since it happens whenever the wood is misshapen or gnarled, whenever the blades do not spin quickly enough or slide out of alignment, or whenever the pressure from the worker's hand on the wood is unevenly distributed. And whenever such an accident occurs, several finger joints or even entire fingers are severed (figure 2).

Not only have all cautionary measures seemed to fail in the face of such risks, so also has every safety device. They either proved to be fully inadequate or they decreased the danger in one respect (by automatically

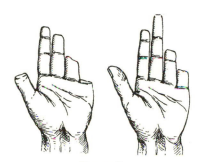

Figure 2.

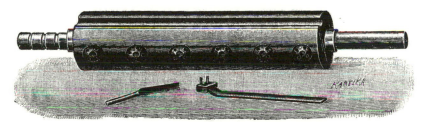

Figure 3.

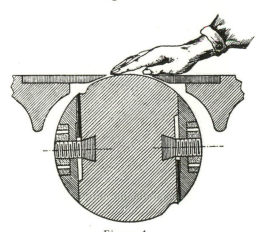

Figure 4.

covering the blade slot with a safety plate or decreasing the width of the blade slot) while increasing it in another respect by not giving the shavings enough room to fall, so that the blade slot became clogged and injuries to the fingers occurred frequently when the worker tried to clear the slot of shavings.

As a comparison to this square shaft, a cylindrical safety shaft from the engineering works of Bohumil Voleský, Prague-Lieben, is illustrated in figures 3 and 4; figures 5 and 6 show an original cylindrical safety shaft for wood-planing machines using the Schrader system, a product of the engineering works of Emil Mau und Co. in Dresden.

The blades of these shafts are completely protected between the flap (Voleský Co. shaft) or between a wedge (Schrader patent) and the solid frame of the shaft. They are fastened securely, unaffected by any strain, and the blades can never snap out, any more than they will be flung out or bent. Should the shaft break, the possibility of the screws' flying out is also minimized because the screws are cylindrical and are sunk deeply into the flaps; moreover, in the case of the Schrader patent, the screws

Figure 5.

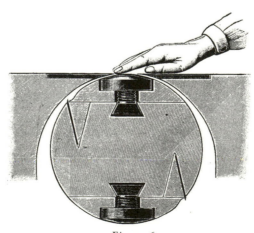

Figure 6.

are exposed to much less strain than those in the square shafts, since in the latter the screws are made to hold the actual blades, while in the cylindrical shaft the only function of the screws is to press the flaps against the wedge—a task that is all the easier because these flaps lie flush only at their outermost ends, being separated for the rest from the frame of the shaft by a space not visible in the illustration.

The fact that the Schrader patented shaft is undercut—this cannot be seen clearly in the illustration either—and very gradually flattens out as it comes closer to the blades keeps the shafts from becoming greasy while making it easy to insert the wood into the shaft and ensuring adequate space for the shavings to fall.

The most important factor from the perspective of safety, however, is that only the cutting edge of the blades protrudes and that the blades can be very thin without danger of breaking, since they are practically of a piece with the shaft.

The described devices eliminate the probability of workers catching their fingers in the slot of the square shaft, and even if fingers are caught in the slot, the resulting injuries are slight, consisting merely of lacerations that need not even interrupt work.

The general effectiveness of cylindrical shafts in regard to safety has flooded the market with a large variety of such products, and most of these perform as indicated, but a few also present some problems along with their protective benefits (shavings easily clog the slots, the blades are not fastened tightly enough, and the like); workers do not willingly use these products, and thus they compromise the effective safety shafts. At any rate, whenever employers were dissatisfied with the functioning of the cylindrical shafts, it has always been a matter of such defective products, and the real effectiveness of the cylindrical shafts remains undisputed. Some people have claimed that reconditioned square shafts are an adequate alternative to the newer cylindrical shafts. We can agree with this opinion only to the extent that the drawbacks we have listed

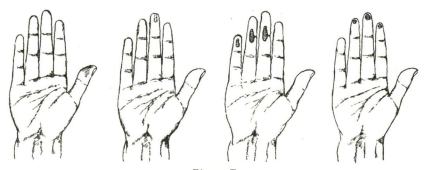

Figure 7.

do not apply—that is, the slots do not become clogged, the blades are fastened tightly enough, the wood glides easily across the shaft, the four rows of screws do not themselves pose a risk of their own, and so forth (figure 8, a shaft reconditioned by the Voleský company.)

Recently a new alternative to cylindrical shafts was recommended for use in wood-planing machines. This is an arrangement that encloses the square shaft in a steel hull, thus decreasing the dangerous gap between the surface of the table and the blade in the same way as do the cylindrical shafts, but it also allows the steel hull to cover the nuts of the screws holding the blades, preventing these from flying off in case the equipment should break. Granted that such a shaft does allow the use of the old blades of the square shaft and the same blade sharpening machine.

II. The cylindrical safety shaft is basically cheaper than the square shaft.

Only artificially tempered blades, at least 8 mm thick, can be used in square shafts, whose exposed blades must stand up to far greater demands, while blades 1½ mm thick of naturally hardened steel are sufficient for the cylindrical shafts.

In addition, it is not necessary to add any other safety devices, an expenditure that cannot be avoided in the case of the old square shafts.

III. The operating costs of the cylindrical safety shafts are less than the costs required by the square shafts.

First and foremost, sharpening these thin blades is, of course, much easier and quicker than the effort required for the heavier blades of the square shafts. Further, the blades on the cylindrical shafts have a much

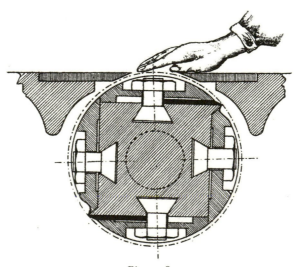

Figure 8.

larger wear-resistant surface. While the surface of the square-shaft blades is only 15–16 mm, the blades of the cylindrical shafts measure 28 mm, or almost twice as much.

Since the blades on the cylindrical shafts encounter far less air resistance than do those of the square shafts, they expend less energy. Therefore they also run much more quietly, and there can be avoidance of the shrieks emanating from the old square shafts—shrieks that literally announced their dangerousness.

IV. The cylindrical shafts are also more efficient.

Since the blades in the cylindrical shafts—those of the Schrader patent, for example—place the entire active pressure of the blades directly on the solid frame of the shaft, a significantly cleaner planing of the wood is achieved, and the blades will not produce such large shavings as those of the square shaft.

The cylindrical shaft can plane both thin and thick shavings, as well as both hard and soft woods. Furthermore, shavings and splinters can be scraped off roughly hewn pieces without any risk; this practice was a frequent source of danger with the old square shafts.

Quick work is guaranteed by the rapid revolution of blades on the cylindrical shafts and above all, by the possibility of incising grooves without removing the planing blades. (Granted, the old square shafts also allowed for this operation, and not all cylindrical shafts have this provision.)

In addition, the cylindrical shafts speed up the work process by allowing workers to proceed without anxiety because of the complete absence of risk.

Commentary 6

In the fall of 1912, Kafka was exchanging love letters and photographs with Felice Bauer, who held a leading position at Carl Lindstroem AG, a Berlin manufacturer of gramophones and dictating machines called "parlographs." The correspondence was not limited to family events. In early December, Kafka, who preferred to think of his future fiancée as working in a "completely unreal" business, offered her a deal:

> Am I to get the pictures of the office? If so, you will get something like our Institute's annual report with an article by me on cylindrical safety shafts! With illustrations! Or even an article on workshop insurance! Or one about safety heads! Dearest, there are many pleasures in store for you. (LF 84, trans. modified.)

In one sense, these illustrations were more than merely fair repayment for photographs of an unreal office. They were a media innovation—the first pictorial elements ever used in the Institute's annual reports. Their function was by no means merely aesthetic; they were the visual part of a precise technical description aimed at an audience of technical experts, mechanical engineers, and business owners. Kafka had taken pains to gain the necessary technical knowledge. At the beginning of the winter of 1909, still a trainee at the Institute, he successfully requested permission from the administrative committee to attend morning lectures at the Institute of Technology in Prague.

The essay shows Kafka to be an expert in social mechanics as well. The deplorable state of workplace safety in Kafka's days was partly due to the fact that the issue of accident prevention was a football between parties to the political conflict over social insurance as a whole. Leo Verkauf, the leading expert in this field among the Social Democrats, bluntly likened the workmen's accident insurance institutes to the employer-biased Austrian bureaucracy:

> It is a widely known fact that only under extreme pressure can employers be brought to pay some attention to the workers' physical safety. What is much worse is that the Austrian bureaucracy has expressed all too clearly its aversion to the sociopolitical demands of the workers and their compliance with the wishes of the industrialists. [. . .] Our accident insurance

institutes are consumed by the same zeal for seeing nothing and intervening nowhere. [. . .] The bureaucrats in the accident insurance institutes
have always resisted all attempts to grant the institutes greater authority in
the area of accident prevention, such as issuing preventive regulations.
They feel a true horror of additional powers, since these could bring them
into conflict with either the workers or the employers.[1]

The employers aimed their criticism at the same "bureaucratic organization" of the Institute but, of course, with completely different conclusions. In their official response to the 1902 program for new social
legislation, the General Committee of the United Chambers of Trade
and Commerce and the Central Association of Austrian Industrialists
argued:

> The reform program authorized the insurance institute to impose sur-
> charges on businesses whose accident-prevention provisions did not meet
> the existing regulations; [. . .] this authorization must give rise to serious
> concerns, given the current bureaucratic organization of the institute.
> When the employers are granted autonomy, these concerns will be relieved,
> and the institutes can be granted all the authority that German law grants
> the trade associations with regard to accident prevention. In particular, the
> insurance institute may be granted the same right that is given in Germany,
> to issue compulsory accident-prevention regulations and to deploy techni-
> cal inspectors to monitor compliance, since the employers' deeply rooted
> and justified dislike of administrative decrees that interfere with the orga-
> nization and operation of their business will disappear.[2]

The model of self-administration suggested here to replace inefficient
bureaucracy boils down to the almost complete exclusion of workers
from the management of social insurance. The price the employers asked
for their good will and cooperation in accident prevention was the
abolition of the existing trilateral governance of the insurance
institutes—guaranteed by an executive body of representatives of the
state, workers, and employers; this group was to be replaced by an executive body consisting entirely of employers.

Against this background, Kafka's technological essay on safety information displays a crucial sociopolitical dimension. As in the case of
workshop insurance in the building trades (doc. 2), Kafka refrains from
siding with either party or from bartering for an *Ausgleich*, the notori-
ous Austrian version of a rotten compromise. Instead, we see him
struggling for a formula that will resolve conflict or, at the least, transform it into a platform for a social consensus. In this case, the shibbo-
leth leading to consensus is hidden in the template of his essay—that
is, in the series of subtitles organizing his line of argument: "I. The

cylindrical safety shaft provides perfect protection." "II. The cylindrical safety shaft is basically cheaper than the square shaft." "III. The operating costs of the cylindrical safety shafts are less than the costs required by the square shafts." This is the ultimate goal of Kafka's incisive technological analysis: an irrefutable line of argument to resolve the antagonism between workplace safety and profit and to deprive the employers of a lever to catapult them into control of accident insurance.

Among Kafka's writings for his institute, the essay on the dangers of wood-planing machines has garnered the greatest scholarly attention. It aims at the fascinating relationship between the illustrations and the technical descriptions of the various types of planing machines and the wounds they inflict and the description of the torture machine in Kafka's story *In the Penal Colony* and the wounds it inscribes. Here, there are two aspects of note. As with all of Kafka's poetic images, a series of stunning empirical "prototypes" has been identified for the torture machine. Among the machines in question (including a typewriter, a psychiatric electrical apparatus, and most notably, a gramophone manufactured by the "completely unreal" business mentioned above—the Berlin-based Lindstroem Company, where Felice Bauer was employed), there is one specimen that has special significance for Kafka's professional field: a machine that both "wounds" and encodes the human body. That is the electric accounting machine (the Hollerith machine) used for processing statistical data from the 1890s on and a piece of machinery well known to Kafka from talks by Heinrich Rauchberg, Austria's leading national statistician, who lectured at Charles University and again at special events for the clerks at the Institute. Electric data processing by the Hollerith system was based on a "counting card" that was first punched according to a specific set of data and then read by the needles of the accounting machine. Owing to his twofold professional responsibility for accident statistics and for accident prevention, Kafka would have been alert to the two interrelated levels of the bodily inscription of power in modern society: its inscription on the individual's physical body (in the form of wounds inflicted by planing machines) and its inscription on the statistical body of social groups (in the form of data, of feeding diagrams, and curves). In fact, much of Kafka's imagery throughout his work is designed to fuse these two currents of power. The ape Rotpeter, in the story "A Report to an Academy," evades the fate of the captured animal, which is to suffer continuous wounding for training purposes, by using the methods of statistical data processing: he organizes his behavior according to the "accumulation of [his] observations" of human behavior (KSS 81). In this fashion, he constitutes himself a social subject. And, again, there is the hunter Gracchus, who demands that his shattered body be transferred to the Beyond; his request is based on the fact that he has fallen victim to a normal employment injury in accordance with his professional routine. Hence, it is more than a similarity of motifs that constitutes the nexus between Kafka's office writings and his literature. Both contain a play of worldviews deeply informed by an analytic grasp of social organization.

7

ON THE EXAMINATION OF FIRMS BY TRADE INSPECTORS (1911)

This is a core document among Kafka's office writings. Kafka wrote this long note of protest to the Minister of the Interior in the summer of 1911, when his department was flooded with appeals from employers protesting the risk classification of their firms. This text belongs somewhere between Gogol's The Inspector General *and Kafka's* The Castle. *At the time the laws governing workmen's accident insurance were established, industrial lobbyists succeeded in having regulations passed that banned the staffs of insurance institutes from their clients' firms, on the grounds of the sanctity of trade secrets. Instead of institute-appointed inspectors, a network of state-approved industrial examiners was set up; these were responsible for the inspection and control of technical and safety standards in Bohemian industries and craftsmen's shops. As the individual firms were literally (closed) black boxes to the insurance institutes, the latter had to rely heavily on accident statistics on the one hand and on the regular reports from the inspectors themselves on the other. Although the inspectorate was conceived as the cognitive organ of accident insurance, in practice it amounted to a monopoly willing and able to misuse its authority. State-approved inspectors deviated from the technical terminology defined in the regulations and invented a language of their own, enabling them to exert illegitimate influence on the whole of Bohemian industry. Kafka's analysis of this situation demonstrates his grasp of the linguistic foundation of the legal norms with which his Institute operated and, hence, of the basis of the social security of the Bohemian work force.*

To the Esteemed k. k. Ministry of the Interior:
The undersigned Institute respectfully takes the liberty of calling your attention to some of the disadvantageous consequences to our classification system that have resulted from the current evaluation practices carried out by the majority of the k. k. trade inspectors. The inspections are part of the appeals process connected with the 1910 reclassification of commercial firms subject to compulsory accident insurance.

The Institute hopes most of all to gain an advantage from this presentation in two areas relating to this subject that we have occasionally mentioned in our specific appeals. When submitting these remarks on the particular expert evaluations of the k. k. trade inspectors, there was no avoiding the fact that every single time the Institute raised serious objections to the factual correctness of an expert opinion, it was considered an exceptional case. Such decisions immediately appeared somewhat questionable, and by the nature of their exceptional status, were not held to require a general remedy. Furthermore, these separate appeals placed the Institute in an embarrassing position as it considered the apparently factual nature of those appraisals; the Institute was thus drawn into a polemic that, viewed from outside, went far beyond the bounds of each case but was always aimed at the biased tendencies the Institute clearly detected as influencing every one of these opinions.

The Institute has repeatedly expressed its opinion of the k. k. trade inspectors' submission of their appraisals in the course of the appeal process; and the Institute arrived at this opinion long before the 1910 reclassification. Even at the time of the 1905 reclassification, the Institute saw itself forced to initiate a procedure to insure that the appraisals of the k. k. trade inspectors are limited to establishing the actual conditions that result in an increase or reduction in industrial risks as these conditions relate to the ordinance. At that time, the Institute was forced to insist that the k. k. trade inspectors' expert opinions avoid any conclusions, since such judgments are outside their area of expertise. This request was of necessity connected with another, to the effect that the assessments make no specific recommendations of risk classes and percentages. The reason for the Institute's request, which culminated in a corresponding petition to the government, is contained in the attached annual report for 1906 (pages 29–31).

This process was completely successful in principle; a decree from the k. k. central trade inspectorate instructed the individual inspectorates to refrain in future from including recommendations concerning risk percentages in all expert opinions dealing with classification. In practice, however, the Institute's procedure proved futile. This particular directive, which was intended to apply to all evaluations—both those submitted directly to the Institute and those issued during the appeals process—appears to have fallen completely into oblivion, and all the Institute's efforts to recall that decree to memory in the individual statements are in vain.

In addition, all the unacceptable conditions that led to the above-mentioned procedure have now grown more serious and place an intolerable strain on the reclassification system. The principal reason for the intensification of these conditions is that the number of trade inspectorates has grown so considerably compared to 1905, and the majority of these new inspectorates have formed new focal points of reporting with a subjectivity prone to every kind of bias. It is true that these unfortunate conditions also have some welcome consequences, in that the problems inherent in the opinions become glaringly clear as a result of the series of conflicting subjective judgments made by earlier and present trade inspectors. So the problems gradually become apparent to the qualified authorities as a general situation and thus cannot help but challenge them to intervene across the board. This is not the place to cite the reasons for the conflicts in the various expert opinions; it is sufficient to note that such contradictions arose even when the separate inspections with radically different outcomes were separated by only the briefest time periods, and that a quite contrary evaluation was rendered even when the later appraisal made it quite clear that the operating conditions of the particular firm had not changed. The inspection reports of the k. k. trade inspectorate in Teplitz are especially illustrative of this trend, as are those of Karlsbad, whose district encompasses several districts that used to be part of the Teplitz inspectorate.

In the course of the administrative procedure regarding appeals against the 1910 reclassification, the undersigned Institute observed that the appraisals rendered by the k. k. trade inspectorate in Karlsbad, which have now been subpoenaed by the k. k. Office of the Governor in the course of this process, fundamentally contradicted the last five years' worth of expert opinion of the inspectorate responsible for Teplitz that had been submitted for reclassification in regard to the Institute. As long as the Institute could study only the materials of separate cases, it had no choice but to approve the more recent of the conflicting evaluations submitted by the inspectorate now responsible, and this was the procedure the Institute followed. But gradually it became evident that the appraisals that contradicted those of the older inspectorate shared the repeated common characteristic that they were unfavorable for the Institute. It then became necessary for the Institute. having studied the contradictions, to take a position against the practices of the new evaluations. The Institute was all the more forced into this position when the submission of such conflicting assessments became a regular occurrence and when then k. k. trade inspectorate in Karlsbad rejected the Institute's classification even when the facts in favor of the disputed classification (i.e., for the report of the k. k. trade inspectorate in Teplitz) were so compelling that even the new appraisal would seem to recommend the previous classification. Thus on occasion the evaluations submitted by the k. k. trade inspectorate in Karlsbad often called for two classifications:

first, classification according to the actual, undeniable findings and second, classification according to the conclusions, which were far afield from the facts.

This phenomenon was by no means limited to the two cited trade inspectorates. The two are noteworthy only because of the remarkable abundance of such conflicting reports and the remarkably consistent, almost hostile type of conflicting findings they contain. These allowed for the relatively early discovery of this subjective effect, which typically colored the assessments of the k. k. trade inspectorate in Karlsbad. The following may serve as examples of the many conflicting expert opinions [here Kafka cites around a dozen opinions—Eds.].

A particularly representative case of such contradictions is shown by an expert opinion rendered by the k. k. trade inspectorate in Königgrätz on April 22, 1911; not only do the conflicting opinions become clear when we compare this evaluation with another, earlier one, but the contradiction is specifically established by an expression of regret in the subsequent opinion. The original submission by the k. k. trade inspectorate responsible for Reichenberg describes undercutting at a quarry (the appraisal formed the basis for the reclassification of a quarrying firm). Now, the later assessment reads: "The undersigned regrets that he is compelled to declare the statement of trade inspector Herr Czerweny to be in obvious error. Not only is there no undercutting in this quarry, but it is probably impossible to undercut here at all."

Establishing the classification system was impeded in another way as well when the appraisals of different trade inspectorates showed conflicting opinions in the cases of those firms for which the classification system had no clear identification; in those instances, different classifications were suggested by different trade inspectorates, whether in the same district or in separate ones. On the one hand, the permanence of the classifications the Institute strove to establish were put at risk by these different classifications, the objectivity of which is in doubt; on the other hand, the uniformity of classification of equivalent firms suffered.

Thus, the undersigned Institute's classification of wooden-spool production was based on the expert opinions of the k. k. trade inspectorates of Tetschen and Reichenberg. Other assessments conflicted with our classification, such as the opinion of the k. k. trade inspectorates in Trautenau of November 23, 1910, and Königgrätz of September 13, 1910.—The expert opinion of the k. k. trade inspectorate in Reichenberg of December 14, 1910, approved the Institute's classification of chain-finishing factories, while the appraisal of the inspectorate in Königgrätz, issued on October 15, 1910, rejected this classification.

Such evaluations largely resulted from the inspectorates' failure to consider all the aspects of the reasons for the Institute's classifications, demanding reclassification without being fully aware of the seriousness of the petitions. As a consequence, the classification system was sucked into a whirlpool of conflicting opinions from which there was no satisfactory escape.

The objectionable elements found in the k. k. trade inspectorate's assessment increased further, as was evident as early as the 1905 reclassification lists. This unfortunate situation was grounded in the fact that the k. k. trade inspectorates had ceased confining themselves to offering concrete proposals—illegal in and of themselves—but since they were unmindful of any restriction, they also took it upon themselves to extend their area of authority.

Thus the ministerial decree of September 18, 1904, in response to a request from the Ministry of Trade and Commerce, points out that the trade inspectors' comments concerning the quality of the technical managers and the workers cannot be allowed because these factors lie outside the sphere of the trade inspectorates; information of this sort can easily jeopardize these officials' position of trust. Given this decree, which clearly forbids comments on the technical management and the quality of the supervising and working personnel, a majority of the k. k. trade inspectors found ways to circumvent these regulations while simultaneously satisfying them—indeed, more than simply satisfying them. They circumvented these regulations and continued to comment on technical management, etc., but they nevertheless did not jeopardize their position with the firms' owners. Rather, they strengthened it by almost exclusively submitting expert opinions during the appeals process that characterized management as good or very good. Now, if the k. k. trade inspectors, as will be shown, still incorporated unsubtle biased distinctions in their evaluations even when addressing facts that simply called for an expert's yes or no, then it seems only natural that their descriptions of good management, so easy to assert and so difficult to gainsay, are worded in extremely general phrases. Not only do these characterizations fail to form a reliable basis for classification; frequently, by following the literal meaning of § 6, they also necessitate a lower classification. In dealings with the opinions from some trade inspectors, the undersigned Institute has become accustomed to finding that very good technical expert management has been discovered in cases without actual risk-reducing factors. The statements about technical management are so numerous that we can cite only a few examples. [...]

Even the few instances we have noted here are sufficient to suggest the principle informing the appraisals of the k. k. trade inspectors—that is, the principle of approaching the Institute in the role of proprietor's advocate. This intention becomes even more evident whenever the evaluations are not limited to the factors they are intended to determine but indulge in special investigations and interpretations of accident-insurance law, of classification regulations and systems, of the wording of legal categories, etc. Of course such investigations and interpretations would be valuable in and of themselves if only they were not included in evaluations of individual cases, where they serve only to blur the conclusive judgment on the individual case by introducing subjective, often very slightly substantiated opinions. Again, these specific investigations and interpretations not only indulge in legalistic deductions in a superficially objective way but are actually intended to argue against the classification made by the Institute. Moreover, the questions addressed here are usually irrelevant and fail to deal with the issues raised in the appeal. We are in possession of assessments in which the way classifications are systematized is misunderstood; these same documents warn us not to classify craft industries under rubrics in which the word "factory" appears (the appraisals of the k. k. trade inspectorates in Königgrätz of November 21, 1910, and in Teplitz of November 28, 1910). Others engage in detailed interpretations in an attempt to exempt excavation sites from compulsory insurance (e.g., the report by the k. k. trade inspectorate in Königgrätz of December 31, 1910), and still others apply an inadmissible interpretation to the Ministry of Trade and Commerce ordinance of May 29, 1908 (the k. k. trade inspectorates in Karlsbad of January 18, 1911, in Prague III of November 7, 1910, and in Karlsbad of November 24, 1910). Further, we have documents in which the ambiguous nature of the provision for exemptions in § 2 of the classification regulations is carefully outlined, and where § 2 can be invoked unequivocally only when it can be turned against the Institute. When it comes to classifying firms specializing in rifling metal rollers—which the Institute previously classified according to accident statistics as well as evaluations of the k. k. trade inspectorate in Reichenberg—other trade inspectorates offer objections by reinterpreting the wording of the rubrics (Tetschen, November 18, 1910). Other documents, rather than evaluating the applicable facts, mistakenly follow their own misunderstanding of the k. k. Administrative Court's findings (Tetschen, March 18, 1911). Some evaluations continue to use the wording of Rubric 530, "Carpenter's Trade," though that appellation has long been abolished and the Institute's position has already been approved by the k. k. Office of the Governor; the overall inappropriateness of such interpretations by the k. k. trade inspectorates becomes all the more obvious (Teplitz, August 8, 1910). Still other appraisals try to support individual cases by reintroducing into Rubric

518 the lower-risk feature of "Construction and Modification of One-Story Buildings," which was excluded from the current classification system for good and sufficient reason, based on accident-statistics (Prague III, December 17, 1910).

§ 3 of the classification regulations provides the possibility of separate classification (as § 4 provides for mixed classification) as a last resort in cases in which a firm that consists of differing departments cannot be classified simply under one rubric because there is no appropriate title that would apply; this same § 3 is used in a number of cases by the trade inspectors as a means of applying for a risk reduction in the classification made by the Institute. We are here dealing neither with cases in which the facts justify the application of § 3 or § 4 nor with instances in which it is possible to raise doubts only about the factual justification of these classifications. Rather, it is a question of cases in which the claim is made for divided classifications regardless of the actual situation and the classification regulations; nor is any consideration given to the fact that such an evaluation blurs the overall accident statistics for the particular rubric, since all it accomplishes is to bring about a diminution in the classification. This inclination to apply for mixed or separate classification became especially evident when the proposed departmentalizing of a firm went only to the point at which no further reduction in the intended risk classification could be made. We refer here to the reviews from the k. k. trade inspectorates in Reichenberg of November 25, 1910, December 14, 1910, and December 15, 1910; from Tetschen of March 18, 1911; from Teplitz of October 21, 1910; from Pardubitz of November 22, 1911, and December 12, 1910; from Pilsen of August 10, 1910; from Prague II of September 6, 1910; and from Prague of December 1, 1911.

Admittedly, the principal explanation for some of the evaluations in question is that the trade inspectorates involved are not sufficiently informed about the overall accident statistics. When we held preliminary discussions with the trade inspectorates about the new classifications, we became aware that a significant number of trade inspectorates, at least at that time, had not been provided with the "Accident Statistical Data, 1902–1906." In such cases, when the statements conflict with the accident statistics, the weight of the evaluation's apparent factuality, which prevails in spite of the differences, is especially regrettable. Such statements include those issued by the k. k. trade inspectorates in Prague III of November 29, 1910, and October 16, 1910; in Pilsen on July 15, 1910, and November 29, 1910; and in Teplitz on August 16, 1910, and January 13, 1910.

The fact that the trade inspectors greatly exceed the scope of the appeal in their proposals for classification is also reflected in their cur-

rent assessment practices; instead of merely examining the facts, as
they are solely authorized to do, they occupy themselves primarily
with evaluating the classification. Although the final judgment on classification can never fully comply with such proposals in light of the
finding of the k. k. Administrative Court of April 30, 1909, the effect
of these reports is nevertheless felt all the way to the final decision;
they may even determine the Institute's position. In many cases the
situation may be such that even when the impracticality of the reviews
that ignore the legal limits is recognized, the proposal adversely affects this recognition. Such documents include those of the k. k. trade
inspectorates in Tetschen of December 21, 1910, and January 7, 1911;
in Pardubitz of November 29, 1910; and in Prague III of December
21, 1910.

The exceptions listed in § 2 of the classification regulations frequently provide the inspectors' assessments with a legal justification to
oppose the Institute's classification. The application of § 2 in the current classification system must rely on the passage regarding revision of
the risk categories as specified on p. 119 of the *Amtliche Nachrichten*
of 1909. This section states that only certain types of commercial enterprises may be considered suitable for the application of § 2, as well as a
limited kind of low-energy engines. But in their eagerness to ally themselves with the owners whenever possible, the inspectorate documents
have been unable to uphold this and the following regulations. Time
and again, we find similar evaluations that purport to discover limited
machine operation in commercial smokehouses, although the particular operating conditions of the smokehouses and their accident statistics contradict such an assumption. Equally unfounded is the request
for the application of § 2 in the case of belt-making firms and factories
producing cleaning and polishing agents. An appraisal by the k. k.
trade inspectorate in Prague of December 14, 1910, calls for classification according to § 2, although no rubric for manual operations of the
kind in question exists anywhere. The appraisal by the inspectorate in
Tetschen of January 22, 1911, asks for classification under § 2 for a
firm although that company uses a steam engine of 30 hp. An evaluation by the k. k. trade inspectorate in Tetschen requests the application
of § 2 in a case that is retrospectively discussed in the discussion of the
risk-category revisions, mentioned above, regarding the illegitimate application of § 2. In many cases, classification according to § 2 is requested although the firms in question include both manual and
machine operations (statements of the k. k. trade inspectorate in Prague
of December 10, 1910, of November 28, 1910, and others).

An appraisal from the k. k. trade inspectorate in Prague of November
22, 1910, also seeks classification according to § 2, although in this

case, motorized firms were separated from firms not employing engines by only one risk category.

The risk-reducing factor of electrically powered machines listed in § 6 of the classification regulations is cited against the Institute in the expert opinions of various trade inspectorates without consideration of the restrictive phrase, "to the extent that mechanical transmission is avoided or significantly reduced." There may be instances in which the trade inspectorate determines the presence of electrical power and consequently proposes a certain risk percentage far below average, again ignoring the restrictive phrase, though the introduction of electricity may have caused a significant increase in risk over the former steam operation, since transmission may have multiplied with the replacement of one steam engine by several electrical motors. Given such documents, it is a lucky break when the actual status of the electric engine is clarified in the proprietor's questionnaire. The following may be cited as examples of such reports: the k. k. trade inspectorates in Pardubitz on December 13, 1910, and January 7, 1911, and in Pilsen on January 14, 1911.

Furthermore, these inspection reports include a very general summary, given as catch phrases, which are indeed intended as such. Such vague formulations have already caused the Institute much grief, both during the discussions with the trade inspectors regarding the reclassification of various firms and during of the earlier risk-category revisions.

Since currently the choice of these catch phrases to describe the structural and safety conditions of the various companies is left entirely to each inspector, the phrases, intended to promote the uniform classification of all businesses, thus reflect the individual trade inspector's personality, and they may be to the point or vague, indecisive or assertive. It is true that at the time of our discussions, the Institute was in a position to work toward some uniformity of these phrases, and especially toward bringing them into conformity with the classification regulations. But because in the assessments issued in the course of the appeals procedure, no trade inspector is prevented from following his momentary preferences, the variety of catch phrases exceeds all bounds, and especially the bounds of the terminology of the classification regulations. Thus, for example, the evaluation of a firm as "appropriate" or "standard" in the sense of the previously established remarks on the revision of the fourth risk category indicates a company equipped according to the regulations enacted for the protection of the life and health of workers in all industries in general and for certain types of firms in particular. As a result, the term "standard firms" and, along with it, the prerequisites for classification in the mean risk percentage of the appropriate category are clearly defined. Nevertheless, some inspection reports seem to feel that they have to invent the term "standard firms" all over again. In such evaluations, "standard firms" can mean any number of things, sometimes more than one in the same document; the term may even have more than one meaning in the same sentence. This all-forgiving vocabulary often serves to bridge the statements of fact and the conclusions, serving to superficially reconcile the two, whereas in reality they would be contradictory according to the classification regulations. Some appraisals declare the equipment of some firms to be standard, others declaring them substandard, and yet both request classification in the middle of the appropriate risk category. Some examples of such reports are those of the k. k. trade inspectorates in Teplitz of August 12, 1910, in Pardubitz of November 14, 1910, and in Prague III of September 21, 1910. Other inspection reports argue that a firm should be classified in the midrange percentage—in other words, as a standard firm—even though the equipment is found to be substandard. Among such reports are those of the k. k. trade inspectorates in Pardubitz of September 9, 1910, and in Königgrätz of July 6, 1910, and August 12, 1910. Other reports admit that the firm in question could not be characterized as exemplary but nevertheless request classification in the lowest risk-percentage category; an example is the assessment of the k. k. trade inspectorate Karlsbad of June 28, 1910. It is only the use of special terminology that turns standard firms into exemplary firms without the need for specific documentation, as in the evaluation by Prague III of December 5, 1910. At times this terminology is encouraged by the idea that these firms' equipment is actually standard but that they should be considered to be relatively better than standard, or if their actual condition is substandard, that they should be seen as relatively normal. This process also occurs in cases where this motivation—which is in no way within legal limits, considering the restricted scope of the supervisory districts of the trade inspectors—does not correspond to the immediate facts. See, for example, the evaluation of the k. k. trade inspectorate Prague III of September 19, 1910.

In their efforts to obtain the lowest possible classification for certain firms, many trade inspectors go even further. The information in their appraisals contradicts the information provided by the proprietors' questionnaires. Of course, in most of these cases, the disparity between the judgments and the questionnaires arises from the fact that a one-time inspection, conducted on an arbitrary date that happened to be especially unfavorable for determining the true facts (particularly in quarries, brickyards, and the construction industries), cannot provide as complete and true a picture of a particular firm as can the questionnaire when it is completely and properly filled out. The k. k. trade inspectors must be aware of this circumstance, but nevertheless, not only do they not acknowledge the difficulty, but they also fail to adjust their conclusions accordingly. Of course, such disparities between the questionnaires and the evaluations can exist only if the questionnaires have been filled out truthfully. And if the bias of an appraisal can seldom be countered even when contrasted with a questionnaire that represents the operational conditions less favorably, then neither the Institute nor the related authorities will ever learn the true conditions. For examples, see the reports by the k. k. trade inspectorates in Teplitz of July 15, 1910, and July 23, 1910; in Pilsen of June 23, 1910, and August 30, 1910; in Karlsbad of February 22, 1911; in Tetschen of January 11, 1911; in Pardubitz of August 9, 1910; and in Prague III of October 19, 1910.

The forms of inspection practices that flout the law that we have described are only those that emerge as typical from the mass of documents to hand. In addition, many more chances arise for the k. k. trade inspectors to protect firms beyond the strict requirements of the law—possibilities that are so closely connected to the nature of each firm that for all practical purposes they form a counterpart to the individualization called for by the regulations and expected of any classification within the law. According to some appraisals, firms formerly found substandard are now particularly well-equipped because the noted flaws have been remedied (the inspection report by the k. k. trade inspectorate in Teplitz of February 26, 1911; and in Prague III of July 19, 1910). Agricultural enterprises, which the k. k. trade inspectors have inspected for the first time only by order of the k. k. Office of the Governor, are promptly judged to be especially favorable, as is shown in the evaluation by the k. k. trade inspectorate in Karlsbad of August 30, 1910. Risk-increasing factors are both asserted and toned down in one and the same report (Karlsbad, July 20, 1910). If no risk-reducing factors can be found in a firm's structure and the safety equipment, one such factor is finally discovered in its technical arrangements—that is, in facilities that may affect performance but not the risk inherent in the firm; such findings are represented in the inspection reports by the k. k. trade inspectorate in Tetschen of December 9, 1910, and in Prague III of December 16, 1910. Some inspection reports that cannot uncover any current risk-reducing factors predict that they will occur in future and therefore request an immediate reduced classification; examples of this practice are Reichenberg, December 30,1910, and January 19, 1911. One classification proposal bases its conclusions entirely on such words as "approximately," "almost without exception," and "possibly"(the report by the k. k. trade inspectorate Prague II of October 25, 1910). Another inspection report by the same inspectorate, submitted on September

17, 1910, supports its conclusions largely by quoting an incorrect mean risk percentage for a certain class. A report by the k. k. trade inspectorate in Tetschen, submitted on January 3, 1911, bases its proposal for a reduced classification for a particular firm on the following characteristic consideration: "Thus (based on the actual facts found) it is more realistic, or at least equally realistic, to assume better than standard conditions than it is to assume standard conditions."

The following is an example of the way different inspection reports on the same company can superficially coincide very neatly for the purpose of establishing a reduced classification outside the legal limits—that is, to obscure actual working conditions. At the time of the preliminary discussions on reclassification, a certain firm was declared to have standard equipment. The evaluation submitted during the appeal process by the k. k. trade inspectorate Prague III on December 7, 1910, explains that formerly—that is, at the time of the first inspection report—this firm was found deficient, but that the noted shortcomings were now remedied and thus (within the guidelines of the general descriptions cited above) a reduced classification is in order. An example of how appraisals that are strikingly different on the surface can be made to coincide, especially when there are more than two of them for comparison, is provided by the following. During the 1904 reclassification, a simulated-leather factory, Ernst Hamburger, in Grünwald was described in such a way that even the highest risk percentage seemed too low. A second appraisal, submitted on August 18, 1906, and based on an inspection of August 7, 1906, upheld this classification. A third evaluation, of October 29, 1906, after a review conducted on October 23, 1906, concluded that at this time, a medium classification should be applied. But then again, a fourth inspection report, submitted on the occasion of the 1909 reclassification and based on a review that, according to the questionnaire, was clearly carried out in 1908, found several safety violations, requiring classification somewhat above the mean. Finally, the inspection report submitted in the appeals process by the k. k. trade inspectorate in Reichenberg on December 15, 1910, concluded the cycle with the surprising revelation that since its founding, the factory had exhibited such serious deficiencies that they justified classification in the highest risk percentage of the appropriate category.

The inspection practices of the k. k. trade inspectors have gradually developed to the present extent of the resulting grievances, and no other authority has had the opportunity to follow the separate phases of this evolution that the Institute has experienced, since all the reports of the k. k. trade inspectors for the past 22 years have passed through the hands of the directors of the department entrusted with the classification system. The Institute was therefore all the more fearful with each

risk-classification review that biased evaluations by the trade inspectorates would adversely influence the classification system; these influences are quite capable of undoing classifications that the Institute,
using all its available resources, had established to reflect as precisely as
possible the uniformity, the letter of the law, and the facts.

With every reclassification, therefore, the Institute has taken steps to
invalidate the trade inspectors' unacceptable reporting practices. § 9 of
the classification regulations leaves it up to the concerned parties to
decide on the ways to bring about the "agreement" required by the
regulations between the Institute and the inspectorates regarding the
reclassification. The current verbal form used to create such "agreements" with the inspectorates developed gradually as the need arose
and was approved retroactively by ministerial decrees, even if it has not
yet been expressly adopted in § 9 of the classification regulations. In its
efforts on the one hand to receive expert evaluations of as many firms
as possible and on the other to keep biases out of these evaluations as
much as possible, the Institute has already attempted, or at least attempted to stimulate, a number of ways to achieve the agreement necessary for the purposes of reclassification. In the risk-category revisions
of 1894 and 1899, the Institute went no further than determining the
risk classification by talking with the trade inspectors about each case
and entering the appropriate notes on the classification forms. This procedure did not prove effective, however, because the authorities charged
with the decision on the objections would not grant to our notes the
validity of an expert report submitted in writing. Of course the Institute's notes had no power against the inspection reports submitted in
the appeals process, which canceled out the preliminary assessments in
a procedure much like that of the present classification, though to a
lesser extent.

Before the reclassification of 1904, the Institute approached the trade
inspectors with a request that they submit a written report based on a
nine-point set of questions developed by the Institute for each firm and
enter their findings in the space reserved on the last page of the questionnaire. We also planned to end these evaluations with a verbal statement. At the time, the esteemed k. k. Office of the Governor recognized
the necessity of this action, and yet the trade inspectorates declined to
take on this final element, and on September 18, 1904, the k. k. Ministry of the Interior issued a decree condoning this refusal. In order to
obtain the agreement required by law, therefore, all that was required
was a verbal statement, along with a brief report prepared by the responsible trade inspectorate. Before the 1904 reclassification, we concentrated on recording as many details as possible, in the hope that
such meticulousness would allow us to approximate the trade inspec-

tors' approach as closely as possible, and to record precisely the details inferred from their investigation forms so as to prevent any change from their earlier, impartial position to an opportunistic one during the appeals process. The outcome clearly demonstrated the uselessness of this procedure and led directly to the action that is described in the Institute's annual report of 1906. Before the reclassification of 1910, the Institute's efforts were therefore limited to recording merely general opinions, adding judgments only in exceptional cases. At the same time, however, the Institute turned to all offices of the trade inspectors with an urgent verbal request that unfavorable evaluations be issued only in instances in which it could safely be expected that successive appeals would uphold the classifications based on these assessments—that is, only in those cases that present convincing grounds for classification to a higher level. We further urged that only those firms be declared normal for which, in fact, no risk-reducing factors as defined in the classification regulations could be demonstrated. In turning to the trade inspectors with such a request, it would seem that the Institute was going against its own interests, since it was encouraging the trade inspectors to completely ignore the Institute's interests that might not be supported by the facts, and even in doubtful cases to issue a report that would favor the firm in question. In reality, however, in asking the trade inspectors to take this course, the Institute was quite aware that it was protecting its own interests, since its classification system can process only classifications that are thoroughly documented down to the minutest detail, along with the greatest possible consistency of such classifications. The Institute is convinced that it has been given at least a majority of such reports. The objection that those reports were submitted only in outline form, made up merely of brief catch phrases, can be countered with the following:

1. The Institute successfully worked toward achieving a uniform terminology in these consultations, which was lacking in the evaluations submitted in the appeals process.

2. Those appraisals represent the essence of documents that were thoroughly revised, often more than once, and based on the investigation forms, by the respective trade inspectors themselves.

3. Finally—and most importantly—it is precisely that which appears to be their greatest drawback, their rapid succession, that actually constitutes their greatest advantage, since the process discourages the introduction of biased effects and considerations. The Institute's intention in obtaining such inspection reports, which demarcate what the Institute could grant the firms and thus the trade inspectorates, was to make it impossible for the latter to issue deviating reports during the appeals

process. In our survey we have already explained that this intention largely failed. Let us merely mention that had we succeeded, the trade inspectors' practice of making specific proposals for classification would have been far less damaging. On the other hand, the failure of our attempt is surely related to the trade inspectors' practices, since the misjudgment of the legal foundations of an institution cannot fail to become evident on every level. The Institute therefore need not again invoke the law against the practices of the trade inspectors; the Institute is currently in a better position as compared with its 1909 effort, however, insofar as it sought to effect an interpretation that is in line with the legal regulations from the k. k. Central Trade Inspectorate, while our current mission is to obtain full compliance with the elements of the interpretation that has come to be accepted.

The crucial point of nearly all the inspection reports, as we have repeatedly noted, is that they contain practical proposals lacking all legal support for the trade inspectorates:

The fifth paragraph of § 14 of the Accident Insurance Law expressly designates the Institute as entitled to classify firms under the individual percentages; the Institute must exercise this authority in its autonomous sphere of influence. Nowhere does § 14 assign the same right to the k. k. trade inspectors, and following this provision alone, specific proposals of classifications cannot be seen as anything but encroachment on the Institute's sole legal rights or on the decision-making rights of the respective authorities appointed to rule on appeals.

§ 28 of the Accident Insurance Law deals with evaluations the k. k. trade inspectorates have submitted at the request of the Institutes. This section, too, makes no provision for the k. k. trade inspectors to participate in any professional activities carried out by insurance institutes. Rather, the trade inspector is entitled merely to convey directly to the insurance institutes the observations made during his inspection.

§ 9 of the classification regulations, which has the greatest validity in this question, again states merely that the classification of firms under risk classes and percentages should proceed as far as possible in agreement with the k. k. trade inspectors. Since § 14 and § 28 of the Accident Insurance Law cannot be repealed by this prescription, the only possible meaning of this section is that the insurance institute, having received an inspection report from the k. k. trade inspectorate, must establish the actual classification; such a report from an inspectorate will record only the conditions encountered in a firm but will never offer specific proposals on any aspect. Consequently, the k. k. trade inspectorates' reviews may contain only an evaluation of actual conditions but not an evaluation of the classification made by the Institute. The decree of the k. k.

Central Trade Inspectorate, to which we have referred repeatedly, reliably confirms this position. The fact that the k. k. Office of the Governor also shares this opinion is proven by the text of the decrees that present the objections to the reclassification to the k. k. trade inspectors for their response; these decrees also specifically specify that the appraisal to be submitted must be worded in accordance with § 9 of the classification regulations—a provision that implies an order to refrain from including any specific proposals for classification.

Yet in spite of these regulations, in spite of the decree by the central trade inspectorate, and in spite of the position of the k. k. Office of the Governor, the encroachment on the Institute's autonomy described here has become general practice, and inspection reports that observe the legal requirements have become such a rare exception that there is only one inspectorate from which we receive them regularly. The k. k. trade inspectorate in Budweis submits these evaluations, which could provide almost all other trade inspectorates with a fine example of adherence to the law. We refer here to the appraisals of September 14, 1910, and December 14, 1910, as examples. These evaluations concentrate entirely on determining the facts and never seek to influence the decisions to be made by the appropriate authorities. They offer no interpretation, no inference about the law, no appraisal of the management, no unfounded revocation, etc. Instead, they list all the facts relevant to insurance-related evaluations, and only such facts, with a precision and thoroughness that allows the Institute to follow these reports with confidence even when they indicate the necessity of revising the Institute's original classification. That reports that conform to the law exist at all within the Institute's area is largely due to the circumstance that chief trade inspector Herr Tusar in Budweis was formerly stationed in Mähren, where the reporting practices of the k. k. trade inspectors generally follow the law.

Proposing specific classifications, the first illegal step in the k. k. trade inspectorates' reports, inevitably led to all further illegality. For just as the evaluations were located outside the law in this respect, they left themselves open to outside influences. Only in this way could that illegal point of view be formed from which the k. k. trade inspectors, even if unconsciously, perceive the risk percentages as the leverage they may always use more or less stringently to reward or punish the employers in their district for matters that have nothing to do with accident insurance. How clearly the illegal aspect of this practice is understood in some instances is shown by the timidity with which various inspection reports state that the Institute would have to find a way to live with this or that very low percentage rate. One appraisal even includes a lengthy deductive argument to this effect, a disquisition that is clearly dictated by a need to justify on the surface what is intrinsically unfair in the application for a reduced classification. This particular report reads: "According to the counterstatement of the Workmen's Accident Insurance Institute, a deficit results in the premium payments as compared to the overall charges of the period 1897–1906. However, since the risk percentage was measured at 40% at that time, it is questionable whether this deficit cannot already be remedied with a somewhat lower risk percentage (compared to the percentage rate in dispute), such as 44% instead of 47%." And this observation, in fact, led this report to propose a lower classification.

If, given the current situation, we return to the original intention of the legislator, who made his opinion clear by subordinating the trade inspectorates to the Institute in questions of classification and to the responsible authorities in appeals decisions, the following picture results:

The insurance institute, for whatever reasons, was not granted the right to do an overall inspection of firms. Thus, in order to ensure the objectivity of the classifications in cases in which other surveys by the Institute were either absent or did not suffice, it was left to expert authorities to support the Institute by supplying information on the actual conditions and to use their documents to intervene where there was no other way to obtain an impartial classification. The fact that the Institute contributes K 10,400 a year toward the expenses of the trade inspectorates in its territory also reflects the inspectorates' place within the classification system.

The current situation does not, however, reflect the intention of the law. The trade inspectorates are no longer auxiliary organizations, especially in the appeals process; rather, they represent the position of the parties, even of the authorities that will make the final decision. Accordingly, the counterstatement of one party disappears under the weight of the illegal appraisals we have discussed, since it is becomes a mere addendum to the inspection report. By the same token, there are cases in which the trade inspector gave illegal advice; for example, a review of August 25, 1909, by the k. k. trade inspectorate in Karlsbad of the clothes-dying and laundry firm Peter Lerner in Eger advised that some departments be excluded from having to carry insurance. Finally, the consequence of such partisanship is that even in those cases where the trade inspectors approve the Institute's classification, the Institute can only half-heartedly agree with the final proposals. But it is precisely this unclarified position of the trade inspectorates in the appeals process, as professional agencies appointed by law on the one hand and as representatives of the interests of the party on the other, that provides them with various advantages over the Institute and gives them such great influence. For as professional agencies, they have the right of inspection, and their evaluations do seem based on fact, but at the same time they favor one side without regard to the facts.

All the reports we have cited support our contention. Further, the trade inspectorates' assessments appear to be reports by professional agencies without personal interests. But currently, even as the statements of specialist agencies, they cannot be characterized as such. The observation has already been made on the occasion of the earlier risk-class revision that the trade inspectors exploit the reports for the purpose of implementing certain agendas of their own that clearly bear no relation to accident insurance. While this practice is not legal, it is easily understandable. For it is well known that the threat of a higher premium payment moves an employer much more readily to obey the dictates of the trade inspectors than would a request from them or from the district authorities. But the reports of the trade inspectors, in their ostensible capacity as protectors of the employers, are even exposed to additional outside influences—though we might mention that in some cases, we could detect biases directed against the owners. The biases that work in favor of the proprietors, however, far outweigh the others. As an example, we may refer to contradictory reports submitted by various trade inspectorates on the same firm, as noted above. Another example: almost all the reports submitted on the belt-making factories in the Gablonz district on the occasion of the discussions before the reclassification were affected by then-Representative Glöckner's interference in the appeals process. In one supervisory district, the reports changed after the intervention of an industrial corporation. Similarly, outside pressure effected the description of the mixed-materials weaving mills in the Ascher district as sheep's-wool weaving mills under Title 303, in spite of the fact that the Institute assigned Title 323, which applies to mixed-materials weaving mills according to the title of the respective subgroup. The Institute is convinced that if the case were such that the risk category for sheep's-wool weaving mills had been higher than the category for cotton-weaving mills, pressure would have been exerted to get the mixed-weaving mills classified as cotton-weaving mills, a change that would, if only coincidentally, have corresponded to actual conditions.

As a result, at present a majority of those tasks assigned by law to the trade inspectorates fall to the Institute—that is, ensuring that classifications are objective and restoring impartiality to those evaluations that were exposed to a variety of biases at the hands of the trade inspectorates; but the Institute can perform this function only to the extent that its limited means allow. In the current state of affairs, however, the Institute is forced by the type of reports to request them only in the most urgent cases; the cooperation of the trade inspectors is thus generally limited to reports submitted for purposes of reclassification—and such reports are rendered only once every five years; and it is therefore mainly with respect to these reports that the Institute, with a budget of K 52,000 every five years, makes its contribution to the costs of the trade inspectorates. But as we have shown, even this sum is only part of the costs imposed on the Institute by the trade inspectors' evaluations.

The preceding discussion makes clear that, if the reports cannot stand up under an inspection using only the methods generally available to the Institute, they will be even less defensible under a real inspection that checks out the facts. The Institute has understandably undertaken such a review only in isolated cases, when chance provided the opportunity. But in every case where such an inspection was conducted, it had the expected result and refuted the main points of the responsible trade inspector's assessment. The following examples, in outline without entering into the details, will serve as illustrations:

The report of the k. k. trade inspectorate in Karlsbad of October 15, 1910, described the safety aspects of a brickyard as being good and its clay pit as closely conforming to regulations. When the Institute initiated an inspection, it was discovered that the property included some steep embankments as well as a runway with a plunging incline that ran very close to a clay wall; the wall threatened to collapse onto the runway, and the runway, in turn, increased the danger of the wall's collapse from the vibrations on the track. Some clay walls were three meters high, only shorter sections of the pit were cut into steps, and these steps were of very recent origin.

A report by the k. k. trade inspectorate in Karlsbad of October 17, 1910, indicated that the steam engine formerly used in the plant had been replaced by an electric single drive and that the clay pit was in complete compliance with the legal requirements. Investigations at the site revealed that an electric single drive is not present in the brickyard and that conditions in the pit are adverse, since there are steep clay walls of up to five meters in height.

A report by the k. k. trade inspectorate in Karlsbad of September 20, 1910, declares a kaolin-extraction site to be a strip mine. Regarding the results of the Institute's own inspection, which completely contradict the report, please consult the Institute's appeal, which was lodged against the decision of the k. k. Office of the Governor on February 20, 1911, to the k. k. Ministry of the Interior on March 16, 1911.

But in other instances, the facts alone were enough to disprove the inspection reports without the intervention of the Institute, albeit too late:

The Institute classified the quarry with stone works M. No. 443/92 as standard equipment and listed it under the mean risk percentage of 59%

in class X according to Title 55, based on the questionnaire. The report of the k. k. trade inspectorate Prague II of November 28, 1910, applied for classification under a risk percentage far below the mean because of the allegedly very favorable quarrying conditions. The Institute does not deny having frequently been influenced by the apparent impartiality of such reports, as was also true in the present instance. In its statement of December 23, 1910, the Institute proposed classifying this quarry under risk percentage 57%, a reduction of 2%. The decision of the k. k. Office of the Governor of January 6, 1911, also under the unavoidable impact of the evaluation, specified a classification percentage of 55%, or 2% lower than the Institute's proposal. The inspection report in question was so persuasive chiefly because it is generally assumed that such definite evaluations must be based on a series of inspections, especially in the case of quarries. And this quarry would finally have been classified at the greatly reduced classification for a five-year period, in total disregard of the actual conditions, as happened in so many other cases, had the quarry not been the scene of a huge accident on April 1, 1911, in which, according to the newspaper stories, one worker was killed and several other quarrymen suffered life-threatening injuries. The accident was caused by the fall of a boulder, an incident that proved that the work was not carried out using terraces, that there were overhanging sections of rock, and that undercutting therefore also occurred; these facts had not only been passed over in silence in the report, they had actually been disclaimed.

Similarly, a very recent serious accident at the previously cited simulated-leather factory Ernst Hamburger in Grünwald, which occurred when a worker became entangled in the transmission line, clearly indicates the contradictions in the various documents that were submitted on this company.

Let us summarize the entire matter:

The Institute fully respects the k. k. trade inspectorates as professional auxiliary organizations, but we must also demand that the inspectors respect the Institute's autonomous area. The Institute defers to the expert evaluations of enterprises by the k. k. trade inspectors, but it cannot in all good conscience bow to positions taken by these agencies that are not within the letter of the law; and finally, while the Institute does not impugn the k. k. trade inspectors' good faith (aside from specific cases) in all the cited assessments, we believe that this good faith is generally based on considerations whose damaging effects can be seen in the risk classifications as intended by law.

In consideration of the above, we request the esteemed k. k. Ministry of the Interior to be so kind as to work toward ending those shortcomings in the current evaluations issued by the k. k. trade inspectors that can be addressed within the Ministry's own sphere of influence and that those shortcomings be remedied in the Institute's territory. Regarding the k. k. central trade inspectorate, we request that evaluations issued by the offices of the k. k. trade inspectorates reflect the limits of the law and be composed in the form of professional reports on technical observations, drawing no conclusions and offering no practical proposals.

Prague, June 22, 1911
The Chairman: The Director:
(Stamp)

Commentary 7

❧

The Prague Institute wrote this note of protest to the Minister of the Interior in the summer of 1911, after a wave of more than 3,000 appeals had challenged the legal basis of the reclassification of Bohemian firms into risk categories. In keeping with the bureaucratic rule, the note was signed by the Institute's director, Robert Marschner, although it was, beyond reasonable doubt, written by Kafka. At the time, he was the responsible official, the only one on the Institute's staff with the competence and knowledge to develop this complex line of argument. Among the documents in this volume, this note reveals most clearly the simultaneous presence of Kafka the clerk and Kafka the writer.

At stake is the need to set down rigorously "the grounds of knowledge" figuring in accident insurance—in a precise word, its epistemology. In the debates preceding the passing of the Accident Insurance Law of 1887, industrial lobbyists, citing "trade secrets," succeeded in restricting the right to inspect individual firms to trade inspectorates established in 1883. The lobbyists deemed these inspectorates to be friendlier than the huge, partly state-run apparatus of the accident-insurance institutes then in the making. This move deprived the institutes of all immediate evidence of the things and persons they insured. Classification of individual firms by risk now relied on two different sets of data: (1) statistical data on the number and types of accidents and sources of danger, and the ratio between the insurance fees paid by the employer and compensation paid by the insurance institute; and (2) descriptive information supplied by firm owners on statistical data-processing punch cards and questionnaires, and expert reports submitted irregularly by trade inspectors. Under these circumstances, each individual firm remained "a black box" or, to quote a humanist critic of the day, "a veiled picture of Sais" for the insurance institute.[1] Hence, the success or failure of the whole system of accident insurance depended on the reliability of the two streams of data.

As far as the trade inspectors' reports were concerned, they were obviously corrupt. Even five years earlier, in the aftermath of the previous reclassification, the Prague Institute had pointed out that the responsibility for reductions in risk classification (and hence in insurance fees) was accumulating around a few local inspectors. It is revealing to compare the demeanor of the Prague Institute in addressing this issue before and after Robert Marschner, the new director, took over. In 1906, the Institute's annual report for 1905 humbly asked the Ministry "to hand down" the necessary orders to the inspectors. In the summer of 1911, relentless realism and dialectics, bordering on sarcasm, replace the earlier attitude. For example, this note of protest confirms that the increase in trade inspectors that the Institute had repeatedly requested from the 1890s on had in no way produced more reliable knowledge of the firms after 1905. Instead, "the majority of these new inspectorates have formed new focal points of reporting with a subjectivity prone to every kind of bias." This growth of corruption was explicitly welcomed insofar as

> the problems inherent in the opinions become glaringly clear as a result of the series of conflicting subjective judgments made by earlier and present trade inspectors. So the problems gradually become apparent to the qualified authorities as a general situation.

These judgments—that is, judgments made by the professional observers, the "eye" of accident insurance—lead to a remarkable perspectival reversal. It is the kind of strategic move we find in most of the papers written by Kafka but hardly anywhere else in the rich documentary material preserved in the archives of the Institute. In Kafka's pages, the inspectors themselves are subjected to close inspection: accident insurance becomes self-referential, in the sense of seeing itself as an operation itself prone to accident. Like the industrial accidents in the Institute's questionnaires and statistics, the malfunctions of the trade inspectors are counted and listed, while "only those that emerge as typical from the mass of documents to hand" are given special recognition in this "second-order" expert report. And it is not by chance that, as in Kafka's long essay of 1908 (doc. 2), language itself is identified here as a prime source of danger. We literally hear Kafka's voice interrupting the monotony of official language when an idiomatic phrase is produced only to be exposed in its emptiness by the recurrence of its key term (here: "bounds"):

> But because in the assessments issued in the course of the appeals procedure, no trade inspector is prevented from following his momentary preferences, the variety of catch phrases exceeds all bounds, and especially the bounds of terminology of the classification regulations.

The pivotal entry in this list of catch phrases is "standard firm." According to the logic of the risk classification scheme (see figure 1), this catch phrase attempts to combine a descriptive and a prescriptive notion. In one sense of the word "standard," a firm's accident risk matches the statistical average risk of the branch of the industry to which it belongs; in another sense, a firm satisfies the technical regulations for accident prevention in its branch. This terminological ambiguity aims to encourage firm owners to fulfill, or even overfulfill, the norms of industrial safety, so as to lower their risk classification and, hence, their insurance fees. In practice, however, confusion increases, since the inspectors add yet a third notion to the catch phrase. They define as "standard" any firm whose technological norms resemble those of most other firms in the region. Kafka's memorandum now proceeds to analyze this fateful linguistic accident:

> At times this terminology is encouraged by the idea that the firms' equipment is actually standard, but that they should be considered to be relatively better than standard; or if their actual condition is substandard, that they should be seen as relatively normal.

In fact, the "idea" developed in the memorandum does not stop at the borderline between Kafka's daytime records and his nocturnal writings. The peculiar bureaucratic machinery in *The Castle* is nicely illuminated by that of the Institute. For example, when Momus, the village secretary, interrogates K in order to "keep a record of this afternoon's happenings," Momus vigorously corrects the landlady's assumption that Momus's "official standing," rather than merely his "official residence," is "restricted to the village." This debate on the validity of records and their official status transcribes into fiction the vital issue of Kafka's 1911 note of protest.[2] It is also part of an ongoing discussion on the relation that might exist between the "lower," ordinary, knowledge available in the village and the assumed "higher," transcendental, knowledge circulating in the castle. Klamm's habitual rejection of the information Momus prepares for him—"'Keep away from me with your protocols,' he usually says"—reminds us of the gap between these two strata.

At this point, the knowledge and skills of Kafka the clerk appear to be seamlessly absorbed by Kafka the poet. The outcome is a mode of writing that reflects and parodies itself by reflecting and parodying the bureaucratic world around it. This observation holds particularly true for the concept of the "standard firm," the central issue of the memo on the trade inspectors. In Kafka's late story "The Burrow," which stages a symbiosis between the author and his work, the animal hero wonders whether it would make sense to check the safety of his burrow against intruders. Observing the entrance from outside, he asks himself whether "the existence of the full scent," which establishes presence in the burrow, is not "the precondition of normal danger." Here, Kafka the poet borrows the key concept of "standard danger" from Kafka the insurance expert to reflect on his house of writing as if it were a firm that is subject to accident insurance.

The interplay between Kafka's two professions goes well beyond converting legal or administrative concepts into literary images. The issue of the "standard versus the less than standard" firm is a pivotal point in most of Kafka's narratives. All his heroes struggle with the ambiguity between the good normality of a state of affairs that corresponds to a norm (be it legal, administrative, religious, or moral) and the bad normality of a flawed or faulty existence that falls short of such fulfillment. When the hero of *The Metamorphosis*, Gregor Samsa, wakes up one morning as vermin, he is neither shocked nor puzzled; he is undismayed and bent on regaining the normal physical abilities of a good employee. The hero in "The Hunter Gracchus" claims that his fatal fall into a ravine was a matter of professional risk or standard business: "Everything went in order. I gave chase, fell, bled to death in a gulch, was dead, and this sailboat was supposed to carry me into the hereafter" (KSS 112). But he does not arrive, owing to the boatman's failure at the helm—a disaster, as the Hunter Gracchus must learn, that is not covered by his earthly insurance. And while his counterpart, the ape in "A Report to an Academy," is much more willing to adapt to the conditions created by his professional accident—to repeat the development of his species in his own lifetime—what he achieves after an unheard-of effort is the "average cultural level of a European," that is, a state of normality that falls well short of fulfillment. The résumé of the ape's autobiographical report—"I can't complain, but neither am I satisfied"—describes Kafka's judgment on the two kinds of "protocols" he left to us (KSS 83f).

8

WORKMEN'S INSURANCE AND EMPLOYERS: TWO ARTICLES IN THE *TETSCHEN-BODENBACHER ZEITUNG* (1911)

❧

These two articles for the daily newspaper of the northern Bohemian industrial town of Tetschen-Bodenbach are a jewel among Kafka's office writings. Moving nimbly between the social and political battle lines, Kafka proceeds to reconstruct the original ideal of workmen's accident insurance—a system meant, after all, to alleviate social conflict—at the very moment that it is had become the object of further conflict between the vested interests of the corporate triangle (state, employers, workers). Kafka employs a subtle authorial rhetoric to close the gaps in the legal texture of social insurance, revitalizing what might be called the spirit of the law. These documents go a long way toward establishing Kafka's deep involvement in the social fabric of the Empire at a crucially formative moment in his career as an author.

A. Workmen's Insurance and Employers (September 13, 1911)

Local papers have recently reprinted excerpts of an article from a German newspaper that subjected the situation of workmen's insurance in Germany to a devastating critique. This article rightly caused a stir beyond Germany's borders, and in our country as well; it was the topic of much discussion and debate. It is therefore appropriate to submit our experiences in Austria in the area of workmen's insurance, and accident insurance in particular, to retrospective scrutiny, especially since discussions about the draft of a social-security law in parliament provide an occasion on another front to do so.

We must begin by saying that the results of our critique cannot help but differ here in many aspects from the results in Germany, because workmen's accident insurance has developed along different paths and is currently at different stages in Germany and Austria. It is well known that from the outset the two countries have found different solutions even to the problem of covering costs. This fact alone has necessarily meant that the German industrial sector was approached with low demands that increased over the years, so that today they may have reached their peak, as is characteristic of the pay-as-you-go system. We handled the approach differently here. From the outset, our fully funded system placed greater demands on the involved groups—and they are the only ones that matter here—and according to the organizational principle of Austrian accident insurance, these demands were not expected to increase significantly with time. While the German system foresaw the growth of the premium requirements from the beginning, so that it came as no surprise, workmen's accident insurance in Austria continually caused new and, it must be said, ever more painful surprises for the industrial groups involved with each one of the never-ending increases in the premium rates, which the system had not planned and which therefore could be caused only by external circumstances rather than being intrinsic to the system.

The extent of the increases is illustrated, for example, in the fact that in 1889, the highest premium rate for K 100 of chargeable wages amounted to K 5.67 for the Prague Institute and has currently reached K 8.59—an increase of more than 51 percent. The simple juxtaposition of these two figures is the most dramatic example of the way workmen's accident insurance developed in Austria, and particularly in Bohemia.

Of course, the steady increase in the premium rates for workmen's accident insurance was not cheerfully accepted by the contributing industrial groups; the chorus of voices raised in protest grew, and the affected groups called for redress with increasing energy. And these were, of course, not the only ways the increase was protested. More than one employer made personal arrangements with the Institute.

This is the place to explain the risk classifications and premium rates in greater detail. The premium contribution in the area of workmen's accident insurance is graduated according to a firm's risk level so that the most dangerous receive the highest risk classification with the highest premium rates, and the least dangerous receive the lowest risk classification with the lowest premium rates. At the very beginning of Austrian workmen's accident insurance, the classification was based on statistical data that were available to the Ministry of the Interior, and we must admit that it was this material that constituted perhaps one of the most disastrous factors in the whole history of Austrian workmen's accident insurance. These data were so defective and inadequate that they did not represent the actuality and resulted in a completely unjustified distribution of the charges among the individual commercial groups. In consequence, a thoroughly skewed perspective was introduced into

Austrian workmen's accident insurance from the outset, and the separate insurance institutes have suffered from these discrepancies ever since, without a way to work their way free of the consequences to this day.

The immediate result was that in the early years of their development—at a time when they had to overcome all kinds of other problems—the insurance institutes had to strive for rectification of the ministerial statistics by adjusting them to actual circumstances, but without being able to acknowledge this actuality by imposing correct premium rates. Until 1897, all the institutes, and especially the Prague Institute, were made to suffer flagrantly under the thoroughly unsuccessful compilation of the rates and the statistics. The proof is the annual accounts of the various institutes, which showed ever-increasing annual losses. In 1897, the first increase in premium rates began, having been preceded by the first revision of the risk classifications in 1895. This revision, however, was also defective, as later revisions made more and more apparent. Here in Austria, we never experienced the final consequences from the statistical results—that is, the various commercial groups were not assigned the risk classifications they properly deserved, instead receiving increasingly lower ones; in these assignments, the determination of the risk classification was regularly controlled by the strength of the influence exerted by the central office in question. The Ministry of the Interior, therefore, could not help but be aware as soon as the new risk classification system was published, that the separate institutes could not break even with the previous premium rates, since, as noted, the results of the statistics had not been fully observed. The Ministry therefore resorted to a measure—which we must firmly condemn from the standpoint of objective financial policy—in that the Ministry increased the premium rate for all employers, not excepting those industrial groups for which neither the increase in risk classification nor the increase in the premium rate was justified by the statistical results. The textile industry, for example, which from the outset always met its requirements, was hard hit by this step, since the general increase in the premium rate obligated this industry to help cover the liabilities of other commercial groups, such as the machine industry, the building trades, agriculture, and stone and soil processing. The same situation arose with every subsequent revision of risk classifications and rate increases. At each of these, the Ministry of the Interior lacked the courage to draw the final conclusions from the statistical results and always thought it more appropriate to spread the losses in certain industrial groups indirectly to the whole and thus to introduce a thoroughly unsuccessful and confused pay-as-you-go system alongside the fully funded one. Incidentally, the Ministry of the Interior seems finally to have realized the error of its policy, for the last risk classification plan, effective as of January 1, 1910, does leave the impression that the Ministry is willing to utilize the statistics fully and to apply them in determining risk classifications. We must, however, point out that this trend has by no means become the general attitude and that the Ministry of the Interior has fallen back into its old ways in the case of a number of groups.

Now we must examine the inevitable impact of this public rate policy on the affected industrial groups and on the insurance institutes.

If we look back on only the most recent years on this point—and we are, of course, primarily interested in the situation of the Prague Institute—we find the following uncovered losses in the balance sheets for this Institute, stated in round numbers: K 35,570,000 in 1907; K 39,200,000 in 1908; and K 40,100,000 in 1909. We must categorically deny that this is purely a paper deficit, which means nothing, and that the Prague Institute's finances are not in desperate straits as long as annual revenues are sufficient to cover annual expenditures. Such a view is utterly wrong, because we must always remember the legislature's purpose in enacting the fully funded system; the system was intended to relieve the industry in the later years of workmen's accident insurance, to protect industry from erratically changing charges, and always to provide industry with positive figures that can be used in planning. These extraordinarily welcome intentions of the legislature have not been realized in the actual development of Austrian workmen's accident insurance—a disappointment not, perhaps, because of the loopholes and imperfections of the law, but primarily because of the completely flawed implementation of its provisions.

It would be unfair, however, to hold the government alone responsible for the present situation, although it bears a large share of the blame, as we have shown. Rather, the Institute's administration and not least the industrial groups involved are also responsible.

We would be closing our eyes to the facts if we were to pass over in silence the fact that the employers themselves have also failed to fulfill their obligations to the new branch of public assistance to the extent the legislature provided for. We have already mentioned that the amount of the premium is set according to each industry's risk level. This level is determined by comparing the charges with total wages, and the result of the comparison is the premium rate. If every employer is to be subject to workmen's accident insurance according to law, the comparison of total wages and the accident charges must correspond to the reality. This correspondence is probably sufficiently ensured by organized labor, which can be counted on to claim the legal social-security pension for every documentable work-incurred disability. The wage totals are a different matter, however. On one hand, these totals must be declared completely in order to be correctly acknowledged in the statistics; on the other hand, however, each employer must not be allowed to avoid the statistical results by declaring a lower, unrealistic wage total in order to freeze the amount of the premium rate. In fact, the true numbers have not been ascertained in either direction. It is only natural that we are talking almost exclusively of the companies placed in a high-risk category—primarily quarries, pit saws, high-rise construction, and railroad construction. We have already alluded to the extent to which the Ministry of the Interior has been the obvious cause of these unpleasant phenomena. Let us note here only that the immediate consequence of every increase in risk classification, and every increase in rates, is the declaration of lower wage totals. Of course, this is not a general procedure; rather, it is always only individual employers who seek to lighten their contribution by this ruse—that is, by incorrectly declaring their chargeable wage totals. However, since the statistics set somewhat of a requirement that has to be covered, the inevitable consequence of the rate and premium policy of a few employers was the increase in the contribution charges for all employers. That is, those employers who took their workmen's accident insurance obligation seriously were compelled not only to pay the sum that was legally imposed on their companies but also to help underwrite the contributions of those employers who handed in defective declarations and thus avoided paying their full premiums. It is therefore in the interest of those employers who make honest declarations that all employers be called upon to fulfill their obligation to the Institute, and it is therefore a misguided belief to claim severity, unjust procedure, or worse in each case in which an insurance institute calls on an employer who has not met his obligation to make a subsequent additional payment. On the contrary, we must always check whether or not the factual basis for the additional payment is a correct one. If the demand is justified, then every employer who fulfills his obligation to the Institute should welcome it, because this is the best guarantee that he will be relieved of the improper contribution imposed on him for the benefit of others in future.

If the representative industrial bodies were to investigate every case, even those that do not objectively deserve intervention, the effect of the action in the interest of those who have clearly been harmed would, of course, be lost. The fact that harshness and infringement that make intervention necessary can and do exist is not in dispute.

What we are saying here is no secret. The unparalleled manner in which the institutes were damaged and their contributions reduced was known both to the government and to the administrations of the various insurance institutes. But until recently, nothing has been done to control these deplorable conditions that fall so heavily on all. That is the harshest reproach that can be laid not only at the government's door, but first and foremost at the feet of the administration of the Prague Institute. The deficit grew, as we have shown, to immeasurable proportions; the premium rate became higher and higher; those employers who made honest declarations almost literally collapsed under the burden of their contributions. Nevertheless, nothing was done; there were plenty of protests on paper, rallies were held, questions were raised, etc., but neither the government nor the Prague Institute's administration took strong measures, and we cannot spare the representatives of the Institute's industries the accusation that they pressed far too little to bring some discipline into the Institute. We cannot demand such an effort from labor representatives; all they needed to do was to ensure that the interests of their delegates were not changed, and these representatives did honestly perform their duty. The proof is, on the one hand, the amount of the social-security pensions granted for serious accidents and, on the other, the excessive number of small pensions in the absence of material injury. The representatives of the industry, by contrast, never made any attempt to understand the situation at the Prague Institute, and acting on a wholly mistaken feeling of solidarity, they never spoke up for any reform aimed to evenly and completely include all employers in paying their contributions.

The situation at the Prague Institute thus developed to the point where one side consisted of employers who had borne unending costs and on the other, employers who had contributed a disproportionately small amount and who went unpunished and without fear of future additional payments. The adverse effect of this situation was clearly shown not only in accident insurance itself but in the entire economy as well. The honest employer was denied any freedom of action, any possibility of fair competition, while the dishonest employer prospered at the honest man's expense.

The Board of Trustees of the Prague Institute emphasized only one aspect in particular—the request for a mandatory wage-list law. This refrain recurs regularly in the Prague Institute's annual reports—set to the tune of ever-increasing deficits but also the best proof of the Institute's own internal weakness. The catchword was not internal measures, but external intervention, and therein lay the fundamental evil, since the government, at which the Institute repeatedly directed its cries for help, was not much more zealous and active than the Institute's board of trustees. The government may have made some attempts to take some action, but it failed to get to the heart of the matter, as did the administration of the Institute itself. This was the situation as it had developed by the end of 1908. This accounting year closed with an annual loss of around K 3,600,000, with premium revenues of K 9,100,000.

Suddenly, however, the involved public was surprised by the official publication in February 1911 of the "Official Bulletin of the k. k. Ministry of the Interior for Accident and Health Insurance," according to which the prescribed 1909 premiums had increased to K 10,300,000 without any outward cause, while the annual loss had sunk to K 870,000. (We hear that the situation in 1910 has become even more unequally favorable, for not only has the yearly deficit been eliminated, but there is even a surplus from this year's performance of over K 2,000,000.)

What brought about this astonishing change? It was widely believed that the cause was the new mandatory wage-list law, which took effect in May 1909. Even a layman will recognize this view as false, however, if he examines the accounting balances of 1909 in detail. The effect of the mandatory wage-list law would have had to have the same effect on the budgets of all the institutes with a corresponding increase of the prescribed annual premium, thus of the prescription for 1909; such a general increase cannot, however, be established. What can be known instead is that there was an unusually large increase in supplementary-contribution revenues from previous years—an increase, that is, under a title that has no connection with the mandatory wage-list law. While these supplements show no increase worth mentioning for other institutes, however, the relevant figures for the Prague Institute are given as K 800,000, or close to the proportion expressing the increase from 1908 to 1909.

In this connection, we should emphasize that other factors have also been responsible for the favorable outcome; these include more sensible compensation management and the especially difficult reorganization of agricultural insurance in particular. A look at the annual report of the Institute provides us with more details about the change that no doubt took place in the Institute's administration. We can read that various employers were required to pay supplements of up to K 100,000 and that these employers willingly paid the additional contributions without resorting to legal recourse. We cannot help asking ourselves at this point: How much must the Institute have been shorted since its inception if now, after twenty years of existence, it can collect such supplementary contributions without arousing resistance? What would the employers' situation have been if from the very beginning care had been taken to make certain that every employer fulfilled his obligation to the Institute? And finally, how much lower would the premiums be today if that prerequisite had actually been met?

The only possible position that the concerned employers can take toward the current measures of the Prague Institute must result from these considerations. To the extent that these measures agree with the legitimate interests of the employers, and to the extent that the goal of the measures is finally to achieve a uniform and fair distribution of premium charges, these measures can only be welcomed warmly and supported by the industrialists. Of course, at the same time we must make certain that the honest endeavor toward redress and reorganization does not turn into pure budgetary concerns and oppressive taxation. In short, industry can welcome and promote the efforts of the Prague Institute only as long as these are aimed at forcing the dishonest employers to fulfill their obligations in order to relieve all honest employers. Any effort beyond that aimed at depriving industries of capital only to amass it sterilely in the Institute's coffers would have to be resisted with all our might. The employers are justified, however, in wanting a consolidation of the conditions of compensation management. A handsome sum is certainly appropriate as compensation for accidents that have serious consequences, and no employer will even consider advocating parsimony in such cases. Conversely, industries perceive it as a serious evil that compensation is also granted in cases where there is no material injury, for the employers rightly fear that it is precisely this practice that has led or will lead to incidents similar to those that Germany is experiencing so severely today.

As in all questions that affect the industrial sector, in this instance the entire industry should also look for protection against possible infringements primarily in its representatives. Only when such protection fails, when the Institute ignores even justified wishes and complaints that come from such representatives, only then is it appropriate for other agents to take a strong position. Finally, however, we must note that it is not useful to the industrial sector when, out of the abundance of cases, we select one or two that are problematic, blow them up, and bring them to the public debate, only to have to admit in the end that these cases were not worth remedying because the employers in question have avoided fulfilling their obligations at the expense of their fellow employers. As in all other instances in economics, it is important not to overlook the larger perspective by concentrating on the meaningless cases, and not flood the government offices, ministries, and parliament with complaints if there is a danger that at the crucial moment, all the institutions will remain closed to any actions that affect the whole and are of vital importance to industry.

B. Workmen's Accident Insurance and Employers (November 4, 1911)

Our last article with the same title in number 73 of this newspaper has met with a certain amount of public attention, both in various trade journals and in the Prague Workmen's Accident Insurance Institute it-self, and finally among other concerned groups. The most valuable statement on the topic, however, appeared in the September 17, 1911, issue of *Die Arbeit* (the official publication of Austrian employers). This article seems especially valuable to us, first, because it presents material that is noteworthy in and of itself, and secondly, because it was our primary intention to arouse interest among the influential in-dustrial leaders in the striking changes in the performance of the Prague Accident Insurance Institute. *Die Arbeit* introduces its essay with the remark that it would not be wrong to assume that the author of our first article must have a close relationship with the administra-tion of the Prague Institute. We will be happy to accept this character-ization if we may interpret it to mean that a person is close to it if, as one of its members, he cares seriously about its growth, if, in the inter-est of industry, he observes to the best of his ability at least the most immediate economic effects of social insurance, and if he is closer to the Institute than is the general public, insofar as he regularly reads its annual reports, which are, sadly, not sufficiently perused by those who are involved.

We considered it necessary to intervene at this particular time for sev-eral reasons. It seemed to us that lately, on a number of occasions, ques-tions had been raised in parliament dedicated to pushing general interests into the background, or concealing them, for the sake of individual wishes whose justification was more than questionable for the uniniti-ated. On the other hand, we had already seen an improvement in the Institute's performance, one that was so vigorously heralded in the Prague Institute's 1909 annual report that it was convincing. Now we gladly admit that until 1909, the annual reports of the Institute, with their figures documenting a deficit that seemed to spread almost like a living organism, offered little encouragement to feel excitement. Instead, these reports succeeded in damping all the Institute's hopes for the fu-ture; the Institute seemed simply to be a corpse, whose only living ele-ment was its growing deficit. The last hope was for a general reform of social insurance, and this reform was therefore the goal of all those who honestly desired improvement. Today, the situation has changed. We believe that the 1909 annual report alone has imposed on all concerned groups the duty of closely following the new vitality in the administra-tion of the Institute, to monitor it, and to support it to the extent that it promised good results, for only general participation can guarantee that the turn to improvement in the Institute is permanent. It is only with this duty in mind that we addressed ourselves to the public in our first article. Our observations were based on the same material available to any of the larger employers in the Institute's territory. The fact that *Die*

Arbeit took such a vivid interest in our article is an auspicious sign that our attempt to arouse general interest was not in vain, and we are ready to step back and leave it to *Die Arbeit*—which is so much better qualified—to keep up the widespread interest in workmen's accident insurance. Nevertheless, it remains true that participation, and therefore cooperation, in workmen's accident insurance can never be excessive, especially since only an open dialogue can resolve the remaining misunderstandings about our article that arose among employers, to judge from the essay in *Die Arbeit*.

We are only now beginning to clear up these misunderstandings, because until now the material available to us did not seem adequate to the task. Our previous article was based on the 1909 annual report of the Prague Institute; the conclusions we drew from its data were justified by a survey of the Institute's growth. The article in *Die Arbeit* sought to refute these conclusions, while we waited for a documented report of additional facts. This report appears in the very recently published annual report of the Institute for 1910, and it unconditionally confirms the conclusions of our previous article.

The annual report begins with the words, "The first positive balance since 1893," and the additional figures cited place the proper emphasis on these words. The year 1910 ended with an annual surplus of K 2,523,295.65 for the Institute. Taking the deficit of K 868,245.55 recorded in 1909 and the losses on stock of K 328,300 suffered in 1910, the total amount by which the financial state of the Institute has increased favorably is K 2,719,841.20. The overall annual deficit of K 40,046,996.81 that accumulated from 1889 to 1909 is reduced by this year's surplus of K 2,523,295.65 to the amount of 37,523,701.16. Assuming that conditions remain the same, the Institute would need another 14 years of regular growth to pay off the deficit incurred over the years.

The annual report gives few facts about the external reason for this drastic turn of events. Only at the beginning is there somewhat unclear and excessive language to the effect that the Institute "initiated and achieved [this turn of events] by virtue of its own strength and ideas." Naturally, this is not enough for the interested reader, who seeks a further explanation in the report and must finally make do with hints found in the notes. Moreover, it cannot be our job to establish the external reasons for the turn of events; that is the job of the state supervisory agency, and we are sure that if these officials have not already set about doing so, they will not be able to avoid their obligation for long. The details of past abuses are, of course, of no interest to the public; instead, the public has the right to expect information in general terms about the findings of the state supervisory agency's investigations as they have been conducted or will be conducted; and the public must continue with this demand until it is satisfied.

In our first article, written after the 1909 annual report was issued, we maintained that the cause of the previous negative standing of the Prague Institute should primarily be ascribed to the fact that employers did not always declare the legally required wage totals to the Institute, and that it is this act of concealing wage lists that was the principal cause of the shortfall in contributions. We base this assertion on the fact that in 1909, the supplementary contribution revenues of the Prague Institute from the previous years amounted to over K 800,000, as well as on the individual instances of large-scale evasions cited on page 14 of the report from 1909. Now, *Die Arbeit* calls this assertion absurd. The magazine makes a grave error in logic here, however. The magazine admits: "Of course some unscrupulous employers stinted on their obligatory contributions at the expense of all the others," and goes on to explain that the Institute's additional revenue from the title of the supplementary contributions "largely represents corrections undertaken as a result of the Institute's stricter inspections and the corresponding enlightenment about the scope of the insurance obligation." While it is true that part of the K 800,000 can be traced back to such corrections, it cannot represent a large share for three reasons: First, because such corrections as *Die Arbeit* has in mind are possible only in the area of small-scale industries, which can never be a matter of large sums; second, because when such corrections occur within large companies, which must surely be familiar with the basic insurance questions, they are not corrections but rather deceitful evasions; and third, because in 1909 the reorganization of the Institute's inspections was still in its infancy, and the itemized inspection of small industry was therefore not yet widespread: inspection was directed almost entirely at large-scale industry in order to rectify the most serious omissions. These K 800,000 can thus have been related only to larger-scale industries and therefore primarily deceitful evasions, as the selected wage evasions cited in the report have clearly shown. This conclusion was necessary and was not an "indiscriminate suspicion," as *Die Arbeit* calls it, but the ascertainment of facts that had been discovered by spot checks, whose number, given the large sum of K 800,000 in supplementary contributions, cannot have been small. Even this conclusion was not an "indiscriminate suspicion" of the employers in certain industries, if only because at the same time, a closer look shows it to have been an indiscriminate defense of those same industries, in order to protect them and all others from those employers who, as *Die Arbeit* admits, "certainly" exist. Nor did it occur to us to accuse all industries, even with a restriction to specific employers; we are convinced, for example, that the large textile and machine-construction industries took no part whatever in these wage evasions. It was quite evident that most of all we were referring to the building trades, though aside from quarries and pit saws, which are also in play here. There are good reasons for the fact that the occurrence is seen primarily in the building trades. There, as in very few other industries, the honest employer suffers from the shortcomings of the commercial code, which cannot protect him and hands him over to the unfair competition of his dishonest colleagues. Of course, the apparently ineradicable evil of "unauthorized coverage" also affects the wage declaration for workmen's accident insurance. An overall position by the Office of the Governor opposing unauthorized coverage, as well as pressure to suppress unauthorized coverage finally coming from the Office of the Governor and spreading to the district commissioners, would support one of the principal interests of the honest men engaged in the building trades, and not only their interests, but also those of the pit saws, quarries, etc., which work closely with the building trades and must endure the same conditions. Finally—something that we do not overlook and did not overlook in our earlier article—is the fact that the psychological blame for the large supplementary contributions must be laid at the door of the Institute's previous completely inadequate inspections (since opportunity is the author of the evasion of contributions, as one industrialist replied in response to our first article); but the actual blame is that of the employers, and if the Institute is currently engaged in putting a stop to the earlier shortcomings, then it is the concern of the interested parties to support its efforts.

Now, the conclusions we drew from the 1909 annual report are, sadly, all too strikingly confirmed by the newly released 1910 report. The revenues from supplementary contributions for the previous year amounted to K 1,121,612.27; the increase by more than K 300,000 from the previous year can in all probability be attributed to the new and more skilled inspections. Over K 1,000,000 of supplementary contributions were prescribed in this year, and almost K 2,000,000 over the last two years. If anyone still wanted to claim that this change is only a matter of corrections, the words would stick in his throat in the face of these figures. In fact, the introduction to the annual report states: "[The Institute] has independently uncovered the causes of the previously incomplete wage declarations and has independently found the generally difficult ways to correctly determine wages and contributions. Through the continued personal mediation of the Institute's administration, it unsparingly exposed the most blatant cases of wage evasion and obtained agreement and payment, sometimes by granting higher down payments and monthly rates—all this in spite of the problems of detecting some of the cases and of obtaining what were in reality very large sums, and all of it was accomplished without turning over even one such important case to successive appeals and thus placing the further stages of the case outside the framework of the Institute and its self-government." It was certainly not a question of "corrections" if in all the more important cases involving a "very large" sum, the acknowledgment of supplementary contributions was obtained while avoiding successive appeals. Page 11 of the annual report states: "In all those cases, in 1910 as in 1909, where significant wage-sum differences and, accordingly, the need for significant supplementary insurance contributions were found, they were discovered only because correct and complete wage lists were finally presented, differing from those the employers had previously given to the agencies of the Institute. The wage lists were therefore actually kept by these employers." In these cases as well—as no one will deny—it cannot have been a matter of "corrections," since the correct and complete wage lists were "finally" presented. And these cases made up the greater share of the large supplementary contributions, as the annual report expressly states; there should be no doubt on this score, at least not without good reason. We further refer *Die Arbeit* to the citations of individual cases on pages 11 and 12, 14, 17, and 32 of the annual report, and we are convinced that if *Die Arbeit* wishes to acknowledge the truth of the facts discussed in the annual report, the journal will also have to become resigned to our assertion, which it called absurd, although we do not doubt that it takes courage to accept such resignation. Furthermore, we have restricted our accusations of employers only to the territory covered by the Prague Institute and continue to do so today, for conditions at other institutes can hardly be seen as analogous in this regard when we consider that the revenues gained from supplementary contributions from previous years amounted to K 1,121,612.27 for the Prague Institute in 1910, while the analogous item on the balance sheet of the Vienna Institute, for example, shows only K 258,284.

In our earlier article we attributed some of the fault for the institutes' deficit to the fact that the final consequences were never drawn in determining the risk classes based on the statistics—i.e., the various industrial groups (and those are the crucial ones) were not assigned those risk classes to which they were properly entitled, instead being placed in lower ones. On this point, we cannot be satisfied with the confession of *Die Arbeit* that it has in its possession many clues suggesting that the strength of the influence exerted by the particular central office decided the determination of each risk classification, even if we are willing to admit that this confession is not lightly made. In truth, this is a question not of particular phenomena, as *Die Arbeit* assumes, but of phenomena with almost universal validity. We need to cite only the following evidence for this: In 1904, a "Memorandum of the Unified Austrian Chambers of Trade and Commerce Regarding the Revision of the Risk Classification of Businesses Subject to Compulsory Accident Insurance" was issued. This paper rendered an opinion on the draft version of the ordinance regarding risk classification at that time, which, as we gather from the discussions of the various titles examined in this memorandum, had no other purpose than to keep the effect of accident statistics as far away from the future classification system as possible. If we leaf through the memorandum at random and make note of some passages, we will read, for example, the following on Title 10: "Though the proposal contained in the government draft [regarding the risk category] corresponds to the statistics, with regard to the intention of levying higher contributions on the mills, it must be taken into account that in the extremely poor economic situation of the milling industry," etc. On Title 27: "Although statistics including sufficient material justify a raise in the risk category, before taking such a step, it should be considered that the shipping institutes, under competition from the railroads," etc. On Title 94: "The application to keep risk category VII, which was determined for the Vienna Institute, as a general risk category as well could naturally only be justified, in the face of the unfavorable statistical situation for this type of firm, on the generally poor situation of mechanized brickworks, especially in Bohemia," etc. We could cite innumerable examples of this kind; we recognize the justified effort that gave rise to these proposals—to help hard-pressed industries in this way—as not unjustified on the part of the chambers of commerce. But it is still a very long way, and a very dangerous one, from this theoretical acknowledgment to a practical application, as the Ministry of the Interior has demonstrated to the chambers of commerce in the final risk-classification plan, as the Institute's annual report form 1906 makes clear. The Ministry dared to take this path and reduced the risk class, compared to the original draft, for 73 work categories, including some very important ones, for reasons explained on pages 5 and 6 of the 1906 annual report. It is, therefore, a fact that earlier reclassifications lowered many categories by more than the statistics required, and even the classification was far from drawing precise conclusions from the statistics, as is evident in the results of the revised accident statistics published by both the Ministry of the Interior and the annual reports of the Institute.

In our earlier article, we emphasized, in an aside, that two further factors influenced the Institute's advantageous financial balance—that is, more sensible compensation management and the reorganization of agricultural insurance. *Die Arbeit* seems to accuse us, first, of having failed to provide figures on these two factors and, second, of justifying our slight treatment of these questions only by omitting figures. The first accusation is justified; it is true that we gave no detailed figures, in spite of the fact that such details might have been necessary; but we did not cite them only because they were not available, since we had no more material at our disposal than does *Die Arbeit*—we probably had less. We still do not have a detailed breakdown of the current state of compensation management, and we will have to save the discussion of this question until the results of the accident statistics for the years 1907–1912 are published. The breakdown on the reorganization of agricultural insurance, on the other hand, is available in the 1910 annual report, and these figures are indeed extremely gratifying, especially when compared with the figures for earlier years. The 1908 annual report indicates that agriculture made premium contributions of K 263,588.12; unfortunately, the flat-rate results for the years 1909 and 1910 cannot be compared with this sum, because regrettably, the annual report does not state the share of additional revenues from the flat-rate contributions that is allotted to the year 1909. Nevertheless, the comparison of the annual result of 1908 with the average results of 1909 and 1910 provides at least an approximate picture. According to these figures, the increase in the average results for 1909 and 1910, compared to the result for 1908, amounts to a total of K 155,167.55, or 58.8%. This increase can only be seen as a success that deserves recognition, considering the short period in which it was achieved—a period that was transitional as well. All the more reason, then, to ask the Institute for an explanation about the kinds of obstacles that arose in the case of the agricultural flat rate, as the annual report states. The passage on page 21 that deals with this topic is completely inadequate. Though it indicates that these obstacles come from the official authorities, there is no actual commentary on this circumstance. And yet industry—which has suffered from deficits in agricultural insurance for such a long time that the deficit has become more a matter of industry than of agriculture—must urgently demand to be informed of everything that is opposed to a reorganization of agriculture by the authorities.

Although we cannot yet present detailed figures on compensation management, and although we have just cited the detailed figures on agricultural insurance, the second accusation made by *Die Arbeit*—that these two factors were wrongly discussed only superficially—nevertheless remains unjustified. We were concerned only with determining the principal factors that were responsible for the Institute's deficits and which employers have the power to influence. And even if the two factors mentioned did influence the Institute's policy, they still cannot change the fact that the determination of risk categories that did not agree with the statistics greatly unsettled the Institute's finances. The beneficial influence of the improved compensation management and reorganization of agricultural insurance cannot change in the slightest either the alarming amount of up to K 2,000,000 of the supplementary contributions that became necessary during the last two years; furthermore, these can only be a symptom of what are actually much higher evasions of contributions.

These three questions—evaded contributions, the influence of the risk-category revision, and the effect of compensation management and the agricultural flat rate—have provoked an apparent conflict between us and *Die Arbeit*. We hope that our discussion has resolved this conflict, and we believe this all the more, since we are essentially in complete agreement. For *Die Arbeit* writes: "Nevertheless, we must agree with the author when he states that industrialists must welcome and support all measures of the Institute with the goal of implementing a final, uniform, and fair distribution of the contribution charges." We believe precisely the same. As long as the Institute simply vegetated for 20 years without actual output, we had to be content with wishing that fundamental reforms would appear, and we were idealists of necessity. Even a rough reorganization of the Institute's finances seemed achievable only with a new law; we forgot that the current law is, in fact, in place and that a long time will have to pass before it is replaced by a new and better one, and that therefore we need to arrange our affairs within the current law as best we can. The principal blame was laid at the door of the fully funded system; this idea was in part openly abandoned only when the memorandum of the Austrian Chamber of Trade and Commerce demonstrated that an immediate transition to the pay-as-you-go system would still not make a significant difference for the industrial sector; however, it would bring about an increase in the contributions very soon. Finally, the size of administrative costs was held responsible for the Institute's situation. This belief was both with and without justification. It was justified because even the lowest administrative costs were too high for an institute that generated only deficits; and it was not justified because the administrative costs bore the least blame for the deficit; only a superficial observer, as the public was, at least at that time, could believe as much. On the other hand, an institute that can demonstrate success will not have overly high administrative costs; the latter is not possible, for success is the sign of good management, and good management will not generate high administrative costs. It is true that the administrative costs of the Prague Institute remain quite high, according to the latest annual report, but the success of the year's performance justifies them, as do comparisons with other insurance institutes in other territories. The Vienna Institute took in

K 9,497,624 in contributions from its members in 1910, while its administrative expenditures amounted to K 1,325,798 or 13.96 percent of the revenues from contributions. The Graz Institute, the only one without a deficit, took in K 2,320,196 and used K 290,368 for administrative expenses, or 12.51 percent of the contribution revenues. The Prague Institute, by contrast, shows K 12,687,948 in insurance contributions and K 1,263,690 in administrative expenses, or only 9.96 percent, and we might add that its territory, compared to that of the Vienna Institute, for example, is disproportionately widespread and would, at least for this reason, justify somewhat higher administrative expenditures. Nevertheless, the Prague Institute has by far the lowest administrative expenses in comparison to the two cited institutes, even if a more businesslike operation could lower administrative costs. Let us only consider that K 150,000 are indicated in the 1910 accounts balance as the cost of investigating general accidents alone, an incomprehensibly high figure, since medical fees are cited in a separate entry as amounting to approximately K 134,000.

But all these general accusations, raised in previous years, against the law, against the fully funded system, against administrative costs, etc., had few concrete results and are somewhat out of date when compared to the figures of the Institute's previous and current annual reports. We thus believe that now, when the Institute is beginning to be effective, it is time to replace these general accusations with an efficient practical policy by the employers themselves and to intervene whenever the facts demand it—a practice in which the latest annual report will prove a useful guide. We firmly believe that no one can any longer deny the Institute's willingness to cooperate, above all considering the most recent annual report, whose voice, grown weak from long years of habit, we have thus endeavored to amplify.

In the new annual report, moreover, the Institute shows employers a new method of working in the area of accident prevention, which was already intimated in the 1909 annual report; previously, those concerned with this matter felt that accident prevention was held too much under the compulsion of the trade inspections, and now it is presented to them in the much more convincing light of accident insurance, or of accident insurance contributions. The impression created by this part of the annual report, as with the report as a whole, is a mixture of both depressing and joyful news. For it is truly depressing that this large Institute, which is entrusted with over 35,000 commercial firms, is only now, after 20 years of existence, becoming conscious of its obligations in the area of accident prevention, even if it is also good news that this consciousness is now awakening. Of course, this work is proceeding much too slowly amid the pressure of the many other probable reforms; the 1909 report discussed only the protective devices for wood-planing machines, while this latest report discusses mainly wood-milling machines, and anyone who is aware of our backwardness in this regard compared to the German trade associations will wish that this work would proceed at a much faster pace. On the other hand, a kind of youthful ridiculousness, as it were, cannot, apparently, be avoided in such a new endeavor. Thus the Institute, as one can learn from this annual report, has started a collection of protective devices in the Institute's building; all those concerned are urgently requested, as the annual report puts it, to visit this collection, though the entire collection appears to include hardly more than 6 items (as they are counted in the annual report), apart from a collection of protective goggles. Nevertheless, no one should disregard the smiles the exhibit arouses, for it has been a long time since the public had an opportunity to smile at the youthful overeagerness of the Prague Institute. And then, by comparison, how much the Institute promises in the area of accident prevention— a promise it will certainly keep, to judge by its explanations, which testify to its best intentions and abilities. This year, the Institute wants to tackle a large initiative that will ensure the general introduction of round shafts in its entire territory, not only for ordinary wood-planing machines, but possibly also for combined planing machines. The Institute will also press for the introduction of safety milling heads wherever possible. It requests that both employers and workers report especially good and especially bad experiences with protective devices; it is committed to processing these reports conscientiously and making them available to all. The Institute is eager to furnish suggestions regarding new safety devices to experts for evaluation; and in safety-related questions, it makes use of trade journals as well as of the professional associations of employers and workers and is ready to lend them plates for illustrations. The Institute also wants to have slides of illustrations of protective devices made and make these available for lecturing purposes. As is briefly mentioned in the annual report, the Institute learned of the great and almost untapped interest that employers have in new protective devices at a lecture given by the Institute at a trade-association meeting, and it is thus surely also prepared to arrange additional lectures on request. Finally, the Institute has approached the Office of the Governor with detailed suggestions regarding protective devices in quarries and in clay, sand, and gravel pits, primarily regarding the agricultural operations of this type of work. We believe that this area is especially important, since in the insurance for quarries, the same relationships exist between the industrial and the agricultural operations on a small scale as exist in insurance as a whole between agriculture and industry on a large scale. To be sure, this is an ambitious program, and the new projects that the

Institute is undertaking certainly do not lack ambition. That is why we believe that employers should clasp the hand that is being offered them here. The support that they contribute to the Institute, however, should not, in our opinion, be support only but should urge the Institute further along this road on which it has at last set out.

P. O.

Commentary 8

❧

O n October 10, 1911, Kafka noted in his diary: "Wrote a sophistic article for the *Tetschen-Bodenbacher Zeitung* for and against the Institute." While this remark refers to the second of the two articles reprinted here, the author of the second document identifies himself with the author of the first one. Moreover, the content, style, and line of argument of the first document strongly indicate that Kafka is, in fact, the author of both. The initialed signature at the end of the second article (P.O.) cannot clearly be deciphered; it may be an inversion of the initials of President Otto Příbram, the Prague Institute's highest officer.

The two articles reveal how deeply Kafka was involved in the issue of workmen's accident insurance in Austria. In a situation that could have gone down in the history of Austrian social insurance as a crucial turning point had not World War I intervened, Kafka obviously acted as the public voice of Austria's largest institute in this field. The place for his public intervention was by no means chosen incidentally. The *Tetschen-Bodenbacher Zeitung* was the oldest and most widely read daily paper of this busy industrial city in northern Bohemia. Tetschen-Bodenbach, situated at the Middle European railway axis of Berlin–Dresden–Prague, was the central junction to the German Reich and the industrial area of Dresden. It was also the outer frontier of Kafka's literary fame, at least according to Franz Werfel's famous verdict, "Once past Tetschen-Bodenbach, no one will understand a word Kafka has written."[1]

The explicit reference in the first article to the critical situation of workmen's accident insurance in the neighboring German Reich is not as casual as it might seem, and it requires explanation. In this final decade of the Hapsburg Empire, national mythologies were spreading in all fields of domestic policy. But the motives of the increasingly "German" orientation among industrialists in northern Bohemia were hardly mythological when it came to workmen's accident insurance. Politically, mounting calls for dividing the Prague Institute into a German and a Czech organization were prompted by the desire to weaken the influence of the (mainly Czech) work force by excluding Czech representatives from the organization of ("German") accident insurance. This political claim was in keeping with general plans to reshape the administrative map of Bohemia in order to create homogenous territories of German and Czech self-administration. The economic purpose was just as radical: nothing less than replacing the capital-based (or fully funded) system established in Austria by the assessment (or pay-as-you-go) system used in Germany. While the former required covering all compensation costs *incurred* in a given year within any firm's annual budget, the latter was restricted to covering compensation that had to be *paid* in any given year. In principle, the former system guaranteed greater financial reliability by setting premiums at a level adequate to cover losses, although it required higher fees in the first years or decades of its establishment. Experts in social insurance in both countries strongly preferred the capital-based system, but the German state acceded to the employers' demand for the assessment system, with its short-term advantages, to strengthen Germany's large industries in world-market competition and win them over for colonialist projects. When it turned out in Austria that the great promise of the capital-based system—stable and calculable insurance fees—could not be fulfilled, calls for a system change in favor of the German plan grew stronger.

At a time when the draft for new social legislation (which had already created the occasion for Kafka's long essay of 1908, doc. 2) was at last discussed in the parliament, the Prague Institute publicly addressed employers with a "retrospective critique" that masterfully combined an unsparing analysis of Austrian workmen's accident insurance with a narrative that opened up a new area of future cooperation. If Kafka's literature is, to a large extent, about subverting and deconstructing false oppositions, these two articles reveal how this attitude had become a practical one in his professional writings. He wrote at the moment when social insurance had been perverted from an instrument crafted to alleviate or even dissolve the antagonism between capital and labor to an object of that antagonism; and these anonymous public interventions were aimed at restoring workmen's accident insurance to its former status.

His first article sets out to prove that the "never-ending increase in the premium rates" was connected to "external circumstances rather than being intrinsic to the system." The first of these circumstances was that the capital-based system strongly depended on sound statistical data, but these data had been lacking on many levels when the system was first established in Austria. Operating on a database in part borrowed from private insurance agencies, and even from the German Reich, Austrian workmen's accident insurance was forced to adapt its premiums to the actual development of compensation paid over time. Moreover, these adaptations were, once again, not based on valid statistics but were the result of deals between the Vienna bureaucracy and the parties to the social conflict. Kafka describes with overt sarcasm the pressure exerted by the industrial lobbies: "the determination of the risk classification was regularly controlled by the strength of the influence exerted by the central office in question." He sums up the unions' strategy with mild irony:

> All they needed to do was to ensure that the interests of their delegates were not changed, and these representatives did honestly perform their duty. The proof is, on the one hand, the amount of the social-security pensions granted for serious accidents and, on the other, the excessive number of small pensions in the absence of material injury.

In a tone hovering now between technical description and bitter irony, Kafka identifies a third unnatural circumstance for the failure of the Austrian premium system: employers' blatantly criminal behavior: "The immediate consequence of every increase in the risk classification, and every increase in rates, is the declaration of lower wage totals." Kafka is here adverting to the widespread practice, on the part of employers, of "balancing" an increase in their risk percentages by a decrease in the wage figures to which these percentages relate.

It is revealing to observe this enumeration of critical factors enabling the transfer of "guilt" from the system of accident insurance to the social groups involved in it. As Kafka digs deeper and deeper into the mud of Austrian insurance bureaucracy, he employs the rhetorical rule of the "devotional mood" he had described in his diary six months earlier, on the occasion of a series of theosophical lectures delivered in Prague in March 1911 by the occultist guru Rudolf Steiner:

> Leisurely discussion of objections raised by the opponents, the listener is astonished at this strong opposition, further comments and praise of these objections, the listener grows concerned, complete immersion in these objections as if they were all there was, the listener now believed that any refutation is quite impossible, and he is easily appeased with the cursory description of the possibility of a defense. (D1 54, trans. modified)

At a crucial juncture in Kafka's critical-historical review—the year 1908—his essay changes rhetorical tactics. He addresses the expert opinion attached to the draft for new social legislation, which contends that Austrian workmen's accident insurance cannot recover from the disastrous budget situation within the established capital-based system. His analytic essay turns into a historical narrative:

> This accounting year closed with an annual loss of around K 3,600,000, with premium revenues of K 9,100,000.—Suddenly, however, the involved public was surprised by the official publication in February 1911 of the

"Official Bulletin of the k. k. Ministry of the Interior for Accident and Health Insurance," according to which the prescribed 1909 premiums had increased to K 10,300,000 without any outward cause, while the annual loss had sunk to K 870,000. (We hear that the situation in 1910 has become even more unequally favorable, for not only has the yearly deficit been eliminated, but there is even a surplus from this year's performance of over K 2,000,000.)

The turning point of a budgetary curve now appears as the dramatic reversal of a process of decay that had seemed beyond repair just a few moments earlier. This surprising relief, however, is in no way connected to the obligation laid on employers by the new mandatory wage-list law passed in February 1909. The reversal results from policies that the Prague Institute established in the course of reforms introduced by Robert Marschner in 1908, policies announced and executed, to a considerable extent, by none other than Franz Kafka.

There is historical evidence that the mode of argument struck in this article is remarkable, and not only from the point of view of a present-day observer. Only three days after the publication of the first article, we find a response in *Die Arbeit*, the official journal of Austria's employers' associations, which strikingly anticipates an eminent characterization of the narrative perspective informing many of Kafka's stories. The contents of these stories, according to the editor of the canonical *Kafka Handbuch*, are presented from a standpoint that is "unreasonable, alien, and at least halfway oppositional."[2] *Die Arbeit* registers that Kafka "comes from" the same "unreasonable, alien, and at least halfway oppositional" perspective of his Prague Institute but nonetheless argues honorably: his argument merits the "greatest" consideration and cannot go uncontested.[3]

The second of Kafka's articles in the *Tetschen-Bodenbacher Zeitung* replies to the piece in *Die Arbeit*. If Kafka's diary terms this reply "sophistic," the qualification must be taken in the full historical meaning of the word. Kafka begins by repeating *Die Arbeit*'s own rhetorical move, characterizing its response as the "most valuable" among the many evoked by his article. He goes on to unfold a crafty arrangement of voices and positions, of speeches and counterspeeches, that succeeds in displacing established political standpoints along the capital-labor divide and in creating a new social subject uniting both sides in an effort to manage the risks of industrial production.

With obvious satisfaction, Kafka notes the employers' uncertainty as to the position of the voice he created in the first article. Remarkably, he confirms the assumption that the author of the first article is "coming from" a place "close to the executives at the Prague Institute" on the grounds, not of his authorship, but of the *readership* of the Institute's annual reports. The reader of these reports is assigned the function of "monitoring" the "new life" of the former "corpse" of the Institute. With this trope, the reader occupies a position like the one Kafka, years later, assigns to his own authorial person in his second-person narrative, "In the Night": "And you watch, you are one of the watchmen. . . . Why do you stand watch? Someone has to watch, they say. Someone has to be there (KKAN2 261). But, unlike this story, which is self-addressed, Kafka's public address on behalf of workmen's accident insurance aims at a collective watch, so to speak—a collective reading of the annual reports by the groups concerned. In fact, the second article is nothing but such a reading. Kafka, who repeatedly confessed his great pleasure in reading his stories out loud to his sisters and his friends, here stages a grandiose public lecture. By reading out the Institute's annual reports to the industrialists (a "reading out," staged in a written text), he invites the industrialists to join the collective readership of the Institute's reports—and hence, to share the position of the Institute's guard—at the same time that he completely deprives them of the means to defend themselves against accusations of illegally withholding insurance fees. The second article, in a word, is designed to redirect the attention of a public, aroused by his first article, to the shadowy existence of those widely ignored annual reports.

What follows is an impressive demonstration of the skill Kafka had acquired as the head of his Institute's appeals department in transcribing statistical data into social meaning, by way of extracting judgments, and even historical truth, from statistics. Kafka's first article placed responsibility for the economic crisis of Bohemian accident insurance with the large industries. *Die Arbeit,* in an attempt to reverse this transfer of guilt, blames the Institute for its slack handling of pension claims and its high administrative overhead. Now Kafka, in an effective dramaturgical move, introduces into his argument the budgetary data of the 1910 annual report—fresh evidence, published just after his first article, to disprove irrefutably these attempts to cover up the blatantly illegal practice of premium evasion abundant in certain branches of industry. And he again insists on the immunity of statistical evidence to the lobbyists' routine clamor, whenever it is a matter of risk classification of their industries, over a depressed economy and domestic or international competition. Like the trade inspectorates a few months earlier (doc. 7), the state authorities themselves are now subjected to a risk classification: from the "theoretical acknowledgment" of this clamor, Kafka's safety report runs, "it is still a very long way, and a very dangerous one, . . . to a practical application [that is, to tampering with], . . . the final risk-classification plan." In fact, "the Ministry dared to take this path and reduced the risk class, compared to the original draft for 73 work categories." Kafka concludes by making it clear that the task of the new social subject created in his article is by no means restricted to safeguarding the control of premium payments and risk classification against lobbyist corruption. Instead, the task of this new reader/monitor/actor concerns the whole system of reforms Robert Marschner had initiated and, in many instances, Kafka himself had put into practice—including accident prevention as well as the Institute's management of pensions and overhead. This new social player is by no means identical with the Prague Institute as it existed in the fall of 1911.

But even if, in this line of argument, statistics appear as a type of superior data, producing judgments "beyond any doubt," the legal scenario Kafka suggests does not mimic that of *In the Penal Colony*, with its transcendent law. The judgment does not result from an authoritative decision. Instead, it is based on an act of collective reading that serves as a temporary substitute for a law owned by and accessible to the people. Instead of simply waiting for that "new law"—an "idealism of necessity" in the days before the reforms—Kafka encourages a more pragmatic attitude: "We forgot that the current law is, in fact, in place and that a long time will have to pass before it is replaced by a new and better one, and that therefore we need to arrange our affairs within the current law as best we can." In the years of the disintegration of the Hapsburg Empire and after, Kafka unfolded his message to the Bohemian industrialists on a wider scale. Especially in "Building the Great Wall of China" and "On the Question of the Laws," it becomes clear that a pragmatics of the law is, in fact, the only viable option—indeed, the "knife edge" between totalitarianism and anarchy. So, in fact, Kafka's articles are sophistic in the full sense of the word. They are instances of a public education that does not rely on submitting individuals to an ideal norm but on their use of human—and statistical—intelligence to build a better society.

9

PETITION OF THE TOY PRODUCERS' ASSOCIATION
IN KATHARINABERG, ERZGEBIRGE (1912)

This case contains a vivid description of the living and working conditions of small craftsmen in the mountainous areas of northern Bohemia. While the craftsmen's petition illustrates the disquieting effects of this new legal practice (social insurance) that no longer operates according to moral norms but rather according to statistical figures (normal and deviant values), Kafka's response to the Minister on behalf of the Institute excels in closing the gap between the two conflicting kinds of knowledge or concepts of justice.

A. From the Trade Association to the Ministry of the Interior: Petition regarding the situation of the toy and wooden-article industry in the Erzgebirge—"Unstable conditions and proposals for their remedy" (April 21, 1912); accompanying letter to the district authority in Most, requesting forwarding of the petition; accompanying letter from the Office of the Governor to the Ministry of the Interior (May 15, 1912)

Letterhead: k. k. Office of the Governor, Bohemia

Prague, May 15, 1912
Trade Association of Manufacturers of Wooden Articles and Toys for the Erzgebirge in Katharinaberg
Re: Accident insurance for association members' businesses
7 enclosures.

K. k. Ministry of the Interior:
    The Office of the Governor hereby respectfully submits the petition of the Trade Association of Manufacturers of Wooden Articles and Toys for the Erzgebirge in Katharinaberg of April 21, 1912, which faults the procedure of the Workmen's Accident Insurance Institute in Prague in classifying the businesses of the Trade Association's members and in setting insurance premiums; in the attached, the Trade Association further

proposes that an expert committee, comprised of Trade Association members, be convened in an advisory capacity in the procedure of the setting of premiums.

For the k. k. Governor:

(signature illegible)

To the esteemed k. k. District Commissioners in Brüx

The undersigned Trade Association of Manufacturers of Wooden Articles and Toys for the Erzgebirge in Katharinaberg respectfully submits to the esteemed k. k. District Commissioners the account, "On the Situation of the Toy and Wooden-Article Industry in the Erzgebirge. Unstable Conditions and Proposals for their Remedy," and asks for support for the requests made therein and for the subsequent forwarding of the petition to the distinguished k. k. Ministry through the appropriate official channels.

Trade Association of Manufacturers
of Wooden Articles and Toys
for the Erzgebirge in Katharinaberg
(Signed:) Alfred Pierschel
Chairman of the Board
Katharinaberg, April 21, 1912

Trade Association of Manufacturers of Wooden Articles and Toys for the Erzgebirge in Katharinaberg

The petition regarding: Relief in the application of workmen's accident insurance law

Is presented to the
k. k. Office of the Governor
in Prague

with the explanation that the industry in question is in its initial stages and in need of special assistance by the state.

The k. k. District Authority:

(signature illegible)

To the esteemed k. k. Ministry of the Interior, Vienna

On the Situation of the Toy and Wooden-Article Industry for the Erzgebirge—Unstable Conditions and Proposals for their Remedy.

Respectfully submitted by the Trade Association of Manufacturers of Wooden Articles and Toys for the Erzgebirge, located in Katharinaberg.

(Signed:) Alfred Pierschel
Chairman of the Board
Katharinaberg, April 21, 1912

For a number of years, the esteemed k. k. government has acknowledged that there is a need to improve the situation of the toy and wooden-article industry in the Erzgebirge, and any unprejudiced person familiar with these conditions must admit that the assistance provided to this industry was not without success. Even if there is no glaringly visible success, there has nevertheless been progress.

But all progress has its unfortunate side effects, as is also the case in the wooden-article and toy industry. These side effects have become so widespread that they not only cancel the progress achieved with such great effort but must surely end in a setback; indications to this effect can already be seen, and its consequences are so unforeseeable that they may well mean the collapse of the entire industry.

In order to prevent a setback with such unfathomable consequences, the undersigned Trade Association of Manufacturers of Wooden Articles and Toys for the Erzgebirge in Katharinaberg will respectfully present the causes that must bring about this setback and ask for redress.

The primary cause is the official policy of the Workmen's Accident Insurance Institute for the Kingdom of Bohemia in Prague.

At the time of the creation of the workmen's accident-insurance law, the toy industry was in such an early stage of development that its current scope was hardly imaginable. At that time, no motor-driven machines were in use, nor was it a case of trade or manufacturing businesses; there were merely a few individual artisans whose work fell into the category of cottage industry. There is no question that at that time the legislature was unable to arrive at the correct solution for an industry that assumed its present form only 15–20 years later, and that shortcomings in the workmen's accident-insurance law for the industry would therefore become apparent. If the same lawmakers were to see now how their work has been handled by the Workmen's Accident Insurance Institute for the Kingdom of Bohemia, they would turn over in their graves. The application of the workmen's accident-insurance law by that Institute is justified neither by the law nor by the facts; it consists of the following:

1. The classification of toy manufacturing in a risk category that is much too high.
2. A mistaken understanding of the phrase "as well as in the facilities belonging to these businesses."
3. The abuse, to their own advantage, of the rights granted them regarding their members.

In order to prove our assertions, we must describe the facilities and working procedures of an average toy-manufacturing business. Such a business might employ eight male and twelve female workers, distributed in three rooms, as well as the same number of employees working out of their homes.

Of these workers, five men are employed in the practical end, producing and supplying the unfinished articles. Their activities include all the work related to the regular operations, such as drying wood, transporting materials, cleaning the machines and work areas, providing lighting and heating, maintaining the workshop facilities, etc. These five male workers are the only ones exposed to the practical dangers of the operation. They are paid K 3,750 per year, for 300 workdays at K 2.50 each. However, approximately 30 percent of this sum at most is for processing wood with the use of machines.

All other tasks are far outside the normal scope of technical operations and their purposes and must be seen as quite separate actions; they include the work of colored-paper pasters, carvers, and varnishers, though these operations connect with a machine-powered carpentry shop. Thus in a second room, 3 workers are engaged in polishing and similar tasks. These 3 workers never enter the rooms housing the technical operations—their work requires nothing that can be found in that station. Their workplace is completely independent of the technical operations, with a separate entrance and exit. The work done by these employees cannot be considered to be essential manual labor linked to the motorized operations, since these workers merely perform additional operations on goods that have already been finished; they are not the first to render them ready for marketing but merely improve their quality. The 3 workers receive a total of K 2,150 [sic] a year, for 300 workdays at K 2.50 each.

A third room houses 12 women. The same description applies to this area and the work performed in it as holds true for the second room. These 12 women employees receive yearly wages of K 3,600 for 300 workdays at K 1.00 each.

In addition to these workers, around 12–15 additional people are employed in their own homes at piecework rates; their yearly wages amount to K 4,000.

Taking into consideration the ordinance of the k. k. Ministry of the Interior of Aug. 2, 1909, the business described should be classified according to § 3 or §§ 4 and 7. Applying § 4 of the relevant ordinance, the risk classification would add up as follows:

For the first five workers, the risk may be roughly the same as is found in carpentry shops, where at most 30% of wages is for machine-powered wood processing. They are put in risk category X, with a percentage rate of 59 percent under Title 425a, while the other operating sites, holding 3 men and 12 women, would be classified under Title 409, the manufacture of small wooden trinkets and notions not requiring the use of motorized machines, in risk category II, with a percentage of 9 percent.

According to § 7 of the decree by the Ministry of the Interior of Aug. 2, 1909, we cite the following figures:

Sum of yearly wages	K 3,750	x	Risk percentage	59%	2,205.50
	2,150	x		9%	193.50
	3,600	x		9%	324.00
Total sum of yearly wages	K 9,500				2,723.00

2,723.00: 9,500—28.6 percent, rounded off to 29 percent

This calculation, as applied to the classification of this firm, results in risk category VII, with a percentage of 29 percent and a premium of K 2.49 for every K 100 of wages, compared to the previous mechanically compiled classification in risk category IX at 50 percent, with a premium of K 4.30.

Businesses equivalent to the average toy factory, including the making of clock cases and the manufacture of casings for telephones and photographic equipment, many of which are also produced locally, are already classified under Title 427 in risk category VI. And yet, toy manufacturers are still grouped with crate makers, large-scale hammer mills, rolling mills, oil companies, arms manufacturers, explosives and cartridge producers, to name only a few—all of them operations that carry a significantly greater potential for danger than even the most dangerous operations that come into play in the toy industry.

Now the Workmen's Accident Insurance Institute maintains that all these elements were considered when the classification was determined. But if we can really assume that so much thought has gone into the decision, then the responsible authorities must lack the intimate knowledge of the toy and wooden-article industry as it operates in this area.

A more appropriate classification can still be accomplished by basing it on § 3 of the cited ordinance by identifying the distinctly disparate operations that are part of every toy firm, treating them as separate businesses. Such a procedure would preclude any routine treatment; classification would automatically be decided component by component, for every full-scale toy manufacturing firm keeps as separate departments a small carpentry shop with motor-powered tools on the one hand, and the rest of the work areas on the other such as the space used for colored-paper pasting, carving, varnishing, painting, polishing, and various other jobs involved in decoration.

The Workmen's Accident Insurance Institute would not suffer any damage from classifying the toy-manufacturing businesses along these lines, because it would allow these businesses to expand, a possibility the current conditions do not offer. Under this proposed method, those employees who worked in their own homes and not now subject to compulsory accident insurance could be included as commercial workers; and those workers who are forced to take jobs in Germany would be able to find employment in their own country. If only for home workers, the reclassification would be a step forward in social progress, for they are the population who are in the worst economic and health situation; they do not enjoy a 10–10½-hour working day, as has been introduced in commercial businesses but must rather spend 12–15 hours working in the room where the whole family lives, cooks, bathes, and sleeps and that also serves as nursery and sickroom. But this situation will not improve as long as the unfair classification of toy manufacturers in such a high-risk category continues; at present, premiums are prohibitively high, and no producer, much less an industrialist, would ever dream of becoming the goose that lays the golden eggs for the Accident Insurance Institute, his only reward an occasional kick as recognition for his service. Continuing to insist on the current view of the functions of the toy industry will result in the decline in income or even the failure of many firms; alternately, some firms will choose to separate out the motorized operations under risk category XII; it cannot get any worse. Some workers will still be employed in these reconstituted firms, and a new proprietor will be found for what remains of the company, and this new owner will operate a business without motorized machinery, which will therefore be reclassified in risk category II. If this plan is followed, and the trade association is determined to do so, then the Accident Insurance Institute's income is sure to diminish.

We should also point out that the Workmen's Accident Insurance Institute really interprets the phrase "and in the facilities belonging to [these businesses]," contained in § 1 of the law of December 28, 1887, very loosely, at least with regard to the toy-manufacturing industry. The Institute includes even the houses of the home workers as such facilities, and bases its view on the fact that home workers are given health insurance. The Accident Insurance Institute pays very little attention to the kind of work performed outside the factory itself or to local work habits; it simply uses its categorizing system to prescribe premiums for these workers; where necessary, these premiums have been allegedly "evaded." The business owner who is burdened by this unlawful regulation is graciously permitted to appeal. And while the appeal is still under review, the affected business owner is expected to pay his premiums promptly. If his firm exists on a hand-to-mouth basis, this situation can mean his economic ruin, regardless of whether or not the Institute had the right to its assessment; and the poor business owner has no help in loosening the noose around his neck because of the medieval interpretation of the law and of rights.

In the course of the appeals process, the Workmen's Accident Insurance Institute for the Kingdom of Bohemia in Prague does not even consider it necessary to explain to an owner—or rather, a delinquent—in response to his understandable query, the grounds for its "calculations." The Institute is presumably anxious to forestall the possibility of any appeal; might it possibly be afraid that some light will shine on some circumstances that the Institute prefers to keep in the dark? The Institute states quite plainly that the record of paid-out wages has been falsified—a claim that it is all the easier to assert when the inspector believes himself to be detective, prosecutor, defense attorney, and judge all in one. We'll use the health-insurance data, they add up to a greater sum, the greater sum is always the right one, the business owner is obviously a swindler, and we'll make short shrift of him. An on-site and professionally conducted standard inspection of the working conditions is merely a minor detail. But God only knows the extent to which this way of thinking and proceeding corrupts the data about actual wages. Part of the fault for the largely groundless classification in higher categories or percentages must also be laid at the door of the k. k. trade inspectors and the k. k. trade authorities. Lacking adequate professional advice, they perceive danger where none exists and are blind to actual danger. This perspective results in opinions and regulations that do not correspond to the facts, as well as the reports on which the Workmen's Accident Insurance Institute bases its belief that greater risk exists than is actually the case and is therefore convinced that the increase is justified. The majority of the business owners in this area submit meekly to all these decisions because in the past, they have learned all too often that their pleas and protests fall on deaf ears.

The k. k. trade authorities mean well in their efforts to support the industry, but at least as far as the toy industry is concerned, they lack the right professionals to advise them in their actions. Clearly, the wooden-article and toy industry covers such a broad range of activities that no professional at the center of it can have a full overview of the whole field. Certainly, it can never be properly understood by someone who has graduated from secondary school, even if he graduated at the top of his class, before acquiring an engineering degree but who has not worked in the field himself. Only someone who has learned the trade and has practiced it can assess an industry, and assess it correctly; it cannot be assessed by someone who merely watches the workers performing their jobs. We are therefore well within our rights in requesting that a professional advisory committee, composed of association members, be formed and consulted about the regulations that apply to this field insofar as they apply to members of the trade association of manufacturers of wooden articles and toys. The undersigned trade association sees this as the only hope of avoiding procedures that complicate working conditions and raise manufacturing costs, so that in the end the industry of the German Reich is able successfully to compete with us in our own country, in spite of all the tariffs imposed on their products. A speedy remedy for this intolerable state of affairs is thus urgently needed, all the more so since the step being taken today should have been taken six or eight years ago. It is an old truth, however, that those to whom life gives little, save their skins only when the situation has become extreme. The toy industry has not seen a single upward and forward step, though skewed reports have maintained as much on various occasions, and the k. k. government cannot help but have noticed how many well-meaning and at times costly provisions for improvement remain unsuccessful and unused. We are not at the beginning of a flourishing new era but in the last phase of a desperate struggle, a struggle for survival in an economically critical time. And in order to win this struggle, we need not only technical ability, diligence, and money, but also moral resolution. We need this strong weapon, and so we hope for the prompt resolution of our problems, freeing us from the danger of falling through the cracks in the law, a danger that grows ever greater the longer we must wait for a resolution.

Trade Association of Manufacturers
of Wooden Articles and Toys
for the Erzgebirge in Katharinaberg
(Signed) Alfred Pierschel
Chairman of the Board
Katharinaberg, April 21, 1912

B. Proceedings of the Ministry of the Interior on the Statement of the Workmen's Accident Insurance Institute (January 5, 1914)

Letterhead: K. K. MINISTRY OF THE INTERIOR

1913
Insurance Department
K. K. Ministry of the Interior
Date: September 9, 1913
Subject:
Trade Association of Manufacturers of Wooden Articles and Toys for the Erzgebirge in Katharinaberg, risk classification of their businesses

The Institute admits that, in addition to overproduction and recent competition, the excessive accident insurance premiums and supplementary payments are, in part, to blame for the critical situation of the toy manufacturers in the Erzgebirge. But we must emphasize that the excessively high category is based on the fact that, in spite of all warnings and supplementary payments, the businesses have repeatedly acknowledged [owned up to—Ed.] only the wages of the machine workers. Admittedly, all these businesses must be treated equally, according to Title 400 or 408. Work done by hand is not as significant a factor as the trade association maintains, if only because only a small percentage of the work can be done off premises. Matters could be improved only with an open and honest account of the wages paid out in the whole industry (though the individual employers would have to be protected from burdensome supplementary payments, notwithstanding the findings legally in force, and that purpose could probably be achieved only by imposing a flat rate), and with a general revision of the classification (in agreement with the trade association). What is crucial for the risk level of the various businesses—and current regulations do not allow sufficient consideration in deciding on the proper category—are the type and number of machines, the type of goods produced, and whether logs or previously prepared boards are used in the production. Some firms work with machinery that is not at all dangerous (lathes and band saws), and others operate highly dangerous woodworking machines (planing machines with square shafts, circular saws). Furthermore, these firms would have to create situations that guarantee safety; the Institute has created a model woodshop, put on display at the crownland exhibition in Komotau, that is intended to be helpful in this effort. Only the combined efforts of the trade associations, other appointed representatives, and the Institute can bring about a resolution, and it is quite certain that discussions to this end will take place in the near future under the leadership of Herr Damm, member of the Reich council and a delegate to the provincial parliament. Since wage inspections carried out in recent years have put an end to the worst abuses in making out the accounts, there is no reason why this issue should be a distraction in these discussions. From 1902 to 1906, Title 408 registered only K 820,303 in wages with the Prague Institute; but from 1907 to 1911, the same account came to K 1,565,312 (according to the annual compilations); after the data are revised, the total will prove to be still higher. Furthermore, the new regular wage inspections showed that the yearly rise in total wages for Title 408 from 1907 to 1912 remained relatively equal.

1907: K 205,958
1912: K 467,234

Insurance Department

We are without doubt dealing here with businesses of the same risk category, though they are by no means identical. The risk classification may have been set too high for this industry because the declared total wages were too low. Since a classification revision is just around the corner and the invitations to nominate representatives to the deliberations will be going out in January, we recommend that for the moment any further investigations be suspended and that the trade association be notified that it may send a representative to the conference. In determining the risk category for Title 408—and that is the main bone of contention—the arguments presented here will have to be seriously addressed.

Vienna, January 5, 1914

(Signed:) Wolf

C. Workmen's Accident Insurance Institute to the Office of the Governor: Addendum to the statement of August 29, 1913 (February 13, 1914); attachment: minutes of the discussions between the trade association and a representative of the Workmen's Accident Insurance Institute, held in the municipal office of Katharinaberg (October 13, 1913)

Prague, February 13, 1914
Trade Association of Manufacturers
of Wooden Articles and Toys for
the Erzgebirge in Katharinaberg.
Risk classification, accident insurance
Complete files
1 enclosure

Esteemed k. k. Office of the Governor in Prague:

As an addendum to the statement by the undersigned Institute of August 29, 1913, regarding the edict cited above, we respectfully submit the attached minutes, recorded at the meeting with the Trade Association of Manufacturers of Wooden Articles and Toys on October 3, 1913, held at the municipal offices of Katharinaberg; these minutes are in addition to the following report:

The discussions with the trade association mentioned in our earlier statement, concerning the wooden-article and toy industry, were held in Katharinaberg and were generally concluded during the negotiations of

October 3, 1913. The immediate outcome is recorded in the attached copy of the minutes. The trade association requested that the undersigned Institute present this copy along with an introductory report to the k. k. Ministry of the Interior, to supplement the association's original submission. Since the negotiations resolved all the significant differences under discussion between the trade association and the Institute to their mutual satisfaction, the Institute stands ready to comply with this request of the trade association, and hereby requests the esteemed k. k. Office of the Governor to forward the copy of the minutes to the k. k. Ministry of the Interior.

To explain the content of the minutes in greater detail, we would like to note here that investigations into the actual conditions basically fully confirmed our original statement. The shortcomings in regard to the insurance of these businesses were just as obvious as their causes, for which the employers were, in all good faith, to blame. A brief overview of the evolution of this industry will make this point clear.

The conditions that exist today in the wooden-article and toy industry of the Erzgebirge are the result of a process that has occurred principally in recent years. Originally, the manufacture of wooden articles and toys was primarily a cottage industry, and only certain wooden parts were produced by machine. This step was carried out in such a way that individual workers rented work spaces in the many existing waterworks and prepared materials for the home workers on their own machines, usually lathes. This type of rental can still be found today, though the renters no longer work for the home workers but are connected to other manufacturers. The next stage involved woodwork using saws—primarily circular saws—by businessmen working for themselves and others, still employing some home workers. The sawmills first registered during this period consist of nothing more than circular saws for cutting wood into boards.

The next step brought the installation of planing machines, to which other special machines have now been added, primarily milling machines. As a consequence, however, home work gradually disappeared and was incorporated into actual workshop labor for its owner. Responding to market demands, attention now needed to be directed to the finishing of the products as well, a development that led to the incorporation of shops using manual labor of many different kinds.

Once a regional power station was put into operation in Obergeorgenthal, the industry as a whole could grow; since electrical motors could now more easily be installed, additional factories became possible.

The official data for the rubric of the greatest importance, Title 408 for the manufacture of wooden trinkets and notions, illustrate this history: in the five-year period from 1890 to 1896, 25 businesses were insured with the Institute, whereas 105 factories carried this insurance in the years 1907–1911. During the interim, total insured wages increased from K 395,900 to K 1,565,500, and the insurance premiums rose from K 3,828 to K 56,428. The risk classification of Title 408 also increased, reflecting the statistics we were given (from 1890 to 1896, the cost coefficient was 2.08; from 1897 to 1901, it was 6.41; and from 1902 to 1906, it was 3.68). This change was due not so much to the actual risk conditions as to the inadequate preliminary classifications, the deficient registration of the businesses, and the flawed declaration of paid-out wages. In 1895, risk classification IV was assigned; in 1900, it was VII; in 1905, the classification was VIII; and finally, in 1910, it was raised to IX. We are not including the increase in the overall premiums during this period. But what placed an especially heavy burden on this industry, and what was the principal reason for its vigorous counterargument, was the fact that the risk category was set at IX just at a time when the progress of this industry had come to a stop and was beginning to experience serious crises. The effort to improve the industry's situation was justified in and of itself, but it was not clearly thought through and therefore gave rise to new problems. The first mistake of the industry was incorrectly declaring wages at the time the insurance premiums were paid. When the wage inspections discovered this inaccuracy, which led to fines, the industry began to falsify the wage lists. When this ploy failed to relieve most of the industry of supplementary payments, it resorted to separating integrated businesses into manual labor and machine-driven operations; these outward divisions were usually accomplished by legally transferring title to the manual-work facilities to the proprietor's wife. The attached copy of the minutes shows how widespread this practice was. The trade association explicitly demanded that all such circumvention of the law be halted.

All these self-serving maneuvers would have resulted in further problems if direct negotiation between the Institute and the trade association had not put a stop to them.

The Institute, working within the framework of the commercial code, sought to meet the interests of the trade association in exchange for the association's formal guarantee that all its member companies would be fully registered, that wage lists would be kept in accordance with the law, that there would be full disclosure of wages paid, and that the ostensible separation of the functions of actually integrated factories would cease. The investigation to determine the precise prevailing conditions in the industry revealed the following:

1. The vast majority of the businesses maintains a strict separation between the work areas used for manual labor and those where machinery is operated.

2. The mechanized work resembles that of carpenters under Title 425b, the only difference being the production of generally very small and light objects. The work makes use of adjustable circular saws with a diameter of approximately 20 cm, planing machines, surfacing machines—some with round shafts—horizontal cutting heads with automatic feed, some vertical cutting heads, drills, and various other specialized machines.

3. Frame saws and large circular saws are not in regular use, since the short, narrow boards the work requires are cut from meter-long wood blocks.

4. Presumably, in almost all the factories, carpentry is also done by hand within the mechanized workshop and almost always in the same room with the machines.

5. The other operations—that is, other manual operations—consist of gluing the various parts together, polishing, painting, pasting, and bookbinding work, as well as finishing, packing, and shipping. Risk category I would seem to be appropriate for these activities, which are similar to Title 419/2.

6. To the extent that individual manufacturers perform metalwork by hand, this activity would come under Title 114 for hand-produced sheet-metal and tin goods. These investigations led to the principles set forth in Point III of the minutes. In accordance with the unique character of this industry, we had to find a special risk classification, in line with § 5 of the classification regulations. The relationship between mechanical operations and manual activities or between the small-scale carpentry work and the other tasks was acknowledged to be crucial in determining the level of risk in this industry. The relationship did not fluctuate greatly between the various production methods. From this aspect, the wage distribution is roughly as follows (as found in the investigation).

Of K 100 in wages, the amount in the left-hand column in the list below comes under the category of small-scale carpentry and all required auxiliary jobs, such as drying wood, cleaning the machines and rooms, heating, lighting, maintaining the facilities, etc. The amount in the right-hand column comes under the related tasks, such as painting, varnishing, polishing, papering, bookbinding work, work with paper, packing, etc.

These are the figures for the production of:

Magic number cubes	K 22.00	K 78.00
Building blocks, medium size	K 30.00	K 70.00
Dominoes "	K 28.00	K 72.00
Checkerboards "	K 20.00	K 80.00
Decorative boxes, polished	K 25.00	K 75.00
Money boxes "	K 24.00	K 76.00
Toy guns	K 25.00	K 75.00
Toy pianos	K 20.00	K 80.00
Fortresses, theater	K 22.00	K 78.00
Pencil boxes, medium size	K 37.00	K 63.00
Writing implements	K 20.00	K 80.00
Wooden handcarts, wheels	K 40.00	K 60.00
Kitchen implements	K 28.00	K 72.00
Toy stores, stables	K 20.00	K 80.00
Doll furniture	K 25.00	K 75.00
Paint boxes	K 24.00	K 76.00

The average wage for small-scale carpentry is K 26.00, and the average pay for all other tasks is K 74.00.

The classifications of Title 410c for the manufacture of moldings, planing, cutting, and milling and Titles 425, 425 a and b, Title 419/2 and 114, were all used to calculate the risk category that generally applies to the above-named factories. We found that risk category VII is the most applicable average category for these businesses according to § 5 of the classification regulations; within this category, risk percentages vary from 25% to 37%, depending on how much of the wood work is performed with the use of machinery; the insurance premium for every K 100 of wages for these businesses now ranges from K 2.15 to K 3.18.

With this reclassification, we reached a complete settlement with the trade association, and the Institute hopes that we have brought about a smooth transition to the next revision of risk classification with no harm to the Institute, thanks to the other guarantees rendered by the trade association in conjunction with this arrangement.

The significance of this arrangement is also shown by the lively interest of the Chamber of Commerce in Eger, as well as by the many discussions of our changes in concerned groups and in the press. The Institute has now initiated preliminary negotiations with the trade association in Kallich that should lead to a similar settlement. An important indirect cause of the great general interest in this matter is the fact that it concerns the continuance of the competitive situation this industry faces in regard to the adjacent German businesses in the same industry; in Germany, accident-insurance premiums were far lower, at least until we arrived at the settlement we have described above; furthermore, German businesses are graded not only according to the proportion of mechanized work to manual work but also according to the various machines used within the machine category.

The Director:

(Signed:) Dr. Marschner

D. Proceedings of the Ministry of the Interior (May 4, 1914)

Letterhead: K. K. MINISTRY OF THE INTERIOR

1914   File No.
Insurance Department
K. K. Ministry of the Interior.
Minutes Number 1459
Date: March 4, 1914
Subject:
Workmen's Accident Insurance Institute in Prague,
Risk classification of the member firms of the Trade Association of Manufacturers of Wooden Articles and Toys for the Erzgebirge in Katharinaberg

In an addendum, the Institute has detailed the progressive growth and change of this industry and has noted (minutes of October 3, 1913) that all differences were resolved in mutual agreement with the trade association. At this time, almost all the businesses are reported to have created a complete division between machine work and manual work. The machine work—where, "presumably, in almost all the factories, carpentry is also done by hand within the mechanized workshop, and almost always in the same room with the machines"—resembles the machine work of the carpenter's shops in Title 425b (except that only very small and light articles are produced), and the remaining manual work is said to consist of gluing the separate parts together, polishing, painting, pasting, bookbinding, finishing, packing, and shipping (Title 419/2, risk category I). According to Title 114, occasional metalwork is to be assessed as category II. Based on the increased proportion of machine work compared to manual work (26:74), risk category VII (graded according to the extent of mechanized woodworking) was determined for these businesses according to § 5, whereby complete agreement with the trade association was achieved without any loss suffered by to the Institute, thanks to the guarantees offered by the trade association (insurance of each firm in its entirety, including the separate auxiliary workshops, which may be located in a nearby settlement; correct and complete wage lists; and accident-prevention measures). Such an agreement was the only way to keep our industry competitive with that of the German Reich, which had previously been classified at a much lower rate.

The trade association's minutes contain the request "that the typical conditions of the Katharinaberg wood industry be considered accordingly in the next revision of risk categories."

Responding to a query submitted to it, the Prague Institute declared its willingness to include a representative of this trade association in the discussions; it is for this reason that the association was invited to send a representative to the negotiations about risk categories.

For your files.

Vienna, May 4, 1914

(Signed:) Wolf

◦❀

As head of the Institute's appeals department, Kafka dealt with complex economic, social, legal, and ethical issues, as illustrated by the petition from the Katharinaberg toy manufacturers to the Ministry of the Interior.

This appeal is not the routine individual employer's rejection of the risk classification assigned to his firm but represents the attempt of a regional branch to address the Ministry in Vienna as the highest accessible governmental authority. These small manufacturers of wooden articles and toys were writing to Vienna, not only from the Erzgebirge in the northwestern borderland of Bohemia but also from the nowhere land of social policy. While insurance law treated their small family firms the same way it addressed large industrial firms, these small firms were, in fact, subcontractors of wholesalers, who usually granted them a mere fraction of the profits. This miserable situation had been aggravated by the German toy industry's tripling exports to Austria between 1900 and 1913 in an effort to preserve its leading position in the world market. Part of the "assistance provided to this industry," modestly referred to in the opening sentence of the petition, consisted of high protective tariffs on toys imported from Germany. The scenario of the "collapse of the entire industry" was only a slight exaggeration of the actual situation.

To make matters worse, these toy manufacturers found themselves in a trouble zone of workmen's accident insurance. From the start, the small firms had feared that they would be "called on to cover the gigantic deficits [in the insurance budget] caused by the big industrial firms and an excessively expensive administrative apparatus" of compulsory accident insurance.[1] In the petition from Katharinaberg, this suspicion is conveyed in the figurative expression of the "goose that lays the golden eggs." But the small industries resisted accident insurance on a more basic level. According to a petition to the Vienna Ministry of the Interior, submitted in October 1912 by the Reichenberg Chamber of Commerce and Industries, the whole system of risk categories and risk percentages inadequately registered the distinctive local conditions of small machine-operating firms. To offer the owners of small firms a way out of the widespread illegal practice of filing false wage declarations, the Reichenberg chamber suggested a legal option of partial insurance for machine operations that were spatially separated from other sections of the same firm. This is but a version of the "Betriebsverdrängung" ("the repression of operations") that we will encounter in full force in the case of Norbert Hochsieder (doc. 10). The following passage from a memorandum from all crownland Institutes warning against attempts to deviate further from comprehensive compulsory insurance highlights the dilemma the Institutes faced as soon as they left the safe ground of positive legal regulations:

> Based on past experience in accident insurance, we must fight decisively against limiting insurance to one segment of a firm, or so-called partial insurance. Aside from the fact that few occupations exist entirely without risk of accidents, it can never be said that one segment of the workers and managers employed in any firm are not subject to the presumed risk of accidents. Any restriction of that sort bears the mark of a certain arbitrariness and is interpreted in different ways. Countless bitter arguments have thus arisen in determining both insurance contributions and accident rulings. It is in the nature of things that in every case, the victim of an accident or his dependents maintain that he was legally insured against accidents; on the other hand, many business owners strive to decrease their insurance contributions and thus to limit the number of insured persons as far as possible. The insurance institute, which has to hold the middle ground against these intentions as dictated by law, thus appears stingy and heartless in the case of accident rulings and greedy in the case of determining insurance contributions.[2]

This is the economic and political background against which the petition has to be read. But it is precisely because the toy manufacturers could not afford to share the point of view of the Institutes that their petition reads as an urtext in Kafka's literary universe. The petitioners claim that the high risk classification established by the Institutes restricts a wide range of workers to the miserable conditions of cottage industry, in which they "must [. . .] spend 12–15 hours working in the room where the whole family lives, cooks, bathes, and sleeps and that also serves as nursery and sickroom." This is an almost literal transcript of K.'s visit to Lasemann's hut in the first chapter of *The Castle*, set in a village whose inhabitants live under the rule of an impenetrable castle bureaucracy. But the most obvious echo to the clamor arising from the Erzgebirge is to be found in the literary complex of *The Trial* and *In the Penal Colony*. A systematic error in the German original, a Derridean rather than a Freudian slip, produces a hidden connection between these two works. Whenever Alfred Pierschel, the actual author of the Katharinaberg petition, refers to the law, he writes the German word *Gesetz* (law) as *Gesetzt* (something set down). This phantasmal creation of a northern Bohemian mountain dweller in fact elucidates the paradoxical origin of written law. Such law is the product of an inaugural act of proclamation (a *Setzung*), and it is at the same time something set in print (*gesetzt*) and distributed as a text or *Schriftsatz*, to use the German collective term for administrative documents. The first aspect of law guarantees its transcendental truth. The second aspect of law, as a text in circulation, attracts additions that are liable to interpretation and, hence, to the law's misuse; in this way the original truth of the law is corrupted. This is basically the message of the priest to Joseph K, in his discussion of the "doorkeeper" legend, when the priest distinguishes the manifold interpretations of the law from what originally stands written—"scripture," *die Schrift*—and is inalterable. At one point, in his desperate effort to reinvest the text of the law with its transcendent truth, Pierschel exclaims, "If the same lawmakers [*Gesetztgeber* (sic)] were to see now how their work has been handled by the Workmen's Accident Insurance Institute for the Kingdom of Bohemia, they would turn over in their graves." He appeals to an instance that is present not so much in *The Trial* as in *In the Penal Colony,* its juridical-political counterpart. Here, the officer in charge of the colony's penal procedure tries to exhume the Old Commandant, the founder of the colony and its archaic, infallible law, when this law is challenged by a modern trend of public opinion, brought to the colony by trade and orchestrated by women's voices. In this light, Kafka the writer evidently considered the petition submitted to Kafka the clerk as something more than a quarry for literary images or themes. He held in his hands, instead, a vivid, real-life symptom of the distress of modern culture, expressed in the desire for an archaic reunion of positive law and transcendental truth. When Pierschel's petition describes the legal procedures enforced by Kafka's Institute, it reveals, however unintentionally, the archaic potential inherent in modern positive law itself:

> The Institute states quite plainly that the record of paid-out wages has been falsified—a claim that is all the easier to assert when the inspector believes himself to be detective, prosecutor, defense attorney, and judge all in one. We'll use the health-insurance data, they add up to a greater sum, the greater sum is always the right one, the manufacturer is obviously a swindler, and we'll make short shrift of him.

This account of a jurisdiction that does not acknowledge different parties—as do both the Roman and the Anglo-Saxon legal traditions—anticipates the legal scenes in *The Trial*, where the attic court deals summarily ("*kurzen Prozess macht*") with K. Again, the petition gives precise instructions to Kafka's narrative: "And while the appeal is still under review, the affected manufacturer is expected to pay." The German is even more instructive: "*Noch ohne dass der Rekurs erledigt ist, wird der Betriebsinhaber* exekutiert." All Kafka the writer needs to do is to take literally the Austrian expression for a routine administrative procedure ("to execute someone," meaning "to legally enforce someone's financial liability") in order to visualize the execution summarily enforced against K in *The Trial*.

According to a remark by Walter Benjamin, it is not politics but organization that defines fate in Kafka's world. Its truth is vivid after a journey into the archive to trace the bureaucratic fate of this desperate message to the highest imperial authority from the "most distant of distances." Here, we catch a realistic instance of the immeasurable space that separates Kafka's Chinese subjects from the Emperor. On April 21, 1912, the petition from the Erzgebirge was signed and immediately sent on by the district authorities in Eger to the governor in Prague. Three more weeks had to elapse before the message was forwarded, on May 15, to the Ministry in Vienna. Now spring turns into summer, and summer into fall, while the desperate toy manufacturers hope in vain for a message from Vienna. On October 23, 1912, however, a trace of this affair emerges in one of the most widely read "love letters" of the twentieth century. On this day, Franz Kafka's desperate longing for a message from Berlin, where his future fiancée and "human tribunal," Felice Bauer, lived, was finally fulfilled. Overflowing with relief and joy, he lost no time in writing his reply from his desk in the office where the letter from Berlin had obviously found him. His response brings a foretaste of what was waiting for Felice in the upcoming months:

> I must tell you that I have spent half my life waiting for your letter—though the waiting period did include three short letters I wrote you during these three weeks (just now I'm being asked questions about insurance for convicts, my God!), and perhaps two of them can now be mailed, while the third, actually the first, cannot possibly be sent. And so your letter is presumably lost (I have just had to explain that I know nothing about a ministerial appeal by Josef Wagner in Katharinaberg) and I will not get answers to my earlier questions. (LF 10, trans. modified)

Longed-for letters and letters lost serve as the common denominator of the agendas of love life and office life as the drama of the former is exposed to the ironic light of the latter agenda.

Josef Wagner, one of the signatories of the Katharinaberg petition, obviously volunteered to investigate the fate of the collective letter. As this letter was by no means a regular "ministerial appeal," which would inevitably have been recorded in the files of Kafka's department, Kafka could only throw up his hands and proclaim his ignorance. In any case, it seems that Wagner's intervention revived the whole process.

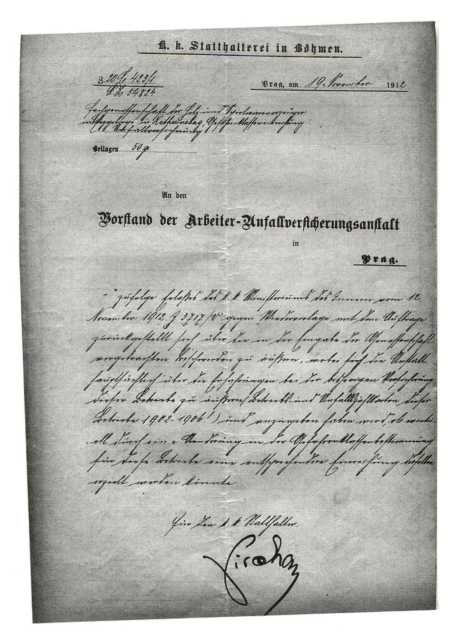

Figure 5a. Note from the Office of the Governor, requiring the Institute's comment on the petition submitted by Katharinaberg Trade Association.

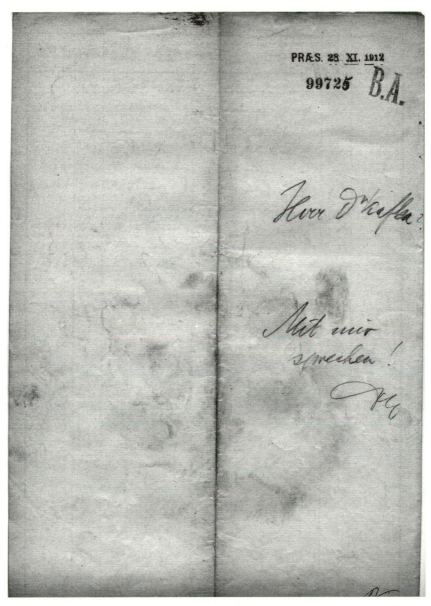

Figure 5b. Reverse: Autograph Robert Marschner: "Herr Dr. Kafka?
Mit mir sprechen!"

On November 12, almost seven months after the message from northern Bohemia was sent out, a record is made for the files in the insurance department of the Vienna Ministry. It confirms the exclamation of a Hofrat in Arthur Schnitzler's 1912 comedy, *Professor Bernhardi*: "As an official you have the choice only of being either an anarchist or an idiot."[3] Having repatriated Katharinaberg from the Riesengebirge—where he had first located it—to the Erzgebirge, the consultant official remarks that the manufacturers' allegations sounded "quite plausible." He expressed the hope that a change of business category might help solve the problems and that, in "any case" or rather, "perhaps," the trade association should be involved in the discussions to establish the impending risk classification. These remarks—far from anarchic—were eventually attached to the petition, which was then sent back to the Office of the Governor and from there to the Institute, where it arrived on November 23, 1912. A handwritten note by Director Robert Marschner on the back of the accompanying letter from the Governor—"Herr Dr. Kafka? See me!"[4] (figures 5a,b)—proves that Kafka, as the head of the risk-classification appeals department, was directly involved in this difficult affair.

Many months followed before Josef Wagner and his cosigners received a preliminary response to their petition. Obviously, the complaint was being taken seriously by the Prague Institute, and a "political" solution outside the formal legal procedure was being sought. So it was not until August 29, 1913, that the Institute responded to the Office of the Governor in a letter indicating that in the meantime, official negotiations with the toy manufacturers of Katharinaberg were being prepared. The stylistic level of this letter clearly indicates that it was not written by Kafka, who was traveling to Vienna as a member of the Institute's delegation at the Second International Congress for Rescue Service and Accident Prevention.

But after the petitioners had met with a representative of the Institute at the mayor's office in Katharinaberg on October 13, 1913 (this representative would not have been Kafka, who had returned just the previous day from a long holiday in Italy), the Institute filed a final statement to the Office of the Governor (selection C). This document, while signed as usual by Robert Marschner, displays all the features of Kafka's eminent competence as a legal commentator on social policy. Its crisp sentences give us a short history of the technological development of wood manufacturing in the Erzgebirge. This account turns into a precise diagnosis of the deplorable conditions described in the Katharinaberg petition. It demonstrates the ways the "justified," if illegal, attempts at "self-help" on the part of the employers in fact only increased their misery; and it explores the methods by which the employers managed to escape the vicious circle only when "direct negotiation between the Institute and the trade association" supplemented the inadequate framework of the law. Like Kafka's two articles in the *Tetschen-Bodenbacher Zeitung*, the Institute's final statement replaces the principle of guilt with an analysis of the legal mechanism at work in accident insurance. From that angle, the Institute and the employers are no longer in opposition. As the Katharinaberg negotiations show, it was in both parties' interest to improve or emend that mechanism where necessary. Social law appears as no longer the product of morality but of efficient engineering.

10

RISK CLASSIFICATION APPEAL BY NORBERT HOCHSIEDER, BOARDING HOUSE OWNER IN MARIENBAD (1912)

This is a special case of Kafka's official writings. Kafka was away from the Institute on his 1912 summer vacation and so did not literally write the Institute's statements to the Ministry. On the other hand, he obviously took notice of the maddening details of this case, which was later to be recorded as a precedent case in the Amtliche Nachrichten, *the official legal records of Austrian accident and health insurance. As hotels with mechanical elevators were liable for insuring their employees against accidents, Hochsieder first contended that the motor for his power-operated elevator was not located in his house but in the local power station, from which he merely received the electrical energy that operated it. Then, after his lawyer had alerted him to his blunder, Hochsieder argued that, while there was, in fact, a motor in his house, the motor was locked in a black box in the cellar and accessible only to the elevator technician, access being strictly forbidden to the other staff members. Finally, Hochsieder argued that, although he was running a "firm" that employed electrical machinery, it could nonetheless not be regarded as a hotel in the first place, since the guests were not being served meals, not even breakfast. Kafka's commentary on this case is not found in the official files but survives, in transfigured form, in a number of his stories.*

A. Hochsieder to the Office of the Governor: Appeal against Classification as a Motor-Powered Business (June 5, 1912)

Norbert Hochsieder, Landlord in Marienbad
Workmen's Accident Insurance
Compulsory Insurance
Marienbad, June 5, 1912
(Stamp and signature of Nadler, attorney-at-law)

Esteemed
k. k. Office of the Governor in Prague:

As a result of the official notice issued by the Workmen's Accident Insurance Institute on May 14, 1912, [. . .] in which all "persons employed for the purposes of operating a rooming house [*Logierhaus*]" in my employ are declared to be subject to insurance under a section allegedly analogous to Section 469/6 that applies to hotels, I consider myself treated unfairly and thus, within the legal time limit, I file my OBJECTION.

I contest the decision and the documents attached thereto in their entirety, including the risk classification and percentage rate.

First of all, I maintain that there is no such thing as a rooming-house business; the term was invented by the Institute merely so that the law governing workmen's accident insurance could be applied willy-nilly to the persons in my employment. In any case, it is incorrect to apply Section 469/6, which is intended for hotels. It is incorrect both from a factual perspective, because what I own is merely a rental property, in which neither food nor drink is provided to the tenants, and from a legal perspective, because the law covering workmen's accident insurance does not permit an analogous application of compulsory insurance regulations.

Apart from the fact that my house is an ordinary apartment house, however, and thus no "business" is conducted in the sense intended by the workmen's accident-insurance law, I do not utilize a motor in my house. The power that activates my elevator is generated in the local electricity plant, and in the house there is only a changeover switch that is locked by the electricity plant and accessible only to its representatives. The control (a knob) is so simple that it can be operated by any of our guests at no risk whatever.

If one wanted to acquire some kind of insurance because of this elevator, one would land in the absurd position of having to insure all occupants of the house and all visitors to the resort, since they are the only ones with access to the elevator, and use of the elevator is strictly forbidden to all others, most particularly to persons in my employ. In reality, however, as noted, we are dealing here with a question, not of the use of a motor in my house, but of the use of a motor operated by the electrical plant. I believe that there is no need for me to cite further evidence, especially since the contested decision makes it absolutely clear that the Workmen's Accident Insurance Institute is sparing no effort in its attempt to subject new classes of people to compulsory insurance without giving much thought to the wording of the workmen's accident insurance law and its rationale.

I petition as follows through my representative identified in Attachment B: I beg the esteemed k. k. Office of the Governor to revoke the Workmen's Accident Insurance Institute's decision of May 14, 1912, as illegal in its entirety.

(Signature :) Norbert Hochsieder

B. Franz Nadler, JD, Attorney-at-Law (Legal Representative of Norbert Hochsieder) to the Office of the Governor: Correction to the Appeal (June 12, 1912)

Representative of Elisabeth Kroha and Norbert Hochsieder
Compulsory workmen's accident insurance
Correction
Marienbad, June 12, 1912

To the esteemed k. k. Office of the Governor in Prague:

As an addendum and correction to the appeal lodged within the legal time limit by myself in the names of Elisabeth Kroha and Norbert Hochsieder against the decisions of the Workmen's Accident Insurance Institute [. . .], I call your attention to the following:

As a result of a misunderstanding in gathering information, I have indicated in the stated appeals that no motor but only a converter is present in the houses in question. That statement does not entirely correspond to the facts. From the perspective of space, there is indeed a motor in the houses. However, it should not be viewed as in use in my house; rather, this motor is operated by the municipal electrical plant—the motor draws its power from this plant, and the plant controls its operation. Furthermore, this motor is always kept locked and is completely inaccessible to my employees, since it is housed under a locked cover in a room that is also kept locked and to which only the elevator operator has access.

No one comes into contact with the motor in order to set the elevator in motion, since this is done by turning the current on and off, an operation for which it is enough to turn a switch, which is at a great distance from the motor. Thus the possibility of danger is completely eliminated; the action is no different from turning an electric light on and off.

Except for these points, I abide by my statements in the cited appeals. I petition as follows:

I beg the esteemed k. k. Office of the Governor to be good enough to take note of this correction and acknowledge it in settling the appeals stated above.

(Signature:) Dr. Franz Nadler.

C. Institute to the Office of the Governor: Statement
on the Hochsieder Appeal (July 12, 1912)

Prague, July 12, 1912
Norbert Hochsieder,
Rooming-House Operation in Marienbad
Classification.

To the esteemed k. k. Office of the Governor in Prague:

The disputed decision pronounced insurance to be compulsory for the entire rooming-house industry, thus correcting a situation that was not clearly covered by the accident-insurance law. That is, until this decision took effect, insurance was required only for the personal elevator used in the business, even though a personal elevator in no way constitutes a separate workplace but can be designated only as a motorized installation within a larger place of business according to § 1, par. 3, point 2, of the accident-insurance law. Since this law provides only for the insurance of commercial establishments as a unified whole, and not for the separate groups of workers who are employed to deal directly with the machinery or are otherwise at a higher risk in the commercial operation, with the singular exception of § 1, par. 4, regarding agricultural and forestry workers, it is therefore clear that the only question reasonably to be raised here concerns the compulsory insurance of the entire rooming-house industry. A resolution of the question of the commercial nature of the rooming house as an industry will comprise the crux of this decision. The undersigned Institute has never viewed the operation of a rooming house as a commercial business within the terms of the commercial code, especially since the commercial code has no bearing on the question of compulsory insurance. However, the operation of a rooming house must surely be regarded as a profession as specified in § 1, par. 3, line 2, of the accident insurance law, where "profession" signifies nothing other than permanent operation for the purpose of gain. In this sense, for example, a private sanatorium is also subject to compulsory insurance as soon as it uses motorized equipment, although such an institution is not covered in the commercial code [. . .].

Most especially, there can be no doubt that rooming houses differ significantly from ordinary rental apartments, which are intended to be rented out on yearly leases. The former are businesses that rent apartments only for defined, relatively brief periods; in particular, they also provide the tenants with breakfast, if not with full board, and finally, they provide special services for all tenants, which is not usually true in apartment houses. In fact, rooming houses stand on the border between full-service hotels and apartment houses, and according to accident-insurance law, they must be classified with hotels. In this connection we refer to the very instructive expert opinion of the k. k. trade inspector in Karlsbad of August 12, 1911, [. . .] which gives a vivid description of the apartment situation in the Bohemian health resorts; according to this document, there is no doubt that rooming houses are a commercial business. A copy of this opinion is attached to our statement of July 12, 1912, [. . .] on the decree of June 15, 1912 [. . .].

Once the commercial nature of the rooming house is established, compulsory insurance for the business as a whole is based on its regular use of motorized equipment. The objection raised in the appeal that the elevator is merely one piece of equipment in the house is not valid, since according to accident-insurance law, if any motors are regularly used in the facility, even though they do not belong to the facility, the proprietor of the facility must be considered their owner; such must be the conclusion drawn from § 11, par. 3, of the accident-insurance law, *argumente e contrario*.

The appellant may offer as further evidence that the rooming house does not operate for the purpose of gain the fact that he pays no income tax. In that case, we must take every precaution to keep the decisions of the revenue authorities, which are guided by various considerations and are frequently influenced by utilitarian and fiscal concerns, from prejudicing the decisions of the Institute, which strives for a social purpose.

The additional circumstance that the rooming house staff does not receive actual wages but depends on tips and providing special services to guests, which these request and pay for, can only reaffirm our opinion. These conditions are the same as, or at least are similar to, those that prevail in hotels, restaurants, and coffeehouses regarding staff income, just as all of the rooming-house industry differs in only a few insignificant points from normal businesses of the abovementioned kind, but such differences are due to the specific conditions prevailing in the Bohemian health resorts. The difficulty, however, of determining the level of payment when the employee is wholly or in part dependent on tips certainly cannot be seen as a serious objection to the compulsory insurance of the business; it is, instead, only a technical question of income audits. These explanations remove any doubt that this business is subject to compulsory insurance; in classifying it, we have taken into account that rooming houses run a lower risk than do hotels, and we have bent over backward to assign to it the lowest percentage rate of Risk Class I, which is indicated by Title 469 b. Given the above, the present appeal appears to be without merit, and we ask that it be rejected.

On behalf of the Director:
(Signature:) Dr. Holeyšovsky
(Stamp)

D. Karlsbad Trade Inspector to the Office of the Governor
Expert opinion on the Hochsieder appeal (no date)
Attachment: Expert opinion on the ministerial appeal of Frank against compulsory insurance for the employees of his resort house in Karlsbad (August 12, 1911)

k. k. Office of the Governor in Prague

The present case undoubtedly involves a resort house [*Kurhaus*], as was discussed extensively in point 2 of the statement by this authority [. . .] on August 12, 1911. (A copy of this statement is attached for all the classification appeals of numerous resort-house owners in Marienbad and Karlsbad.) In this house, a motor-driven elevator is available for the greater comfort of the guests taking the cure.

Although this house cannot at present be classified as a commercial business according to current legal regulations, it nevertheless cannot be classified as an apartment house let out to tenants on a yearly basis. In our estimation, compulsory insurance for this resort house would, in practice, be as justified as it is for hotels; such a decision would be based on the motor-driven elevator in the building, since this elevator presents the same risk of accident for the staff of the house as in any hotel equipped with an elevator, and such hotels are already legally subject to compulsory accident insurance for all their employees.

It should be noted further that, as far as this authority learned in a similar case, the k. k. Ministry of the Interior has already officially declared insurance to be compulsory for two resort houses equipped with motorized elevators (the houses "Asgart" and "Mittgart," owned by Dr. Kilian Frank, in Karlsbad).

The k. k. Trade Inspector:

(Signature:) M. Schutt

Attachment:

Copy

K. k. Trade Inspector—Region of Supervision: Karlsbad

Copy of the statement by this authority [. . .] on August 12, 1911, concerning the resort houses "Asgart and Mittgart" owned by Dr. Kilian Frank in Karlsbad, submitted as evidence in the ministerial appeals lodged by Dr. Frank regarding the compulsory insurance of the staff in these houses.

In order to decide whether or not the houses belonging to Dr. Kilian Frank in Karlsbad, "Asgart" and "Mittgart," are subject to compulsory accident insurance in their entirety because of the elevators in them, it is necessary to begin by examining more closely the existing accommodations for guests in Karlsbad.

During the resort season, three different types of accommodations are offered to guests both in Karlsbad and in the other Bohemian resort towns (Marienbad and Franzensbad). These are: 1) accommodations in hotels and inns licensed by the government; 2) those in the so-called resort houses, which do not require a license; and finally, 3) subleases in accommodations leased on a yearly basis to tenants.

1. Hotels and inns. Some of these are in year-round operation, while some operate only during the resort season, as in the overwhelming majority of cases in Karlsbad. Rooms are rented to guests on a daily or a weekly basis; most of them contain restaurants, which not only serve food and drink to the guests of their hotel but are also open to others, making use of all the rights listed in § 16 of the commercial code. The hotels and inns are subject to the provisions of this code without exception, and the entire staff becomes insured against accidents as soon as motorized elevators or other motorized devices are installed.

2. Resort houses. These are certain residential buildings with various owners (the same landlord may own several such houses), usually built much like hotels, with fully furnished rooms, not meant for tenants on yearly leases (with the exception of the landlord, the only one who usually lives on the premises all year) nor equipped for such a purpose; these buildings are designed only to accommodate guests during the resort season. They are therefore empty during the greater part of the year (except for the residence of the landlord, if the house is his permanent residence) and are frequented by guests only during the season.

These houses in health resorts are not subject to the official licensing requirements and should therefore serve only to accommodate visitors, and this only for at least weekly and not daily rental; by the same token, they are not permitted to serve food and drink, as hotels and inns are, according to § 16 of the commercial code. In reality, however, food and drink are served in the majority of these so-called resort houses, though only to resident guests and only at their express request.

As is the case in hotels, the staff required in these houses consists of janitors, servants of various kinds, elevator operators, housekeepers, chambermaids, and possibly kitchen staff. They are hired for the season, with a specified ending date, and their pay is agreed on in advance. As proof of employment, they usually have their paybooks; the law does not require them to be insured against illness with a health-insurance agency, but they usually have voluntarily taken out a policy with the municipal wage earners' health-insurance agency.

Since none of the owners of these houses believes his property to be a commercial business (though he will readily admit that the house is intended to turn a profit), and since to this day no decision on the legal standing of these houses has been handed down, so that the governmental authorities do not view these houses as commercial businesses, the entire staff of such resort houses must currently be seen as not subject to the provisions of the commercial code.

3. Subletters of tenants with one-year leases: The apartments rented by landlords to tenants on a yearly basis (so-called yearly tenants) with three months' notice to terminate the lease are rented out during the season room by room to resort guests while the actual tenants make do with various secondary rooms and crannies, often in questionable condition, during this time.

The present case concerns two separate residential buildings of three and four stories that belong to the attorney Dr. Kilian Frank; there is no question that these are resort houses as defined under (2) above. The attorney maintains an apartment for his own use in one of the houses, while he rents all the other living spaces in both houses to resort guests during the season; these spaces are furnished in the manner of hotel rooms (nearly 50 rooms per house). During the rest of the year, all these rooms are unoccupied.

For the comfort of the guests, a motorized (hydraulic) elevator has been installed in each of the two houses. Three elevator operators attend them. In addition, around 20 other persons of both sexes are employed in the two houses during the season; they work as room servants, janitors, housekeepers, maids, and kitchen staff.

As these explanations show, the two houses in question cannot be classified either as private resort spas (since they offer no spa treatment) or as licensed hotels; nor are they purely rental apartments, since the landlord rents the apartments in the houses not on a yearly basis but exclusively as rooms to visitors to the resort, who in this case, do not count as subletters.

In the estimation of this authority, in practice, the obligation to insure the motorized elevators is beyond doubt, since the elevators serve exactly the same purpose as do those in hotels, other commercial businesses, and sanatoriums. Though houses in health resorts as described here are considered neither hotels (i. e., commercial businesses) nor as private sanatoriums, at the present time legal grounds for regarding the elevators as subject to compulsory insurance are absent. Nevertheless, it is also difficult to establish that such personal elevators are not legally subject to compulsory insurance, since such establishments are also a different matter from rental apartments as these were codified in the decision by the Administrative Court on April 27, 1895, line 2158.

The k. k. Trade Inspector:

(signed) M. Schutt

E. Hochsieder to the Office of the Governor: Reply to the Statement
by the Institute of July 12, 1912 (undated draft)

With regard to the representations made in the statement by the Workmen's Accident Insurance Institute of July 12, 1912 [. . .] to hand, I hereby make the following counterclaim:

1. I protest the fact that the source of income resulting from renting rooms to outsiders, especially guests at the resort, is designated and handled as a "business."

I repudiate as incorrect the wholly inapplicable assertion that renting rooms in my house comes close to its being a "hotel."

The hotel business is characterized, for one thing, by the fact that it is operated as a commercial business and that its commercial activities consist of serving food and drink to transients according to commercial principles (purchasing in order to resell) and of providing accommodations for travelers.

All that happens in my house, by contrast, is the rental of furnished rooms to resort guests (not transients), thus to persons who are staying in Marienbad for a greater length of time. If some of them are actually served breakfast, we perform this service at cost, out of a desire to oblige, and usually only for people who are ill or confined to their rooms by inclement weather. There can thus be no question of a room rental combined with board, a combination that does not exist in Marienbad at all.

Now the Workmen's Accident Insurance Institute maintains that the workmen's accident-insurance law "provides only for the insurance of entire businesses and not additionally for individual groups of workers who work directly with the machines." Since, however, neither a commercial nor a professional "business" exists in the present case, there can be no question of compulsory insurance, and I was therefore not obliged to insure the elevator operator, who is the only person who has access to the elevator.

2. The distinction made by the Workmen's Accident Insurance Institute between commercial and professional is far-fetched; the workmen's accident-insurance law does not recognize such a distinction. § 1, line 2, of the law mentions only "commercial businesses" and the "singular instance" of agricultural and forestry businesses. Furthermore, by using the expression "singular instance," the Workmen's Accident Insurance Institute reveals that the legal term "commercial" is not to be interpreted in a wider sense.

3. The fact that most of my staff receives no wages from me seems to be an argument for the fact that my house is not a commercial institution, as a hotel might be, for example.

4. The fact that I pay no income tax on the rental of my property speaks for the reality that mine is not a commercial business. But the objection of the opposing party that "the decisions of the revenue authorities may prejudice the decisions of the Insurance Institute" is out of place because it is not the financial authorities but the esteemed k. k. Administrative Court to which "utilitarian and financial" intentions can certainly not be imputed, which has repeatedly found that the rental of rooms to resort guests is not subject to income tax.

I have far greater justification, however, to turn the tables and say: I protest the fact that the opinion of the k. k. trade inspector of August 12, 1911, [. . .] is taken into consideration in deciding on my impartial appeals, because it is sufficiently well known that the trade inspector is a product of sociopolitical intentions. Since I was never told the actual wording of that opinion, I cannot, of course, discuss it in detail. One thing is clear, however: Whether it corresponds to the facts or not, that opinion deals only with conditions in Karlsbad, and these are entirely different from the situation in Marienbad.

To sum up, I repeat that since there cannot be a question of a "business" and a "commercial nature," renting out rooms in private houses to resort guests does not fall under the authority of the workmen's accident-insurance law, and I therefore stand by the statements made in my appeals.

(Signatures :) Norbert Hochsieder
Dr. Franz Nadler

F. Hochsieder to the Ministry of the Interior: Ministerial Appeal against the Classification Decision (January 3, 1913)

Norbert Hochsieder, Landlord in Marienbad
"The Golden Angel"
Appeal regarding the decision [. . .]
of the k. k. Office of the Governor in Prague of
November 28, 1912
Marienbad, January 3, 1913
By and to Dr. Franz Nadler, JD
(Stamp and signature of Franz Nadler, Esq.)

To the k. k. Ministry of the Interior in Vienna:

I hereby lodge within the legal time limit the following further appeal against the decision of the k. k. Office of the Governor in Prague on November 28, 1912, [. . .] in which my appeal against the decision of the Workmen's Accident Insurance Institute in Prague on May 14, 1912, [. . .] was not upheld:

My appeal against the decision of the Workmen's' Accident Insurance Institute in Prague of May 14, 1912, and especially the explanations in my statement against the findings of the Workmen's Accident Insurance Institute in Prague of July 12, 1912, [. . .] are not refuted by the contested decision.

For the sake of brevity, I therefore refer to my statements in the appeal and in the cited counterclaim. In order to establish that I have an obligation to assume insurance, concepts are being fabricated that have no legal foundation and minor issues are being turned into central issues. But these devices fail to consider all those circumstances that the authorities should keep in mind in the public interest and in favor of our local health resorts. Above all, I must again protest against calling my house a " resort-house business" and especially against the claim that it closely resembles a hotel. My house, "The Golden Angel," [. . .] is not a hotel, for in order to be one it would require a license from the authorities according to § 16 of the commercial code, and I have no such license. I am thus in no way entitled to perform those actions that characterize the hotel business—namely, to serve food and drink to strangers, transients, et al., according to commercial principles, and I certainly do not engage in such practices. What remains is thus merely the rental of rooms to visitors to the health resort; their visits usually last for only a short time, which, as a rule, physicians limit to 3 to 4 weeks. Renting out apartments is, therefore, not a commercial business and is not subject to the regulations of the commercial code; thus, it cannot be turned into a business simply by means of interpretation. Since the accident-insurance law provides only for the insurance of the entirety of businesses and not separate groups of workers, and since in the present case, no "business"—either commercial or professional—exists, there can be no question of compulsory insurance.

Accordingly, I am not obligated to insure even the elevator operator, the only person who has access to the elevator. I have stated above that minor circumstances are being made into central issues in an attempt to prove that I am liable to insurance, and that the interpretation that is supposed to make me subject to compulsory insurance does not grant the local health resorts the consideration they deserve. Most of the houses that cater to guests of the health resort do not have elevators, and those that do have such an amenity actually offer their guests nothing more than a convenience. The elevator cannot, then, be considered a facility intended for or succeeding in making a profit for the landlord. In all foreign health resorts, as in Germany, all the better houses are equipped with elevators. Resort visitors from abroad—and those from

Germany alone amount to 90 percent of the visitors to our health spas—therefore expect this amenity at no cost, not added either as a direct fee or an inclusion in the price of the room. The simple explanation is that such equipment belongs in any health-resort house, is offered everywhere abroad, and thus, must also be offered here if the resort is to lay claim to the reputation and rank of a first-class or even world-class resort.

All in all, then, the elevator has nothing to do with the administration and use of the house for rental as a whole; instead, it is a piece of equipment that serves only the guests' convenience and in no way furthers the owner's advantage or profit.

The German health resorts enjoy the support of the state directly, in the form of large subsidies. Many health-resort facilities (spas, colonnades, etc.) are built directly by the state and are given over to public use, without burdening private citizens with the cost of construction, as is the custom here. The taxes paid by resorts abroad are minimal compared to our property tax—how, then, are we to remain competitive against resorts abroad, seeing that we are required to make all kinds of further payments in addition to the high taxes?

We must not fail to recognize the great economic significance of our resort areas, not only for the immediate area and the crownland, but for the entire kingdom. Foreign capital comes in, remains here, and benefits not only the town and its neighborhood but the crownland and empire as well. Trade and commerce benefit from the foreign capital spent on the operation of the resorts, and even a great percentage of the railways, etc., share in the benefits. There is therefore every reason to support the resorts, if not directly with subsidies and other contributions, then indirectly by refusing to overburden them with taxes and relieving them of all payments not directly mandated by law.

We observed that this year the volume of visitors to the principal resort areas of Karlsbad, Marienbad, and Franzensbad declined significantly, while it increased by the same amount abroad. The decline can be traced to the fact that the cost of our accommodations and services must be relatively high, so that we can cover our expenses for the entire year during only the few months of the resort season (less than five), since we cannot break even charging the rates that can usually be charged abroad. In time, this decline will become even more perceptible if newly imposed payments, such as will be the case with accident-insurance premiums, put pressure on us perhaps to increase our rates in order to meet the increased costs.

When it comes to care for employees who are ill—and the only ones we employ in our houses are maids, janitors, and elevator operators—that matter is already provided for by § 20 and §21 of the service regulations.

Then, the municipality has made provisions by setting up an officially approved servants' fund directly connected to the municipal hospital under municipal administration, which ensures medical treatment and care in the hospital free of charge for all servants who require medical care. If the establishment of compulsory insurance subjects us to additional payments, relief medical care for our staff places a hardship on the employer, who deserves at least the same consideration given the employee, since, after all, the employer provides the worker with his income.

Both the notice given by the Workmen's Accident Insurance Institute and the contested decision are taking refuge in an unfounded analogy in order to establish the compulsory insurance that I dispute. All statements refer to my house only as one that involves occupancy carried out "in the manner of a business."

I thus again contest my insurance obligation and make the following request:

That the k. k. Ministry of the Interior revoke the contested decision of the k. k. Office of the Governor of November 28, 1912, [. . .] and uphold my appeal against the decision of the Workmen's Accident Insurance Institute for the Kingdom of Bohemia in Prague of May 14, 1912 [. . .].

(Signature:) Norbert Hochsieder

G. Decision of the Administrative Court (November 22, 1913)

In the Name of His Majesty the Kaiser

The k. k. Administrative Court, under the chairmanship of the k. k. Senate President Dr. Freiherr von Schenk, in the presence of the councilors of the k. k. Administrative Court: Freiherr von Hock, Dr. Edlen von Schneller, Karanowicz, and Dr. Kamitz, and of the Secretary k. k. Judge Dr. Hatschek, has in all justice found as follows, regarding the complaint of Norbert Hochsieder in Marienbad against the decision of the k. k. Ministry of the Interior on March 13, 1913, [. . .] regarding accident insurance, after the public oral hearing conducted on September 26, 1913, and after listening to the presentation of the examiner as well as the statements of Dr. Eduard Petschner, court lawyer in Vienna, as representative of the complaint, and the counterstatements of the k. k. Office of the Governor secretary Dr. Rudolf Breschar, as representative of the responsible ministry:

The complaint is dismissed as unfounded.

Grounds for the Decision

The contestant, who regularly rents out the furnished apartments in his house to a succession of visitors to the health resort, contests the decision that declared his business to be subject to accident insurance because of the use of an elevator run by elemental power, with the following objections:

His business is allegedly not a commercial business within the terms of the commercial code; he claims that only businesses so designated fall under the accident-insurance regulations, and that under no circumstances does the law require that the employees in his business need to be insured for accidents by law except for those employed to operate the elevator.

In both respects, the court was compelled to find the complaint unfounded—without investigating the matter of whether the business in question is not, in fact, a commercial enterprise according to the commercial code, for which the contestant was simply in error by failing to procure a commercial license. Reference was made to the legal opinions of this court, set down in numerous findings and invariably upheld, according to which not only businesses covered by the commercial code are to be understood under "commercial businesses" in § 1 of the accident-insurance law, but so are all occupations carried out professionally, and thus all operations conducted in the manner of business with the intention of turning a profit. Further, according to these legal opinions, it is not only the workers and supervisors working directly with the motor who need to be covered by insurance; everyone employed in the business must, by law, share in the benefits of accident insurance. This circumstance is so by virtue of the principle of collective insurance, which, according to accident-insurance law, applies to all commercial businesses—in contrast to agriculture and forestry—and especially to the hotel business.

Finally, when the complaint maintains that it allegedly contravenes the law to classify the business as a "rooming-house business" under Title 469 b for "Hotels and Inns," when this description does not occur in the definitive regulations, we need only point out that § 5 of this ordinance provides for the case of businesses that cannot be suitably classified directly under a certain risk category rubric. It is surely the meaning of the law that businesses whose classification is not based explicitly on this ordinance will be classified in the same way as the listed occupations of similar type and risk.

Vienna, November 22, 1913

Commentary 10

☙

If Michel Foucault has read Flaubert's oeuvre as a "fantastic library"—writing spurred not by the author's imagination but by knowledge stored in libraries and archives and bent, thereafter, on reorganizing this knowledge into a surface of literary images—then Kafka's work can be read as a "fantastic office." In many cases, the fantastic transformation of technical and legal facts can already be found on the official side of Kafka's written records, in the real world of his insurance files.

Technological change posed a challenge to the language of the law in the case of Norbert Hochsieder's rooming house in the fashionable resort of Marienbad, as it did in the case of Christian Geipel's weaving mill (doc. 5). In 1889, the Otis passenger elevator—invented as early as 1857—was equipped with the electric engine developed by Werner von Siemens a few years earlier. In 1903, the Otis Elevator Company became a global player with a new invention: the gearless elevator that could be installed for any elevation and, depending on size, at any desirable speed.

These innovations had complex consequences for workers' accident insurance in the spa triangle of Karlsbad–Marienbad–Franzensbad, a region thriving on tourism. In 1905, Austrian law subjected all hotels operating electric elevators to comprehensive compulsory accident insurance. The hotel trade association urged that the law be restricted to elevator operators. The 1908 draft of new social legislation suggested that this limitation would be an acceptable compromise. But as the draft was still under discussion during the reclassification of businesses in 1909, the insurance agencies continued to enforce the comprehensive legislation of 1905.

In April 1910, the hotel trade association opened a second battlefront, this time waging war against the increasing number of rooming houses and boarding houses operating the new gearless elevators but still getting away without insurance. Sailing with the wind of powerful outcries over unfair competition, the Prague Institute expanded its campaign to require insurance of these smaller, often family-run, accommodations that tried to take advantage of the blessings of progress without paying the price.

Most of these operators were outraged when they received their notices from Prague requiring insurance payments. Their customary appeal against the notice was based on a linguistic argument. Compulsory
insurance was limited to businesses run as commercial (German: *gewerbsmäßig*) enterprises; the rooming-house owners argued that, since
they were not members of any trade association (hence, in German:
gewerbemäßig), they were not commercial firms, and therefore they
were exempted from compulsory insurance.

Hochsieder's first note of protest to the Office of the Governor made
this argument in somewhat exaggerated fashion. He claimed that there
is no such thing as a rooming house, that in fact, "the term was invented
by the Institute" to make his domestic servants liable to accident insurance (doc. 10A). But this was not the end of fantasy in the quest for
exemption. Even if he owned a rooming house, his appeal continued, his
house should be exempt from compulsory accident insurance, since he
was not using a motor in his house. "The power that activates my elevator is generated in the local electricity plant, and in the house there is
only a changeover switch that is locked by the electricity plant and accessible only to its representatives. The control (a knob) is so simple that it
can be operated by any of our guests at no risk whatever." This fantasy
of motorless motion was only partly created by the imaginative potential of technology (belief in the miraculous capacities of electric power,
the gearless elevator); its deep structure was an understandable predis-
position among Bohemian business owners that could be called *Betriebsverdrängung* ("repression of operation"), in an allusion to Freud's key
term *Triebverdrängung* ("repression of drives").

In practice, the institutes left an escape route from comprehensive insurance where it could be established that only a clearly defined part of
the staff actually worked with the engines that gave rise to insurance coverage. As a consequence, Kafka had to deal with letters of protest teeming
with closets, side rooms, and storerooms where engines were kept under
lock and key, accessible only to qualified personnel. In these Bohemian
industrial fantasies, it is not the "contiguity of desire," as Deleuze and
Guattari suggest in their structural reading of Kafka's narratives, but the
contiguity of danger "that causes whatever happens always to happen in
the office next door."[1] That Hochsieder's first note was merely an extreme
case of this contiguity of danger (issuing from *Betriebsverdrängung*) is
proved by the follow-up note to the Office of the Governor sent only a
week later by his attorney, Dr. Franz Nadler, a sober-minded professional
and a former mayor of Marienbad. Hochsieder admitted that the first description of his elevator "does not entirely correspond to the facts" as seen
"from the perspective of space": the motor of his elevator was indeed

located in his home. However, in a technical sense, he claimed, the motor was on a remote control from the electric-power plant. Accordingly, the motor itself was a doubly sealed source of danger, covered by "a locked cover," which, in turn, was located in a "room that is also kept locked and to which only the elevator operator has access." Notionally, the motor played no part in propelling the elevator!

In response to these contortions (doc. 10C), the Institute insisted that the restriction of accident insurance to the elevator staff had created "a situation that was not clearly covered by the accident-insurance law," to which it was now putting an end. To close Hochsieder's other escape route—his claim of noncommercial status for his house—the Institute pointed to the detailed description of the hospitality industry provided by the trade inspectorate of Karlsbad as early as the summer of 1911. The heading of this expert report (a copy of which is attached to the statement of the trade inspector in the Hochsieder case; see doc. 10D) shows that the newly adopted strict procedures at the Institute caused an avalanche of appeals from hospitality companies operating below the level of full hotel service. But both the Institute and the trade inspector concluded that, despite the absence of legal regulations, accommodations less than standard for hotels should not be exempted from compulsory insurance.

Thereafter, Hochsieder took his case to Vienna, complaining that the Prague Institute had constructed "concepts . . . that have no legal foundation" with the sole purpose of subjecting his house to compulsory insurance (doc. 10F). When the Minister also turned down the appeal, Hochsieder appealed to the highest authority, the Administrative Court. Here the judges put an end to Hochsieder's linguistic hair-splitting by going back to the regulations of the accident-insurance law, which, under § 1, explicitly included in compulsory insurance, not only those firms allied in a particular trade organization but any commercial occupation aiming to realize a profit.

The Hochsieder case highlights the relationship between Kafka the clerk and Kafka the writer in an unprecedented way. The Institute's only statement (doc. 10C) was written during his summer vacation—hence, according to the evidence of the archive, Kafka never contributed even a single line to the dispute in this case. But this fact is only part of the story. The absence of Kafka's writings in the Hochsieder files is compensated by Hochsieder's presence in Kafka's poetic files. On September 26, 1912, three days after Kafka sentenced himself to literature by writing *The Judgment*, but also three months after Hochsieder launched his fantasy appeals against being sentenced to accident insurance, Kafka resumed his America novel, *The Man Who Disappeared*, a project he had abandoned in 1911. The novel owes a lot to

Hochsieder and the rooming-house owners of Marienbad. In chapters 5 and 6, the nexus between *Triebverdrängung* and *Betriebsverdrängung*, between repressed drives and repressed operation, is most obvious. When Kafka's hero Karl takes up his new job as an elevator operator in the Hotel Occidental,

> what disappointed Karl most was that all the operator had to do with the mechanism of the elevator was to set it going by merely pushing a button, while repairs on the motor itself were exclusively assigned to the hotel's own engineers, so that, for example, although he had been working the elevator for six months, Giacomo had personally seen neither the engine in the cellar nor the gears within the elevator, although—as he himself clearly said—it would have given him great pleasure to do so. (A96, trans. modified)

Eventually, Karl is fired for violating the regulations for operating an elevator and moves on in his descending order of houses: his uncle's house in New York; the country house near New York; the Hotel Occidental; the dusty apartment of the fat singer Brunelda; a whorehouse; and finally, the promise of the house of houses, the Nature Theater of Oklahoma, providing a safe haven for all the outcasts of Kafka's Amerika. This descending order—a crucial part of the novel's narrative—might be seen as yet another literary extension of the Hochsieder files, especially of the trade inspector's report on the categories of houses in Karlsbad (doc. 10D, attachment). Furthermore, for boarding establishments to be required to carry insurance, it was crucial that guests be served meals, and especially breakfast (doc. 10C, D, E)—a theme recurrently marking turning points in *The Man Who Disappeared*. Karl's informal position as a servant in Brunelda's household is put to the test when one day he is ordered, at four in the afternoon, to put together a breakfast for his mistress from the leftovers of a nearby kitchen.

The most fantastic return of Hochsieder's *Betriebsverdrängung* is to be found in Kafka's dream story, "A Country Doctor." When the doctor, called to a sick patient's bed one night, searches for a horse for his carriage, the exclamation of his maid announces a turning point in the story that resonates with the Hochsieder appeal. She cries, "You never know the things you have in your own house." What happens next may be described as the return of the repressed in the context of *Betriebsverdrängung*: the uncanny horses, "powerful animals with strong flanks, [. . .] their bodies thickly steaming," emerging from the pigsty (one of Kafka's abundant closets), connotes a standard metaphor for the locomotive (the "iron horse"). The horses point to the first paragraph of the Austrian accident-insurance law, which stipulates that the use of "engines [. . .] driven by elementary power or by animals" subjects a business to carrying accident insurance. Since at the same time, it is the power of the horse Pegasus that stands for poetic inspiration, we can observe Kafka the writer turning into a client of Kafka the clerk—and sniffing out hidden places of dangerous operation. Here, too, together with "repressed operation," "repressed drives" emerge in the person of the servant who will rape Rosa, the maid, while the country doctor prepares for his trip abroad on the steaming horses.

11

LETTERS TO THE WORKMEN'S ACCIDENT INSURANCE INSTITUTE IN PRAGUE (1912–15)

In his long letter of December 1912 appealing for a raise, Kafka adopts the role of spokesman for his entire group of officials. His last letter addresses the slow pace of his career as compared with the advancement of his colleagues, never explicitly mentioning what was probably the true reason for this delay: anti-Jewish discrimination.

A. Letter to the Workmen's Accident Insurance Institute in Prague (Prague, Wednesday, August 31, 1910)

Esteemed Board of Directors:

The undersigned respectfully submits a request to the honorable Board of Directors for an increase in his base salary from K 1,800 to K 2,400, for the following reasons:

In 1907, the esteemed Board of Directors saw fit to increase the base salary of the Institute's law clerks from K 2,000 to K 2,400, in consideration both of the general increase in the cost of living and of the base salaries granted law clerks in state, crownland, and other public services. In comparison, the base salary of the undersigned amounts to only K 1,800 and thus does not even reach the level of the Institute's law clerks' base salary before 1907.

The undersigned respectfully begs to point out that, on the one hand, as a law clerk, his duties—like those of all law clerks in other posts—include the drawing up of licenses and other documents (correspondence; commenting on and composing pleadings, appeals, complaints, and reports of all kinds) and that the continually increasing cost of living places a hardship on him, as it does on all others. These are the circumstances that have urgently forced the undersigned to state his request, which he hereby submits for the consideration of the esteemed Board of Directors.

Prague, August 31, 1910

Dr. Franz Kafka, JD

B. Letter to the Workmen's Accident Insurance Institute in Prague
(Prague, Saturday, May 13, 1911)

Esteemed Board of Directors of the Workmen's Accident Insurance Institute for the Kingdom of Bohemia:

The undersigned respectfully submit a request to the esteemed Board of Directors for an increase in his base salary to K 2,600, for the following reasons:

His age, his educational background, his personal circumstances, and the general increase in the cost of living face the undersigned with commitments that he cannot fully meet, given his current salary. In view of work performance, the salary levels of law clerks in public service, and the salary levels within the Institute itself, the undersigned believes that he is justified in submitting this request for the favorable consideration of the esteemed Board of Directors.

Dr. Franz Kafka
Prague, May 13, 1911

C. Letter to the Workmen's Accident Insurance Institute in Prague
(Prague, Wednesday, December 11, 1912)

Esteemed Board of Directors!

The undersigned respectfully submits a modest request to the esteemed Board of Directors for the effective adjustment of his salary and title, requesting that the Board be so good as to take the following reasons under advisement.

It is an undisputed fact that for a number of years, the cost of living has been rising until it has reached a level that is most oppressive to everyone. The esteemed Board of Directors has not ignored this circumstance, and recently, and especially in 1910 and 1911, it has effectively adjusted the salaries of the major groups of Institute employees. This adjustment, which met the most pressing needs of those who were so compensated, applied not only to all the civil servants in the narrower sense of that term—i.e. those employees who, according to the current Civil Service Act, are required to have a secondary-school diploma—but also to the entire male and female office staff. The adjustment included even the janitorial staff; all in all, the adjustment addressed the ubiquitous rising cost of living, which had become untenable.

The Board's resolution: increasing the housing allowance from 30 percent to 40 percent and raising its upper limit from K 1,400 to K 1,600, as well as increasing the supplemental cost-of-living allowance from 10 percent to 15 percent of the base salary and the housing allowance. This increase applied to the large group of the Institute's civil servants with secondary-school diplomas and to the office staff (directors, secretaries, and law clerks) and senior clerks, since all, with three exceptions, seem classified in the general civil-service salary scale. However, a salary adjustment of this scope could not have fully satisfied the two excepted groups of above-named Institute civil servants, who differ from those with a secondary-school diploma by having a higher educational background (usually university) and by their more demanding and responsible jobs at the Institute. Any salary adjustment that did not exceed that granted the civil servants with secondary-school diplomas would have undeservedly lowered the level of their earnings in relation to that of the large group of above-named civil servants and thus would have unfairly decreased the difference between their previous earnings. The esteemed Board did, in fact, take this problem into account by adjusting the earnings of the office staff far beyond the amount described above but with the exception of the law clerks (that is, only the directors and secretaries).

The Institute's law clerks were left quite uncompensated in these salary adjustments—an undeniable consequence of the increasing cost of living—although an adjustment in the salaries of precisely this group of office staff should have been the most extreme if their salaries were to be placed in a correct and fair relationship to those of the civil servants with secondary school diplomas, on the one hand, and those of the civil servants of the senior office staff, especially the secretaries, on the other. The very first prerequisite of such an effective adjustment would have been, first, to raise the salaries of the law clerks to the level of 1904, and only then to adjust these salaries, brought to the old level, in proportion to the acknowledged reality of rising costs—as was, incidentally, done for the senior office staff. While the earnings of all other Institute employees experiences a natural increase, in incremental stages from year to year, in line with the alarming increase in costs, the law clerks' salary level not only did not increase, but, moving in the opposite direction of the salary increases granted all other groups of civil servants in recent years, was actually decreased to an even lower level. However, on the occasion of the large-scale salary adjustments for the Institute's civil servants, the base salary of the law clerks was not increased even to the 1904 level. Much less was this level punctually recalculated, accounting for the general consequences of rising costs.

The undersigned is convinced that the esteemed Board of Directors will not ignore the evidence of the following figures that illustrate these facts:

| | *Actual increasing in the entry-level salaries of law clerks* | | | | *How the salaries of the law clerks would have changed had the base salary level of 1904 been kept, i.e., without adjustments* | | | |
Year	Base salary	Housing allowance	Allowance for in-creased costs	Total salary	Base salary	Housing allowance	Allowance for in-creased costs	Total salary
1904	2,000	600		2,600	2,000	600		2,600
1910	1,800	540	234	2,574	2,000	600	260	2,800
1912	1,600	640	336	2,576	2,100	840	441	3,381

In comparison, the salary paid to civil servants with secondary-school diplomas has increased as follows:

Year	Entry-level salary	Housing allowance	Cost-of-living allowance	Total entry-level salary
Nov. 1, 1900	1,600	(20%) 320	0	1,920
After Nov. 1, 1900	1,600	(30%) 480	0	2,080
After Jan. 1, 1906	1,600	(30%) 480	(10%) 208	2,288
After Nov. 1, 1911	1,600	(40%) 640	(15%) 336	2,576

In addition, after 1906, the civil servants were granted salary increases every three years instead of the previous four years, and after 1910, each salary bracket was increased by K 50, an adjustment that is not shown in the above table.

Comparison of the Starting Salaries for Civil Servants
with Secondary-School Diplomas and for Law Clerks

| | | | Total starting salary | |
Year starting base salary	Servant	Law clerk	Civil servant	Law clerk
1904	1,600	2,000	2,080	2,600
1910	1,600	1,800	2,288	2,574
1912	1,600	1,600	2,576	2,576

Increase in the Salaries of Civil Servants with Secondary-School Diplomas,
and Decrease in Earnings of Law Clerks, Expressed in Percentages

| | Starting salary | | Total starting salary | |
Year	Civil servant, increase	Law clerk, decrease	Civil servant, increase	Law clerk, decrease
1910 vs. 1904	+0%	10%	+10%	1%
1912 vs. 1904	+0%	20%	+20%	1%

As these figures clearly show, the law clerk—who is generally classified
at the very least in category X, even in the admittedly low-paying government service—has been demoted in the Institute to the level of a civil servant with only a secondary-school diploma, or category XI.

The unjustifiably low position of the undersigned and his closest colleagues in the matter of salary becomes even more apparent when you
consider that, conversely, the Institute has established a starting salary of K
2,400 or K 2,800 for the official position of civil servant with only a
secondary-school diploma. This is a salary, in other words, reached only in
category X in government service, and then only after several years of employment in that category; the necessary previous experience is not at issue
in this comparison, since law clerks must complete a longer apprenticeship
in the Institute before they can be appointed to the position of law
clerk—unless, that is, they cannot give proof of previous experience. The
material situation of the undersigned is as unfortunate as that calculated in
the comparison with the other salary levels within the Institute when his
salary is compared to that of a law clerk in other public services and in our
sister institutes. Conditions in the Royal Bohemian Crownland Committee
and its institutes in Prague would offer the closest comparison to the situation in other public services, because this authority is also a public body,

on the one hand, and its location and the territory it covers are the same as those of the Institute, on the other. At present, the situation at the k.k. Office of the Governor need not be examined in detail because—as the government has openly recognized—the earnings of government employees do not reflect currently rising costs, and the law regarding employment regulations and the promotion schedule, which revises the earnings of government employees, has not yet been passed.

	Starting base salary of law clerks		Total starting salary of law clerks	
Year	In Crownland committee	In Institute	In Crownland committee	In Institute
1910	2,400	1,800	3,120	2,574
1912	3,000	1,600	3,900	2,576
Increase	20%	11%	20%	0%

After three years of employment as a law clerk, the situation is as follows:

Employer	Base salary	Total salary	Title
Crownland committee	3,600	4,680	Vice-Secretary
Institute	2,350	3,783	Law clerk

A comparison with the corresponding salaries at those sister institutes that have supplied us with the applicable data yields the following:

Minimum Salary of a Law Clerk at the Accident Insurance Institute

In:	Base salary	Housing allowance	Regular cost-of-living adjustment	Total
Graz	2,200	768	260+300	3,528
Brünn*	2,400	720	360	3,480
Salzburg	2,200	960	300	3,460
Prague	1,600	640	336	2,576

*Our colleagues in Brünn receive an additional special allowance of K 200 or K 150 per year (thus totaling 3,680 or K 3,630). As of January 1, 1913, the Brünn Institute begins a general salary adjustment, which is not included here.

After some years on the job, the salary chart looks as follows:

	After no. of years	Base salary	Housing allowance	Cost-of-living adjustment	Total salary	Title
Graz	3	2,800	960	280+300	4,340	Commissioner
Salzburg	3	2,800	1200	300	4,300	Commissioner
Brünn	1	2,800	840	420	4,060	Vice-Secretary
Prague	almost 3	2,350	940	493	3,783	(unchanged) Law clerk

The difference between the lowest salary for a law clerk in Prague and the highest in Graz thus amounts to nearly K 1,000. The above table shows that after three years of service, the difference—quite aside from the superior conditions at the Brünn Institute—still amounts to K 600. In the following table, the undersigned respectfully further points out the difference between the lowest base salaries of the office staff and those of the civil servants with secondary-school diplomas in various posts:

Type of service	Civil servant with secondary-school diploma	Office staff	Difference in K	in %
Government service	1,600	2,200	600	37.5%
Crownland committee	2,000	3,000	1,000	50%
Mortgage bank	1,800	3,000	1,200	66.66%
Accident Insurance Institute, Prague	1,600	1,600	0	0%

Because of the above-described conditions, the undersigned has labored under a significant economic disadvantage. Past shortcomings can no longer be remedied, and the future can be improved only by a truly effective adjustment that fully takes into account all the crucial factors listed here.

The undersigned therefore most respectfully requests the esteemed Board of Directors effectively to adjust his salary and title in a way that places him on a level in both respects with his closest colleagues in the Royal Bohemian Crownland Committee. With regard to the salary adjustment, he requests that the base salary be seen as the crucial element, since it is the only element that distinguishes the civil servants from one another by category and title, while the so-called secondary earnings, which are relatively identical for all civil servants, are intended merely to add to the base salary in order to compensate for the increases in the cost of living. In the Royal Bohemian Crownland Committee in Prague, a staff member is appointed to the position of Vice-Secretary, with a base salary of K 3,600, after three years of work as a law clerk. Accordingly, the undersigned respectfully requests the honorable Board of Directors to assign him to the first salary bracket of category III (K 3,600) of the salary scale for the Institute's civil servants and give him the title of Vice-Secretary or Commissioner (as in our sister institutes in Graz and Salzburg).

Prague, December 11, 1912

Dr. Franz Kafka, law clerk at the Institute

D. Letter to the Workmen's Accident Insurance Institute in Prague (Prague, Wednesday, January 27, 1915)

Esteemed Board of Directors of the Workmen's Accident Insurance Institute for the Kingdom of Bohemia in Prague:

The undersigned once again respectfully submits the request he first submitted two years ago for an adjustment in his earnings; at that time, his request was granted only in part. He respectfully requests that the same plea may now be granted, for reasons that have arisen in the meantime and are described in detail in the following.

There is no need to list once more the figures compiled for the earlier request. The current request to substitute the previous application—which asked that the undersigned be moved to salary bracket 1 of category III—with an application that he be assigned to salary bracket 2 of category III is based on the fact that two further years in the same position have passed. The honorable Board of Directors may want to note that an automatic increase in the base salary of K 600 is granted the law clerks employed by the Royal Bohemian Crownland Committee.

Special emphasis should be placed on one fact that the undersigned first noted two years ago: a striking disparity exists between his earnings and those of both the secretaries on the one hand and his less-experienced colleagues on the other—a disparity based neither on the number of years of employment nor on the type of work performed.

In order to alleviate this disparity, the undersigned requests

1. classification in the second salary bracket of the third category;

2. the same attention given to this request for promotion as was granted his less-experienced colleagues beginning on January 1, 1915,

keeping in mind that the salary adjustment of 1913 became effective on the same date for the undersigned as it did for those gentlemen.
Prague, January 27, 1915
Dr. Franz Kafka
Vice-Secretary of the Institute

E. Letter to the Workmen's Accident Insurance Institute in Prague
(Prague, Monday, February 5, 1917)

Esteemed Board of Directors:

The undersigned respectfully submits to the esteemed Board of Directors a request for appointment as Secretary along with a corresponding adjustment of his salary, for the following reasons:

As the Institute's affairs grow and new problems and new lines of work arise, new and increased demands are made, especially of the law clerks; the undersigned has always done his best to deal with them.

Furthermore, the present request conforms with the previous position of the esteemed Board, which has been pleased to grant appointments to the position of secretary six years after granting appointments to the position of law clerk. Seven years have now passed since the undersigned received his appointment to the position of law clerk. Finally, the undersigned respectfully points out the extraordinary increase in the cost of living, which inexorably forces him to make this request.

Trusting that the esteemed Board will not ignore these reasons, the undersigned requests that it may be pleased to appoint him to the position of secretary and promote him to the fourth bracket of the third salary classification.

Dr. Franz Kafka
Prague, February 5, 1917

Commentary 11

༄

K afka's correspondence with his employer was dominated by letters asking for a raise until the spring of 1917, when, after he
suffered the outbreak of tuberculosis in the late summer of that
year, they were replaced by letters requesting leave. We include Kafka's
five letters asking for raises, written between 1910 and 1917, for the
light they shed on Kafka's specific position within the Prague Institute.
Two features of these letters are especially remarkable.

Although the promotion of Austrian public servants was highly stan-
dardized, Kafka's career advanced at a significantly slower pace than
that of his colleagues. As the letters show, this imbalance was not merely
limited to a period of time but continued over the entire Hapsburg period of his career. We can safely conclude that this delay was just one
more instance of discrimination against Jews in the Empire's public service. In the letter of 1915, we read Kafka's somewhat cryptic remark
that

> a striking disparity exists between his earnings and those of both the secre-
> taries on the one hand and his less-experienced colleagues on the other—a
> disparity based neither on the number of years of employment nor on the
> type of work performed.

This claim seems to imply that Kafka was well aware of the actual reason but preferred to leave it unstated.

The long letter of December 1912 points to a different aspect of the
covertly political mode of writing Kafka was compelled to develop in his
job. This letter has been read through the lens of his personal situation
as an expression of his dissatisfaction with his job and, again, as a
timely attempt to rise to a position and wage level worthy of Felice
Bauer's future fiancé. Because of Kafka's seeming impatience, as one
critic has suggested, Kafka's superiors would fulfill his request only at a
later date and only in part.[1] In fact, the matter is more intricate—and
more interesting.

On the afternoon of January 9, 1912, the Verein der deutschen
Beamten der Arbeiter-Unfallversicherungsanstalt (Society of German
Officials of the Workmen's Accident Insurance Institute) was consti-
tuted, with Franz Kafka and his next-door office mate, the statistician
Alois Gütling, as treasurers. The formation of this association might be

considered a reaction to the Czech staff's establishing its own group the previous year, a sign of the national conflict paralyzing Austrian social policy in the prewar period. At the same time, both bodies may be seen as symptoms of the growing political consciousness of public servants all over Europe—that is, the so-called *Beamtenfrage* (the problem of officialdom). True, it was with the provision that it "not engage in political activities" that the German group's official agenda was conceived: it aimed to represent the interests of its members, advance their professional skills, and improve their economic condition by other means. But this explicit expression of obedience to the Hapsburg state, its employer, was also in the best interests of the German staff, whose dominant position over the Czech's depended on preserving the political status quo. Kafka's remarkable letter pleading for a raise demonstrates the manner in which this somewhat paradoxical mission—of representing group interests without taking political action—was carried out.

Kafka's letter formally makes the case of the individual petitioner but is political from first line to last. The opening paragraph mentions the increased cost of living, which in the prewar years had a depressing effect especially on public servants, who had received only small wage increases. But while the letter readily acknowledges the Institute's general attempt to deal with this situation, this attitude quickly turns out to be a mere *captatio benevolentiae*. What follows is the precise and relentless reconstruction of the gross imbalance in the wage dynamics of the specific group of clerks to which Kafka belonged—that is, the *Concipisten*, or law clerks.

Two aspects of the letter should be highlighted: (1) The detailed statistical data—not only for the Institute, but also for other public institutions—were probably made available to Kafka by the Verein der deutschen Beamten. (2) The injustice he complains of is not presented as bearing on his own case alone. This fact creates a remarkable contrast with Kafka's other letters on the same subject. Nowhere in this letter do Kafka's detailed accounts compare his own salary and advancement record with those of his Prague colleagues. Instead, he makes comparisons (a) with other staff ranks in the Prague Institute; (b) with the same rank (that of law clerks) in the sister institutes; and (c) with equivalent ranks in similar institutions. Whatever Kafka's personal motives in asking for promotion and a raise, it is clear that his letter makes the case for an entire group of clerks. Hence, the seemingly arbitrary point of reference in his request to:

> the esteemed Board of Directors effectively to adjust his salary and title in a way that places him on a level in both respects with his closest colleagues in the Royal Bohemian Crownland Committee.

As a result, the Board of Directors could hardly have complied with his request without acknowledging Kafka's general line of argument with regard to promotions and raises for all law clerks. This, and not their dissatisfaction with an "impatient" young clerk, was the reason the Board turned down Kafka's request or, rather, granted it only partially a few months later, in March 1913, by promoting him to Vice-Secretary.

Very much like his accounts of the conflicts between employers and the Institute over risk classification, Kafka's long letter of December 1912 makes a political claim without a single allusion to the class struggle. And like so many of the earlier appeals, this conflict over conditions of employment resonates with Kafka's literary writings. While Kafka's letter to the Board of Directors argues that the Institute's wage policies "have demoted [the official of his rank, the law clerk with academic education] in the Institute to the level of a civil servant with only a secondary-school diploma," his "American" hero Karl Rossmann seems to reflect this degradation when, toward the end of an ever-declining career in the New World, he introduces himself to the Nature Theater of Oklahoma as a former "European secondary-school student." Although this providential institution promises to put an end to all social competition and exclusion, its offices are located on a race track. Upon declaring his educational status, Karl is directed to "a booth on the outermost verge, not only smaller but also lower than all the others," foretelling his continual decline in the course of the—unfinished—novel.

12

CRIMINAL CHARGE AGAINST JOSEF RENELT FOR THE ILLEGAL WITHHOLDING OF INSURANCE FEES (1913)

෬

Renelt, the owner of a small quarry and apple orchard in a little village near Aussig in northern Bohemia, is a namesake of Renell, a character in Kafka's America novel The Man Who Disappeared. *Both are explicitly characterized as rogues attempting to skirt the law for their own amusement. For ten years, Renelt refused to pay insurance fees for his quarry workers, claiming that they were employed only as orchard workers. In 1913, he was finally taken to criminal court in Aussig, with Kafka representing the Institute at the trial. The case was lost in court but not in historical memory. It leaves its traces in Kafka's letters to Felice, his fiancée, who was living in Berlin, and thereafter in the Institute's archive in Prague, giving us further insight into the complex web of Kafka's professional duties.*

A. District Court of Aussig: Decision in the Renelt Case (May 15, 1913)

In the Name of His Majesty the Kaiser:

The k. k. District Court of Aussig, Department IX, today held a final hearing in the case brought by the prosecutor against Josef Franz Renelt for crimes against property, according to § 197, 461, Penal Code. Present at the hearing were the public prosecutor, Anton Fechtner; the defendant Josef Franz Renelt, who is not in custody; defense counsel, Dr. Gustav Kahn, attorney-at-law in Aussig; and Dr. Franz Kafka, Vice-Secretary of the Workmen's Accident Insurance Institute, representing that Institute, which has a private interest in the matter. After today's hearing, conducted in response to the prosecutor's request for legal judgment and the petition of the privately interested party for indemnification of K 68 and the petition of defense counsel for acquittal of the charge and for ordering the accusing party to bear all expenses according to § 390 St. P. O., the court finds as follows:

The Defendant
 Josef Franz Renelt
 52 years of age, Catholic, married, owner of a quarry in Pömmerle, is acquitted according to § 259 Zl 3, Code of Criminal Procedure, of the charge that in the first half of the year 1911 he misled the Workmen's Accident Insurance Institute for the Kingdom of Bohemia through deceptive actions, namely, by paying out wages of K 1,542. 77 in his sandstone quarry in Pömmerle during that period, yet declaring paid wages of only K 266.40, as a result of which the above-named Institute allegedly sustained damages not exceeding K 200 and in fact did sustain damages in the amount of K 68, and that the defendant thereby committed fraud according to § 461 Penal Code.

In accordance with § 360, Code of Criminal Procedure, the Workmen's Accident Insurance Institute for the Kingdom of Bohemia in Prague is referred to the civil court to press its claim.

Grounds for the decision:
 Based on the statements of the witnesses Franz Richter, Heinrich Pieschel, Clemens Schmidt, Heinrich Puschmann, Franz Heller, Wenzel Hamprecht, and Josef Franze as they relate to the defendant Josef Franz Renelt's defense, the court was unable to accept as proven the facts as detailed in the findings.

The witness Julius Schönfeld stated that he was sent to Kleinpriesen as the authorized representative of the Workmen's Accident Insurance Institute for the Kingdom of Bohemia in Prague to meet with the former quarry foreman of the defendant's business, Franz Richter, in order to investigate the defendant's accident-insurance premium payments. He testified that Franz Richter gave him his record book, which listed wages paid to the quarry workers from January 7 to May 6, 1911, and indicated that the defendant's above-named firm paid out wages in the amount of K 1,542.17 [sic] in the first half of 1911. When questioned, Franz Richter confirmed that these wages were paid out in the quarry, as Schönfeld noted in his deposition. He then established, through statements by Heinrich Puschmann, Klemens Schmidt, and Franz Heller, that the defendant's orchard and fields were not within the confines of the quarry and that only K 266.40 in wages could be assigned to work done in the quarry during the first half of 1911, while all other wages were said to have been paid out for work done in the defendant's orchard and fields.

However, the three above-named witnesses confirmed that a calculation of 300 work shifts per year for work in the orchard and fields was a highly optimistic guess on the part of the defendant.

Schönfeld indicated that he also noted these statements in the record and communicated the matter to the Workmen's Accident Insurance Institute for the Kingdom of Bohemia in Prague, which denounced the defendant.

Schönfeld stated that he became convinced that if the defendant—who must surely acknowledge that the above-cited circumstances are correct—declared, or ordered declared, the sum of K 266.40 for the first half of 1911 as the amount of wages subject to accident-insurance premiums, this statement did not correspond to the truth. Schönfeld also based this hunch on the fact that a short while thereafter, when the Institute laid the charge against the defendant, Franz Richter sent a letter to the Institute demanding the return of the book in which he recorded paid wages; the handwriting of the letter, however, was very similar to that of the defendant.

The charges made by the Workmen's Accident Insurance Institute, based on the facts as determined by the witness Julius Schönfeld, state only that the defendant's firm was classified as having a premium rate of K 5.33 per K 100 of applicable wages, resulting in a difference of K 68 compared to the amount actually paid by the defendant and amounting to the loss the Institute claims to have suffered during this billing period.

The defendant Josef Franz Renelt denies all guilt and defends himself by citing the facts that his business employs not only quarry workers but other workers as well, that these workers also help out in the fields and the orchard, and that when it comes to compulsory insurance, he declares only that part of the wages that are actually paid to the quarry workers, so that the declared wages of K 266.40 is entirely truthful.

All the witnesses who testified not only confirmed the defendant's argument but also completely refuted the statements made by the witness Julius Schönfeld.

The witness Heinrich Puschmann, for example, stated that he knew nothing whatever about field work and that he relied on the estimates of Klemens Schmidt; the witness Franz Heller signed the deposition without reading it.

These witnesses, as well as the witness Klemens Schmidt, stated that they told Julius Schönfeld at the time of his investigation that the defendant employs four workers for three months to work in the defendant's fields, which would amount, not to 300, but to at least 360 working shifts, covering only the harvest.

Further, these witnesses indicated that their statements covered only the possible employment of field workers, but that they could not offer a precise figure, nor did they claim that the workdays for the defendant's fields were estimated generously, but rather that they considered them correct to the best of their knowledge and that Julius Schönfeld's testimony on this point was therefore, in all probability, incorrect.

The witness Franz Richter next stated that he did not give Julius Schönfeld his actual wage-record book but only three or four of the notebooks with his jottings and that he had told Julius Schönfeld that he, as foreman, had paid out the wages from January 7 to May 6, 1911, and not that the work had been performed only in the quarry; rather, he had told Schönfeld that the workers Klein, Franze, and Hamprecht had also been sent to work in the fields. It was true, Franz Richter agreed, that Julius Schönfeld took notes and read them aloud, whereupon he, Richter, signed the paper, but he stated that he was unable to make out the context and that, in particular, he overlooked the fact that the record contained the statement: "I make available to the Institute these records, which list only and exclusively wages paid quarry workers and stonemasons for work performed in the quarry for the time period from January 7 to May 6, 1911." He could not confirm this point because it would have been incorrect, nor did he desire to confirm that he had made the records available, because he would have needed the book the following day.

The defendant had no way of knowing for what kind of work the wages were paid, since often he was away and had to rely on what Richter told him. Richter also claims not to have told Renelt that only some of the wages were paid for work in the quarry and the remainder for other kinds of work.

Richter also testified that he had not pressed Julius Schönfeld to take the record book but that on the following day the book had disappeared, and that was the reason he commissioned the teacher Adam Schückel to write a letter to Julius Schönfeld asking for the return of the book, because it had been surreptitiously taken from him and removed from his possession without his permission.

The witness Adam Schückel also fully confirmed Richter's statement regarding the letter, so that there were no longer grounds for accusing the defendant of having written the letter to the Institute. The witness Heinrich Püschel further testified that the quarry is not worked every day and that the quarry workers are also used in the fields; they are therefore day laborers, since they were paid no matter where they worked.

The witness Wenzel Hamprecht confirmed that he worked in the quarry only occasionally and that his principal employment with the defendant was in the fields. The witness Josef Franze stated that the defendant had him work both in the quarry and in the fields and the orchard more or less equally, as was also true for the worker Klein, and that aside from Richter, only he, Franze, and Klein were employed as workers, and that the defendant employed no other workers.

On the one hand, the statements of these witnesses make it sufficiently clear that Julius Schönfeld's testimony is based on incorrect assumptions that arose during his investigation, so that his credibility appears completely in doubt.

On the other hand, all the witnesses confirm the defendant's defense, most particularly his statement that he did not knowingly provide a lower figure of paid wages for compulsory insurance than he was obligated to declare according to the extent and operation of his quarry.

Since there seems no proof that fraud was committed, the defendant was acquitted in accordance with § 259 Z. 3, Code of Criminal Procedure.

Aussig, May 15, 1913.
Dr. Roth m. p.
Suppan m. p.

B. Workmen's Accident Insurance Institute to the Office of the Governor in Prague: Statement on the appeal to the official in charge against Controller Schönfeld; Enclosure: Record of the examination of the foreman Franz Richter (June 25, 1913)

Prague, June 25, 1913
Josef Franz Renelt in Pömmerle,
Quarry
Insurance premiums
Enclosures

To the esteemed k. k. Office of the Governor in Prague:
Before addressing the details of the various items of the appeal under consideration, we must begin by noting that the behavior of this quarry owner has compelled the Institute from the beginning of his business to determine the amount of insurance premiums the Institute is required by law to collect. The Institute had no other recourse but to resort to direct inspection of wages paid and other forms of investigation. This situation arose because of the employer's incomplete and, as he himself has admitted, random wage declarations and of the equally admitted extreme

disorder that reigns, at least outwardly, in his various statements of account, both those rendered to the Institute and those given to the health-insurance institute.

We respectfully add the following details that pertain to the appeal under adjudication:

I. The case in question, for which a copy of the sworn deposition by the Institute's controller is enclosed, was not in any way an inspection of the business. Rather, it was simply an investigation of the wage situation "on site," which the Institute is legally entitled to carry out according to § 23 of the accident-insurance law. In many different cases, it becomes necessary to begin the investigation, not at the main office of the business—in this case with Renelt in Pömmerle—but at the employer's nearest work site—in this case, with the foreman at the quarry. As we have noted, we certainly have this legal right. The practical reason entitling us to proceed rests on the fact that everyone is concerned to conduct an investigation without the employer's exerting his influence, since in many instances, workers are notoriously dependent on their employer, and this effect can be reflected in statements taken down in evidence. Additionally, in the specific case, it is more likely that wage records will be found at the quarry; or it may be that no wage lists are kept at all, so that we must rely on the statements of the quarry foreman. Furthermore, § 23 offers no provision whatever to the effect that such on-site investigations must be conducted in the presence of the employer himself or that the employer must be informed or even that his consent must be obtained. We will cite only the findings of the k. k. Administrative Court of January 31, 1896, [. . .] among other judicial rulings.

II. The above remarks infer that the records can be requested, not only of the employer himself, but also of anyone entrusted with overseeing the business as intended by § 23. The employer himself is irrelevant in such investigations because the matter in question does not involve legally binding statements by the employer but only the determination of the actual circumstances as learned from the records of the business, though these may of course be supplemented and clarified by interviews.

III. As far as the record book of wages kept by former quarry foreman Franz Richter is concerned, it merely aided in setting the premium, which had to be determined "on the basis of other investigations," since there were no usable wage lists in the sense of § 1, par. 7, of the law of February 8, 1909. [. . .] The enclosed copy of the minutes taken by the Institute's controller on December 13, 1912, in his meeting with Franz Richter is correct and complete, except that the closing expression, "Read and declared correct," is missing, as are the signatures of Franz Richter and the Institute's controller. This record was not, as the appeal claims, submitted to the communal authority in Pömmerle for signed certification, so that the record could be certified in its entirety by the authority. Such certification would, of course, have been both impossible and pointless, nor was it required. Rather, the Institute's controller sent a letter to the Pömmerle authorities on December 17, 1912, asking for confirmation of a copy of this record; the controller expressly noted that he was concerned "only with confirmation [. . .] that the working conditions described by Franz Richter reflect the true state of affairs."

It is true that, subsequently, Franz Richter retracted the statements placed in the record when he became a witness in the criminal proceeding against his employer for crimes against property. At this later time Richter testified that though the Institute's controller had, in fact, read the minutes to him, he had been unable to make sense of them, so that he did not know what it was that he actually signed.

IV. Richter did, in fact, maintain his previous statements with regard to the wage book, which the controller had seen at the quarry on November 25, 1912. The copy of the Institute's controller's deposition enclosed by the employer is incorrect in so far as the Institute controller stated that he had seen a "light-brown-marbled book, not a blue-marbled book." Furthermore, the Institute's controller states in his deposition that, while leafing through the book, the employer said, "Oh, these are just old records, from 1904," while in the enclosed copy the year 1905 is given. This discrepancy is significant, since the Institute's controller states that on November 26, 1912, instead of the light-brown-marbled book, mentioned above, which he saw very clearly and whose format and binding he (the son of a bookbinder) could assess very accurately, a black, or at least very dark, notebook of a completely different format and thickness was presented to him, which contained no records whatever for 1904.

V. During his deposition, the Institute's controller never expressed his suspicion that Franz Richter's letter of January 13, 1913, was written by the employer himself. As indicated in the two concluding paragraphs of the Institute's controller's deposition, a copy of which is enclosed, the controller merely stated that the handwriting in this letter is very like that of Renelt in the documents in the Institute's possession. This is in no way to say that the letter might have been written by Renelt; a striking similarity was pointed out between two handwriting samples found in two closely related documents. Thus all that was noted was the possibility that the same person—who certainly did not have to be the employer—could have written both documents.

Prague, June 25, 1913.
The Director:
(signed:) Dr. Marschner
Enclosures

Minutes taken on December 13, 1912

On this day, the sworn representative of the Workmen's Accident Insurance Institute called on me and asked me for the wage records I kept when I was foreman at the quarry and stone works of J. F. Renelt in Pömmerle.

Of the records I kept, I have in my possession only the quarry lists for the period January 7–June 6, 1911. According to this payment book, the following wages were paid out in the quarry and stone works of J. F. Renelt:

In January 1911, K 265.32; in February 1911, K 261.10; in March, K 190.91; in April, K 334.78; and on May 6, 1911, K 70.06.

In addition to these wages, I received a weekly salary of K 20 as quarry foreman; thus 18 weeks at K 20, or K 360, are added to the wages listed above. Further, a coachman was also employed at the quarry and stone works of J. F. Renelt for roughly two to three months a year.

I make these records available to the Institute. For the period January 7–May 6, 1911, they contain only and exclusively the list of wages paid to quarry workers and stonemasons for work performed at the quarry.

I am no longer in possession of additional records, and I declare that in the years 1901–1911 no work was performed in the quarry and stone works of J. F. Renelt during the fruit harvest and during hard frosts. Since the quarry workers were also employed for agricultural work in harvesting grain and hay, it is a fair assumption that all work in the quarry was always performed only during nine months of the year and that the average situation was as indicated in the record book presented in evidence. In each year during the nine months stated above, around three to five workers, or sometimes more, were employed in the quarry and stone works of J. F. Renelt, depending on the order book.

Read and declared correct:
Franz Richter by his own hand
Engineer Julius Schönfeld, sworn controller, by his own hand

C. Workmen's Accident Insurance Institute to the Office of the Governor in Prague: Statement on the Renelt Trial (June 28, 1913)

Prague, June 28, 1913
Josef Franz Renelt in Pömmerle
Accident-insurance premiums
Enclosures

Esteemed k. k. Office of the Governor in Prague:

I. Before the criminal proceedings against Renelt (a copy of the decision is enclosed), the Institute was in possession of the following information:

1. The employer declared paid out wages of K 266.40 for his sandstone quarry and stone works for the first six months of 1911. The fact that this declaration is incorrect follows from the comparisons cited below:

a. The health-insurance premiums of 4% for the regional health-insurance plan in Aussig amounted to K 68.88 in the first half of 1911; the theoretical sum of the wages would therefore be K 1,722.

b. The employer kept records of wages paid out in 1912. Actual wages paid from March to June 1912 were 32% higher than the wages subject to health insurance, according to the premiums for the corresponding months. Applying this ratio to the first half of 1911, the total wages at that time would have amounted to over K 2,200.

c. According to the wage records, the wages paid for piecework alone from March to June 1912—clearly, stonemasons' wages (daily wages are also paid in the quarry)—amount to 46% of wages, according to the health-insurance lists. Applying this ratio to the first half of 1911, stonemasons' wages alone would have amounted to K 800 at that time, or more than three times what was actually declared.

d. According to Franz Richter's record book, K 1,542.17 were paid out in the quarry in the period from January 7 to May 6, 1912 (the record book lists specific figures only for this period). According to the book, wages paid for piecework—thus, again, no doubt, stonemasons' wages—for these five months came to K 380.49, while the employer had declared only K 266.40 for piece work for the entire six months.

e. The quarry foreman Franz Richter drew a weekly wage of K 20, and occasionally more, in 1911. His wages alone would thus have amounted to over K 500 in the first half of 1911.

2. Furthermore, the Institute had the use of Franz Richter's book recording paid wages. According to the statement of the Institute's

controller, Engineer Julius Schönfeld, when he submitted the record (a copy of which is enclosed), Franz Richter had made this record available to the Institute.

3. The Institute initiated investigations regarding the extent of Renelt's activities in fields and orchards. By questioning the Pömmerle authorities, we learned that the employer's total agricultural operation encompassed only 31 yoke, 390 fathoms [ca 44.4 acres—Ed.]; furthermore, most of this land—16 yoke by 586 fathoms [ca. 23.3 acres—Ed.]—is forest land, so that the business in its entirety might be regarded as medium-sized; considering the small dimensions of the cultivated land, however, it must be regarded as a small business. This status was confirmed by an official statement from the Pömmerle authorities on December 14, 1912, which is cited word for word in the appellant's petition. Thus, the extent of the orchard business appears to be completely established, though we should stress that the extent of the field work, and especially work in forestry, can have no immediate and important significance for the criminal proceedings, since, strictly speaking, only the time from January 7 to May 6, 1912, is in question—a period of time, then, in which the least amount of field work and almost no orchard work was performed.

II. In order to characterize the difficulties in determining the wages paid by this firm, the following must be emphasized:

1. In dealing with this business, the Institute has always been compelled by the absence of reliable wage lists and declarations to determine the amounts due by doing extensive checks on paid wages, investigations, and scrutiny.

2. The employer makes a habit of referring to the carelessness that prevails in bookkeeping in his business, and he does so in the criminal proceeding as well. He thus implicitly admits that the information he provides is only approximate, nor did he during the criminal proceedings precisely indicate the calculations or records that formed the basis for his declaration for the first half of 1911. During the preliminary hearing, he even conceded that he could not dispute the possibility of an incorrect declaration. He further stated in the preliminary hearing that in the first half of 1911 "absolutely no more than 165 days of work were performed in the sandstone quarry. If these days are calculated at an average of K 3.10, you will get the declared amount." But that calculation is incorrect, because the total would be K 511.

3. The employer gave an incorrect figure even for the health-insurance premiums, so that, according to the health-insurance data, the theoretical wages would also have to be higher. In 1910, for example, he employed the workers Franz Klein, Josef Franze, and Franz Püschel, whose

names also appeared in the copies of wage list for 1910 that the employer subsequently submitted; according to these lists, 30 hellers were deducted weekly from each for health insurance. However, they were not registered with the health-insurance institute in 1910, any more than they were in 1911.

4. The report by the Institute's controller on the wage inspection conducted on November 25, 1912, shows the difficulties that had to be overcome in the immediate inspection of the wages in this business. We will cite only the following characteristic passage from this report: "The proprietor, who insisted in his apartment in Pömmerle that he did not have the wage book at home, was eager to check if the book we wanted to see might perhaps be in the quarry, and had a locked chest opened for this purpose. In this chest we observed among other items a book approximately 1½ cm thick, with a light-brown marbled hard cover. The employer picked up this book, leafed through it, and said: 'Oh, these are just some old records from 1904.' Since an official action by the k. k. district authorities in Aussig regarding the Institute's provisions for the business of J. F. Renelt for the premium periods from the second half of 1901 to the first half of 1905 was scheduled for the following day—November 26, 1912—I was interested in this book; and since I had seen that piecework wages and other records important to the official action were listed in this book, I insisted that I be granted a look at it, and I referred to my authority as a <u>sworn representative of the Institute. Though the employer acceded to my wish, he was so agitated that he was shaking, and he held the book by its covers with both hands, so that I could only leaf through it hurriedly. Since I feared that his agitation, as well as that of the quarry foreman (we were alone in the wooden shack at the quarry), might degenerate into something worse and that they might not be able to control themselves toward me, I gave up for the moment using the book for the purpose of establishing wages.</u>"

III. The criminal proceeding itself, insofar as it concerned the Institute's evidence, had the following results:

1. Franz Richter largely retracted the statements he had made in his deposition (a copy of which is enclosed) by declaring that the Institute's controller had indeed read his record aloud to him but that he had been unable to make sense of it, so that he did not know what he actually signed.

2. As is indicated by the wording of the depositions cited in the appeal under adjudication, the witnesses from the Pömmerle authorities—Heinrich Puschmann, Klemens Schmidt, and Franz Heller—modified their statements to the effect that

(a) the facts they had testified to were not certain but only possible; (b) they took into account all work, not only harvest work but also field and orchard work (from January to May, or the time to which Richter's wage book refers), pruning bushes, fruit trees, and forest trees and sowing and cultivating the fields; however, they provided information only to the effect that four workers were engaged for three full months, a time span that does not equal 256 work shifts, but at least 360.

3. The decision rendered by the k. k. Regional Court in Aussig, Dept. IX, on May 15, 1913, U IX 51/13–18, in listing its grounds, explicitly stated that the Institute's controller can in no way be held responsible for these changes in the depositions and the change, in part related to the foregoing, in the significance of the evidence. "[. . .] Julius Schönfeld is not to blame for the fact that the record on which the penal charge was based included information that later proved to be incorrect; instead, it was only through the negligence of the above-named witnesses in signing the minutes that the inaccuracies and errors in Julius Schönfeld's investigation were authenticated."

IV. The Institute's evidence remaining valid after the criminal proceeding, insofar as it was influenced by the criminal proceedings:

1. Most importantly, we must insist on the fact that, if legally prescribed wage lists are not available, it is impossible to arrive at a reliably precise list of wages. Instead, we are restricted to trying for the most accurate possible approximation. Paragraph 7 of § 1 of the compulsory wage-list law states that if the employer does not meet the regulations for compulsory wage lists, an official assumption made on the basis of other investigations can be contested only if it is based on the nonapplication or incorrect application of the law or on obviously incorrect factual stipulations. In the latter case, that is, it can be contested legally only if the closest possible approximation to the facts that can no longer be precisely established was not arrived at under the given circumstances.

2. The Institute tried to achieve a close approximation of this kind, first by securing a book in which wages were recorded and whose general correctness could not be disproved in the course of criminal proceedings (in fact, the three wage sheets presented by the employer increased the book's evidentiary value because of their agreement with its data). Second, the Institute obtained the expert opinions of three members of the local council so as to be able to evaluate the employer's field and orchard business. This latter information remains unquestioned after the criminal proceedings, since the Institute was aware from the outset that what it had been given were not certain but only possible data, and since the principal witness, Klemens Schmidt, supported these possible data in the criminal proceedings.

3. The Institute considered it important to compensate for all possible sources of error from the beginning, aware that the supplementary payments were calculated only with approximate figures, especially since the employer himself had not provided a helpful way to arrive at precise figures, even in the course of criminal proceedings, and the method he had chosen for his previous declarations was not based on figures. The Institute's efforts at achieving some reconcilable figures consisted of calculating the supplementary payment as favorably as possible for the employer, even at the risk of losing a part of the claims, which are surely justified. That is, in calculating the supplementary payment, we assumed that no work was done in the quarry and stone works in December, January, and February, and that therefore no health-insurance premiums would be charged for this period. We established this fiction in spite of the fact that Richter's record book showed quarry work for January and February, even and particularly piecework. Further, wages for the month of December are shown in the copies of the wage list for the second half of 1910 that were later produced. Finally, accidents had previously occurred in the quarry during these months, most notably accidents involving Wenzel Püschel on January 14, 1898, and Eduard Hanke on January 22, 1902. This fiction worked entirely to the employer's advantage. The following calculation shows how it reduced the supplementary payment: For December, January, and February of each year in the period in question from the second half of 1909 to the first half of 1912, health-insurance premiums were deducted from the start. They amounted to K 18.02 in the second half of 1909, to K 63.48 in both half-years of 1910, to K 38.03 and K 25.94 in the first half of 1912, for a total of K 145.47. At the premium rate of 4% set by the health-insurance institute, these amounts correspond to a theoretical wage total of K 3,636.75; with the adjustment rectification by an additional charge of 29%—a sum of K 1,054.66—the total of wages was K 4,691.41. This total was simply disregarded in calculating the supplementary payment in the employer's favor and to compensate for possible sources of error. In the face of this sum, of course, the objection that the local council members claimed that 360 work shifts must be applied to field work, though the minutes reveal that they considered 300 shifts sufficient, carries no weight. For 60 work shifts at a daily wage of K 3.35, total only K 200 per year, or K 600 for the six half-year periods in question. Apart from the facts that the employer's property amounts to only around 17 acres cultivated land and that the figures provided by the local council members are clearly described as approximate (both rounded up and rounded down), the difference of K 600, compared to the wage total of K 4,691, excluded in the employer's favor, appears insignificant and largely compensated for.

4. Finally, we will once more respectfully point out that the employer has failed to raise an objection to the supplementary payment and that it has thus become legally binding.

The Director:
(Signed:) Dr. Marschner

D. Renelt to the Office of the Governor: Comment on the Statements of the Workmen's Accident Insurance Institute to His Complaint to the Official in Charge (August 14, 1913)

With regard to the statements issued by the Workmen's Accident Insurance Institute for the Kingdom of Bohemia on June 25, 1913, and June 28, 1913, I respectfully offer the following comments:

My appeals of March 21 and June 7, 1913, are complaints against the conduct of a public official or disciplinary charges against the controller of the Workmen's Accident Insurance Institute, Mr. Julius Schönfeld, engineer. These charges accuse him of performing the duties of his office in a manner contrary to regulations, incorrectly documenting facts established in performing the duties of his office, and uttering unfounded suspicions.

I have proven these accusations in the enclosed complaints; surely it would be hard to misunderstand them. The statements of the Workmen's Accident Insurance Institute are largely concerned with the factual side of the supplementary payment for the second half of 1911, without actually disproving or being able to disprove the substance of the complaint.

Even had my wage declarations been incomplete and random and the Workmen's Accident Insurance Institute had therefore thought it necessary to determine the premiums actually owed by means of direct wage inspections and other scrutiny, such investigations would nevertheless have to be conducted only within the framework of the existing regulations and would not justify the investigating Institute's controller, Engineer Julius Schönfeld, compiling untruthful records, harboring groundless suspicions, and exceeding the authority of his office.

I thus maintain my complaint in its entirety and can only characterize the statements of the Workmen's Accident Insurance Institute as illogical and far-fetched in the extreme.

For example, the difference between "on-site investigations" and "inspection" is incomprehensible to me, in spite of the careful wording in the Workmen's Accident Insurance Institute's statement.

The Workmen's Accident Insurance Institute certainly has the right to conduct "investigations"; investigations on site, however, are always necessarily connected to the "inspection" of the business and are therefore permitted only when the owner of the business is present.

Considering that my quarry is located only a short distance from the village of Pömmerle and that I employ 4–5 workers there, the fine distinction between "main office" and "work site" elicits an involuntary smile.

The Workmen's Accident Insurance Institute's remarks passed completely over a number of facts, and these were never refuted, so that they must be considered to be truthful. These facts are that in the minutes of his interview with Franz Richter, Engineer Schönfeld included the remark that Richter had made his record book available to him; but Richter testified before the court that Engineer Schönfeld had misappropriated the book; Engineer Schönfeld let this testimony stand unchallenged; the witness Richter declared that the record kept by Engineer Schönfeld was incorrect and that he had never made such a statement for the record, nor did Engineer Schönfeld take steps against Richter on this count. When the claim is made that in his testimony, the Institute's controller, Engineer Schönfeld, never expressed the suspicion that I was the author of the letter dated January 13, 1913, instead of Franz Richter, and if this claim is intended to whitewash Engineer Schönfeld on this point, we can only call such an attempt a completely unsuccessful one, since it is clear from Engineer Schönfeld's testimony on this point that all he wanted was to place me under suspicion of being the letter's author. Whether or not my wage records or my declarations were materially correct is not the subject of my disciplinary charges, and however difficult the inquiries into the correctness of my premium returns might have been, Engineer Schönfeld, as I stated, had no right, as Franz Richter testified, to misappropriate the record book; Schönfeld had no right to place in his record the exact opposite of what Franz Richter and the information officers at the Pömmerle authority had told him about wage conditions; and Schönfeld had no right to express his suspicion that I, not Franz Richter, had written the letter of January 13, 1913, to the Workmen's Accident Insurance Institute. It seems all the more peculiar to me that the Workmen's Accident Insurance Institute's statement continues to refer to Franz Richter's wage record, although Richter testified that this book was unreliable as a source of information about wage conditions in my business, and when the Institute cites inquiries made with the Pömmerle authorities, although the inaccuracy of these inquiries has already been testified to by impeccable witnesses.

I am entering a petition to access the files of the k. k. District Court of Aussig concerning the decision of May 15, 1913; these will clearly show the blatant and outrageous actions of the Institute's controller, Engineer Julius Schönfeld.

Similarly, the reports of the Institute's controller, Engineer Schönfeld, are not sufficient to justify his actions, which have repeatedly been described, since the verdict of the k. k. District Court of Aussig, rendered on May 15, 1913, established by law that Engineer Schönfeld's statements are in no way credible. If the court accepts as proven by the evidence presented that Julius Schönfeld's records are inaccurate, then surely no credence can be given to Schönfeld's report regarding the wage inspection of November 25, 1912, another document he confirmed on the witness stand. The decision of the k. k. District Court of Aussig, Dept. IX, on May 15, 1913, states only that the inaccuracies and errors in Julius Schönfeld's records remain as they stand because the witnesses were negligent in signing; the cited passage of the District Court decision distinguishes precisely between inaccuracies and errors on the part of Julius Schönfeld.

To the extent that the statements of the Workmen's Accident Insurance Institute deal with justifying the inaccuracy of the supplementary payment for the first half of 1911, they lie outside the scope of my disciplinary charge, and since I have submitted a separate complaint in this matter, there is no reason for me to comment further.

I respectfully request that I be informed of the results of the disciplinary investigation, since it is my earnest intention to seek compensation in a civil court to recoup the great expenses I incurred as a result of Engineer Julius Schönfeld's actions, and since the wider public, and especially the relevant groups of employers, are interested in the outcome of these precedential proceedings.

Aussig, August 14, 1913
Josef Franz Renelt

Commentary 12

∽

In the accident-insurances files from the days of the Hapsburg monarchy found in the Czech national archives, the case of Josef Franz Renelt, owner of an orchard and a quarry in the northern Bohemian village of Pömmerle, ranks among the most protracted and voluminous, while the value in dispute amounts to an entirely negligible sum. In 1905, the Institute suspected Renelt of an "incomplete wage declaration" of the amount paid his workers, so that the declaration he submitted illegally reduced his accident-insurance premiums. When the Institute demanded supplementary payments based on health-insurance data, Renelt appealed to the Office of the Governor (1908) and to the Ministry of the Interior in Vienna (1909). The Institute, meanwhile, gathered additional evidence by interviewing Renelt's workers in the office of the mayor of Pömmerle. Renelt's appeal was rejected both times. He decided to take his case all the way to the top and appeal to the Administrative Court. In return, the Institute demanded additional supplementary payments for the five-year period from 1905 to 1909.

On October 14, 1910, the Administrative Court overruled the decision of the Vienna Ministry to turn down Renelt's appeal on procedural grounds. The reason for this decision points to a gray area in Austrian insurance law—an area responsible for many of the appeals Kafka dealt with: the piecemeal extension of compulsory insurance to the business firms of the Empire. Renelt's rural "firm" consisted of an orchard and a small quarry with stone works. It was even easier for him to take advantage of that fragmentation than it was for most of Kafka's insured employers.

Because of the hybrid and low-tech nature of his business—the quarry and stone works were subject to accident insurance, but the orchard was exempted, though the same workers were assigned to both operations—Renelt obviously would, and in the years before the mandatory wage-list law of 1909, easily could, attribute as much as possible of the wages he paid to the orchard. The Administrative Court ruled that the Institute had failed to establish with sufficient certainty "the ratio between the labor intensity of the orchard on the one hand and quarry and stone works on the other hand." However, the Institute gathered additional evidence against Renelt, including the case of a worker who claimed compensation for an accident suffered in the depth of winter, a period when, according to Renelt, both parts of his business were idle and no wages were paid. As a compromise, it offered a settlement, reducing Renelt's supplementary payments from K 890 to K 444.68.

On November 17, 1911, the Vienna ministry ruled this compromise to be legally binding, but Renelt filed another appeal to the Administrative Court. On September 30, 1912, the court again overruled the Ministry on the grounds of insufficient evidence. But the Institute was not prepared to give in. In November and December, it sent its controller, Julius Schönfeld, to Pömmerle for further investigations. Based on his findings, the Institute issued a third notification for supplementary payments for the period from the second half of 1909 to the second half of 1912. Renelt again contested Schönfeld's findings. The Institute finally decided to escalate the conflict. It filed criminal charges of insurance fraud. The amount in dispute (K 68) indicates that its motive was certainly not financial.

Since, within the legal frame of insurance law, the burden of proof for wage calculations rested with the insurance institutes unless the employer's wage declarations could be classified as fraudulent, the Prague Institute found itself obliged to proceed to criminal prosecution, with "Renelt" as a test case.

The Renelt case, marked by the defendant's stubborn resistance and transparently criminal intent, unmitigated by the slightest attempt to justify his behavior, yields rich information on the internal organization of the Institute and Kafka's role within it. By the time Kafka came on the scene, Renelt had succeeded in involving three major units in his case. The actuarial department was struggling to establish the wage basis for his insurance premiums, calculated from repeated investigations by the controls department, while the appeals department was busy producing legal opinions. The first of a number of remarks we find in Kafka's letters to Felice Bauer on the criminal procedures against Renelt furnishes clues to the nature of his involvement in the case. On March 26, 1913, after a visit to Berlin at Easter, Kafka wrote, "I am almost beside myself with sleepiness, exhaustion, and anxiety, and still have a big stack of files to study in preparation for tomorrow's proceedings in Aussig." The following morning, on his way from the Aussig railway station to the district court, he sent off greetings on a picture postcard to Berlin: "to start the day in Aussig with something worthwhile"; on another postcard, written that same evening, he summed up the day's events: "All successfully concluded, but I'm tired, and my head twitches" (LF 229, trans. modified).

These bulletins obviously refer to the "pretrial hearings" (doc. 12B), where Renelt "conceded that he could not dispute the possibility of an incorrect declaration." Kafka's protests about "stacks of files" that required preparation indicate that his involvement in this K 68 dispute was not as the head of the appeals department, where he was disputing cases involving hundreds of thousands of crowns. We may assume that the Institute deliberately entrusted its sharpest legal mind with the strategically significant mission of fighting this test case of wage-list fraud, although it would actually have been the responsibility of the actuarial department. On April 20, two days before the preliminary trial in Aussig, Kafka continued coquettishly to introduce into his wooing game a mixture of annoyance and pride in the trust placed in him: "Stayed in bed far too long, with the gloomiest thoughts, and I can't stop feeling a great distaste for all of the preparations, no matter how essential, for the court hearing in Aussig on Tuesday," he wrote to Berlin on Sunday morning, continuing in another letter written that same evening: "So now it's Sunday evening, just before bedtime, and nothing as yet ready for the Aussig trial, really, though I'll have hardly any time to take care of it in the morning, and though I should have a thousand details neatly arranged in my mind for this complicated pleading if I wish to appear in court with even the slightest hope of success, or at least some confidence that I won't be making a fool of myself. But I can't, I can't. Certainly, if it were only a question of studying the files, but between me and this task there are rocks to indicate my reluctance, and I would first have to clear these away" (LF 244, trans. modified). It does not, therefore, come as a surprise when, two days later, we see Kafka resorting to magic. His picture postcard, sent in the morning from Aussig to Berlin, notes, "One of the engineers from our institute, who is a witness at today's hearing while I'll be acting as a kind of prosecutor, is sitting opposite me and wants briefly to discuss a number of things; I insist, however, that I must first (at this moment he is reading to me) write a postcard, otherwise the trial is bound to turn out badly." But the postcards sent that evening add this ambiguous codicil: "It has turned out badly after all, though it's not quite over yet. What can you do, don't be mad at me, it's not my fault. And I don't really care, a letter is waiting for me in Prague, and that is all that matters" (LF 246, trans. modified). This laconic message once more exemplifies Kafka's technique of connecting different streams of writing and reference. It not only implies that the main trial on May 15 was lost for the Institute before it even began; it also anticipates the bottom line of July 12 of the following year, when Kafka and Felice Bauer dissolve their engagement in what would become known as "the tribunal in the hotel," while it leaves no doubt about the actual purpose behind describing these official and private scenes: to receive and to send letters, to continue the traffic of writing.

As far as the Aussig tribunal is concerned, the reasons for the verdict (doc. 12A) make clear why the Institute—and Kafka—never had a chance to win. The Institute's strategy of convicting Renelt of "deceptive actions" based on carefully prepared evidence failed even before the tribunal evaluated it. It collapsed at the threshold between oral and literal communication. In court, the witnesses who had been so carefully selected by Schönfeld claimed that their responses to the interviews were a result of misunderstandings, flawed memories, and some illiteracy (although signatures are found on the minutes of interviews that the undersigned claimed to have fully understood), so that eventually "his credibility appear[ed] to be completely doubtful." While Renelt may have taken advantage of this defect, the style and grammar of the written verdict (clearer in the German original) indicate that he and his workers had not made it up out of whole cloth.

The verdict of the district court was not the final episode in this picaresque case. Before the preliminary trial in Aussig, Renelt launched another counterattack (June 25, 1913, statement by the Institute to the Office of the Governor, doc. 12B). On March 21, Renelt had filed an appeal to the official in charge, blaming Schönfeld for interviewing Renelt's workers behind his back. The Institute distinguished an "inspection of the firm" (requiring due announcement) from "investigations on site," covered by § 23 of the accident-insurance law. The reason for such data raids highlights a significant difference between risk classification and wage control. In the former, immediate contact between employers and the Institute was the exception, not the rule. Relevant data were provided in questionnaires, forms, statistics, and trade inspectors' reports. In the latter, however, the physical underpinning of insurance data dominated. As the following two accounts of control visits show, the physical element might at times even manifest itself with a vengeance.

Three days later, on June 28, 1913, the Institute issued a detailed summary and evaluation of the Renelt trial in which it elaborated the difference between the mathematical and the physical aspects of insurance data. We can safely assume that Kafka was its author. His official responsibility for and knowledge of the matter are matched by the style and presentation of argument. Following a reconstruction of the available data, section II of the statement details the resistance the Institute met when trying to gather data on small and medium-sized firms. A widespread strategy of the employers consisted of obstructing access to systematic and reliable knowledge by using negligence or bad memory as a defense against charges of fraud. But as Kafka's reconstruction shows, there was also a physical obstacle to gathering data on wages. In quoting from the report that the controller, Schönfeld, wrote after his investigation in Renelt's office in November 1912, Kafka hints at some employers' archaic instinct to defend their territory physically. When a wage book suddenly appeared from a locked closet, Schönfeld demanded a closer look at it:

> Though the employer acceded to my wish, he was so agitated that he was shaking, and he held the book by its covers with both hands, so that I could only leaf through it hurriedly. Since I feared that his agitation, as well as that of the quarry foreman (we were alone in the wooden shack at the quarry), might degenerate into something worse and that they might not be able to control themselves toward me, I gave up for the moment using the book for the purpose of establishing wages.

Note the underlining. A verdict of the Kuttenberg district court in a previous case explains the controller's fear that this scene might get out of hand. Six weeks before his trip to Pömmerle, Schönfeld had been sent to inspect the construction business of one Vinzenz Kruml in Goltsch Jenikau, a small town southeast of Prague. The rationale of the verdict contains a burlesque scene that highlights the physical aspect of the will to knowledge inherent in social insurance.

We may safely assume that Kafka had read this document and therefore could quote from it at length. Upon arrival at Kruml's office, Schönfeld, accompanied by another controller, Karl Broz, produced his credentials and demanded to see the current wage lists. The lists seemed flawed; the controllers then asked Kruml to produce his cash book, but Kruml claimed not to possess any written evidence other than the lists. The controllers continued copying the obviously flawed data from the lists into the Institute's forms while Kruml left the office:

> Then Karl Broz took out a document from a bundle of files in the bookcase not far from the table, the edges of which were sticking out on top and which, judging from its format and ruled lines, he had identified as a wage list the minute he had entered the office. He then handed the document to Julius Schönfeld, who, recognizing it as the original wage-payment list, immediately took out from the bookcase the entire fascicle of the wage-payment lists for the lumber business containing the real wage payments for the period from January 1, 1911 to May 10, 1912, and he read out to Karl Broz the final sum from these ledgers. After about two minutes, the head of the construction company, Herr Kruml, returned and remarked that the Inspector could make his job easier by using the combined wage lists that had been assembled in the business office. To this, Julius Schönfeld replied that he had already read off the payments from the correct ledgers and would like to have an end to lies and to open all the wage lists, a right to which he was entitled by law. At this, Kruml flew into a rage and shouted out more or less the following words: "Just for that I'm not going to give you either

the real or the doctored ones, and you just make sure to clear out of here." Then he leaped to the table in an attempt to get hold of the original ledger. But Julius Schönfeld took it from the table, along with the remaining files, and held them firmly in his hand. Kruml then came from the back and squeezed Schönfeld's right hand and tore the files he was holding from his hand. All this pulling files back and forth left both Schönfeld and Kruml with slight injuries. But as Schönfeld was physically weaker than the head of the construction company, Herr Kruml, he began to cry for help, where-upon Kruml let go. Schönfeld, from whose hand some of the files had fallen to the ground in the meantime, bundled them together again and ran out crying for help. Throughout this scene, Karl Broz continually warned Herr Kruml about behaving violently and put himself in his path so that he could not run after Julius Schönfeld. Kruml knocked into him a number of times. In a few moments, Julius Schönfeld returned to the office, announc-ing that help was on the way. Both inspectors then picked up the torn files, left the office, and continued on to Caslau, where they reported the inci-dent at the Imperial Police Headquarters, there depositing the true note-books and a bundle of the papers that had been written over [that is, doctored—Eds.].

Kruml, who was obviously less able to control himself than was Renelt, was sentenced to fourteen days in prison, including one day on bread and water. Renelt had been bold enough to refer to the Kruml in-cident in his appeal against Schönfeld in order to cast doubt on the pro-fessional soundness of Schönfeld's investigative procedure. On July 9, 1913, the Institute filed a brief statement with the Office of the Gover-nor regarding this allegation. In view of the sarcastic precision of the response, we may assume that Kafka, still in charge of the case, was its author:

Between the case of Vinzenz Kruml and the present affair, there exists no concrete connection whatever that might serve to support the complaints of the employer in his own case. The sole connection consists in the fact that Vinzenz Kruml also attempted to deprive the Institute of documents that were its due and that the same inspector was entrusted with the examina-tion of the wage lists. [. . .] And so there is no further conclusion to be drawn from the entire Kruml affair, which had been adduced as compara-ble, other than that in the case of certain employers and certain wage lists, the Institute's inspector has to contend with obstacles of all sorts, and not only those in the way of establishing an authentic wage list.

In the final section of his long statement on the Renelt trial (section IV of doc. 12), Kafka explains with great precision the legal foundation of the Institute's proceedings against Renelt, frankly admitting that in cases where "legally prescribed wage lists are not available," the Institute would have to resort to "the most accurate possible approximation." Thus, while in view of its investigations into the Renelt case, the Institute had been well aware that "what it had been given were not certain but only possible data," it had made sure "to compensate for possible sources of error." Hence, the credibility of Schönfeld's witnesses should never have been an issue in the Aussig trial.

In the fat volume of the Renelt files, we find the clearest and most penetrating reconstruction of this complex case in the one document we can absolutely attribute to Kafka as its author. The German original of this and other appeals reveals the ways in which Kafka's office writings excel in style and sophistication, while hardly ever transgressing the strict rules of legal-administrative language. But such skill would not necessarily add up to success in court. On August 13, 1913, Renelt filed a response (doc. 12D) to the Institute's statements (doc. 12B and C). He discards the Institute's matter-of-fact argument and shifts the focus back to Schönfeld's methods of investigation, informing the Office of the Governor of his determination to take the case to civil court if his appeal was rejected. And indeed, after the Vienna ministry again ruled that Renelt was liable to a supplementary payment of K 444, the Administrative Court again revoked that ruling because of procedural issues, specifying that Renelt should have been informed in advance that Schönfeld would be interviewing his workers. Eventually, in the spring of 1914, the parties met twice for negotiations in the office of the Aussig district authorities. After nine years of continuous legal procedures, they agreed on a settlement, reducing Renelt's debt to K 222.

This epic struggle between a ruthless scoundrel and the law left some clearly detectable traces in all three of Kafka's novels. The first, the America novel *The Man Who Disappeared*, was, to a large extent, written between October 1912, when the controls department had intensified its investigations into Renelt's quarry, and January 1913, when the Institute decided to take the case to criminal court. In chap. 6 the hero of the novel, Karl Rossmann, falls victim to the machinations of one of his fellow elevator operators at the Hotel Occidental, a cunning scoundrel named Renell. Rossmann eventually loses his job. In the wake of his rather abrupt dismissal, he acts out a promise hidden in the name of "Rennelt" (this recurrent misspelling in the written verdict of the Administrative Court immediately evokes the association of the German word *Rennen*="running" or "race"): a race against the law. Lacking his overcoat and his identity papers, Rossmann runs straight into a policeman. After a brief interrogation, he decides to run away to avoid arrest. While the arm of the law chases Karl "at an easy lope that gave evidence of both great strength and practice" and in the middle of a busy street, "it was lucky for Karl that the chase took place in a working-class quarter. The workers had no great liking for the authorities. [. . .] He saw the occasional worker halting on the pavement, watching him calmly while the policeman shouted, 'Stop him!' and kept pointing his nightstick at Karl."

Finally, a second scoundrel, Delamarche, comes to Rossmann's rescue. "From time to time," he observes, "racing with the police is a useful exercise," thus summing up this episode, as well as Renelt's nine years of legal quarrels with the Institute.

A few months later, Kafka began writing *The Trial*. The Renelt case is one of a series of—literal and metaphorical—trials that haunts this novel. As "Renelt" oscillates between insurance law and criminal law, the accused Joseph K—who, like Renelt before the Aussig district court, "is not in custody" (doc. 12A)—tries in vain to identify clearly the jurisdiction he is dealing with. His later reflections on his strange trial duplicate Renelt's attempted shift of focus from the factual to the procedural aspects of the legal dispute and its ensuing transformation into an out-of-court settlement: "There was no guilty verdict. This legal action was nothing more than a business deal, such as he had often made to the advantage of the bank—a deal within which, as always happened, lurked various dangers that had simply to be averted" (T 125, trans. modified). But whereas Renelt succeeds, K does not.

Finally, in a deleted passage of Kafka's last novel, *The Castle*, we find this laconic comment on the burlesque struggle for the physical possession of written evidence in the office of Vinzenz Kruml:

"And the proceedings?" K asked. "Stay in the briefcase," Momus replied. "I would have liked to take a look," said K, and almost instinctively, he reached for the case, he already had hold of its edge. "No, no," the secretary said and pulled the case away. "What do you think you're doing?" the hostess asked, lightly slapping K's hand. "Do you really think you can use force to get back what your recklessness and arrogance lost you? You evil, horrible person! Would the proceedings be of any use if you had them? They'd be a flower mowed down in the meadow."

<h1 style="text-align:center">13</h1>

SECOND INTERNATIONAL CONGRESS ON ACCIDENT PREVENTION AND FIRST AID IN VIENNA (1913)

When, in September 1913, the world's leading experts in accident prevention met in Vienna, Kafka was selected to accompany the two principal representatives of the Prague Institute, Robert Marschner, its director, and Eugen Pfohl, the head of the Institute's business department. Though Kafka's name does not appear on the list of speakers, his correspondence with his fiancée and a recently discovered letter from his correspondence with his uncle Alfred Löwy clearly indicate that he wrote both speeches. These two texts contain an implicit, and at times explicit, theory of the development of social institutions and the organization of administrative power. In this sense, they constitute a striking analogy with two of Kafka's literary texts on technical and military safety. "A Page from an Old Document," like Marschner's speech, stresses the danger resulting from a weak center, whereas "Building the Great Wall of China," like Pfohl's speech, advances a decentralized organization of state institutions. The dissolution of antitheses into a subtle balance of viewpoints is a strategy common to both Kafka the bureaucrat and Kafka the author.

A. Accident Prevention within the Context of Accident Insurance, with Special Consideration of the Prague Workmen's Accident Insurance Institute

Address delivered by Dr. Robert Marschner, Director of the Workmen's Accident Insurance Institute for the Kingdom of Bohemia (Prague).

I. The Original Relationship between Workmen's Accident Insurance and Accident Prevention

The connection between workmen's accident insurance and accident prevention within the confines of social-policy legislation is not as old, from an organizational standpoint, as we might suppose. In theory, the connection existed from the beginning of the more recent actions in social legislation. If we examine the situation in Austria alone, we find an appeal in principle to the basic idea that "accident insurance and accident prevention must augment one another" as early as no. 4 of the *Amtliche Nachrichten* of the k. k. Ministry of the Interior on workmen's accident and health insurance, issued on October 15, 1889—almost at the same time as our principal laws regarding accident insurance took effect.

On a practical level, however, at the beginning, such a connection was made difficult by the fact that at the time, accident insurance and accident prevention did not carry equal weight. For accident insurance, there existed a complete legal system, at least in its essential features; accident prevention, on the other hand, was only in its beginning stages, at least in Austria. The reason for this disparity, of course, lies in the nature of both areas. Workmen's accident insurance began as a very generalized demand, along with the transformation of Germany into an industrial nation; the demand arrived at legal form relatively rapidly, urged on by political, social, and civil impulses. Thus, accident insurance was connected to the development of insurance in general and needed only to find its particular formulation.

Efforts at accident prevention, on the other hand, are extremely recent, triggered by the dangers, previously ignored, of the new production methods involving machinery and factories. The result of these dangers as regards the frequency and cost of accidents was processed in the context of accident insurance, with consideration given to the growing body of statistical evidence. The possibility of preventing accidents, however, required study before its necessity could be recognized. Of course, a type of accident prevention had existed in Austria going back to the time of Emperor Joseph II; however, it had been practiced only in mining and metallurgy—the primary large-scale enterprises of the premechanical era—and this to a very limited extent. But quite apart from the actual development of accident insurance and accident prevention, their paths were markedly different from the start. For even if accident insurance continues to build on many separate experiences, it must proceed as rapidly as possible from general principles to the practical realization of its efforts. Accident prevention, on the other hand, even in its most complete formulation, must always keep every slightest experience in sight. For this same reason, a version of accident insurance will be adequate for some years, while accident prevention is in a permanent process of reformulation, since it must follow both the development of industry and machine technology as well as the developments of accident prevention technology.

II. Accident Prevention in Employers' Liability-Insurance Associations and in Territorial Insurance Organizations

That both areas belong together has been acknowledged from the outset; this fact may even have been overestimated, owing to the inadequate statistical basis of accident insurance, but a satisfactory connection could not be organized at that time. In principle, Austria was actually in a more favorable situation because its accident-insurance law was enacted $3\frac{1}{2}$ years after Germany's commercial accident-insurance law, so that the statistical data of this time period could be utilized. However, the difference between Austria and Germany in organizing accident insurance presented an obstacle. The German trade associations proved capable of developing accident prevention quickly, systematically, and with a scope that far exceeded the provisions of the German law. In Austria, on the other hand, accident prevention remained outside the framework of territorial accident insurance. Furthermore, this difference lies in the nature of both areas, quite aside from legal factors. Accident prevention, proceeding from individual cases, needed to find within the trade associations an organizational form that was appropriate and capable of encompassing this new creation, as well as being attuned to a uniform and limited area of production. At the same time, the territorial organization was much too broad—both when it was founded and for a long time thereafter—to be effectively coupled with accident prevention. One of the reasons provided for the Austrian workmen's accident insurance bill stated that the fully funded insurance approach was ideally suited to meaningfully promote accident prevention, since accident- prevention measures give employers the tools with which to lower the firms' risk percentages. However, the adverse financial results soon felt at least by the largest workmen's accident insurance institutes have unfortunately had an inhibiting effect on the development of accident prevention.

III. Accident Prevention in the Legally Defined Agenda of the Workmen's Accident Insurance Institutes

The workmen's accident insurance institutes in Austria were given the task of evaluating the risks in firms subject to compulsory insurance, comparing those risks to others, observing them over time, and finally, being the ones to carry the burden.

At first they had no opportunity to become immediately familiar with the operating facilities of the affected firms. In order to gauge the adverse situation of the insurance institutes in this regard, we need not set up a comparison with the employers' trade associations of Germany, where information about industrial operations was heavily concentrated; we need only a simple comparison with private insurance institutes. Even today, after almost twenty-five years of workmen's accident insurance in Austria, the institutes have still not been granted the right to inspect the firms they insure; they must rely on information provided by employers and derived from accident reports. Nor do the institutes have the right to take their own measures against poor operating facilities, apart from placing them in a higher risk category; their only recourse is to report such firms to the authorities, whose effectiveness is questionable because they, too, are not allowed direct access.

IV. The Workmen's Accident Insurance Institute in Prague

Practical needs, and in part the growth of accident prevention as well, forced the institutes to take the initiative in improving the collected information about firms as best they could, given that they had no right of inspection. They undertook this effort on their own initiative and in spite of the lack of corresponding legal requirements. In and of themselves, these efforts did not make a direct impact on accident prevention, but at least, they provided it with an indirect benefit.

The following description is limited to the Workmen's Accident Insurance Institute for Bohemia in Prague. The general conditions we have mentioned have, of course, had varying effects in different territories, and therefore as a characteristic example the Prague Institute will suffice.

1. Deepening Knowledge of Operations on One's Own Initiative

Most of all, the Institute could not be satisfied with the official registration form for firms subject to compulsory insurance; the form consisted of only eleven general, systematized questions, and only four related to the actual operating equipment. After extensive preliminaries that gradually crystallized in final drafts, therefore, the Institute developed various questionnaires for the primary commercial categories. If the employer filled these out in detail, they gave a clear picture of the firm. They also yielded a number of observations important for any form of promoting safety. Contrary to expectation, any employer is generally happy to fill out such questionnaires; he is glad to describe his operations in answer to a framework of objective questions, since he is thus given the opportunity of himself throwing a new light on his operation, as it were. The questionnaire also gives him the assurance that, by law, the information he provides is intended for the insurance institute only and thus cannot threaten him in other ways. He is also willing to describe his operation, since in this instance, contrary to other admissions made to the authorities, reporting the best possible operational facilities is to the employer's greatest advantage; he must, of course, remain aware of the fact that the control questions as well as other resources allow for verification of the answers. At the same time, the questionnaire tells the employer the requirements set forth for his business in the matter of safety. He realizes that his firm is actually subject to regular, if not immediate, inspection of his safety measures by the Institute. All these aspects together provide a kind of tacit education—if not directly leading to improving the firm's safety, then to alertness and readiness regarding questions of safety. This is, of course, nothing more than a *surrogate* of safety promotion, but the Institute had to remain satisfied with surrogates as long as no other comprehensive safety ordinances have been issued that would lend greater significance to the Institute's right to report violations.

2. The Safety Ordinances of the Accident Prevention Commission and the Workmen's Accident Insurance Institute

The basis for issuing these ordinances was first created in 1900, with the founding of the Accident Prevention Commission as an advisory body of the Ministry of Trade and Commerce. The first ordinance, however, did not appear until late in 1905. Though since that time, a series of very carefully crafted safety ordinances for various industries and trades has been issued, this normative action is not backed by any organization that would also insure its thoroughgoing promotion and enforcement and that would be equipped with the necessary resources for the task. The following example shows the significance of this lack: An ordinance issued by the Ministry of Trade and Commerce on February 7, 1907, a document produced by the Accident Prevention Commission itself, contains detailed regulations for preventing accidents and protecting the health of workers employed in construction. The ordinance also lists regulations for the workers and obligates the employer to post these regulations at every construction site or face penalties. It also determines penalties for failure to follow all other regulations. In 1910—by then, the ordinance had been in force for three years—the Institute had an opportunity to gather information about the spread of awareness of the ordinance. A questionnaire the Institute sent throughout the building trades included the question: "Are you aware of this ordinance, and in what ways do you take it into consideration?" In responding to the question, the vast majority indicated that the employer was not aware of the ordinance. One employer, for example, stated that he had been aware of the decree for the past forty years. Another declared that he was familiar with all the laws and ordinances. Others answered innocently with a request that they be sent the ordinance, since it would be of interest to them. Many avoided the question altogether and simply emphasized in very general terms the absence of danger in their methods of construction. The wide variety of answers thus descended in stages down to those who simply responded "No."

Even with these ordinances, then, the involved employers were free to decide whether or not to adopt the suggested practices. As far as the provisions of the ordinances went, only the trade authorities were in a position to observe them, but the means and organization available to these agencies were not such that they could effectively exploit them, as experience shows. Since the issues involved required the judgment of experts in the field, the trade authorities had to begin by consulting these; this need in itself results in delays that adversely affect the dissemination as well as the enforcement of the regulations.

3. Three Characteristic Safety Measures Taken by the Prague Institute

The possibilities for intervention available to any of the territorial institutes in these matters, on the other hand, and the ways they utilized them can be illustrated with three examples from the practice of the Prague Institute, which are especially clear because they can be followed statistically.

a. Protective devices for agricultural machinery. At the suggestion of the Prague Institute, in 1907 the Office of the Governor issued an ordinance regarding accident prevention in agricultural operations using machinery. Though this ordinance was carefully worked out in consultation with the Agricultural Council, it would have had little impact, if for no other reason than the relative imperviousness of farmers, especially when it came to information about safety. In fact, the Institute had attempted various measures regarding the safety of agricultural mechanized equipment before this ordinance was issued, quite without success. The Institute had sent out large posters listing safety regulations; either these were entirely overlooked or they were misused, being utilized for such purposes as covering broken windows. The ordinance would have met a similar fate, since various earlier measures, such as sending copies of it out with premium invoices and announcements sent to the local governments had proven ineffective. But then, again at the instigation of the Institute and with great cooperation by the k.k. Office of the Governor in Prague, a specific monitoring organization for this special safety area was successfully created in such a way that the district commissioners undertook yearly and systematic safety inspections of agricultural mechanized operations. Such a measure is, of course, possible only in this particular case, since no expert examinations are necessary; all that is needed are inspections to check whether the pre-scribed protective devices are provided for each mechanized agricultural operation. The following figures prove that every specific organization in the area of safety arrived at immediate success, even under today's conditions. For the Prague Institute, the number of compensated acci-dents in agricultural concerns was 377 in 1907 and 380 in 1908. The numbers were thus fairly constant. But in 1909, which saw the first suc-cesses of the Office of the Governor's ordinance and the organization created for it, the number of compensated accidents was abruptly re-duced to 338; it remained roughly constant, with 339 in 1910, and fell to 336 in 1911. (We should also remember that, because of the natural increase in insured concerns and workers, the number of accidents can be expected to increase over the years.) All other figures for accident trends show a similar decrease, and even if other circumstances outside our scope have also had an impact on these conditions, the main effect remains due to those ordinances issued by the Office of the Governor.

b. Cylindrical safety shafts for wood-planing machines. The Institute introduced a second comprehensive measure for the introduction of cy-lindrical safety shafts for planing machines—an action that is all the more remarkable because the safety regulations for woodworking firms to come from the Accident Prevention Commission are still under dis-cussion, so that no official ordinance is yet in force. The Institute's ac-tion was necessary, since it is precisely woodworking machines—and at least second among them, planing machines—that rank among the equipment posing the highest risks, and since almost infallible protec-tive devices exist for these very machines. The Institute had to begin by trying for an alternative to the absent general regulations by obtaining a decree from the Office of the Governor directed to the government agen-cies. This decree was duly issued; it obligated the district commissioners to urge the universal introduction of cylindrical shafts. It was only at this point that the Institute's real work could begin. Illustrated articles on the advantages of the cylindrical shafts were published in the annual reports. Trade journals and calendars were provided with articles and plates on the subject, and a small collection of protective devices for woodworking machines was exhibited at the Institute itself. In written correspondence, every opportunity was taken to point out the impor-tance of the cylindrical shafts. Their introduction was rewarded with a lower insurance classification. Products that had proven themselves were repeatedly recommended. Most importantly, however, the most accu-rate possible list of planing machines used in firms subject to compul-sory insurance in the Institute's territory was compiled; and with the help of this list, the Institute attempted to enforce the use of cylindrical shafts by means of letters, notifications to the authorities, and keeping record of the replies, all the while regularly checking the results against the accident reports. And again, it was only the organized effort that led to the following statistics: In 1907, accidents on planing machines in the Institute's territory resulted in 50 short-term and 59 permanent benefits. It was in 1908 that the Institute first became effective; in that year, there were 50 short-term benefits, these remaining constant, but 72 permanent ones, or 13 more. But in the following year, already, 1909, there was a significant a improvement compared to the previous steady increases. Admittedly, short-term benefits increased to 65, but permanent pensions decreased to 69. In 1910, there was again an increase in short-term benefits to 71, while permanent payouts continued to fall to 59. In 1911, a significant decrease in temporary compensations was seen as these fell to 54, and permanent benefits sank further, to 42.

To summarize the results of these five years: In 1908, the year the effort began, 122 accidents were caused by planing machines, and in 1911 the total was only 96, or a decrease of 21%. But even this comparison does not give the full picture. What is crucial to the downward trend of accidents are those that have resulted in permanent benefits, and that category decreased from 72 to 42—almost half the total, or 41%. It is thus the permanent benefits that decreased the most, without a significant increase in short-term benefits, since these increased only from 50 to 54, or by 8%. The factor that decreased the danger, and whose effects began in 1908, thus did not decrease permanent benefits at the cost of short-term ones but prevented some accidents resulting in permanent benefits from happening in the first place. But the bare figures for permanent benefits could also be deceptive, since it may be that the 1911 accidents were unusually severe, so that they offset the decrease in the actual number. But such is also not the case. The average amount of the permanent benefits in 1908 was approximately 16 percent of the yearly earnings of the worker who suffered the accident, and the average amount of the permanent benefits in 1911 was also approximately 16 percent of that figure. These constant figures prove that the permanent benefits in both years were the result of uniform causes, and that in 1911 these causes were simply reduced, while the remaining causes continued to have the same effects as before. The quite insignificant increase in short-term benefits, incidentally, may be due, in part, to the fact that the workers become less cautious when they begin to work with machines equipped with cylindrical shafts, and that the shafts that are first introduced are not cylindrical enough. These are not adequately undercut and obstruct the necessary discharge of shavings, clogging the opening between blade and table and forcing the worker to clear the opening manually. The cylindrical shafts manufactured today by some specialized firms with no other purpose also eliminate these disadvantages.

The increase in the number of short-term benefits is merely a transitional phenomenon, however; if statistics for short-term benefits were kept, it would be easier to realize that these numbers have no significance, for even imperfectly constructed cylindrical shafts cause only minor lacerations that do not disrupt work. Finally, we may ask whether other conditions might not have had an effect on the decline in the accident trend, and why, precisely, the entire effect is attributed to the introduction of the cylindrical shafts. From the perspective of accident statistics, however, the case of planing machines is an extraordinarily clear one. The square shaft was more than the principal danger—it was the only danger connected with use of the planing machines; any reduction in the risk of these machines must therefore be credited to the fight against the square shafts, especially since even the greatest improvement in work supervision cannot significantly counter the danger of such shafts. Furthermore, the number of planing machines in the Institute's territory of course increased during the years under consideration, and this increase remained without effect on the frequency of accidents because most new machines are equipped with cylindrical shafts.

c. Improvement of work supervision in quarries and small-scale industries. While the two examples of protective devices for agricultural machines and cylindrical shafts for planing machines demonstrate success primarily because of the proper arrangements of promotional and informational materials, a third example will show how much can be achieved in certain types of operations by educating employers in the practice of better work supervision. This is above all the case in quarries as well as in small-scale industries.

The principal problem in quarries is not the use of protective devices (aside from the use of protective goggles, good explosive materials, etc.) but of careful quarrying. The occasional regulation of working conditions is not enough; we must demand that this caution in quarrying be practiced continually, since the formation of the quarry changes continually with the progressive work of crushing the rocks. This circumstance is the reason for the need for constant work supervision. A sizable large group of quarries, owned by an important construction company, is located within the territory of the Prague Workmen's Accident Insurance Institute. In 1904 (to pick a typical past year), the costs of accidents in these quarries amounted to K 14.29 per K 100 of insured wages. These untenable conditions, as well as a clear understanding of the type of accidents, led the Institute to enter into negotiations with the employer, explaining to him that it was possible to remedy the situation by indicating the causes of the accidents and to persuade him to engage in stricter work supervision, cleaner quarries, and better quarrying techniques. The successful result was that in the five-year period from 1907 to 1911, the costs of accidents in these quarries amounted to only about a third of what they had been—K 5.02 per K 100 of insured wages.

The significance of work supervision in small-scale industries is evident from the fact that here, where the employer shares in the manual work, and the workshops are small, so they can be easily overseen, possibilities for work supervision exist that could never be achieved even in the best-managed large firms. A speaker at a cooperative assembly once formulated the point thus: "A slap by the master protects the apprentice better than the best safety devices." This is a drastic statement, and it is certainly not completely accurate, but there is some truth in it, and if someday, aside from the introduction of protective devices, we will also have succeeded in convincing the master of the necessity of the strictest work supervision, then a great advance in protection will have been made.

To the extent that the current scope permits and requires, the Prague Institute has now made contact with cooperatives and cooperative associations in an attempt to motivate them to make some efforts in the interest of accident prevention. And there has been no lack of cooperation. However, these efforts are still very recent. There is, as yet, no authority that studies accident-prevention statistics in the way the Ministry of the Interior handles accident statistics.

V. Overview of Additional Accident Prevention Efforts by the Prague Institute

The three projects described above are meant to serve as isolated examples; in reality, they are related to the entire activity of the Prague Institute in the area of accident prevention; the Institute is making step-by-step progress in its efforts to deal with every area it can reach. Today the accident-prevention work of the Prague Institute is divided into four areas:

1. Direct influence on separate firms—i.e., the Institute presents a safety-related demand and immediately puts it into effect.

This most important practice is, as we have mentioned, largely denied to the Institute by law, and the only direct executive power consists in the gradations of the risk classifications. This measure, however, is not very effective, either in a positive or in a negative sense, especially since the law allows the category gradation merely to act to establish categories and to set financial amounts for them, but the Institute is not granted executive authority. For example, within the current risk-classification regulations, it is not possible to increase the risk classification of a large woodworking firm that still uses square shafts in its planing machines by more than 2 percentage points. Such an increase adds to the premium at most 18h[eller] per K 100 of insured wages and is therefore an infinitesimal increase.

2. Indirect influence on separate firms by means of a legal notice, according to § 28 of the Workmen's Accident Insurance Law.

According to this section, based on the reports of the trade inspector, the Institute may request the court to issue an order about the employer's obligation to make the proper arrangements for preventing accidents in his firm and to observe the proper behavior for the same purpose. But this measure is also not very effective, if only because the Institute lacks the right to inspect the facilities. Furthermore, this method consists of a number of time-consuming actions: the Institute's request to the trade inspector to inspect the firm; the inspector's visit to the firm; the report of the results to the Institute; the Institute's application to the trade authority; the trade authority's investigation of the case, which actually represents the third investigation of the same matter after the investigations of the trade inspector and the Institute; and only then the court decision, subject to successive appeals and the final communication of the decision to the Institute. And all these activities may not result in success, since the Institute, whose petition is seen legally as only an application, has no legal recourse if its claim is not upheld.

3. The actions left to the Prague Institute are therefore principally ones not specifically assigned by law.

Such actions must, therefore, be addressed not so much to individual firms as to whole business categories. This means, above all, enlisting the collaboration of other elements better equipped, either by law or by the actual situation, to engage in protective measures. The Prague Institute therefore submits proposals to the Office of the Governor for the issuance of safety-related ordinances and decrees. Aside from the previously discussed cases of agricultural machinery and cylindrical safety shafts, this effort has occurred with regard to agricultural quarries and unauthorized coverage in the construction industry (a prime example of risk increase resulting from an absence of supervision in the workplace), various protective measures in construction, the limitation of child labor in conjunction with agricultural machinery, the restriction on evenings of dance music, etc.

The contributions of the k.k. Office of the Governor in Prague in supporting the Institute were repeatedly recognized by the Institute's board of trustees. On some of these occasions, the Institute also approached the district commissioners. The Institute maintained a permanent connection with the Agricultural Council regarding accident prevention in agricultural concerns, and here the Institute gratefully acknowledges the involvement of all parties' rural representatives. Some safety-related issues were handled jointly with the chambers of trade and commerce.

Negotiations have taken place and will take place with cooperatives and other groups in matters of accident prevention in the respective industrial and commercial categories.

4. The Institute's Own Initiatives in Publicity and Promotion

This work must, of course, begin with the appropriate correspondence. In addition, the Prague Institute has organized lectures at cooperative meetings and in workmen's associations. Annual reports described effective protective devices in images and text; and along with the case for cylindrical shafts, a case was made for the introduction of safety milling heads and the widest possible replacement of circular saws with band saws. Plates and articles were made available to trade journals and calendars, pamphlets with descriptions of typical accident cases were distributed, leaflets that specifically and convincingly summarized the content of the ministerial safety ordinances were issued. A small collection of protective devices was set up in the Institute building, from which individual objects were loaned for lecturing purposes. The Institute has made itself available to employers as an information office for safety questions as well as for suggestions for new protective devices. On the occasion of various inquiries by technical schools, the Institute has tried to work toward having accident prevention included in the curriculum. The Institute has also participated in an effort to raise funds to be used to grant assistance to workshop owners to defray their insurance premiums and possibly for the purchase of safety devices.

Finally, the Prague Institute is participating in this year's industrial exposition in Komotau with a rather large safety exhibit that will bring home to any viewer the advantages of protected woodworking machines.

VI. Measures Considered for Future Implementation

In addition to the activities already mentioned and the expansion of the existing ones, the following measures are being considered for the near future.

We will suggest proposals to the appropriate agencies about limiting alcohol abuse, the special supervision required for assembly workers, preventing workers from falling asleep at their machines, and preventing workers from skipping work on Mondays, with the indirect effect of increased danger because of the workers' doubling up on work near the end of the week. Special attention will have to be given to first aid, and it will be especially necessary *to set about establishing a connection between the Institute and Good Samaritan organizations, similar to the collaboration between German trade associations and the Red Cross.*

Among its direct informational and promotional activities, the Institute will strive to gain greater influence on supervisors and foremen in matters related to safety by sending the Institute's relevant publications directly to them. We will consider the question—in spite of many reservations that exist to the contrary—whether individuals should be rewarded for accident prevention. We will initiate negotiations to exclude the delivery of machines not provided with any protective devices altogether—a step that will involve some difficulty, since, in contrast to the situation that prevails in Germany, the Austrian insurance institutes have no legal recourse against suppliers of machinery in this regard. Work will continue with the goal of replacing dangerous machines with less dangerous ones as far as possible, so that, for example, the technically dispensable and very dangerous shingling machines disappear. Attempts will be made to have the accident-prevention regulations read out in the workplace at regular intervals. Typical accident investigations will be photographed and the pictures distributed. And finally, work will be done to expand accident-prevention statistics.

VII. The Position of the Institute in the Framework of Accident Prevention as a Whole

So the circle of accident-prevention measures that radiate out from the Prague Workmen's Accident Insurance Institute will continue to expand, though the two gaps we have described will remain open, because of the law and of the Institute's limited scope and resources. The position of the Prague Institute within the entire area of Austrian accident prevention is thus as follows: Today's program of accident prevention in Austria suffers from a lack of organization; there is no shortage of material, but its wealth is not practically applicable. The disadvantages of such disorganization are only too clear. At the moment, accident prevention lags far behind its counterpart in Germany, and its growth has been seriously disorganized, with details in a discontinuous sequence. Basically, however, there are also advantages to this disorganization, in that it represents a transitional stage within which those factors that have the capacity of advancing accident prevention in spite of unfortunate conditions can work all the more visibly. In a sense, there is free competition within Austrian accident prevention; after the practical selection of the effective powers, this competition must lead to a legal determination. This determination, in turn, will have an empirical foundation that is unquestionably solid. In any case, the Workmen's Accident Insurance Institute will, given its previous achievements, be entitled to claim a special position within the final organization, and the proof will be provided that accident prevention can be combined with territorial insurance just as closely and organically as it is with insurance organized by trade associations, though the evolution has taken longer.

B. The Organization of Accident Prevention in Austria

Address delivered by Eugen Pfohl, Senior Inspector of the Workmen's Accident Insurance Institute for the Kingdom of Bohemia (Prague).

Whatever final organizational form accident prevention strives for, it must always first pass through four principal stages. The transitions, the course and duration of each stage can be very different, depending on different sociopolitical conditions, but the four stages that will always be recognizable are: those of private initiative, incorporation, governmental provisions, and finally, the beginnings of general organization.

Private initiative must mark the beginning of all accident prevention. Taking its cue from various experiences, each firm must initiate its own accident-prevention program. While only the largest enterprises can afford to organize something that might replace health insurance, for example, or even accident insurance, accident prevention must be established in the smallest firms as well as in midsize and large companies. And this first stage of accident prevention is enough to indicate the need of a particularly sweeping organization.

Private initiative is followed by incorporation. The growth of private efforts and the need for accident prevention lead to a situation in which the initiatives proceeding from separate firms are assumed by a group of companies, along with the care for their further elaboration. Aside from the merely analogous organizations of preindustrial times, the first obvious example of a safety organization is the one founded by Engel-Dollfus in Mühlhausen in 1867; others followed its example.

But since accident prevention does not appear as an isolated phenomenon but is connected with the most important interests of public law and industry, it must, along with these interests, pressure the government into taking a position. It is at this point that the third stage of accident prevention begins. Today, the focus of governmental aid for accident prevention is § 74 of the amendment to the laws governing trade and industry of March 8, 1885, which was recently further extended by the law of April 21, 1913. In accordance with its general provisions, the section consists of only the general outline of a "Provision for Unskilled Labor," to use the law's own wording. For the sake of thoroughness, we must add that a series of separate decrees regarding accident protection preceded this legal determination in principle. The earliest of these decrees was issued by a court in 1784 and dealt with quarrying gravel and clay. The last of these separate, unsystematically issued decrees are from 1885. Translating the full body of legal material into practical application resulted in the institution of the trade inspectors. There is, unfortunately, no room in the scope of my topic to praise the all-encompassing activity of these institutes, which unfolded their work in the area of workmen's protection during the last three decades under the most difficult of conditions, and which have effected a transformation of our entire industrial and commercial life with unparalleled rapidity and thoroughness. But accident prevention is only a small part of this larger area.

Accident prevention in Austria has passed through the first three stages to the extent that the beginnings of organization that are now apparent could lead to a large umbrella organization. As long as such an ultimate organization is not yet in place, however, as long as obsolete and unnecessary separate organizations have not been discarded in favor of a total organization—and such is still the case in Austria—all elements of the historical development must remain both on the books and in effect.

As a consequence, there are still many Austrian firms that seek to perfect their safety facilities completely independently, even establishing their own accident-prevention offices.

The corporate measures are in effect alongside these private initiatives. A very few examples will suffice. The Electrotechnical Society (Elektrotechnischer Verein) in Vienna has, on its own initiative, issued safety regulations for high-voltage electrical plants; these were officially recognized in 1909 by a decree of the Ministry of Public Works. A chamber of trade and commerce in Bohemia subsequently opened its own technical information office for accident prevention. The Agricultural Council in Bohemia has advocated the dissemination of safety regulations for agricultural concerns. The Crownland Commission for Child Protection and the Welfare of Youth in Bohemia has initiated an action against child labor in agricultural work. These and many other organizations' initiatives were followed by government provisions, for which a central office was established in 1900 in the Accident Prevention Commission, which is assigned to the Ministry of Trade as an investigative body in questions of accident protection, and which by 1911 had issued nine safety decrees for various business categories. Additional government support has taken the form of laws, such as the 1909 law concerning the prohibition of the use of white and yellow phosphorus in the manufacture of matches. In addition, decrees on safety provisions have been issued by regional authorities, such as those in Bohemia,

Lower Austria, and Styria, for the prevention of accidents in agricultural-machine operations.

The fourth stage of development, the onset of an umbrella organization, can be seen most of all in the safety-related work of the various workmen's accident insurance institutes, just as accident prevention has crystallized in the area of workmen's accident insurance in general, or at least is forming as such. Regional government authorities engage in additional initiatives, which, unfortunately, can act through giving and enforcing orders only on a case-by-case basis of accident prevention. Finally, this cluster of general measures includes the various museums and collections of safety-related material.

This is an extremely brief overview of the currently available positive material in favor of accident prevention in Austria. All these efforts, however, have their opposing forces, which have so far prevented the completion of an umbrella organization.

The cases of private initiative must remain isolated and far from substantial as long as there is no central headquarters for matters relating to safety, an organization to which the individual employer feels solidly connected. The same applies to the measures taken by the various Institutes. The interest in accident prevention shown by an individual Institute, which is overburdened with very different tasks, must be short-lived if that interest is not upheld and encouraged by other offices dedicated solely to accident prevention. To give an example, the previously mentioned technical information office of one chamber of trade and commerce has long since ceased to exist in its original ambitious form.

Within the scope of government provisions, the distribution of safety regulations and, even more, their enforcement shows the lack of agencies intended *exclusively* for these purposes and directed from a central authority. The sphere of operations of our trade inspectors is much too large for accident prevention to gain the necessary recognition, as the reports of the central inspectorate repeatedly emphasize. As a consequence, there are far too few inspections. In 1912, for example, the Austrian trade inspectors conducted 33,940 inspections of businesses subject to compulsory insurance, while the technical representatives of the trade associations of Germany conducted 376,536. And we must remember that this figure does not include the German mining and maritime associations or inspections by the *state* supervisors of Germany, and the fact that only some the audits of the trade inspectors extend *exclusively* to safety inspections. In absolute numbers, for every inspection by our trade inspectors, there are eleven by the German representatives of the trade associations. If we relate the number of inspections to the number of firms subject to compulsory insurance, there is a little less than one inspection by the inspectors for every four firms; in

Germany, on the other hand, there are somewhat more than one inspection by the supervisors for every two firms. We must also keep in mind that in Germany, a greater number of companies is subject to compulsory insurance than is the case in Austria; the German category also includes a great number of small-business categories that need no insurance here.

Given these general conditions, it becomes our task to uncover all existing efforts while fending off all impediments. But this can happen only by means of a well-rounded organization, one that identifies the existing efforts that show the potential for combining with others, and strengthens and links them on a legal basis as well. In Austria, such an organization can only be territorial, if only because of the political conditions.

I will speak here only of the most basic principles guiding such an organization.

There are clear advantages for accident prevention in an arrangement by profession, limited to a small circle of similar companies that are easy to survey and can be dealt with equally, since accident prevention is primarily concerned with individual firms, and these advantages have been proven in practice by the way they have been worked out in Germany. But a territorial organization also has advantages that should not be underestimated, especially for us. These lie, above all, in the possibility of easily answering overall questions, the close mutual supervision of operating groups, the formation of powerful organizations able to produce leverage, the analogy that is thereby created to the territorial arrangement of the governmental trade authorities, and finally, the simplification of the central organization. The principal advantages of the organization of trade associations need not be relinquished, for the compulsory trade associations that exist in Austria will, of necessity, have to be put to use as secondary associations subsumed in an umbrella organization for accident prevention.

This territorial organization would have to be established by a law that would arrange for the creation of a mandatory regional committee composed of a senate of employers and a senate of workers. The creation of a completely new organization will not be necessary, since it is only a matter of linking what already exists and is almost completely developed. But since among all organizations today, the accident insurance institutes are the ones that possess not all, but the most and most promising resources for accident-protection efforts, an arrangement of the regional committee as close to the institutes as possible—something like the present court of accident arbitration—will be of great advantage.

The costs of the regional organization will be relatively low, since this is not a question of an independent institution with independent requirements but only of an aid to organization. The organization will, most of all, have to concentrate on bringing in the cooperatives and industrial associations—with, of course, the greatest possible support from the governmental authorities, for whom the regional committee will save a great deal of work—so that the latter should become the actual focus of accident protection efforts. Finding the necessary funds will also present few difficulties, because a concentration of the resources that were previously scattered will have a place in the regional committee as a concentration of all previous accident-prevention efforts.

Aside from the general publicity campaign about industrial safety, for which the German trade associations offer perfect examples and on which our Workmen's Accident Insurance Institutes are already engaged though with respectively fewer funds, the main task of the regional committee will be to issue accident-prevention regulations; these must then be made public through prescriptive channels, with penalty sanctions and generally binding force. The penalties for flouting the regulations can be divided into two groups affecting the employers—an increase in premiums set by the institutes, and fines the regional committee is entitled to impose.

The regional committee would be given substantial control over adherence to the safety regulations by the fact that the Institutes would be granted the right to inspect firms, and the cooperatives and other associations would also be entrusted with official control. The example of Germany shows the easy coexistence of the state and other work supervision.

The regional committee will perform direct practical work from a perspective much too much neglected today, in that it will get in touch with companies that produce proven safety devices and arrange for their sale in large quantities at a discounted price, possibly stimulating the production of products here that were formerly produced in other countries. The foundation of a comprehensive museum for safety-related material will be associated with these activities at no cost.

The regional committee will be the agency that can represent safety-related matters most dependably to all authorities. The desired uniformity in practice in civil, penal, and commercial legal matters will thus be achieved for questions of safety.

The regional committee will gain direct influence on the ministry's consultation on safety regulations that today is essentially denied to both employers and workers.

Finally, it will be inevitable that rescue service will also be included in the regional committee's sphere of activity.

With this territorial organization, Austrian accident prevention would arrive at a satisfactory overall conclusion, in spite of the fact that, as it developed, it was often confronted with nearly hopeless forecasts. The reason for this pessimism lies in an unfair comparison between the trade association and the territorial forms of organization. A territorial organization, working with larger complexes and greater considerations and obstacles, arrives much later at the appropriate stable end state, in which all tasks are dealt with fairly, than does a trade safety-and-insurance association that works in small groups and can be equal to these tasks much more quickly. In the same way as today, after the last unexpectedly favorable annual statements of account of the workmen's accident insurance institutes, we are experiencing a justification for workmen's accident insurance within a territorial organization and the fully funded insurance system that goes with it—in the same way, again, if the present signs of a crucial end stage are not neglected, we are facing, after many years of accident prevention seemingly given over to chance organization, the first territorial organization of accident prevention in Austria.

Commentary 13

In September 1913, the world's leading experts in accident prevention met in Vienna for the Second International Congress on Accident Prevention and First Aid, and Kafka was asked to accompany Marschner and Pfohl. (The published records of the conference list Kafka as a member of the Prague delegation.) The two speeches made by the Prague representatives appear under the names of Marschner and Pfohl; however, Kafka's letter to Felice Bauer dated April 28, 1913, and the newly discovered letter from his uncle Alfred Löwy, dated March 12, 1914, reveal that Kafka composed both speeches.

> I read both speeches with interest, and as they came from your pen I congratulate you sincerely on your thorough knowledge of the subject matter, which emerges. One has the solid impression that this could have been written only by someone who has a complete mastery of the subject; and everything is explained in such pure and clear language that even a layman reads it with pleasure and understanding, which is a rarity where such reports are concerned. That your supervisors put their names to the reports written by you is not a rare occurrence. (KKAB2 582)

The Vienna experience, including the correspondence with Alfred Löwy, is preserved in cryptoautobiographical fragments playfully scattered throughout Kafka's work. In "Building the Great Wall of China," the narrator describes himself as one of those "leaders of the lower rank" who, while inferior to the "upper level of leaders, indeed even the leaders of the middle rank, saw enough of the manifold growth of the Wall to sustain their intellectual and moral strength" (KSS 114). And still they "stood intellectually [so] far above their outwardly petty tasks" that they "had to be provided for differently" to keep up their morale. So the "system of partial construction" was established; and after the completion of each section, "they were sent far, far away," pausing "at the compounds of higher-ranking leaders, who bestowed medals on them" (KSS 115). This is the action to which Franz Kafka basically submitted after his superiors in the Institute decided "at the last moment" to add his name to the list of the Prague delegation. This autobiographical reading adds some ironic, even sarcastic, spin to Kafka's Chinese reflections, since it is precisely the leader of the lower rank—Kafka—who, in fact, depicted to an international audience "the manifold growth" of the wall of Bohemian accident prevention.

On this occasion, Kafka's semiprivate game goes even further. In the letter cited above, his uncle Alfred, after musing on the different punctuation marks occurring at the end of the address line in different countries, proposes the following research topic to his nephew: "How varied different peoples are in even the slightest matters. To the best of my knowledge, no philosopher has yet studied this question, and so I offer it to you without claim to a patent." Kafka obviously passed this generous offer on to his Chinese expert in nomad prevention, who at one point in his report admits that "while the Wall was being built and afterward to this day, I have been occupied almost exclusively with comparative ethnography—there are certain questions whose nub, so to speak, one can get to only by this method" (KSS 118). At the same time, this passage shows how Kafka's ongoing game with life and literature immediately moves onto the more serious plane of a debate at the highest level of contemporary political and philosophical thought, notably with Friedrich Nietzsche: "Just because they were poorly informed and not even very curious about different peoples, times, and past ages," Nietzsche criticizes the moral philosophers, "they never laid eyes on the real problems of morality; for these emerge only when we compare many moralities."[1]

These apparent digressions take us to the heart of Kafka's mission in Vienna. The two speeches delivered by Kafka's superiors, Marschner and Pfohl, prefigure the issues of his Chinese narrative. In the story, the distinction between accident prevention in the German Reich and in Austria is reproduced in the difference between an all-encompassing defensive wall and an inexpedient system of piecemeal construction.

In Germany, accident prevention proceeded from individual cases. As industrial accident insurance was provided by trade associations, these cases could be swiftly adjudicated by being referred to rubrics listed according to distinct branches of industry. In Austria, however, the territorial organization was much too broad to be coupled with accident prevention in a purposeful way.

In "Building the Great Wall of China," the task of constructing the Wall has to respond to both the continuous development of building technology and the continual movement of the nomads. "Those sections of the wall left abandoned in barren regions can easily be destroyed, over and over, by the nomads, especially since at that time these people, made anxious by the construction of the Wall, changed their dwelling places with incomprehensible rapidity, like locusts, and so perhaps had a better overview of the progress of the Wall than even we ourselves, its builders" (KSS 113). These same difficulties are anticipated in

"Marschner's" report on accident prevention: "accident prevention is in a permanent process of reformulation, since it must follow both the development of industry and machine technology as well as the developments of accident-prevention technology." Like Kafka's Chinese narrator, Kafka's Prague experts in accident insurance are fully aware of the fact that they can learn from the nomads—that is to say, from the accidents—how best to organize their defense. In 1916, Alois Gütling, the head statistician at the Prague Institute, Kafka's next-door office mate, welcomed the 1913 German translation of Frederick W. Taylor's *Principles of Scientific Management*, in the belief that breaking down the process of production into minute steps would make it possible to establish statistically the precise accident risk of every single movement made by every individual worker.

There is another strong resonance between Chinese nomad prevention and Bohemian accident prevention on the question of political authority and the law. Consider "Marschner's" summary of the responses obtained to a circulated questionnaire checking awareness of a three-year-old safety regulation in the construction industry: "In responding to the question, the vast majority indicated that the employer was not aware of the ordinance. One employer, for example, stated that he had been aware of the decree for the past forty years. Another declared that he was familiar with all the laws and ordinances. Others answered innocently with a request that they be sent the ordinance, since it would be of interest to them." The Chinese architect describes political-legal awareness among his people as follows: "A lot of this sort of thing is learned by rote at school, but the general uncertainty in this respect is so great that even the best students are drawn into it. In our villages, long-dead emperors are set up on thrones, and one who lives on only in song has recently issued a decree that the priest reads aloud in front of the altar" (KSS 120). Even the explanation given for these "Oriental" conditions is the same. "Pfohl": "There are far too few inspections"; Kafka's Chinese narrator: ". . . [O]nce, once in a lifetime, an imperial official touring the provinces accidentally comes into our village" (KSS 121).

The most striking and, in a sense, most far-reaching analogy is to be found at the level of textual organization. As Kafka's literary notebooks show, he wrote two safety reports—one based in Vienna and one in China. While the architect-narrator of "Building the Great Wall of China" praises the weakness of a political organization that leaves room for a variety of viewpoints, even contradictory ones, on law and authority, the Chinese cobbler of "A Page from an Old Document," witnessing the havoc wreaked by nomads raiding the capital, replaces the point of view of the safety expert with the point of view of the victim of a major cultural accident, ending with a complaint that revokes the former's praise of a weakly organized state: "To us craftsmen and businessmen the salvation of the fatherland is entrusted; but we are not up to such a task; certainly we have never boasted of being capable of it. It is a misunderstanding, and it means our destruction" (KSS 67). It is fascinating to see Kafka, the Institute's ghostwriter for the contributions at the Vienna Congress, anticipating this confrontation of two basic philosophies of optimal social organization. As "Marschner," he pleads for a degree of disorganization in the field of accident prevention as the precondition of a newly emerging order:

> Basically, however, there are also advantages to this disorganization, in that it represents a transitional stage within which those factors that have the capacity of advancing accident prevention in spite of unfortunate conditions can work all the more visibly. In a sense, there is free competition within Austrian accident prevention; after the practical selection of the effective powers, this competition must lead to a legal determination. This determination, in turn, will have an empirical foundation that is unquestionably solid.

On the other hand, the conclusion Kafka arrives at in the paper delivered by Pfohl is literally in keeping with the wisdom of the cobbler in "A Page from an Old Document": "The cases of private initiative must remain isolated and far from substantial as long as there is no central headquarters for matters relating to safety, an organization to which the individual employer feels solidly connected."

These echoes from Kafka's office writings in his literary work are far too audible to be dismissed as accidental; neither are they a matter of thematic or stylistic "influence." Through the Viennese-Chinese metamorphosis, Kafka's art projects key concepts from his professional field of social insurance onto large-scale political and cultural constellations. These projections are driven by something more than an instinct for literary game playing. They are stimulated by adjacent real-world events, new encounters, cross-disciplinary infusions of knowledge. In World War I propaganda, social insurance came to be highlighted as an integral part of the national defense: Social welfare regulations, wrote the Brunswick lawyer and city councilor von Frankenberg in 1916, "represent, as a whole and in all its details, a part of the iron bulwark against our enemies."[2] Kafka's Chinese construction project is also informed by details of Theodor Herzl's *The Jewish State*: Herzl's Zionist program of 1896 projects the state of Israel as another element in the defensive constructions against the enemies of culture, "a portion of a rampart of Europe against Asia, an outpost of civilization as opposed to barbarism."[3]

In Kafka's days, Zionism and accident prevention did more than share a metaphor; they shared a city. During his stay in Vienna in September 1913, Kafka attended two international congresses. On September 2, the Eleventh Zionist Congress had opened, and five days later, Kafka visited this event, which had been widely covered in the newspapers. In the pages of the *Neue Freie Presse*, which had begun its reporting on the Congress on Accident Prevention and First Aid the preceding weekend (September 6), the two congresses were covered side by side for a whole week; in fact, the two series of reports display striking similarities on the issue of centralized versus decentralized organization. As if arranged by an invisible hand, reports from a third conference also appeared in Vienna's papers during the time of Kafka's visit—a meeting that represented the newly discovered basis of both accident prevention and Zionist colonization: the International Statistical Institute had summoned a plenary gathering to clear the ground for the establishment of the International Statistical Bureau in The Hague.

14

ACCIDENT PREVENTION IN QUARRIES (1914)

A lively and occasionally picturesque report on the working conditions of Austrian quarrymen, this remarkable essay is itself a quarry for images scattered across Kafka's literary work. And in this case, the images are not mere metaphors. Historians of the media will be interested to learn of Kafka's employment of photographs as a means of recording the sites and circumstances of quarry accidents. The photographs around which the report is organized are themselves impressive.

Accident Prevention in Quarries: Statistical Findings

The means currently available to the Institute and the possibilities and rights the law provides for its work in the field of safety have led its efforts in particular directions. The Institute is unable to address the entire field of accident prevention, as the German trade associations do, but must limit its activities to intervening where there is an urgent need from both a social and a statistical standpoint, and where there is the strongest prospect of success at the least possible expense. These were the considerations in dealing with the provision of safety equipment for agricultural machines. The financial stability of the Institute was threatened by excessive costs for some time, but record keeping and inspections are easy with the aid of the municipalities and district authorities, and they have proven to be so. The process was similar with the universal introduction of safety shafts for wood-planing machines. There is a safety device that functions almost perfectly for these tools, which are the second-most dangerous woodworking machines. With the help of precise records from the affected firms, listing the number, type, and arrangement of the planing machines, and with the assistance of governmental authorities, the Institute succeeded in limiting the use of the old square shafts to an increasing extent, as recent figures clearly show.

Unlike the German trade associations' work to achieve safety measures, before each such effort, the Institute must first call on all parties who can be assumed to have a special interest to participate and collaborate. While the German trade associations can work independently in this area because they have the necessary means and legal authority, for the present, the Institute is limited to motivating outsiders, and only when their participation is assured can the Institute become involved. For this same reason, each undertaking evolves slowly and shows concrete results only after a long period of preliminary work.

All these considerations apply especially to the Institute's endeavors to restructure in its territory the quarries whose safety regulations have been neglected in order to install rational operating procedures.

The figures on the costs for the most important business titles in question are clear enough.

If we concentrate on the five most important titles, they show the following losses in the two decades from 1890 to 1911:

Title 55—Quarries That Include Material Processing	K 493,231
Title 57—Gravel Quarries	K 688,656
Title 60—Other Quarries	K 738,344
Title 61—Extracting and Breaking Up Erratic Boulders	K 54,019
Title 62—Sand, Pebble, and Gravel Pits	K 167,762
Total Deficit	K 2, 142,012

This deficit occurs in spite of the fact that the titles in question almost entirely designate the highest-risk categories. These excessive costs are even more striking considering that, according to the statistics, a large part of these accidents could have been prevented with efficient excavation practices and even the slightest effort at supervision. The issue here is not unforeseen chance occurrences during the operation of machinery but primarily the correct application and management of human labor. The lack is not so much of safety equipment as it is of supervision at the worksite and, at an earlier stage, training for both the employers and the workers. More than in any other dangerous operation, each worker is left to his own devices, and here, more than elsewhere, the entire operation remains without supervision by the employer or the authorities.

Only from this perspective can we understand the percentage distribution of the separate causes of accidents in the overall costs.

For example, in the period from 1897 to 1911, under Title 57—Gravel Quarries—an average of 32–33 percent of the total costs were for accidents caused by flying shards during stoneworking. Under Title 60, that same cause of accidents accounted for around 13 percent. A great part of these accidents—most commonly eye injuries—could have been prevented if protective goggles had been worn. Such goggles have largely been perfected; some goggles, such as those listed in the catalog of the company St. Scheidig & Son, neither impede the work nor are bothersome in any other way yet still fulfill their purpose. And yet, safety goggles are seldom used.

It is true that safety goggles are frequently issued to the workers, but the men find them impossible to use, or they are prejudiced against using them, so that the goggles are usually found in the workers' pockets during the workday. Such a situation can exist because supervision of the operation is either inadequate or altogether lacking.

Between 32 percent and 33 percent of the total costs under Title 57 for Gravel Quarries was for the collapse of rock masses and falling rock; this figure was between 34 percent and 35 percent under Title 60 for Other Quarries, and it went as high as 70 percent under Title 62 for Sand, Pebble, and Gravel Pits. These accidents are chiefly caused by an absence of efficient excavation practices: employers and workers lack a complete understanding of the potential and the advantages of proper excavation practices; inadequate inspection by the authorities; and particularly in many areas of the Institute's territory, the adverse effect of adjacent mining operations. Similar reasons account for accidents involving workers falling from high locations. They amounted to around 8 percent under Title 57, approximately 9 percent under Title 60, 5 percent under Title 62, and 8 percent under Title 63.

Approximately 12–13 percent of the total costs under Title 57 were the result of blasting; this figure was 13–15 percent under Title 60 and correspondingly lower under the other titles. If lack of training bears a large part of the burden for the previously mentioned causes of accidents, it bears the largest part here. Working with blasting materials requires workers to be familiar with all the possible dangers, and they must be given thorough and repeated training. Such precautions are all the more necessary because no special proof of knowledge of working with explosives is required.

Status of Laws Protecting Workers in Quarries

At the outset, such detrimental conditions were countered by merely minimal governmental measures.

Quarries call for a kind of inspection that differs from that required by other operations. In this work, it is not a matter of safety devices that, once acquired, will last and be useful for long periods of time; what matters is efficient excavation, which has to be planned over and over so as to fit with the ever-changing soil conditions. For this reason, the oversight needed is not so much thorough and time-consuming; it should be as frequent and systematic as possible. Such checks were never initiated, however, because the official inspections are not attuned to this perspective, and it is frequently difficult to carry out even one-time inspections of the many quarries situated in sites of the district that are nearly inaccessible.

But a great many quarries—the so-called agricultural quarries—elude all forms of inspection, and since the distinction between agricultural and commercial quarries is not precise and can be blurred in practice, many commercial quarries are among those that are never inspected.

Nor are there any definitive principles that might have been authoritatively applied at any inspections.

[. . .]

The Institute's Control of the Dissemination of Safety Regulations

The Institute therefore took it as its mission to arrange for implementation of the safety regulations as well as give them wider application and to extend this activity to the agricultural quarries.

The details of how to conduct the inspections may be reserved for a later time.

The first opportunity came with a dissemination of the ordinance in the form of posters. Since previous attempts of this kind regarding safety regulations for agricultural machinery had not proved successful, however, this effort was abandoned. What mattered here was not so much bringing to the attention of employers and workers a summary of the ordinance in poster form but rather enforcing observation of safety regulations in the first place.

Once this end had been achieved, our attention could be turned to entire safety regulations just as well as to individual excerpts.

From the outset, the complete indifference to safety regulations had to be overcome. The Institute had no doubt from the beginning that this could best be done by direct personal training by experts in the field. But at present, such a step is still not possible. The Institute had, therefore, to be satisfied with printing up copies of the ordinance, which were sold at cost; these were also provided to organizations free of charge. The printed copies have been widely distributed, especially because the Institute's questionnaire for firms put a set of questions concerning safety devices and regulations and asked directly whether the employer had a copy of the safety regulations and had posted them.

Call for Safety Measures at Agricultural Quarries

The Institute's further effort was directed to imposing the safety regulations on both agricultural and commercial quarries, so as to allow for their official inspection. In particular, agricultural quarries had to be defined more precisely than had been the previous practice. Only those operations that served agricultural purposes exclusively were to be regarded as agricultural quarries, whether they served the purpose of the farmer himself or the purpose of agriculture in general. Therefore, all those quarries that derived a profit from the resale of the extracted materials, though they might belong to the farmer, would be separated from the category of above-mentioned agricultural activities. Until this time, such quarries were often designated and managed as agricultural quarries. These conditions made it easy to conceal a quarry's transition from agricultural to commercial operation, as all too frequently happened. In a petition to the Office of the Governor, the Institute pointed out that the concept of an agricultural quarry had to be defined precisely but that it was important as well to take safety precautions even in firms claiming to be purely agricultural quarries. At present, these dangerous quarries are outside the scope of the safety regulations and therefore beyond the reach of official inspection.

This situation led many such quarries to neglect registering with the Institute and coming forward only after an accident occurred.

At that time, the Institute made the following retrospective suggestions as they affect agricultural quarries:

Call for the Supervision of Agricultural Quarries

1. The district authorities should assign permanent supervision of the quarries to those state agencies that have to assure the public safety. Since the regulations for these businesses involve merely separate measures to be observed in all businesses, the particulars of these measures can easily be communicated to the authorized agencies. In this instance, too, what matters is frequency of inspections more than their thoroughness. A cursory inspection is therefore adequate to establish the current safety conditions that obtain in any such business, and it will not be necessary to call upon these agencies for inspections merely for the Institute's purposes; it will be enough if the inspectors note the prevailing safety conditions in these firms during their visits—which experience has shown to be required for other official reasons and which occur quite frequently—and if they report any conditions that do not meet the regulations.

2. The majority of the agricultural quarries are the property of municipalities, which let their citizens work in the quarries without concerning themselves with the methods used in the excavations.

In this respect, the influence the district authorities exert over the municipalities in general can be used to bring about the most efficient excavation in the municipal quarries.

3. Stricter attention than before should be given to the transition of a quarry from an agricultural to a commercial operation, and in such cases commercial registration will have to be urged immediately, thus directly subjecting the firm to the effect of the Ministry of Trade and Commerce ordinance of May 2, 1908, [. . .].

4. All quarries that can be considered commercial businesses under the more precise interpretation of the definition but that have not previously obtained a trade license need to apply for a license at once.

The same petition did not, however, address agricultural quarries exclusively but also asked the Office of the Governor [. . .] to replace the cited circular decree, which is already outdated, with a new decree to remind the government officials once again of the provisions of the safety decree and give instructions regarding the above suggestions that would apply to both agricultural and commercial quarries.

[. . .]

Alcohol Abuse in Quarries

Without losing sight of the final goal of general and systematic safety audits for all quarries, the Institute used every opportunity for minor measures, and while these might not lead to the principal goal, they nevertheless approached it indirectly. Three endeavors should be stressed in this regard:

1. Various experiences during inspections by Institute agents demonstrated the danger of locating canteens close by the quarry. The Ministry of Trade and Commerce ordinance of May 29, 1908, lacked adequate provisions in this regard. Though § 34 ordered that only the most experienced and reliable workers be employed in blasting, and § 52 stated that anyone who is intoxicated is to be relieved from this work altogether, this provision fell far short of prescribing everything that needed to be done on this front. The Institute's experiences in one district in particular spurred it into action on this matter. There are a number of slate quarries in the area where the quarry workers' alcoholic consumption has reached an extraordinary degree, and in almost the same manner.

The immediate cause of this excess is the fact that providing the workers with brandy is, to all intents and purposes, stipulated in their labor contract. In these quarries, this custom has been observed so irresponsibly that the workers will not even report for work if they are not first promised their quota of brandy.

A typical example of this practice will show how such abuses can arise. One quarry owner was also the owner of an inn located about 10 minutes from the quarry. Every day the foreman would, as one of his most important tasks, bring large jugs of brandy from the inn to the quarry and distribute them to the workers, keeping records of their consumption.

The wage book, like the separate scraps of paper the foreman used to compile it, contained just as many notes on alcohol consumption as it did on work in the quarry. Of course, the notes on alcohol consumption were disguised under the heading "On account."

Accounts were settled once a week, and the procedure that was followed deducted the listed "amount" from the wages the worker was entitled to for the week's work; and apart from the very insignificant health insurance deduction, "On account" referred entirely to the cost of brandy. These deductions were exceptionally large overall—though it was not possible to determine the sums allotted to alcohol precisely because there were gaps in the wage lists. In any case, however, the amounts charged some of the workers for brandy consumption amounted to as much as 30 percent of the worker's total wages. In effect, the workforce of this quarry was made up largely of men who were, to a greater or lesser degree, drunk. Once, while walking along the upper rim of the quarry, a patrol of constables found a cartridge on the ground; during the closer inspection of the quarry that followed, the constable asked to see the place where the dynamite was kept. In the shack where the dynamite was stored, the constable found a tobacco pipe. These conditions aside, the quarry in itself is very dangerous if only because of the way the rock is stratified, as is true of all the quarries in the area. These quarries have high, rather steeply sloping sides, and the workers must be let down to the face where they will work by means of a rope. This particular quarry is only one example in the area, however. In other quarries, alcohol is brought in from unrelated shops, but there are no essential differences between quarries. The universal results of these circumstances are the demoralization of the workforce, loss of wages for the family, and extreme danger to the workers.

Since barrooms, besides providing the workers with brandy as payment in kind, are widespread phenomena, the Institute petitioned the Office of the Governor as follows:

a. Connections between the operation of an inn and work in quarries (with the exception of special cases in which no adverse effects are to be feared from such a connection) should be eliminated by the threat of or actual revocation of licenses.

b. Bars in immediate proximity to quarries should be shut down altogether.

c. The provision of brandy as payment in kind by the employer should be prohibited or limited as much as possible wherever possible.

The Institute was not satisfied with this general petition, however, but sought to bring about improvement in specific cases that came to its attention on the occasion of wage inspections or other reports or even from some of the workers themselves. With the help of the district authorities, this process has been quite successful.

Use of Safety Goggles

2. Unending complaints about the workers' refusal to use safety goggles caused the Institute to look into this matter specifically. The complaints pour in from all sides; inspections by the authorities find again and again that safety goggles are not being used; employers complain that the workers do not use the goggles made available to them; the workers complain either that they receive no goggles or that the goggles hinder their work and diminish their earnings. Even in the Institute's questionnaire, in which every employer strives to depict his workplace as being as well-equipped as possible, employers often openly admit that safety goggles are not used. And the figures for accidents all too clearly show the justification of these complaints.

The Institute approached the firms, requested models of proven safety goggles, tried to advocate their use, especially if they were domestic products, and displayed them for inspection at the Institute as well as at the exhibition in Komotau.

We must, however, admit that this effort did very little good, since nothing of lasting value can usually be achieved solely by promoting something in the absence of systematic inspections of the entire enterprise.

Measures Designed for Agricultural Quarries

3. The effort to impose some safety regulations on the agricultural quarries continued after the k. k. Office of the Governor issued the decree mentioned above. A petition from the Office of the Governor to the

Ministry of Agriculture, sent at the Institute's instigation, led to the Ministry's decree of January 31, 1912, [. . .]. This document stated that there were legal reasons for excluding agricultural quarries from the provisions of the ministerial ordinance of May 29, 1908, [. . .]. Since this decision had already been pronounced in the cited decree by the Office of the Governor, the Office of the Governor should proceed in agreement with the Crownland Committee for the Kingdom of Bohemia to regulate this matter independently with the issue of an ordinance. Various evaluations were gathered, namely from the Ministry of Agriculture's expert, Privy Councilor and Professor H. Friedrich; the Crownland Committee; and the two sections of the Agricultural Council for the Kingdom of Bohemia.

The Institute kept this matter in constant view and got in touch with the crownland agricultural council directly; after lengthy discussions a draft was agreed upon, which is now waiting for the Office of the Governor to accept it. In devising this draft, the parties assumed that the various reasons why the men were endangered would first have to be established on the basis of the figures and according to the degree of their severity. Following the same arrangement, the means for combating these risk factors could then be addressed. The plan would have to make sure that there was a clear distinction between those elements that were essential and those that were not, because it was important, especially in dealing with the agricultural quarries, to issue brief, clear instructions. In order to strengthen the force of the decree, the Institute proposed providing it with small sketches. In its present form, this draft appears as follows:

Draft of an ordinance for agricultural quarries and gravel, sand, and clay pits

1. The provisions of this ordinance shall apply to all agricultural quarries and gravel, sand, and clay pits.
2. All rubble and all loose material along the quarry walls must always be removed.
3. Excavation must take place from the top down and must carve out terraces or steps, of no greater distances than of a man's height at most.
4. Undermining is prohibited without exception.
5. Splitting or chipping away is also prohibited, unless it is performed without undermining and below the regular gradient.
6. Excavation in loose and rolling material may be conducted only below the natural gradient, which may not exceed 45°.
7. Solid material may be excavated in terraces (steps and stages) or vertically. Vertical excavation is permitted only if the material, including

rubble, is arranged in layers no higher than a man's height; otherwise, only steps or stages may be excavated to that height.

8. Blasting may be done only by trained workers and according to the regulations stipulated in the decree. The use of loosely gathered explosives is prohibited. All explosives must be stored safely.

9. When working in hard stone and when breaking rock to gravel, workers must be provided with safety goggles. In making gravel, the work stations must be set up at least $1\frac{1}{2}$ meters apart and separated by protective screens.

10. Every quarry and gravel, sand, and clay pit must be provided with safe supply and disposal routes and be securely enclosed by an exterior wall $1\frac{1}{2}$ meters deep.

11. Dangerous spots in the quarry and the cited pits must be specially enclosed, and excavated cavities must be filled in.

12. Only workers who are known to the employer to be reliable and sober are to be employed.

13. When there is a thaw, workers must start their shifts with the greatest caution. Work is to be discontinued in case of heavy fog and rain.

14. The employer shall provide for constant supervision of all operations.

15. Abandoned quarries must be secured by appropriate enclosures and by filling in all pits in such a way that there is no possibility of accidents.

16. If agricultural quarrying is performed by means of underground shafts and tunnels, all safety measures for securing the shaft, the pit, and the trench entrance are to be closely observed.

Reasons for Demanding Constant
and Overall Inspections for All Quarries

A very typical case gave new impetus to our efforts to establish overall and systematic inspections of all quarries. The Institute had long complained of its powerlessness in the face of firms that carried out destructive despoiling without regard for the safety regulations and that sought to present themselves in the questionnaire as being managed with particular care, going so far in this deception that they succeeded in concealing their actual operating conditions from the authorities even when occasional inspections were carried out. The Institute itself could not as a rule crucially bring about the discovery of such poor conditions, lacking both the right to inspect the firms as well as lacking the necessary authority. Furthermore, in the various cases in which the Institute actually did inspect a firm and discovered adverse operating conditions, all we achieved was our word against the firm's, so that further inspections were required, and in these, the employer's deceptive practices might succeed again. And this is where the particular typical case represented a turning point.

The case involved a quarry that also practiced stonecutting; the re-classification of 1905 had classified it in risk category X, with a risk percentage of 61 percent under Title 55—Quarries that Include Material Processing.

The risk percentage, actually only 2 percent above the median, had been selected because, according to the findings of the inspection, the walls of the quarry were very high—from 10 to 15 meters—while the mass of rubble rose 3–4 meters high and was severely disintegrated, and because only some of the workers wore safety goggles. These conditions were evident in the answers to the questionnaire, but this document described the excavation method as following the natural gradient and claimed that rubble was always completely cleared away before excavation was begun. At the time, the employer lodged an appeal with the Office of the Governor concerning the classification, and based on another inspection, the firm was judged to meet the standard and was reclassified in the median-risk percentage, like all standard firms.

For the 1910 reclassification, the Institute was presented with an expert opinion as the result of an official inspection, according to which the business was to be considered as having all standard equipment and arrangements.

In consequence, and in consideration of the above-mentioned decision, the Institute classified the firm in the median-risk percentage category of 59 percent. According to the description of the firm's operations given in the questionnaire, conditions had even improved; the stratification was very convenient; all excavation was terraced—the claim even included a sketch—allegedly there was no undermining, rubble was regularly removed, and safety goggles, the Institute was assured, were always worn.

There seemed no obvious reason, therefore, to deny the firm the 59 percent classification, even if at that time, the firm's accident charges already raised the alarm against lowering the classification, for some serious accidents had been caused by flying stone chips and falling rock. The employer was still not satisfied with reclassification in the median-risk percentage either, however, and he lodged a new appeal with the Office of the Governor; based on a new inspection, a further reduction to 55 percent—4 percent below the previous 59 percent, foreseen for standard operations—was granted. The reduction was based on supposedly advantageous conditions for excavating. Not quite four months after this decision, there was a serious mass accident in the quarry when a projecting layer of stone, eroded by rain, collapsed. One worker was killed, and two others were very seriously injured. The charges for these three accidents alone amounted to more than K 10,000. At this point, it was no longer possible to conceal the true conditions in this firm. In addition, the accident figures for the five-year period from 1907 to 1911 spoke volumes. The firm's accident charges were far too high, amounting to K 33,000; in order to acknowledge this excess, classification in risk percentage 144 percent would have been required for the year 1915.

Photographs of Large Commercial Quarries

Given these circumstances, the Institute could no longer stand idly by. It therefore decided not only to have its own authorities conduct an inspection but also to have the results of the inspection documented photographically here and to do the same in other quarries.

It was not possible to take nearly as many photographs as the Institute would have liked. But what we seek to show is that only systematic and continuing inspections can help to reduce accidents in quarries, while sporadic inspections often serve to conceal actual conditions rather than clarify them.

All the photographs show quarries in intensive industrial use.

Figure I

Figure I shows a granite quarry where the formation of projecting columns and simultaneous ledges can be seen very clearly at the top right. Neither trash nor rubble has been removed. The entire site is a desolate heap of ruins. Even the formation of narrow paths between ravines to the right and the left is visible. Access to the separate quarrying areas is almost barricaded by trash. If there is a projecting piece of rock that might endanger a worker, he will find it almost impossible to bypass it, given the conditions on the ground. The dangers that arise when blasting is carried out under these circumstances are inconceivable. Moreover, in this quarry, blasting is done exclusively with loose black powder.

Fig. II. This photograph shows even more clearly than the one of the previous quarry that rolling debris is not cleared away and that rubble covers the full height of the quarry. The deep shadows bordering various rocks show the extent to which they project. The railing bordering the top of the quarry is set so close to the edge that it is quite impossible to remove the debris accumulated at the top; the work must therefore proceed while debris hangs over the workers; work should no longer be allowed, and the quarry should be shut down altogether, at least at this site. Even projecting rocks are still loaded down with debris. To better evaluate the danger posed by these quarries, note that in this case, as in the next, the walls of the quarry are 10–16 meters high and that the rubble rises to 1–3 meters; the debris consists of broken stone of various

Figure II

sizes, from 1 cubic decimeter to 1 cubic meter, which are layered in soft soil, so that the entire layer of debris must start rolling at the slightest impetus, especially in spring when the thaw sets in.

Fig. III. At the center of the photograph I saw a projecting rock wall with distinct three-sided slanted columns. In this instance as well, the rubble and debris have not been removed, and rubble and workable blocks lie close together and intermingled. Large areas have been hollowed out in the crumbling material to both the right and the left. The questionnaire this firm returned denies that there is any evidence of undermining.

Fig. IV. At the very top to the right in the debris, marked with "B," a loose stone block, 1 cubic meter in size, lies almost suspended above a projecting rock wall. At the center of the picture, marked "S," a man can be seen to be working at a dangerous spot, 4 meters above ground, without being attached to a rope. Debris is not removed, and quarrying work has been pushed forward almost to the edge of the walkways shown through the railing.

Fig. V. The reverse-wedge formation is so prevalent here that we might be tempted to say that the quarry would meet the safety regulations much better if it were stood on its head. Here, too, we see rubble and debris everywhere. At the center of the picture, at the top, there is another, nearly suspended, projecting stone block.

Figure III

Figure IV

Figure V

Fig. VI. A quarry with vertical rock walls. After inspecting quarries, such as those in the previous illustrations, this one almost seems more properly excavated, although it follows the wording of the regulations perhaps even less. What is missing are the step fragments obstructed by rubble seen in the previous pictures of quarries. However, the lighter parts at the left side of the picture also indicate projecting walls. Nor is the debris removed, it forms a solid layer. Keeping the quarry free of rubble also contributes to the better impression it creates. After inspecting the other quarries, we are at first not even aware of how far this quarry also is from fulfilling the regulations. At the bottom right we note a worker busy crushing gravel who is working without safety goggles.

Fig. VII. At the center we see a man crushing gravel without safety goggles, and to the right, the last section of rail of a narrow-gauge railway hangs loose over the embankment of rubble and debris. Further, the rails are not bent upward at the free-hanging end, nor are there braking or stopping devices on this track. Since the track has a noticeable incline from the quarry to the heap of debris, so that the loaded car not only does not need uphill propulsion but must even be braked, any transport of the debris and especially emptying the car above the loose-hanging track runs a significant risk of accidents.

Fig. VIII. Again, columnar formations along with ledges with projecting rock walls. Although this quarry is located on a hill approximately 100 meters high, it has a considerable amount of ground water, as the

Figure VI

Figure VII

Figure VIII

photograph shows, which in places reaches a depth of 5 to 6 meters. This photograph was taken in winter, but since this quarry is worked all year round, the picture is realistic. The snow points out the narrow ledges and the steep walls immediately over the water. Note the carelessness with which the rock wall between the excavated and the active quarry is treated, although the wall is also hollowed out by ground water.

Fig. IX. The background indicates the beginnings of a proper excavation. But much less concern has been taken with working the rest of the quarry. The debris is not removed, the quarry is not cleared of rubble; indeed, this detritus makes the quarry quite inaccessible. At the left of the picture in particular, the loose rubble threatens to come crashing down. Given these conditions, the part of the excavation that is properly cared for counts for nothing at all; it even increases the danger because it gives the workers a sense of safety. As is clear from the masses of stone framing the quarry, the stratification of the rock is far from adverse, so that proper excavation would easily be possible, as the section of stepped excavation shows.

Fig. X. A narrow-gauge railroad leads to this quarry through a passage approximately 20 m long and 3 m wide. The rock has so many fissures that in March, when the ground thawed, the whole length of the roadbed was blocked with rolling rubble. The lower edge of the picture shows only a small section of the railway. The life-threatening danger implicit in this quarry must be obvious to any layman. Shards of stone

Figure IX

Figure X

never stop rolling downward, and the echo of stones crashing against one another is a constant background noise. Using the worker at the center of the picture as a frame of reference, the rock walls can be estimated to rise approximately 20 m.

Fig. XI. The sight of this quarry is alarming. Debris, rubble, and refuse cover everything in sight. The rock is so heavily fissured that the original columns and ledges of the stone have to be surmised rather than seen. A worker is standing above the mark (a), barely visible in front of the 40-m-high rock wall. The debris above where he is standing, which can be estimated at approximately 1000 cubic meters, collapsed during the thaw of March 1914. Fortunately, the workers were having their afternoon coffee break at the time of the rock fall, or all of them would have been buried alive. The extent of the rock fall is indicated by the fact that the employer plans to install motorized gravel production to process this pile of stone, which he had obtained quite without cost.

Fig. XII. This close-up of a block that crashed down during the thaw serves to illustrate the rock masses that can be set in motion during a thaw because excavation has been performed without regard to the regulations.

Fig. XIII. Debris that has been completely neglected; even trees are left standing close to the quarry wall, as seen by the exposed roots. It

Figure XI

Figure XII

Figure XIII

would seem that the fact that the tree roots hold fast to the debris does away with any obligation to create appropriate berms. Loading work is carried out in the area where the debris rolls down, as the overturned loading platform indicates; this practice is, of course, all the more dangerous in that the entire slope is in a permanent state of sliding. A part of the shed and the smithy also appear to lie in the area of rolling debris.

Fig. XIV. Here we are dealing with what is actually a newly opened quarry, which is located near the tracks of a local train. Even though it is in the area of the train's operation, there is no evidence that the rubble is cleared away.

All these quarries share certain characteristics in spite of their individual differences.

The regulations of the decree are insufficiently complied with. And yet the operation of these quarries has continued along the same lines, sometimes for years. The Institute has never received a notice that special penalties were imposed upon the employers for violating the regulations or that one or another quarry was shut down.

The accident statistics for these quarries show very costly accidents, even accidents involving a number of workers, and where accidents have not yet occurred, there exists a very strong probability that they will happen any given day. It is not only the workers themselves who are

Figure XIV

endangered, however, but also outsiders who come near the quarry, as can be seen in the quarries that are worked up to the part set off by railings (figs. II and IV), as well as in the quarry that threatens the nearby railroad with its great piles of trash (fig. XIV). And we must always keep in mind that these are only examples, whose number can be multiplied at will. These observations agree with the general comments of today's official inspectors; one such report for the year 1913 stated: "Undermining [for which we could easily substitute "excavation contrary to regulations"] cannot be eradicated, in spite of all official efforts, and there is little hope that there will be a significant improvement in this regard in the foreseeable future."

Means for Remedying These Poor Conditions

Based on earlier experiences, however, the Institute, for its part, nevertheless believes in the possibility of improvement. But to bring about this improvement, we believe that very different means must be applied than any used heretofore. The Institute makes the following principal demands in this regard:

Systematic Inspection

1. The current sporadic inspections are generally inadequate from the perspective of safety given the many opportunities open to employers to conceal the actual operating conditions—as shown by the above example of the quarry that won increasingly lower ratings as a result of inspection reports, though conditions kept deteriorating. These inspections can in reality be misleading. A different arrangement for inspections must therefore be found; a model of correct inspection is available.

This model is the inspection of agricultural machines as conducted annually by the district authorities. In this area, too, precise lists must be kept of all commercial quarries as well as of all agricultural ones (after the projected decree on this matter has been issued), and annual general inspections of these quarries must take place based on the continuously revised lists. Involving the agencies for public safety is, of course, essential for this purpose to a greater extent than was provided for in the most recent decree of the Office of the Governor.

Inspection of Blasting Practices

2. Special attention must be devoted to all blasting in quarries. The provisions of the ordinance are perhaps the least adequate in this respect. What is important on this point is not sporadic training after the fact, but advance education. Just as the German trade associations regularly provide lectures for blasters, we must make similar arrangements here. Blasting in particular is hampered by old, deeply rooted prejudices that forbid the introduction of better methods. Training is of no use, but frequently on-site demonstrations can help. In many cases, for example, workers' doubts about the usefulness of the wooden ramrods can be allayed only by having an expert come to the quarry to show that wooden ramrods can certainly do the job even in shallow drill holes. The following description, provided by a forest service, of a fatal accident will demonstrate the naïveté that prevails regarding blasting, even in areas where we might assume that adequate training had been provided. The account reads: "The victim of the accident was gently heating 4 dynamite cartridges on a shovel at a small fire, because the dynamite, having just been taken from cold storage, had solidified. The cartridges exploded (in a manner not yet explained!)."

Fig. XV will show the exemplary fashion in which the principles of blasting according to regulation are demonstrated by the German quarry

Figure XV

trade association. This illustration represents a model from the social-security organization's permanent exhibition in Charlottenburg. The nature of the measures to be demonstrated here is unfortunately such that a mere illustration cannot render them with sufficient clarity. However, the photograph indicates the available opportunities to exert a strong effect in this area.

A lecture on blasting held in front of this model cannot fail to be highly productive. The model represents four ideal quarries in full operation, with all the details of blasting in actual size, structure, method of excavation, and color. To the left granite is being extracted, and next to it greywacke and sandstone, and limestone to the right.

Between granite and greywacke, a transitional rock in the form of a filled cleft has been inserted. All four types of rock are extracted by blasting.

On the outer surfaces of the rock ledges, the drill holes are shown in their actual direction and size, but they are cut through, while the blasting cartridges are fully in place and show the preliminary steps for ignition, removing duds, etc. The blasting charges are, following regulations, identified with black-lettered signs, while two signs with red lettering prohibit touching the exhibit. The granite, which steps down in four terraces and is layered with thin rubble, has been given a drill hole almost two meters deep, filled with safety explosive and ready for ignition of the fuse.

Next to the transition rock, a crack holds a blasting cartridge filled with powder and with electric ignition to demonstrate the impact on the stone of such charges when loose powder is used (the crack concerned here has been made to be very deep).

Among the other depictions, the removal of duds shown in the second terrace of the sandstone is of particular interest.

Two charges can be seen. One has misfired and must be removed by working from a drill hole created at its side. In this case, the new drill hole must be slanted in such a way to avoid the dud's blasting charge being hit by the drill. That is why the drill holes slant slightly away from one another. On the lowest bank of greywacke, the three most common methods of securing the charges against being hurled are shown: protecting them with fascines, railway ties, and wire mats. The right side of the model illustrates pillar blasting in limestone. Two pillars fashioned from the layered rock are each provided with two horizontal drill holes filled with safety blasting cartridges. The electric battery stands ready to detonate these charges and thus to bring the rock wall tumbling down. An emergency rope with a safety grip hangs in front of the limestone quarry; the workers can use it to climb up and down the quarry wall easily and safely.

Photographic Documentation of the Situation after Accidents

3. We must call on photography to aid us in judging operating conditions on a large scale, not so much to establish operating conditions in general—the foreseen systematic inspections will take care of that aspect, apart from very special cases. Rather, as is the practice of the German trade associations, the photographs should retrospectively document the characteristic situation that led to an accident. In this way, we can significantly increase our understanding of the factors giving rise to accidents in individual quarries and in general.

Cooperation with Employers

4. General improvements in the operating conditions can never be forced, as experience shows, and cannot succeed without the cooperation of the persons involved.

It is, in any case, highly desirable to undertake the proposed systematic inspections, not only on the part of the authorities but also by including representatives of the employers and the workers of the district. These representatives must, of course, take their responsibility very seriously. Even if this arrangement cannot be put into practice at present, the Institute can nevertheless report considerable progress on this front. We have succeeded in reaching agreement with the central association of licensed master stonemasons of the Kingdom of Bohemia in Prague on the principles to be applied in evaluating all firms in the stone working industry, including quarries. The chairman of the central association, the architect Josef Seiche, greatly aided the negotiations with his expert knowledge, objective judgment, and sociopolitical insight. The Institute was pleased to be able to confirm the agreement with the central association recently on the occasion of an evaluation of the objections raised by members of the quarry industry against reclassification. It must be granted, however, that the expert opinions of the central association were limited to evaluation of the material in the files, since the means for experts to conduct on-site inspections are not available. Nevertheless, the value of truly expert, unprejudiced intervention in the appeal process became apparent.

The Institute is equally pleased to endorse the findings of such expert opinions in cases in which the original classification turns out to have been too high.

Even the relatively few earlier expert opinions have produced an abundance of material well suited to eliminating various preconceived ideas that became established in the previous evaluation of factors that would increase or decrease risks. We will note only that the proportional numbers of the actual quarries and stone work have been set on a new basis and that, for example, the use of gravity planes was found to be a risk-increasing factor in individual cases, in contrast to earlier expert opinions, and that the same was found to be true for piece-work payment almost without exception, especially when it is in recompense for transportation work.

The reduction of erratic boulders to small pieces was designated as altogether risk-increasing, even when it occurs in fields, although this does not involve risky transportation; the reason for this finding is that field work lacks even the most primitive safety measures. Stone dams were found to be an entirely inadequate replacement for safety fences in stone working, since the stones cannot be piled high enough and keep rolling downward because of the natural gradient, in themselves presenting a danger.

This new evaluation method allows us to hope for a further understanding between the involved factions and the Institute, and it signifies the best prognosis, especially for accident prevention in quarries and their supervision.

Commentary 14

❧

One of the minor consequences of World War I was that the Austrian workmen's accident insurance institutes fell behind in filing their annual reports. On May 30, 1916, Kafka sent the Prague Institute's annual report for 1914 to Felice Bauer, noting on an attached postcard, "As a sad diversion, my Institute's latest report, of which approximately pages 10–80 were written by me" (LF 470).

Kafka's long account of accident prevention in quarries is closely related to his literary work, and most of all to his Chinese scenario on national security and the construction of a defensive wall. As in the first of the two speeches Kafka wrote for the International Congress in Vienna (doc. 13A,B), he begins by contrasting accident prevention in Germany (where trade associations would "address the entire field of accident prevention") with the fragmented Austrian system (which had to "limit its activities to intervening where there is an urgent need from both a social and a statistical standpoint"). Like his Chinese architect of 1917, Kafka goes on to discuss the gaps in the protective system, in this case the "quarries whose safety regulations have been neglected." Often "situated in sites of the district that are nearly inaccessible" and difficult to supervise, they anticipate those especially endangered "sections of the [Chinese] Wall left abandoned in barren regions" that "can easily be destroyed by the nomads" (KSS 113). And while in the Chinese account, the nomads, "made anxious by the construction of the wall, changed their dwelling places [. . .] like locusts" (SS 113), in the Bohemian report the "ever-changing soil conditions" prevent "safety devices, once acquired, [from] last[ing] and be[ing] useful for long periods of time." In both scenarios, the sources of danger are sources of information as well: while in one Bohemian quarry only a "serious mass accident" made it impossible for the owner "to conceal the true conditions in this firm" to the Institute, the nomads, owing to their "incomprehensible rapidity, [. . .] perhaps had a better overview of the progress of the Wall than even we ourselves, its builders" (KSS 113).

Kafka's extensive use of photography as a source of information on accident prevention is remarkable. He ingeniously exploits the fact that in the case of quarrying, photography is not restricted to reproducing the surface (the horizontal dimension of a terrain) but can reproduce the depth as well (the vertical layers of the soil). Here is a model of a

Kafkaesque literary text: like this image of the quarry, the text yields its full richness only to a gaze directed both to the surface and to the depth—the multitude of verbal citations and echoes evoked and concealed by this surface. Indeed Kafka himself used quarrying to denote the empirical pole of his empirical-transcendental model of aesthetic production, as in this lustrous fable from his scrapbook:

> Everything submitted to him for the construction. Foreign workers brought the marble stones trimmed and fitted to one another. The stones lifted and placed themselves according to the measuring movements of his fingers. No construction ever came into being as easily as did this temple—or rather, this temple came into being in true temple-fashion. Except that on every stone—from what quarry had they come?-was scratched, with instruments obviously of a marvelous sharpness, the clumsy scribblings of senseless child-hands, or rather the inscriptions [better: entries, *Eintragungen*—Eds.] of barbaric mountain dwellers, in order to spite, or to desecrate, or to destroy completely, for an eternity outlasting the temple. (DF 205)

Kafka had a precedent for introducing photographs into his report in the practice of the German trade associations, who used "photographs [to] document retrospectively the characteristic situation that led to an accident." This practice finds a reverse echo in his Chinese stories. Instead of a new medium, it is an explicitly old medium ("A Page from an Old Document," the title of the narrative postscript to "Building the Great Wall of China") that retrospectively records the "characteristic situation" resulting from the disastrous intrusion of the nomads into the cultured space of China. Note, too, the presence in the Bohemian protection scenario of "rational operating procedures" and the "correct application and management of human labor." Both functions play a mirror-image role in the reflections of the architect of the Great Wall. Kafka's Chinese "have really only come to know [themselves] as a result of poring over the decrees of the highest leadership" (KSS 116). In Kafka's Institute, the "architects" are busy devising regional regulations and ordinances so as to close the gap between the inexpedient legislation of the "highest leadership" in Vienna and the industrial reality of Bohemia.

15

JUBILEE REPORT: TWENTY-FIVE YEARS OF THE WORKMEN'S ACCIDENT INSURANCE INSTITUTE (1914)

The remarkable history of the Prague Institute's Jubiläumsschrift *(twenty-fifth-anniversary volume) can be reconstructed from the files of the Ministry of the Interior in Vienna. While the original project of compiling a comprehensive source book of statistics from the workmen's insurance institutes of all the crownlands was obstructed by the outbreak of World War I, the Prague Institute continued with a publication of its own. The existence of this outstanding historical source is owed to the fact that in Prague two exceptional essayists were available for the job: Director Marschner, a renowned Goethe scholar, and Kafka. Therefore, the volume as a whole resonates with the mixed music of Marschner's "Goethe's German" and Kafka's crisp memorandum style. The sections presented here document the gap between the regulations of the central government on the one hand and their actual interpretation and application to local circumstances on the other. In this sense, they exhibit a recurrent feature of the bureaucracies depicted in Kafka's literary works.*

A. Periodic Revision of the Risk Classifications Based on the Applicable Ministerial Regulations

The implementation of the new risk classification [. . .] showed the typical development of the Institute's previous classification plan. The first effort aimed at creating the most complicated apparatus, one that had the capacity to account for every possible situation. Next, after the subject had been studied as intensively as possible, the system could be refined to make it simpler and to show greater precision. This trend can be seen at each stage of reclassification.

In brief, the Institute's proposals relating to general questions before the 1914 classification were as follows:

a. The upcoming stabilization of the statistics, the result of the disclosure and elimination of the principal sources of error of the previous five years, requires us to draw all the consequences from these statistics in such a way as to understand that the most important titles are burdened by the deficits of several five-year periods. We must also understand that the increase in total wages for the last five years is not based on the very nature of these firms and that it will thus not continue to grow nor permit all too favorable consequences for the financial status of these titles, even if we were to take this five-year period out of the equation.

b. An increase in the previous base figure of 7.10, which does not correspond to the actual statistical conditions. The current stabilization of the statistics for the most important titles, as well as the end of the deficit of agricultural insurance, will allow for greater precision of the base figure.

c. In § 1 of the classification regulations, the "firm as a technical unit" is to be placed above all other distinctions.

d. The exceptional provision of § 2 concerning the case-by-case classification of mechanized firms as manual operations must be given greater precision, since currently it leaves open a number of questions that require definitive answers and thus makes the classification system more difficult.

e. The classifications according to § 5 of the regulations occurring within a five-year period are to be determined immediately in the next risk-category revision by introducing new titles. Every classification according to § 5 should similarly be subjected to special approval, as is done with firms to be insured voluntarily.

f. Any reference to the safety regulations that have appeared or will appear must specifically be mentioned along with those factors increasing or decreasing risk that must absolutely be considered.

g. The fourth paragraph of § 10, concerning the questioning of experts from among the employers and workers in legal proceedings before the k. k. Ministry of the Interior, should be stricken, since as a rule, the Institute is no longer heard before the k. k. Ministry of the Interior and usually is not vouchsafed any glimpses into the results of the proceeding before decision is rendered. Once the decision is handed down, however, most of the factors that the Institute might have called to the Ministry's attention and thus might have influenced the decision can no longer be brought to bear on the matter, since the Administrative Court cannot consider them. This petition has been repeated before each risk classification.

h. It would best meet the practical requirements of classification if the current risk-percentage distribution were reversed, the high-risk categories of the more homogeneous groups of firms receiving only a few risk-percentage points and the number of points increasing in the direction of the groups of firms with a lower classification. In general, the large number of risk percentages in the various risk categories makes it more difficult for the Institute to arrive at precise and uniform classifications. In part, this proposal repeats a proposal made by the Institute before the risk-category revision of 1904, to the effect that the "midrange risk percentage" for the medium-risk categories should be eliminated, substituting "standard percentages" for all titles, corresponding to the statistical outcomes.

i. A collection of authoritative technical interpretations for each title should be published.

As early as 1904, questionnaires were sent to all categories, except to subsidiary building trades; these firms also received the questionnaire in advance of the risk classification of 1910.

An additional task remaining in connection with the questionnaires includes sending out reminders in cases of questionnaires that were not returned in time, using correspondence in order to complete inadequately answered questionnaires, collecting and sorting the returned questionnaires, and comparing the data they contain with those of earlier questionnaires.

Obtaining Expert Opinions from the k. k. Trade Inspectors

1. In the risk-classification revisions of 1894 and 1899, the Institute restricted its involvement to establishing risk classifications one by one in talks with the trade inspectors and entering notes on these discussions in the classification forms. This procedure has not proved valid, however, because the authorities did not recognize those entries as having the evidentiary validity of a written opinion.

2. In consequence, in 1904, the Institute turned to the trade inspectors with the request that they submit a written opinion for each firm using a set of questions developed by the Institute; an appropriate space for this opinion was reserved on the final page of the questionnaire.

Finally, to follow up the expert opinions, we planned a face-to-face discussion. The trade inspectors declined to assume this task, since they believed it to be too extensive. The Institute thereupon offered a modified proposal: we would proceed by making verbal inquiries, always consulting Institute officials fully familiar with the risk categories; these would be responsible for keeping a written record of the verbal opinions. On September 18, 1904, following a petition by the Institute, the k. k. Ministry of the Interior issued a decree approving this procedure. [. . .]. In gathering expert opinions in this manner in 1904, the Institute, wanting to conform to the classification regulations as closely as possible on our part, attempted to take note of as many details as possible.

3. In the reclassification 1909, without changing the method of collecting opinions, the Institute limited its participation as a rule to recording general judgments, leaving detailed judgments to exceptional cases only.

4. Since the results of this procedure also proved inadequate, the Institute will change its approach. The primary possibilities here lie in direct negotiation with employers.

The Actual Reclassification

This reclassification will primarily take the following factors into account:

1. The provisions of the classification regulations or the various safety regulations;
2. the general and particular statistical results;
3. the new questionnaires;
4. the previous classification and earlier questionnaires;
5. the expert opinions of the k. k. trade inspectors;
6. additional classifications of the commercial category in question;
7. additional classifications within the district commission or the particular industrial sphere.

Approval of the Classifications by the Institute's Board of Trustees

In accordance with the statute, the Board of Trustees determines each reclassification, basing its decision on the Business Department's proposals submitted to the Board of Trustees by business group and title along with all questionnaires and decisions.

Registering the Reclassification and Subsequent Tasks

Reclassification is now entered into the business registry by business title, risk class, and risk percentage, along with the year of the particular classification regulations. Subsequently, the change in classification is entered in all manuals and statistical compilations.

Publishing the Reclassification Decisions

At the present time, the reclassification decisions that previously assigned different versions in different business categories are now reduced to three versions for all firms.

Appeals Process

In the last classification, the number of appeals against these reclassification decisions was reduced significantly only for agricultural enterprises. The reason for this reduction is that in the previous classification, changes were made only in the rarest of cases, removing any cause for appeals. In the case of commercial firms, on the other hand, the number of appeals did not significantly decrease.

A new factor entered into the classification system and appeals process, however, because for the present, the Institute has begun to negotiate directly at least with the largest firms—the same process it has initiated within the limits of its agenda. The expectation is that after a private inspection of the firms—some before the decisions were issued and some during the appeals process—reclassification could be determined by mutual agreement. This effort has been a complete success: Some of the most burdensome appeals, which had occupied all the authorities, the trade inspectors, and the Institute for years at the time of the last classification, were prevented from being filed.

B. Special Measures by the Institute concerning Classification of Firms and Premium Collection [excerpts]

The Insurance of Wooden-Toy Manufacture in the Erzgebirge

Two principal problems make it difficult to insure these firms.

The firms in question produce children's toys such as blocks, construction sets, dominos, checkerboards, boxes, piggy banks, toy guns, pianos, castles, toy theaters, pen and pencil boxes, writing utensils, wagons, wheels, kitchen utensils, toy stores, toy barns, doll furniture, and paint boxes. In and of themselves, these are, of course, wooden trinkets and were designated as such by the trade inspectors and classified as such by the Institute. This classification was too high, however, because this was not a question of the production of trinkets in the sense of the classification regulations but rather a very special kind of operation, with an unusually high amount of handicraft, such as painting, polishing, papering, bookbinding, paper processing, making cardboard packaging, etc. On the other hand, the classification was also too low, because for decades the declared wages were too low and did not correctly reflect the facts.

Originally, the products were, for the most part, manufactured as home work. Only certain wooden components were prepared by machine; each worker rented supplies in the numerous waterworks and worked on his own machine. The next stage was the introduction of woodworking using saws, mainly circular saws, by independent contractors, some of whom still worked out of their homes and prepared materials for themselves and others to refine at home.

The insurance registration of the circle cutters—which are simply circular saws used to cut wood into splinters—dates from this period. As the industry evolved, planing machines were installed, and special machines were added recently, mainly milling machines. Work from home diminished gradually as these machines were introduced, however, merging into real workshop labor performed for the workshop owner's profit. In response to the demands of the market, the products had to be given special textures. This consideration resulted in the affiliation of the various handicraft shops. Working from home thus lost its last use—decorating and packaging the goods. Especially at this stage of the work process, the product cannot run the danger of damage during repeated transportation from the workshops to the houses of the home-workers and back again. The establishment of a district-wide power station allowed electrical motors to be installed, thus providing an impetus for setting up additional workshops. Some employers also set up power plants that were used by neighbors who had established their own machines in others' workshops. Because of the combined effect of these circumstances, the insurance plan grew increasingly unfavorable. The statistics of Title 408, in which these firms predominate, required the risk classification to be raised again and again; it increased from IV in 1895 to VII in 1900, then to VIII in 1905, and finally to IX in 1910. For their part, the employers sought to protect themselves by reporting lower wages, and they transferred the manual work to another name under trade law, in spite of the fact that the firms actually formed technical and commercial units.

In 1913, the Institute entered into direct negotiations with the appropriate trade association of manufacturers of wooden trinkets and toys, and after an inspection of the principal firms and preliminary statistical studies, a single negotiation, held on October 3, 1913, and we arrived at mutual agreement on what truly seems the permanent settlement of all open questions; this achievement will presumably be extended to all Erzgebirge trade associations.

[...]

Insurance for the Building Trades and Their Subsidiary Trades

By their nature, the building trades and their subsidiaries require a form of insurance that stands apart from insurance as a whole.

The Institute has always aimed at incorporating the full scope of the building trades into insurance plans, since the evident anomalies could be mastered only on the broadest insurance base. The Institute therefore submitted a petition to the k. k. Ministry of the Interior as early as 1890 requesting the official expansion of compulsory insurance to workshops.

In 1896, a principal item in the restructuring of the Institute was the idea that accident insurance should be extended to workshops in the building trade and its subsidiaries.

The finding of the k. k. Administrative Court of April 19, 1906, recognized the Institute's belief [. . .]; but the same court's finding of May 22, 1908, deviated from this view [. . .].

All the defects that could have been remedied by the acceptance of and adherence to the original proposal arose once more after the second decision. A change occurred only when obligatory insurance was extended to the workshop labor of the building trade and at least most of its subsidiaries in consequence of the law of April 29, 1912, [. . .], making moot the question of the interpretation of the original law. During the interim periods, when the Institute's interpretation of § 1 of the accident insurance law could not be implemented in the form of obligatory insurance, the Institute endeavored to implement it in the form of voluntary additional insurance to the greatest possible extent.

Wherever it was necessary and possible, the Institute pursued the goal of voluntary additional insurance with flat-rate premiums.

The phenomenon of unauthorized coverage has taken on special and generally harmful significance in the competitive struggle in the building trade, though it has no immediate effect on accident insurance because of the introduction of obligatory insurance. Even the authorities who were most concerned with eliminating unauthorized coverage declared themselves powerless against it. The reason for the spread of unauthorized coverage as insurance became obligatory is that it offered the easiest way to withhold accident-insurance contributions from the Institute and to proceed recklessly, without regard to safety. The practice flourished because the Institute learned about most of the buildings in question only indirectly, when construction was already completed. Furthermore, the building owner, who is not a craftsman and whom the authorities do not formally recognize to carry out the work himself, ignores the provisions of the accident-insurance law. Finally, as a rule, the actual builder cannot pay the insurance premiums even if he wanted to, because he does not know the wages being paid on the project. When it comes to actual safety, of course, it is impossible to observe the regulations in such buildings, since steady supervision, provided by a specialist, is lacking. As a consequence, construction with unauthorized coverage had great competitive advantages. These circumstances also led to better countermeasures, however, once the Institute took action in terms of its own competence.

In 1891, at the instigation of the insurance institutes, the k. k. Ministry of the Interior issued a decree urging the district commissioners and municipal authorities to take severe measures against this misconduct, in consideration of the damage unauthorized coverage was inflicting on the insurance institutes. In 1896, the Institute proposed countering the unlawful practice by having the building authorities introduce mandatory notification of every construction project.

In 1897, the k. k. Ministry of the Interior issued another decree ordering stricter application of all available means available against unauthorized coverage.

As a result of the Institute's proposals, the k. k. Ministry of the Interior determined in a decree on April 1, 1899, that:

1. The local councils must draw up annual lists of all new buildings, additions, and rebuilding projects and submit these lists to the government authorities, and
2. the Institute must receive such lists from the district commissioners by municipality.

In 1903, the Institute initiated specific construction monitoring and repeatedly requested that wage lists be made compulsory by law.

When this legalization was introduced, the Institute used wage audits to determine which building projects were in private hands and then, using official channels, issued rulings based on health-insurance data.

On May 13, 1899, the k. k. Ministry of the Interior issued a decree that again outlined the measures to be used against unauthorized coverage.

In its annual reports, the Institute never ceased to point out the prevailing conditions. The steadily increasing spread of unauthorized coverage in the Institute's territory in spite of these measures brought about the k. k. Office of the Governor's standard edict of July 6, 1906, which regulated the filing of reports on observed punishable offenses.

The Institute's introduction of a special survey for individual construction projects signified further progress. Based on its experiences, the Institute identified four basic forms of unauthorized coverage:

The building owner always controls construction completely independently, without construction permits and without consulting any authorized building experts (master builder, mason, carpenter, etc.), in that he alone hires, pays, and fires workers. This defines the private building project proper.

Alternately, the licensed building foreman (master builder, mason, carpenter) has no funds and lends his name and even his license to the building project for a disproportionately small compensation, without further concerning himself with the construction. The building owner pays for the materials and the wages, and also hires, pays, and fires the workers (this is the form of direct coverage by licensed contractor).

A further possibility is that the building owner has appropriated only the procurement of the building materials. The construction itself is executed in the same way as above by an unauthorized third party under the coverage of a craftsman (master builder, mason, carpenter) who is actually authorized but lacks funds. This third party, such as an unauthorized building foreman, takes over construction, possibly also hiring, paying, and firing the workers. This is the most common case—the form of indirect coverage with masters' licenses.

In the final case, the building owner has kept for himself only the procurement of the material and the administration of the funds necessary to pay wages, but a licensed contractor (master builder, mason, carpenter, etc.) hires the workers, pays, and fires them himself and supervises the building continually, either in person or through his deputies. His only recompense is a fee, which is determined in various ways. This case fulfills the requirements of the building-trade law of December 26, 1893 [. . .].

In view of these circumstances, the Institute used a specific questionnaire, intended, for the present, to facilitate setting premiums and possibly preparing to report offenses. The questionnaire proved so effective in clarifying the relationship between the building owner and the actual craftsmen that it was employed even more broadly. The governorship's edict of July 26, 1909, and that of the k. k. Ministry of Trade and Commerce of March 11, 1909, referred to this questionnaire and recommended its use to the k. k. district commissioners. The four principal forms of unauthorized coverage listed in the ministerial decree essentially coincide with the Institute's findings in its 1905 questionnaire.

With the help of the law of February 8, 1909, the Institute generated new possibilities regarding unauthorized coverage and the reorganization of wage supervision:

a. The general identifications collected by the health-insurance plans of the people they insure were refined with reference to the building trades and were regularly requested and collected.
b. All civil servants delegated by the Institute in whatever outside matter were obligated to record their observations on buildings in a separate report and to submit such reports to the accounting department as evidence, in this case primarily regarding private building projects and unauthorized building coverage.

c. Forms for identifying buildings were enclosed with the premium assessments for building firms, in separate versions for independent construction and private building projects. If they were filled out correctly, these identification papers listed the name and residence of the building owner, information on the location, type, and duration of the construction, information on the number of floors and the area of the building in square meters (the latter for estimating construction costs in order to comply with official ordinances), the name of the master carpenter on the project, the applicable overall wage total, and the health-insurance company that carried the building's insurance. All this information, once established, was used for systematically reporting offenses to the authorities and with the documented evidence. In the matter of unauthorized coverage, as in all checks on wages, the direct connection between the Institute and employers brought about the decisive turn. Direct communication between the associations of building craftsmen and the Institute is increasing, and the trade associations are reporting unauthorized coverage to the Institute directly and providing the material for uncovering each case more and more systematically. Where this material alone does not appear adequate for successfully imposing supplementary payments and reporting offenses, the Institute and the associations discuss the matter and jointly conduct further investigations. This method has already resulted in the complete resolution of complicated cases of unauthorized coverage, including one case in which the district commissioners declared themselves to be powerless to proceed against this type of coverage. The reports of offenses also seem more significant when the trade associations and the Institute file simultaneous reports regarding the same case and both parties insist on its urgency. The Institute sees a great opportunity in this joint approach, which will be expanded further and further, of suppressing unauthorized coverage with increasing speed.

A further possibility, which at this time lies almost completely in the future, is that a generous flat rate for the insurance premiums in the building trade (for which the foundations have already been laid) could relieve some of the supervisory personnel currently occupied mainly with checking wages of these chores, so that instead they could pursue the problem of unauthorized building coverage.

C. Accident Prevention

From the outset, the Institute's Board of Trustees not only spontaneously expressed a lively interest in the important issue of accident prevention but also let no occasion pass without reminding the k. k. government of the subject's importance and fervently supporting all proposals of the management. It was especially the group of workers' representatives and at its head long-time Board of Trustees member Wilhelm Černý who never wavered in their interest in accident prevention. This response was seen at the very beginning of the Institute's operations, for several members of the Board of Trustees and civil servants participated officially in the accident-prevention exhibition held in Brünn in 1889.

In appreciation of the humane goals of the museum of industrial hygiene established in Vienna by Dr. Franz Migerka, k. k. ministerial councilor and central trade inspector, the Board of Trustees further resolved at its meeting of December 20, 1890, to make a one-time contribution of 1,000 gulden as foundation funding and, provisionally, to appropriate an additional 500 gulden a year to the museum to support its goals. Subsequently, the Prague Institute contributed the same amount for the museum in the years 1892 to 1894.

A study of the situation that pertained to accidents determined that many accidents were caused by the fact that there was a total lack or an inadequate supply of the necessary safety equipment for the cogged wheels of some machines and for transmission gears or that the machines were oiled and cleaned while they were in operation, in defiance of the rules and regulations. The Institute therefore turned to the k. k. trade inspectors and all trade authorities of Bohemia as early as 1890; referring to § 74 of the trade regulations, the Institute requested that all employers and other insured parties be made aware of the need for strict observation of the accident-prevention regulations and adherence to the provisions of the separate factory regulations, and that the authorities impose penalties if necessary.

From the very beginning, the building trade and its subsidiary trades stood out among the vulnerable trade groups. Along with inadequate wage reports and insufficient premium payments, early on the Institute learned from the accident data that provisions made for excavating, actual construction, and assembling the scaffolding did not meet the requirements set for workers' safety. In addition, it was learned that, in this case, a number of workers in other building trades entered into the risky space created by the master builder or master mason.

At its meeting of September 6, 1893, the administrative committee therefore resolved to submit a petition to the k. k. Office of the Governor, indicating the inadequate provisions for accident prevention in the building trades in Prague and its surroundings. The petition requested that arrangements be made for the authorities and agencies charged with supervising the works not only to advocate strongly for conditions guaranteeing the safety of construction workers and the provision of safety and accident prevention measures, but also to see that the required safety provisions be implemented in a way that guaranteed that their purpose be attained under all conditions.

At that time, however, no effective action to prevent building accidents in Prague and its environs was taken, though, as far as responsibility was involved, the director of the Institute was able to cite certain blatant examples, based on experience gained in Prague and the rest of Bohemia during the official investigation conducted in Vienna from November 25 to December 5, 1895. These examples demonstrated the careless ways in which even the most ordinary technical principles, or simply structural principles, were ignored in construction and illustrated the opportunities the Institute subsequently found, in a plan based on §§ 45 to 47 of the accident-insurance law, for laying claims for damages against the building craftsmen. After the Institute was not granted the legal power to exert some influence on the introduction of accident-prevention measures, its only recourse was to direct a legal request to the appropriate trade inspector to examine the individual cases of operations where an accident could clearly be traced back to the lack of the proper safety arrangements. Though as a rule this method repeatedly resulted in safety measures being installed, what was missing was action that would exert a broad influence on all firms.

A new stimulus for further progress in this direction came from the workers' representatives on the Board of Trustees; they proposed the election of a committee that would make concrete proposals to the Board.

Responding to these proposals, the Board of Trustees resolved to appeal to the k. k. Office of the Governor to convene an official inquiry conducted by the parties involved and by experts as soon as possible in order to discuss the introduction of accident-prevention measures. In addition, the k. k. Office of the Governor was called upon to persuade the k. k. government to influence the domestic machine factories to keep safety mechanisms in mind in the construction of the machines and to deliver only machines equipped with proven safety devices. The k. k. government should also be made aware of the urgent need of expanding the institution of the trade inspectors and thus support an increase in their number.

In March 1896, the Board of Trustees charged Director Haubner, JD, along with Dr. Marschner, JD, at that time a law clerk, to make a study trip to Germany to investigate the organization and results of the policies of the German trade associations. The report on the matter also made suggestions regarding accident prevention. This act by the Board of Trustees was closely followed by discussions on this topic at the afore-mentioned accident-insurance inquiry in Vienna; both the chairman of the board, Dr. Otto Příbram, JD, and the director, Dr. Jacob Haubner, JD, participated, representing the Institute.

At this meeting a special wish was expressed to expand the scope of the accident insurance institutes to enable them to dedicate funds to accident prevention, not for individual firms, but for accident prevention in general.

A further proposal suggested that the institutes be allowed to allocate funds to set up a commission, composed of employers and workers with practical experience in various professions as well as consulting engineers and architects; this commission would be empowered to evaluate any proposals and award bonuses for outstanding accident prevention. It was further suggested that the Institute be granted the right to hire officers chosen from the ranks of specialists in the field who would visit the various firms and make certain that the regulations were being observed and applied.

In 1897, the Board of Trustees took two further actions. First, it turned to the agricultural council of the kingdom of Bohemia and the k. k. Office of the Governor with a suggestion to bar schoolchildren from working with agricultural machines. Second, the Board paved the way for an agreement with the agricultural council on the joint development of separate accident-prevention regulations for the operation of agricultural machinery.

In response to a communication from the Institute of May 6, 1897, the k. k. Office of the Governor also issued an edict on May 26, 1897, to the k. k. district commissioners to adequately alert the rural population to the danger of allowing children to work with agricultural machines and to take steps to prevent employing children in agricultural mechanized operations.

At the same time, a decree issued by the k. k. Office of the Governor on August 26, 1897, informed the Institute that its earlier communication had been submitted to the k. k. Ministry of the Interior because of the question it had raised regarding legislated steps to prevent accidents involving school-age children working with agricultural machinery.

In 1903, separate regulations for accident prevention in companies using agricultural machinery were issued; this measure was the consequence of joint preliminary work by both sections of the agricultural council for the kingdom of Bohemia. His Excellency Governor Karl Graf Coudenhove intensively promoted the move. Following his governmental edict of July 10, 1904, the k. k. district commissioners, working through the municipal authorities, issued the accident-prevention regulations in the form of a poster to all employers in companies using agricultural machinery, which effectively stressed the importance of the regulations.

His Excellency further requested the presiding authority of the higher regional court to alert the lower courts to the existence and distribution of accident-prevention regulations, so that this situation would be taken into consideration in any pending criminal proceedings arising from accidents that occurred during the operation of agricultural machinery.

In 1904, "Regulations for Preventing Accidents during the Operation of Agricultural Machinery" were implemented; they were published jointly by both sections of the agricultural council for the kingdom of Bohemia. One result of this measure was seen at the Prague agricultural exhibition of May 1904, in the rivalry that broke out among the participating machine manufacturers about the safety devices with which they had equipped the machines they were showing; but a lively interest in accident prevention regulations became apparent among the smaller machine manufacturers in that they brought original models of accident-prevention devices to be exhibited. The exhibition jury happily recognized these efforts with a large number of awards.

In consideration of the continuing increase in accidents, the Board of Trustees, along with the other agencies in the Institute's area, resolved in 1905 to address a cumulative petition to the k. k. Ministry of the Interior for the speedy proclamation of the accident-prevention regulations developed by the accident-prevention commission of the k. k. Ministry of Trade and Commerce.

More welcome progress was to be seen in the field of accident prevention in 1906, in that the first of the ordinances developed by the accident-prevention commission was issued. This was the ordinance of the k. k. Ministry of Trade and Commerce in agreement with the k. k. Ministry of the Interior of November 23, 1905, which provided general regulations for the protection of the life and health of workers in commercial firms, based on § 74 of the law of March 8, 1885, regarding the revision and supplementing of the industrial code. This ordinance was followed by the ordinance issued on July 18, 1906, by the k. k. Ministry of Trade and Commerce in agreement with the k. k. Ministry of the Interior and the Ministry of Agriculture and Railways, which set forth rules for the production, use, and maintenance of facilities for distributing and utilizing combustible gases (gas regulation). In turn, this ordinance was followed by one of February 7, 1907, regarding the commercial construction of tall buildings and the execution of construction associated with it.

In 1907, the Institute was helped by the ordinance of the k. k. Office of the Governor for Bohemia, issued on March 12, which prescribed special safety equipment for agricultural machinery. This effort resulted in a statistically proven decrease in the number of accidents and their severity.

The Institute's Board of Trustees gratefully recognized the enactment of this ordinance, which appears suited to control certain conditions that manifested themselves most unpleasantly. It was a well-known fact that agricultural workers' safety was almost entirely neglected and that our farmers made no efforts to guarantee safety; and that especially when purchasing machines for agricultural use, they never considered whether or not the machines were appropriately equipped for safety. Farmers are usually concerned primarily with obtaining the lowest possible price. Given this state of affairs, the use of machinery for cultivation, which increased annually, naturally brought about a constant and unusual increase in serious accidents. It was expected that the legally binding regulations of the ordinance regarding the equipment of agricultural machines with safety devices would successfully counteract the previous indifference and deplorable circumstances.

In a meeting of April 19, 1907, the Institute's Board of Trustees resolved to express its deepest thanks to His Excellency the governor for issuing the ordinance, which once again showed the warm solicitude for the Board's accident-prevention efforts.

In order to spread awareness of the ordinance widely and to motivate farmers to meet its regulations, in July 1907 the Institute enclosed a copy with the premium-calculation forms to all municipalities in its territory and to the larger agricultural concerns.

The following stand out as further successes of the Institute's efforts to increase safety:

1. At the Institute's suggestion and with the cooperation of the k. k. Office of the Governor in Prague, the Institute created a supervisory organization by asking the district commissioners systematically to conduct yearly safety inspections of the firms in their districts using agricultural machinery.

2. On August 9, 1909, the Institute introduced a second comprehensive measure with its petition, Number 43,802, concerning the introduction of cylindrical safety shafts for wood-planing machines—an initiative that is all the more remarkable in that the safety regulations for woodworking firms are still under deliberation by the accident-prevention commission, and therefore no ordinance has yet been issued. The Institute's step was urgently necessary because it is precisely the woodworking machines, and at least in second place among them the wood-planing machines, that are included in the machinery that poses the greatest risk, and yet almost completely effective safety devices exist, especially for these machines. The Institute's initial action was an attempt to make up for the lack of general regulations by effecting the

Office of the Governor's decree of March 23, 1910, addressed to the governmental authorities. This decree made the district commissioners responsible for promoting the general introduction of cylindrical shafts.

Illustrated articles on the advantages of the cylindrical shafts were published in the annual reports; articles and plates on the subject were made available to trade journals and calendars; and a small collection of safety devices for wood-planing machines was put on exhibit in the Institute itself. No opportunity was overlooked to point out the importance of the cylindrical shafts in all correspondence; their introduction was rewarded with a lowered classification, and products that had proven themselves were repeatedly recommended. Above all, however, we compiled as detailed a list as possible of all wood-planing machines used in the firms subject to insurance in the Institute's territory; the institute used these lists to try to urge the employment of cylindrical shafts; this argument was promoted in letters, by reports to the governmental authorities, and by cataloguing the responses. We used accident reports to check on results. Once again, it was only the Institute's organization of this initiative that led to favorable statistical results.

3. In quarry work, the main issue is not actually the use of safety devices—except for safety goggles and the proper blasting materials—but rather the exercise of caution in quarrying. This is not a place where occasional compliance with the regulations of working conditions can be considered satisfactory, however; we must insist that caution be exercised continuously when it comes to quarrying, since the physical conditions of any quarry also change constantly as the work of breaking stones progresses. This situation, however, calls for constant supervision.

The Prague Institute therefore established contact with trade associations and their umbrella organizations to interest them in accident prevention. These initiatives in matters of accident prevention on the part of the Institute were highly successful, and a number of others followed. A large number of demolition projects in Prague, for example, have shown an enormous increase in the number of construction accidents—especially since concrete has become a common building material—caused by projecting nails and by wires and spikes. Although the occasions of these accidents are minor in and of themselves, they frequently have serious and long-lasting consequences because they lead to blood poisoning, which itself is seriously injurious to health. Since the ministerial ordinance of February 7, 1907, did not consider these factors, the Institute turned to the k. k. Office of the Governor with a request that a decree be circulated to the government authorities calling attention to these dangers and making suitable provisions for avoiding them.

The constantly rising accident rate in quarries led to the May 29, 1908, ordinance by the Ministry of Trade and Commerce that set out regulations for the commercial operation of stone quarries and clay, sand, and gravel pits. These regulations provided a number of exhaustively enumerated standards for evaluating the commercial operation of companies of subgroups IVa and in part IVb of the plan. Nevertheless, the accident statistics show no impact from this decree, although it has been in effect for over six years.

What is characteristic of operating conditions in the above-named groups is that the kind of risk incurred depends on the way the concern is managed; the most salient task is therefore to introduce care into the act of excavating, which must, of course, proceed with greater care, the more unfavorable the material conditions are in the particular quarry. The quarry employers need to be systematically trained in the safety regulations. For this reason the Institute approached the k. k. Office of the Governor with the request that, in order to implement the ministerial ordinance of May 29, 1908, an edict be issued to the governmental authorities to remind them once again them of the provisions of the ordinance and issue directives along the lines of the above suggestions that appeared appropriate for realizing the intentions of the ordinance. The Institute asked for a similar ordinance to apply to agricultural quarries. The matter is still under advisement.

On October 20 and November 8, 1912, the Institute also had the opportunity to issue a statement urging issuance of a new decree regarding using children to work with agricultural machinery—a regulation that had been suggested by the regional commission for the protection of children and youth. The Institute took special satisfaction in this statement, since we had paid close attention to this matter from the beginning. The Institute was also happy to welcome a step taken by the Chamber of Trade and Commerce in Reichenberg that aimed at creating a technical information office about accident prevention.

In this section, we must finally recall the little collection of accident-prevention models put on display in our offices; it has already attracted many interested visitors.

It remains only to mention developments in the topic of accident prevention with regard to the public.

Fueled by the wish to interest broad segments of the population in the issues of accident prevention, the Institute had repeatedly taken the opportunity to make the development of accident prevention accessible to the public by using diagrams and graphic illustrations at exhibitions. We had to conclude that this topic aroused no greater interest. Journalists kept their silence; the topic may have been too unintelligible and remote.

Next, on the occasion of the German-Bohemian crownland exhibition in Komotau in 1913, the Institute made an attempt to publicize accident prevention by a method that departed from previous practice. We set up a special exhibit of machines for the woodworking trade; its special importance lay in the fact that it displayed machines that were well-constructed and efficiently arranged, demonstrating to workers in the trade the methods by which the machines must be secured against serious industrial accidents and the arrangements that must be made on the shop floor to make them clean enough by eliminating the buildup of dust. The exhibition of woodworking machines had special significance for Komotau because group XI companies are heavily represented in that area.

A reference chart that stretched across the entire back wall of the exhibit provided information on its purpose as well as on the Institute's reason to mount the exhibit.

The statistics illustrate the most frequently occurring causes of accidents. In the five-year period from 1902 to 1906, accidents caused by the following factors resulted in the expenses indicated for the Prague Institute:

Flying shards in stone- and metalworking	K1,293,669
Industrial railroads	K 930,189
Belt drives	K 628,066
Pressing, dies, and stamping machines	K 230,841
Carding	K 309,407
Mechanized looms	K 276,774
Circular saws for woodcutting	K 966,461
Wood-milling machines	K 148,586
Wood-planing machines	K 546,061
Cleaning and lubricating machines while in operation	K 586,240

The reference chart shows the precautions in an employer's control that would enable him to avoid or at least significantly reduce these serious accidents. Most of the protective measures were on display at the exhibition. There was a complete collection of goggles that would protect eyes during stone- and metalworking, for example. Direct electric drives for machines, avoiding the need for transmission, as well as the greatest possible limitation on belt drives served to reduce accidents occurring with the operation of power-transmission systems.

A screened timber-sizing machine and a planing machine with a cylindrical safety shaft provided proof of the possibility of almost entirely eliminating accidents in connection with wood-planing machines.

A milling machine with a safety head and protective wire guard and a circular saw with splitting wedge and protective hood ensured that accidents with these especially dangerous woodworking machines were kept to a minimum.

The band saw on exhibit was a good example of a well-protected machine; indeed, only the opening for inserting the wood was exposed, while the rest of the machine was otherwise completely sheathed.

The safety devices on all these machines as well as on the sanding machine and drill also on exhibit were painted a bright red to make them easy to recognize. The exhibit also included an exhaust system to suck up the shavings created in planing, milling, and sawing. A mechanic demonstrated the system in operation.

A sizable number of components for power-driven work systems were demonstrated on the exhibit table. The main item of interest was a comparison of the square shaft with the cylindrical shaft in various models, a safety milling head, a safety butcher's saw, and a ladder scaffold. A complete collection of safety goggles and protective masks was displayed on the rear of the exhibit table.

The Institute also summarized its earlier achievements in accident prevention at international forums—once at the 1902 International Industrial Insurance Congress in Düsseldorf in the presentation by Dr. Robert Marschner, JD, at that time secretary of the Institute, titled "The Current Status of Accident Prevention in Austria"; and a second time, at the Second International Congress for Rescue and Accident Prevention, held in Vienna in September 1913, in the presentation by the Institute's director, Dr. Robert Marschner, JD, titled "The Prague Workmen's Accident Insurance Institute and Accident Prevention," and in a talk by the Institute's chief inspector, Eugen Pfohl, titled "The Organization of Accident Insurance in Austria."

Some of the experiences gathered at the latter congress were immediately put into practice.

Commentary 15

❧

In his postcard to Felice Bauer of May 30, 1916 (com. 14), Kafka mentions the Institute's anniversary report as another potentially "sad diversion" for his fiancée: "You will be spared the Jubilee Report, running to 100-odd pages" (LF 470). In view of the highly official status of this document, we may reasonably assume that most of the text was produced by the Prague Institute's two most skillful writers, Franz Kafka and Robert Marschner. Our selection covers only the sections most closely related to Kafka's professional responsibilities.

The holdings of the Ministry of the Interior in the Austrian State Archive permit some revealing insights into the genesis of this report and, at the same time, into the outstanding position of the Prague Institute among all Austrian institutes.[1] On April 4, 1913, Kafka's Institute submitted this petition to the Ministry in Vienna:

> At its last meeting, the association of territorial institutes suggested publishing a commemorative volume on the occasion of the upcoming twenty-fifth anniversary of Austrian workmen's accident insurance, together with a series of simply written brochures in each of the national languages. The association decided to request the Ministry to act as the editor of these materials. [. . .]

> The territorial institutes will be happy to provide the necessary data for this purpose and to contribute to the volume and its various sections. (Fascicle 61)

Attached to this petition was a detailed outline of the planned volume and relevant data. In fact, this magnanimous project seemed to its planners an ideal representation of the complex unity of the multiethnic Empire, since it was designed to bridge social as well as national lines of conflict. All aspects of Kafka's Chinese scenario—the system of partial construction, the nexus between social and ethnic unity on the one hand and national security on the other; the crucial and opaque role of the "highest leadership"—are assembled in this one major, and probably most comprehensive, sample of Kafka's office writings.

In Vienna, the initiative was received enthusiastically. A file document dated April 9, 1913, reads, "In Germany, too, the twenty-fifth anniversary of workmen's insurance was celebrated last year, along with various observations, among them a commemorative volume."

Interestingly, we are dealing here with a hitherto unappreciated forerunner of the ominous "parallel action" that occupies the (empty) center of Robert Musil's great novel *The Man Without Qualities*. That novel tells of the attempt of a group of Viennese government officials to match the upcoming 1918 celebration of the thirtieth anniversary of the German emperor's accession to the throne with a corresponding Austrian program to commemorate the seventieth anniversary of Emperor Franz Joseph's coronation the same year. The Viennese proposal continues with one of those "sketchy [. . .] plans" (KSS 116) that once again conjures up Kafka's Chinese construction project: "The plan of the volume cannot be established in detail at this point, but it will essentially follow the attached outline." On December 23, 1913, a ministerial decree officially put the project on track, and as early as January 24, 1914, the Prague Institute declared that extensive sections of the presentation had already been completed, that the Prague authors were engaged in eliminating the remaining gaps, and that the entire volume would soon be submitted to the Ministry. By April 23, 1914, four letters from Prague announced the completion of further parts. However, the Viennese archive does not contain any of these parts, nor is any bibliographical reference available for a nationwide volume on workmen's insurance. We must therefore assume that the outbreak of World War I in the summer of 1914 interfered with the imperial project and that Kafka's Institute took the occasion to proceed with its own jubilee volume. In fact, the introduction to that report seems to confirm Prague's view of itself as *primus inter pares* among all Austrian institutes:

> By both its size and its organization, however, [the Prague Institute] reflects accident insurance throughout Austria. A general survey of the Institute's growth during these twenty-five years seems all the more desirable, since the political situation in Bohemia has compelled the Institute to increase its staff during elections to the board, in dealing with its internal affairs, and in all its official activities involving employers and insured employees. Even so, the Institute has succeeded, during the last five years of its first quarter-century, in substantially improving its financial situation, which was precarious at the outset, by taking appropriate measures within its own scope.

The sections of the report included here yield a wealth of insights into major fields of Kafka's professional agenda: from (a) risk classification through (b) so-called "special measures"—that is, extraprocedural agreements with employers—through (c) the struggle against wage-list fraud in the construction business to (d) accident prevention. Owing to the public-relations nature of the jubilee report, these sections provide a rich background to the preceding documents in this volume.

16

RISK CLASSIFICATION AND ACCIDENT PREVENTION IN WARTIME (1915)

∾

Both sections of this report document the application of the terminology and mathematics of insurance to military mobilization and conflict, as well as the limitations of this practice. After 1945, West German historians coined the metaphor Betriebsunfall der Geschichte *(an occupational accident in the historical process), which they applied to both wars. Kafka would have rejected this metaphor for World War I by confronting it with the genuine meaning of the term. This text employs imagery remarkably similar to that of* In the Penal Colony, *which was written (in three nights or fewer) at about the same time, around mid-October 1914.*

A. Wartime and Risk Classification

The current extraordinary economic conditions have had little effect on risk classification in general, in spite of the fact that many employers have mistakenly used the situation as an argument for changes in classifications. Classification has been influenced most strongly, relatively speaking, by the fact that industry has increasingly adapted to the new demands it faces as many firms have begun to produce goods completely different from their former work. We must distinguish here between firms that have completely or significantly switched to different machinery and those where no such change has occurred. The former, of course, have encountered no obstacles in immediately implementing the respective new classifications. Such a decision has not been so simple for the latter group of firms, however. While they have not changed as far as their machinery is concerned, their production has indeed become significantly different. Special consideration has to be paid to the fact that the machines, even when they have been kept on, are often not well suited to the heavy tasks they are now usually expected to perform; this fact alone increases the risk factor, especially as the pace of operation was pushed.

Another fact that needs to be addressed is that firms often failed to adapt in their entirety but have held on to some part of their traditional products. For example, one section of a metal-button manufacturing plant has remained reserved for that operation while other spaces have been converted to pressing and rolling detonators for grenades and shrapnel explosives, using the old machines. Admittedly, there are other cases of firms that have been partially transformed for the production of war articles, where the dangerous aspects of the operation have become restricted while the less dangerous elements have been expanded.

Where production has been changed while continuing to use the old machines, wherever possible, attempts have been made to go on using the previous classification. If this has not been possible because the difference in the levels of risk is too great, the risk percentage was changed. If this change, too, was insufficient because of the complete incompatibility of the two kinds of production, the new method has been classified separately. Mixed classification has been rigorously avoided in such cases. In the early days of the war in particular, cases piled up in which firms requested a lower classification because of the complete cessation of motorized operations, referring to § 19 of the accident-insurance law.

Such requests were generally turned down according to § 19, since the motors were not dismantled, and only the general extraordinary circumstances caused the temporary cessation; therefore the complete outward and actual change in a whole firm required by § 19 was absent. In fact, many of these firms gradually reintroduced motorized operations even while letters regarding the matter were still going back and forth; thereafter, these firms limited their requests to the even less justified plea for a change in classification for the relatively brief period in which motorized operation had been discontinued.

Firms that have completely ceased production and as a rule engage only in direct labor and cleaning work have also requested changes in their classification. In these cases, too, no change in classification has been made, since we were dealing with part-time work done by a primary firm that, though shut down for the present, nevertheless is a genuine entity, and thus any work it performs is necessarily included in the firm's classification.

[. . .]

B. Accident Prevention

The war has brought not only an interruption in the promising improvements of accident insurance, especially within the Institute's area, but, in part, even the destruction of what has already been achieved. All that remains is the hope that, after the war, so much unleashed economic power—which even in wartime is having such extraordinary success—will see the onset of a new era of increasing demands for accident prevention, which will far exceed the currently inflicted damage.

Effect of the War on Accident Prevention

We can therefore tailor our publicity concerning safety only to preserving the current status, without addressing additional improvements. We cannot demand of those firms that are operating only in a limited capacity because of the present situation that they shoulder the cost and adjustments in operations required by new accident-prevention measures. And yet again, those firms that must dedicate all their efforts to fulfilling military contracts or in other directions are faced with the practical impossibility of devoting sufficient care to accident prevention. Additionally, the current state of the labor market makes it difficult to obtain the necessary machinery quickly enough, even with the best intentions, and all the more difficult to obtain the necessary safety equipment, especially when operations depend on the work of craftsmen.

While new accident-prevention equipment is hard to procure, actual need for such equipment has increased dramatically. In the many firms that have now been working at an accelerated pace for a significant period, the risk of accidents, and therefore the necessity of preventive measures, has greatly increased. This situation has come about because it became necessary to hire large numbers of unskilled workers, in particular women and young people; night shifts and overtime have been introduced; frequently there are not even enough supervisors; and even the unqualified labor pool is subject to strong fluctuations. It is also unavoidable that unskilled women and young people are employed to operate relatively dangerous machines, such as drills, lathes, presses, even milling machines. The consequences can be seen even in large firms that have long been regarded as using exemplary equipment and that certainly endeavor even now to go to the utmost extreme to prevent accidents. Nevertheless, in one such firm, for example, the number of accidents—injuries to the eyes and the penetration of foreign objects into the cornea—has increased since the beginning of the war at an alarmingly consistent rate.

During a five-month observation period, 311 accidents involving injuries to the eye occurred at this firm, and 232 occurred in another firm during the same period. It is worth noting that before the war, one of these firms had actually been particularly attentive to protecting the workers' eyes; clear proof of this care is provided not only by the firm's low accident rate but also by the excellent leaflets on protecting their eyes that it handed out to the workers. These leaflets attempted to address appropriately all the possible dangers threatening the worker's eyes, including penetration by foreign objects, blunt-force traumas, burns and corrosive injuries, heat radiation, gases and steam, and finally blinding as the result of glare. The instructions given to workers on how to proceed if they suffered an eye injury were exemplary. That is how matters stood before the war; now, however, an enormous increase in accident figures set in. The Institute, which had always met with the greatest cooperation from this firm in matters of accident prevention, wrote to the firm to call its attention to the situation.

Not unexpectedly, the crucial passage in the firm's response read: "Under the present unusual circumstances, when we must make do with many untrained outsiders and with the work of inexperienced employees, it is difficult to strictly enforce safety regulations." Here we seem to have found the outer limit of what accident prevention can achieve, at least in its present state. Special recognition is due to the fact that since the universal use of safety goggles clearly cannot be implemented, this firm has increased the use of other preventive measures, especially the installation of protective screens on the lathes to guard against flying chips.

A further decline in the quality of the technical equipment at the various firms from the standpoint of accident prevention set in because it became necessary to fulfill the new production requirements by old and sometimes inadequate machinery. Not only were older machines—few of which would ordinarily have been kept in use—put back into operation, but also coarser and heavier work, especially processing material for which the machines had never been intended, now had to be performed with machines designed for earlier, often lighter production methods. Firms that had previously manufactured precision instruments or snap fasteners abruptly switched to completely different tasks, such as preparing detonators and their components and twist-off pins [. . .] for grenades, etc., without significantly altering their mechanical equipment. Naturally, they had to make do with the available machinery, without giving much thought to accident prevention. Lathes, for example, were used as milling machines, and a great variety of such substitutes proved to be necessary. But omission of accident-prevention measures applied to existing machines—usually out of necessity—was not the only sin committed. As the result of various unavoidable laws, the same trend also made itself felt in the firms' other arrangements, for example in the case of insulation, where iron and zinc were now substituted for copper and aluminum, sheet-metal casings with paper insulation were introduced, and zinc cables were sheathed in recycled rubber. The association of German electrical engineers has been forced to consider all such replacements legitimate for the duration of the war.

It would have required very strict industrial supervision to ameliorate this general decline in accident prevention even slightly. But, as noted above, great gaps in the personnel of foremen and supervisors have arisen; in many cases, even company managements have been taken on by men who have simply been deputized but who are not really familiar with the workings of the firm. Even where this was not the case, whenever a new production method was introduced, the employer and the supervisory personnel themselves did not understand the new procedure well enough to take the necessary steps to increase accident prevention in the context of such stopgap and interim arrangements, a precaution that would be difficult even for experts.

It has been in this connection that some of the accident-prevention regulations—and the Institute's publications, which we redistributed as widely as possible—fell partly into oblivion. The dissemination of the accident-prevention ordinances and the leaflets has come to a standstill; there have been instances in which there seemed almost total unawareness of the accident-prevention regulations.

A large district health-insurance agency wrote:

> Since the factories have become so heavily occupied producing war materiel, many eye injuries have recently occurred in our iron-working factories, caused by metal filings while the employees failed to wear safety goggles at work. The accident-prevention regulations we consulted, however, unfortunately gave us no determination for the circumstances that obligate employers to provide safety goggles; on the contrary, the employers turn to the undersigned health insurance agency to provide those protective articles. But we do not believe that we have any obligation to acquire such goggles and to pass them on to the insured workers, however, so long as they are not already injured. § 74 of the industrial code contains some paragraphs about provisions for accident prevention, but there is no mention whatever of an obligation for ironworks and metalworking shops.

And yet, § 1 of the ordinance issued by the Ministry of Trade and Commerce on November 23, 1905, which consists of what amounts to an addendum to § 74 of the industrial code, provides as follows: "Those workers who, in consequence of their work, incur the possibility of danger to the eyes from fumes, caustic or hot fluids, splinters, or glowing or molten substances must be equipped with safety goggles, protective screens, or face masks. For the protection of all other workers, protective shields or safety nets are to be installed wherever desirable."

From the outset, Germany attempted to counter the progressive weakening of accident prevention, some of which was expected. A regulation from the National Insurance Office (Reichsversicherungsamt), which was circulated as early as August 25, 1914, stated: "Monitoring the accident-prevention regulations is to be sustained if at all possible, since such supervision is a matter of protecting workers' life and health. Furthermore, the employment of a large number of unskilled workers must be taken into account."

We should also mention that some countervailing forces have developed precisely in response to the extraordinary conditions prevailing in the area of accident prevention. These forces gradually do work to improve some aspects of the situation, even without direct official pressure. Among other factors, the military management of some firms, which may serve as a measure of accident prevention, should be kept in mind; but even more significant is the fact that, where accident prevention is concerned, the factories and firms increasingly show a gradual adjustment to the new conditions. Thus the new production methods are gradually being mastered, the factories are gradually adopting the appropriate arrangements to meet the new excessive demands, and the continual, unvarying production to satisfy military requirements may also have had an effect on accident prevention.

Germany is further attempting to exert some influence on this front by appealing to the employers' and workers' patriotic feelings when it comes to the war and exhorting them to pay attention to accident prevention wherever possible, in the interest of the people. Finally, the forced retrenchment in some industries, in response to the commercial situation or the difficulty of procuring materials, may also help to prevent accidents.

Accident Prevention for Chimney Sweeps

In accordance with these conditions, the Institute's direct accident-prevention actions have been limited only to individual cases that presented themselves and that had some significance both as they represented a principle and as there seemed some promise that they could be helped. In the case of new construction, the Institute has pressed for better observation of certain regulations that observation has shown to be regularly violated. The building trades, which came to an almost complete standstill, particularly in the early days of the war, made it especially possible to enforce observation of the regulations, even though in many jobs—such as the construction of military barracks—the work was often just as stepped up as in other industries working to equip the army.

At this time, the Institute has particularly called for observation of those safety regulations that covered provisions significant for preventing accidents not only in actual construction but also in its ancillary and cleaning tasks, such as the activities of chimney sweeps.

Accordingly, the Institute has petitioned the Office of the Governor to set out measures with respect to the following:

1. Frequently, the catwalks in buildings under construction are not installed according to regulations. Either the planks are too weak, or instead of using one strong board, two weak boards are nailed together. Even when the boards are strong enough, the catwalk may still become unsafe because of an insufficient number of supports, so that the ends of the boards, unsupported, protrude into space.

2. Great deficiencies were also found in the way the catwalk railings are secured. In many cases, they are merely screwed to boards that are inadequately fastened, and as a result, they provide more danger than safety. Yet official inspections rarely discover these deplorable conditions, since from the ground, such railings may easily appear to meet regulations; it is not, however, possible to conduct a closer inspection, because wherever there is a chance that a reprimand might be issued, the access ladders are removed before the inspector's visit.

3. Risks arise for chimney sweeps specifically because buildings lack long ladders, so that the chimney sweep must improvise by setting his own ladder, which is too short for most tasks, on top of chairs or crates, where it cannot be adequately secured.

In response to this petition, the Office of the Governor sent the Institute a copy of a memorandum in which the Office of the Governor, citing the noted deficiencies, requested the crownland administration commission as the highest authority in matters of construction, to take the steps necessary to improve these conditions.

[. . .]

Employers' Interest in Accident Prevention

Those firms that have demonstrated their concern for accident prevention of their own initiative deserve all the more gratitude therefore. Special mention must be made of the accident-prevention office of the Skoda works in Pilsen under the direction of the engineer R. Hríbal; this office has issued notable publications, especially since the beginning of the war, dealing in particular with such topics as the firm's welfare provisions and such safety precautions for the operation of electric cranes as they were realized in the Skoda works.

Accident Prevention and Relief for Disabled War Veterans

A new problem in accident prevention, almost entirely unknown before the war, is becoming increasingly critical, requiring the Institute's special scrutiny. It is a question of employing disabled war veterans in firms subject to compulsory insurance. The Institute first became aware of this situation as a number of separate problems arose. For example, one master plumber asked whether he might be exposing himself to the danger of liability if he employed a veteran who had contracted epilepsy as a consequence of a shrapnel wound.

He added that his modest operation and the scarcity of workers as well as the paucity of commissions would make it impossible for him to restrict the veteran's activities to the workshop; he would have to use the man for construction work as well, though he would not, of course, place him in dangerous situations. He emphasized that the disabled man was diligent and skilled and would be unable to find other jobs in his line of work and would be driven to despair if he could not be hired by this master. Nevertheless, the master would have to reject him, he pointed out, if he would be risking liability in case of an accident.

The essential features of the entire problem are clearly outlined on this one example, taken at random.

Like the employer, the Institute certainly has an interest, quite apart from the general societal interest, in preserving for the entire insured industries the pool of workers who are skilled in performing the necessary operations of their respective firm and who have been working for that firm until now. Therefore, in its own interest (and not merely as an agent of the Public Crownland Agency for the Relief of Returning Soldiers), the Institute is supporting all endeavors directed toward the re-employment of workers and supervisors returning from military service. For this purpose, in July 1915, the Institute circulated an open letter with a registration sheet to employers in firms subject to compulsory insurance. The letter explained in detail why it was requesting each employer to rehire those workers and supervisors who had been working in the firm before reporting for military duty to the extent that their wounds were healed and they were fit for work and to return them to their earlier positions wherever practicable. It was requested that employers employ those workers who were now disabled as the result of military service and to consult with the Crownland Central Employment Agency in Prague (the subject of this initiative by the Institute) in this matter.

Germany has also taken steps aimed at restoring disabled veterans to their previous occupations. Note was especially taken of the necessity not only of employers' willingness to cooperate but also of the participation of the foremen and workers themselves—groups that have been admirably in agreement for this mission.

But there is something of a limitation on the aspects accident prevention must enforce. Germany considered this factor as well. An open letter circulated by the National Insurance Office on August 30, 1915, addresses the question in detail. Among other matters, it states: "Disabled veterans may never be exposed to occupational risks that they are no longer able to withstand. That caution is a self-evident requirement of accident insurance both in their interest and in the interest of their insured fellow employees." We are in possession of the relevant decisions in the various accident-insurance ordinances on this aspect. The ordinances of February 7, 1907 (safety regulations for buildings), and August 22, 1911 (safety regulations for sugar factories), for example, are nearly identical:

> Persons whom the employer knows to be suffering from epilepsy, convulsions, occasional fainting fits, dizziness, impaired hearing, or other bodily failings or debilities to the extent that such infirmity exposes them to excessive risk in the performance of certain tasks or that their infirmity may give rise to such risks, may not be employed in work of this kind. — Especially dangerous tasks may be entrusted only to such persons as have considerable familiarity with the work and the risks it entails and who possess the necessary skills.

The ordinance of May 29, 1908 (regulations for the commercial operation of quarries and of clay, sand and gravel pits) contains the same provision but restricts it to work at the sites where the material is won. The ordinance of September 25, 1911 (safety regulations for paper manufacture) includes these instructions and adds, "Under-age workers, as well as employees with impaired or sensitive lungs, tuberculosis, and open sores may not be charged with direct handling of rag fibers."

All these decisions, of course, apply across the board to the employment of disabled veterans as well. Some conditions, however, arise in the employment of disabled veterans that have not been considered in these decisions. Above all, at present the labor market differs fundamentally from the pre-war situation, and the current state will continue for a long time. Some occupations suffer from a shortage of workers, while in others, employment is not possible as the market is saturated; we will see great changes in this situation once the war is over. As we consider possibilities for employing disabled veterans, we must keep all these points in mind. Further, many of the disabled veterans who are to be given jobs in their former occupations have a great deal of professional experience and, on the one hand, are too old to be able to change occupations, and on the other, are so thoroughly skilled in one occupation that the potential danger in some tasks must be assessed differently from the evaluation that applies to other workers who are new to the particular occupation. In addition, it will be necessary to make different judgments when assessing occupational capability in men who suffer war-engendered mutilation and illness from decisions made in individual cases before the war. On the other hand, of course, in individual cases, such as judging the occupational ability of former masons who have lost an eye in the war and where serious risk to their remaining eye may be connected with continued practice of their occupation, though they might otherwise be well suited, the limitations to occupational ability detailed in the cited ordinances must also be somewhat intensified.

The sum of these considerations is that it is impossible for the accident-prevention regulations to establish strict, rigid principles regarding employability in particular occupations of disabled veterans as was previously possible in similar cases. What has been an abstract question will now be a fact, and all we can say in response to such questions is: The same human consideration that advocates employing disabled veterans in their former occupations must also keep us from hiring them to do work that, because of their infirmity, may predictably place them in unusual danger.

Accident prevention must take steps on another front as well when the disabled return to their occupations. The cited letter from the German National Insurance Office states:

> Just as medical treatment of disabled veterans has fortunately been further developed during the war—professional training was the preparatory school for this treatment—interest in the reemployment of disabled veterans should equally provide motivation for improvements in accident-prevention techniques.
>
> By this means, not only can many more disabled veterans' work be better safeguarded, but permanent gains might be achieved for everyone who has restricted ability to earn a livelihood, including people injured in accidents. In particular, an effort should be made to arrange the safety equipment, to adjust machines, to move loads, etc., tasks that heretofore required two healthy arms or legs, in such a way that one of these limbs will, if necessary, be sufficient without increasing the risk of accident.

The National Insurance Office has also initiated contact with trade associations to urge initiatives along these lines. In this country, as far as we know, a significant initiative along these lines has not yet been undertaken. Of course, we will also reap the benefits of any findings that result from the German research and proposals for accident prevention here, if only we have the will for it.

Let us cite only a few examples of what we are striving for: The shifting device that regulates the feed on die cutters, presses, and similar machines, will have to be redesigned so that it can be operated with the left hand or with the foot. A supporting seat will need to be built for workers with leg or foot injuries. Tools and equipment will have to be

provided with handles that fit prosthetic devices. The dangerous components of drive wheels and flywheels, for which a simple rail was previously found to be adequate, as it may well have been, will have to be
sheathed in order to be operated by disabled veterans so that they cannot accidentally catch an arm or a leg in them. These are only a few of
the examples cited at a conference of the Association of German Engineers. Accident-prevention technology is offers a wide possibility of ad-
aptation.

Accident Prevention and the Training of the Disabled

It will, of course, be essential to make disabled veterans aware of the
new dangers that their condition exposes them to in their former or new
occupation and to train them to prevent accidents. Their training will
therefore have to place special emphasis on accident prevention.

Possibilities for Additional Techniques to Promote Safety

The entire overview of current accident-prevention measures shows that
very little can be done at present but that the postwar period expects
that much greater and more pressing tasks need to address
accident-prevention technology and promotion. Even now the Institute
must prepare for its part in this work. At this time we intend, once normal conditions are resumed, to make the fullest possible use of the authority granted the Institute by § 28 of the accident-insurance law: the
authority to require the trade inspector to inspect any firm. Using the
resulting information, the Institute can apply to the lowest governmental authorities to enact and implement appropriate directives. This authority granted the Institute should be exercised in conjunction with
every accident that is shown, with some probability, to have been caused
by violation of accident-prevention regulations. Only by making a systematic study of the histories of accidents obtained by studying the regulations can we hope to effect a gradual improvement of the deplorable
conditions in the area of accident prevention that are the result of the
current situation.

Caution in Employing Prisoners of War

Last year, attention was called in Germany to a special problem of accident prevention related to the war. Thankfully, so far, the Institute's
territory has not seen any case even remotely similar, but the matter deserves attention nevertheless.

The case was as follows. A prisoner of war was employed as operator of a large overhead crane. One day, for no good reason, he set the crane's hoist motor at full power. When the hoisting cable broke, the pulley block shot up into the air and flew into the workspace behind, without, as it happened, hitting anyone.

There was no doubt that the prisoner of war's principal intention had been to disable the crane and to disrupt the flow of work. The German authorities recommended that any firms employing prisoners of war make certain that these are not called upon to perform tasks on which the welfare of the operation depends.

Commentary 16

∾

The two sections selected from the annual report for the year 1914 deal with Kafka's two principal areas of responsibility: risk classification and accident prevention.

The Institute's annual report for 1914 is a source text for studying the transition from a peacetime economy to a wartime economy. In section (A), on risk classification, Kafka argues that the laws of statistics and probability need to be defended against the exceptionalist rhetoric of employers. The passage from peacetime to wartime must not be considered grounds for discarding the statistical perspective; such continuity must be preserved.

The second section, on accident prevention, presents a different picture. In times of war, national security and workplace security are intimately connected. The relation is more than metaphorical, as our commentaries 2 and 13 suggest; it is literal and practical. On the one hand, the rhetoric of war propaganda is part of the overall framework of national defense, and social insurance plays a major role in such propaganda. On the other hand, Kafka's report shows how wartime conditions literally and practically enter the framework of accident prevention. Not only do they stand in the way of further development of accident-prevention measures; they have also brought about "in part [. . .] the destruction of what has already been achieved" in this area.

The report elaborates this damage by documenting the impact of the war economy on the four major dimensions of risk in workmen's accident insurance: risk is increased by the *human* factor, when a depleted workforce is supplied with increasingly unskilled workers; by the *mechanical* factor, when "new production requirements" are demanded from "old and sometimes inadequate machinery"; by the *material* factor, when industrial production must make do with "a great variety of [. . .] substitutes" for materials needed for the war effort; and by the *supervisory* factor, when vulnerable situations follow from the "great gaps in the personnel of foremen and supervisors."

More than the technical essay on wood-planing machines, on which there has been considerable commentary, it is Kafka's treatment of accident prevention in the 1914 report that forcefully connects his office writings with his early wartime story, *In the Penal Colony*. On October 3, 1914, the President of the German Insurance Office, Paul Kaufmann, delivered a propaganda speech at Kafka's Institute, declaring, "It is a sign of the strength abiding in our people that in times of war, the mechanism of social insurance continues its quiet operation as in the days of peace."[1] Now consider, in this light, Kafka's report on disintegrating machinery and work flow in *In the Penal Colony*: the officer observes that "the [penal] machine was obviously falling to pieces; its quiet motion was deceptive." This remark reads like a direct reply to Kaufmann.[2] Furthermore, as was the case in the Bohemian war economy, the disintegration of the penal machine is linked to a shortage of material. In a seemingly innocuous passage early in the story, the officer remarks, "Unfortunately, spare parts are very hard to come by here." And later, commenting on a torn strap that was supposed to tie the condemned man to the machine, he adds, "If I send for a new strap, the torn one is demanded as proof, and it takes ten days for the new one to get here, and then it's of an inferior make and of almost no use" (KSS 38, 46). As in many Bohemian factories during World War I, the machine at the center of the story is supervised by an officer rather than a civil expert. When the officer eventually turns himself over to "his" machine, the machine literally follows the script of Kafka's annual report on accident prevention, being obliged to "process material for which [it] had never been intended," and so it is bound to disintegrate.

17

A PUBLIC PSYCHIATRIC HOSPITAL FOR
GERMAN-BOHEMIA (1916)

Kafka invests his literary skill in a plan to establish a psychiatric clinic for veterans in the northern Bohemian village of Frankenstein (near Rumburg). In both texts, he manipulates the "biopolitical" ideology of his day to produce an effect opposite to that intended by the jargon. In Kafka's inversion of the meaning of stereotypical terms, "life" ceases to figure as an asset of the war-mongering imperial state and is restored to the individual as his inalienable possession. Here, Kafka demonstrates his loyalty to the ethical postulate of human existence in the "bio state": when life itself becomes the object and battleground of political power, it is no longer habeas corpus *but* habeas vitam.

A. A Major War Relief Plan Demands Realization: Establishing a Psychiatric Hospital in German Bohemia (*Rumburger Zeitung*, October 8, 1916)

Soon after the outbreak of war, a strange apparition, arousing fear and pity, appeared in the streets of our cities. He was a soldier returned from the front. He could move only on crutches or had to be pushed along in a wheelchair. His body shook without cease, as if he were overcome by a mighty chill, or he was standing stock-still in the middle of the tranquil street, in the thrall of his experiences at the front. We see others, too, men who could move ahead only by taking jerky steps; poor, pale, and gaunt, they leaped as though a merciless hand held them by the neck, tossing them back and forth in their tortured movements.

People gazed at them with compassion but more or less thoughtlessly, especially as the number of such apparitions increased and became almost a part of life on the street. But there was no one to provide the necessary explanation and to say something like the following:

What we are seeing here are neuroses, most of them triggered by trauma but other forms as well. No matter how many of these trembling, jerking men we see in the streets, their actual numbers are much larger. Furthermore, this is merely one kind of nervous illness, not even the most serious kind, simply the most conspicuous. Just think of all the cases of neuroses related to frontline service—neurasthenia, hysteria, epilepsy. Even now we have statistics to show that well over 2,000 such patients are already housed in the hospitals of Cisleithania[1] alone. But that's not all. We must also include in the category of neurological diseases numerous disorders of speech, hearing, and the facial muscles; over 1,000 such cases have been reported so far in the hospitals of Cisleithania. But even these figures do not exhaust the total number of nervous disorders. A large part of all mental disorders must be included in this same category. The total numbers for the Cisleithanian hospitals come to almost 3,000. And even now the number of cases of neurological diseases is not yet complete, for these figures, of course, count only those afflicted men who are placed in the hospitals in the rear of the frontlines. But many these have been given medical discharges and sent back home, and a subsequent official medical investigation has shown that at least 10 percent of these cases of nervous disorders are still in need of treatment. If we take from these overall figures only those that apply to Bohemia, we can count over 2,000 of the war disabled with nervous disorders who have been discharged but still require a cure, and more than 2,500 are in hospitals, thus making a total of close to 5,000. But remember: this figure is not only a minimum; it is merely provisional. It does not include those men who suffer with nervous disorders and are kept away from the front lines nor the army of those whose nerves are afflicted, a group that science can safely alert us to expect once the war is over, the prisoners of war return, and tensions abruptly ease. Then the numbers will increase beyond measure. For all these conditions, however, there is a nearly equal consolation: The greater part of these disorders, as we have already learned from this war, are completely curable, while others can be brought close to a cure. Of course, cures can be achieved only by the proper residential therapy and not through outpatient treatment. Where the latter fails—as it most often does—the former can still work wonders. Most patients, in the absence of residential treatment, are condemned to a life of ever-increasing suffering, and for many it means a lifetime of living in an insane asylum.

And such indispensable residential treatment is impractical today, at least in Bohemia. The few small, expensive sanatoriums that exist cannot, of course, serve this purpose. The only other existing facility is Professor Margulies' temporary psychiatric hospital, housed in barracks on the Belvedere in Prague. Granted that this outstanding scientist and physician is doing everything humanly possible, in this instance the possible cannot meet the need. His hospital can serve only as an interim

location: it is too small, shoddily built, lacking in equipment and supplies, short of the most basic necessities. The excellent results this facility has achieved within its limitations are only a faint indication of what
a large, fully equipped psychiatric hospital would be able to achieve under such an excellent director.

This irrefutable compelling need should surely have led the Provincial
Central Administration for the Welfare of Returning Veterans to make
plans for such a facility. Of course, for obvious reasons we cannot pay
too much attention to the first project that presents itself—an Utraquist
institution to serve all of Bohemia.[2] We should devote all the more effort
to studying the feasibility of a facility to serve German Bohemia.

And this opportunity, we may safely say, has now arrived; it virtually
offers itself, waiting only for helping hands. We are not suggesting that
a large new building is required; given the urgency of the need, all outward embellishments are best avoided. Nor should we want to see too
much money spent on the project, and we should not have to wait too
long before the facility can be put to use. Expert scientists and planners
have engaged in exhaustive discussions and have found the plant at
Geltschbad to be especially suited to such a facility. Here is a plant that
can be put to use in the shortest possible time without major changes;
the location is healthful, with good air, plenty of woods, and excellent
water for hydropathical therapy. At some later date, the plant could easily be expanded, and most particularly, it offers an opportunity for patients to work in the fields, gardens, and workshops—one of the most
important therapies used in the treatment of neurological disorders.

We might object that establishing such a large facility for what is a temporary need—the limited aim of postwar rehabilitation—is questionable.
But viewed correctly, this objection is one of the strongest arguments in
favor of the plan, not against it. Even in peacetime there was an urgent
need for a public psychiatric hospital, but we could hardly hope that this
need would be met, given the limited resources of the normal peacetime
economy. However, the need itself was never in doubt. The consulting
rooms of neurologists have been crowded with people from the lower
middle class: teachers, civil servants, business managers, merchants, men
and women; physicians were helpless because they had no access to the
necessary residential treatment, and only such treatment had a reasonable
chance of successfully rehabilitating these patients. Even more urgent and
inaccessible to the physicians, however, were adequate treatment for the
wealth of traumatic neuroses caused by industrial accidents incurred by
workers and accidents suffered by the general population especially in
connection with the railroads, that have been known to increase by all
possible stages to the point of compensation hysteria. The costs that have
accrued through these groups of neuroses to the social insurance agencies,

the railway administrations, and the public at large are huge but they have largely been wasted, because the goal—a cure—could not be achieved for lack of a public psychiatric hospital. In addition to the great loss of capital, a number of curable workers were doomed to infirmity.

Now the war-relief effort is practically forcing this psychiatric hospital upon us. What can now be seen only as an act of patriotism—establishing a psychiatric facility for men returned from war with nervous disorders—once peace is concluded, will become a greater and greater social blessing, in which not only social-insurance institutes and railroad administrations, but also all elements of industry, trade, the civil service, and agriculture have a vital interest. The psychiatric facility that is to be established now is intended to become a public psychiatric hospital, accessible to the whole population, after the war.

Accordingly, we must think of generating the funds to establish and operate the facility. Too many demands are made on the Provincial Central Administration from every side; it cannot be expected to provide large amounts for this purpose from its own coffers, but we can reasonably expect the government to participate significantly in the effort. The financial participation of the social-insurance institutes and railroad administration can be regarded as equally certain. And the information need only be presented in an urgent and organized manner for the widest circles of private charities to be stirred to action.

We can count on all these plans coming true—but only when the seed money has been raised to start this effort. All that is needed for the time being is that one or more generous persons lend their support to lay the financial cornerstone of the whole. Once that is done, the whole project is certain to be completed easily and swiftly with the assured help of the public and the government. But whoever it is who lays the cornerstone will earn the everlasting thanks of his German-Bohemian home and will have performed a patriotic and social deed of abiding value. The Prague Central Administration surely stands ready to get in touch at any time with anyone who will take such an interest in the project and to provide whatever information is helpful. But we must always remember that, in this instance, it is never too soon to begin.

B. German Society for the Establishment and Maintenance of a Public Veterans' Psychiatric Hospital for German Bohemia in Prague

Fellow Countrymen:

The World War, in which all human misery is concentrated, is also a war of nerves, more so than any previous war. And in this war of nerves, all too many suffer defeat. Just as the intensive operation of machinery during the last few decades' peacetime jeopardized, far more than ever before, the nervous systems of those so employed, giving rise to nervous disturbances and disorders, the enormous increase in the mechanical aspect of contemporary warfare has caused the most serious risks and suffering for the nerves of our fighting men. And this in a manner that even the well-informed can hardly have imagined in full. As early as June 1916, there were over 4,000 disabled veterans with nervous disorders in German Bohemia alone, according to conservative statistical data. And what more is yet to come? How many of these men with nervous disorders are lying in hospitals outside of Bohemia? How many of them will return from being prisoners of war? Immense suffering is crying out for help. The nervous men who shake and jerk in the streets of our cities are only relatively innocuous emissaries from the enormous horde of sufferers.

What shall we do? We have a choice: We can let everything continue on its present course. We can stand by, and the men with nervous disabilities come back from the front and flow into the veterans' hospitals, and we can see that only a tiny number of them are admitted to the limited special wards for nervous disorders, the rest being housed only in regular wards for the military. Of course, in the special wards we see some successes, showing improvement and cures, as good as is possible, given the deficient and makeshift resources available. But how few fortunate men receive this treatment! And the majority of veterans with nervous disabilities who are housed in regular hospitals—what becomes of them? Even the best will in the world and greatest medical skill cannot help them today. For them there is no help in their country, which they have defended with their lives and for which they have risked their future and that of their families, for only careful treatment in a psychiatric hospital with modern facilities can help them. Since no such hospital exists, however, the fate of these unfortunate men is sealed. They will be released to their homes, their disorder still in place, thus multiplying the number of peacetime sufferers from neurological diseases, victims of never-ending, constantly increasing suffering, a torment to their families, a loss to the German-Bohemian people's power, and candidates for the insane asylum. Is this to be the way German Bohemia rewards its sons?

But another possibility exists. German Bohemia—that is, all our German countrymen—could use our own means to establish a large *public psychiatric hospital.* Of course, such an effort requires corresponding contributions from the government (which has a vital interest in such an institution in wartime as it does in peacetime) and from public and private insurance companies, the railroad administration, large landowners, industry, and all those kind-hearted people who are willing to help, no matter how small their gift might be. A rich blessing could spread over German Bohemia from such a *public psychiatric hospital*, fully supplied with all the necessary equipment in the exemplary fashion of the German Reich. Now, and for as long as necessary after the war, such a hospital could serve disabled veterans from German Bohemia exclusively, but once this need is met, the hospital can be dedicated to its *long-term purpose*—accommodating and treating *indigent* German Bohemian countrymen who suffer from nervous afflictions. This plan offers an opportunity to use the weapons of philanthropy and science in order to alleviate one of the great miseries of war as well as of peacetime, if not completely, at least to a large extent.

We must choose one of these two courses of action—rather, there is really no choice. Even if the chance that our help would be crowned with success were not such a strong and promising enticement, it would still be our natural human and patriotic duty as a people to intervene here with all our powers. Since success does seem assured, however, the urgency is all the greater.

The first steps have already been taken. On October 14, an assembly of representatives of all political parties, professions, and walks of life in German Bohemia took place in the German House in Prague. With a rare show of unanimity and readiness for sacrifice, the necessity of active assistance was recognized, and it was decided to found a *German Society for the Establishment and Maintenance of a Public Veterans' Psychiatric Hospital for German Bohemia,* located in Prague. This society is envisaged as part of the popular German Bohemian war-relief effort and will be represented for the present by the undersigned *preparatory committee* elected in that assembly.

The first order of business is procuring the resources. To this end we request you most respectfully to participate in this great German Bohemian undertaking, to which there is nothing yet similar in Austria, to the utmost of your ability and to advocate the plan among your fellows.

Participation can take the following forms, according to the statutes:

1. Through voluntary donations.
2. Through becoming a sponsor of the Society by donating K 5,000 or more; joining as a *sponsor* by contributing K 5,000 will entitle that individual to nominate a patient for care at the hospital.
3. Through becoming a *founding member* of the Society with a one-time contribution of K 1,000 or more. The names of the sponsors and founders will be listed on a permanent memorial plaque in the hospital.

4. Through becoming a *full member* of the Society, with a yearly contribution of at least K 5. A one-time donation of at least K 200 may be substituted for yearly contributions.

We are confident that our request is not made in vain, *since it is the request of our beloved homeland as well.*

Contributions may be sent, by an enclosed money order. For the time being, please send to: "German Society for the Establishment and Maintenance of a Public and Veterans' Psychiatric Hospital in German Bohemia, Prague—Poříč 7, Workmen's Accident Insurance Institute."
Prague, November 1916

Commentary 17

⁓

In a letter to Felice Bauer of October 30, 1916, Kafka identifies the second of the two documents concerned with veterans' rehabilitation (doc. 17B) as his own work. The same letter indicates that he had written a number of other texts on this issue. The elaborate style of the first document (doc. 17A), published under the name of Eugen Pfohl, excludes the possibility that Kafka's boss had, in fact, written this article. As Kafka was the responsible officer for this project, and as both texts are connected by a quite particular line of argument (see the following commentary as well), we can reasonably assume that Kafka once more acted as Pfohl's ghost writer, as he had done on the occasion of the Vienna congress (doc. 13).

In his introduction to the famous 1919 volume on the *Psychoanalysis of War Neuroses*, Freud locates the conflict between a peacetime ego, used to a life of security, and a wartime ego, suddenly facing the risk of death, as the basis of war trauma and, hence, the national army as the nourishing soil for that psychic disorder.[1] The concept of a discontinuity, even contradiction, between war and peace implied in this explanation is squarely contested in the opening passage of Kafka's public appeal: "Just as the intensive operation of machinery during the last few decades' peacetime jeopardized, far more than ever before, the nervous systems of those so employed, giving rise to nervous disturbances and disorders, the enormous increase in the mechanical aspect of contemporary warfare has caused the most serious risks and suffering for the nerves of our fighting men." Replacing the opposition between "war" and "peace" by the opposition between "machine" and "human nerves," Kafka highlights the strategic center of both documents, which asserts the continuity of a battle that began well before the war and that, more importantly, would continue after its end.

During the war, neurological disorders, such as traumatic neurosis (or shell shock), spread so quickly that they were soon considered a "psychic epidemic." But their origin reaches further back in history. While nervous dysfunction without corresponding physical impairment was first diagnosed in the mid-nineteenth century in connection with railroad accidents—so-called "railway spines"—these recognized cases significantly increased toward the end of the century, when public accident insurance was introduced in industrialized Europe. It soon became evident that the phenomenon could not be adequately explained as im-moral or illegal behavior. A clear-cut distinction between malingering (the intentional simulation of injury), aggravation (the exaggeration of symptoms), and pension neurosis (a psychiatric dysfunction of traumatic suggestion, triggered by the collective consciousness of the very exis-tence of accident insurance), could not be established. But the general air of suspicion that grew up alongside the benefits of the welfare state seemed to be blown away by the winds of war. As the propaganda ma-chine needed heroes, wounded warriors received a better press than wounded workers, even if the German language had created the generic category of *Drückeberger* for shirkers of all stripes. The two documents under review (docs. 17A,B) try to take advantage of this constructive constellation.

As with the other documents in this edition, a factual issue is entan-gled with an ideological issue. Both texts explicitly refer to the problem of the public perception of neurotic disorders. The Rumburger newspa-per article (doc. 17A) especially highlights the danger of the public gaze's getting used to the phenomenon of a mass derangement as part of life on the street. In the connecting sentence, we notice a subtle literary device that clearly points to Kafka as the author of this article. The nar-rator inserts into his report a second narrative voice, one marked by its conspicuous absence in the public debate on the welfare of war veter-ans—"there was no one to provide the necessary explanation and to say something like the following"—thus adding to the gaze of the man in the street the statistical knowledge of the man in the field. This bifocal gaze on the particular case (man as individual) and on the statistical field to which it belongs (the "average man") is an epistemic figure, cut-ting across the borderline between Kafka's office writings and his litera-ture.

The line of argument taken by these two documents, as well as their rhetoric, cannot be fully understood except with a view to the contem-porary nexus between war and welfare. If World War I was conceived of as a catalyst for the development of the welfare state, this relation could easily be inverted. High-ranking experts, such as Paul Kaufmann, the president of the German Insurance Office, whom we have encountered (com. 16), argued that the military superiority of Germany was based on the excellence of its welfare system. On October 2, 1916, six days before "Pfohl's" article was published in the *Rumburger Zeitung*, the Crown-land Agency for the Welfare of Returning Veterans had invited Kauf-mann to lecture in Prague. We can safely assume that, owing to his responsibilities within the Agency, Kafka would have been in the audi-ence at Kaufmann's speech. But even if he had not attended, he certainly would have read the concluding sentences in the *Prager Tagblatt* the following day: "Protecting against any unfitness for work is more important than caring for those already disabled. Each life thus kept fit is a national asset."[2]

In the Prague Crownland Agency, this approach was shared and developed further by the eminent national statistician Heinrich Rauchberg, Kafka's former professor at Charles University and now a member of the Agency's training board. In a widely published essay on the welfare of war veterans aiming at a national homestead plan, Rauchberg defines "national power" (*Volkskraft*) as the basis for "military power" (*Wehrmacht*).[3] The former is by no means a mythological construct but represents a complex empirical index. It consists of such statistical factors as birth rates, employment figures, and the national rate of sick leaves. Based on this formula, Rauchberg proposes a distinction between the two fields of war veterans' welfare. On the one hand, the homestead scheme would have to be considered a long-term investment in national power; on the other hand, medical care for wounded soldiers (that is, the area Kafka was assigned to) would have to be considered a merely temporary task, posed by the war and bound to disappear soon after its end. In his public appeal for a psychiatric hospital (doc. 17B), Kafka seems to advert to Rauchberg when he warns of "a loss to the German-Bohemian people's power." But in fact this ethno- and biopolitical terminology serves only to dispute the distinction between the welfare of the nation and the welfare of the individual. The treatment of men disabled by neurotic disorders is not a temporary problem, related to war. It came into being long before this particular war and would not disappear with its end. Here, and not on the level of patriotic rhetoric, we find a specific textual feature that may be assigned to Kafka the writer. Whereas national leaders in biopolitics, such as Kaufmann and Rauchberg, were struggling to rally social welfare, as it were, Kafka/"Pfohl" moves in the opposite direction by welcoming an "act of patriotism—establishing a psychiatric facility for men returned from war with nervous disorders—[. . . as] a greater and greater social blessing" in a future peacetime world. Within such a conceptual frame, life is no longer considered an allotment to a national asset but a value indissolubly connected to the individual.

18

"HELP DISABLED VETERANS! AN URGENT APPEAL TO THE PUBLIC" (1916/1917)

In this polemical piece of wartime journalism, Kafka uses the principle of ha-beas vitam as the starting point for a model of the interaction between individual and state. It includes a vision of a federalist and democratic organization of a postwar Austria. Like Kafka's "Building the Great Wall of China," a story about national defense and political freedom, this article can be read as a direct criticism of Werner Sombart's influential pamphlet Händler und Helden, w*hich celebrates collective self-sacrifice.*

A. "Help Disabled Veterans! An Urgent Appeal to the Public"
(*Prager Tagblatt*, December 10, 1916)

Let this appeal be heard everywhere, and let everyone respond! Our disabled veterans have suffered and are suffering for all of us, and they have the right to ask all of us to help alleviate as much as possible a very painful and worrisome future. Every day the war claims new victims, every day the trains carrying the wounded roll into the hinterland, and every day the hospitals accept new patients as they discharge the earlier ones. Of course, the physicians' skill manages to heal wounds inflicted by war entirely for many thousands, but for a great many more, the wounds go too deep, the bones are too shattered, the destruction wrought by shrapnel and grenade is too great. These unfortunate, needy men are maimed for life. The number of the maimed, crippled, blind, and deaf increases with every day of this long and harsh war. Modern medicine brings some relief of the deep, prolonged suffering; it replaces missing limbs with ingenious prostheses, it teaches the deaf to read lips and thus to hear with their eyes, it gives Braille to the blind, and by these means brings about a bearable existence where a black and hopeless life seemed fated. But even modern medicine cannot make the disabled fully able to gain useful employment; it cannot give them back the courage to live or the confidence inspired by a healthy body.

The disabled remain in need of help, and providing them with help is our sacred duty.

The state, as an organization, has done its duty with regard to disabled veterans by establishing, in every crownland, government offices that provide aid to returning soldiers in general and disabled veterans in particular. The responsibility for these eminently important and, in the best sense, patriotic tasks, however, lies with each citizen as well. Each of us has our victorious armies to thank for the safe enjoyment of his property, his personal security, and the guarantee of a happy future under a freely elected leadership. And should we now abandon those who gave everything for us in battle, who staked their possessions for ours, who endangered their lives for our security, and who shattered their future for our pleasant continued existence? Can it really be true that selfishness remains so strong in these times, which teach us love of fatherland, that an appeal on behalf of disabled veterans goes unheard? We hope not. The hundreds of thousands, even millions, of kronen needed to provide for our returning frontline soldiers and disabled veterans must be raised; each one of us, according to his ability, must ease the hardships of war there where they are felt most acutely, having caused irreparable loss.

We must not keep the idea of the state and the totality of its citizens in separate categories. The war has clearly shown that all of us are the state, that none of us stands outside the concept of the state, that the state's success is success for each one of us, and that a blow against the state is felt by each of us with equal force. That is why we may not justify a reluctance to give with the poor argument that it is the job of the state to care for disabled veterans, that it is not our duty but that of the state to heal the wounds dealt by the war, and that this solicitude is not a private but a public matter. Those who thus try to cast their own miserliness in a familiar and general light lack all understanding for the very fact that they themselves are the state, that every public matter impacts the private citizen in return. What they seem to want is that the organization of the state prescribe their specific contribution to war relief, and that such revenues should be enforced in the form of taxes—revenues that, were they freely and willingly given as donations, would have the value of a patriotic declaration of loyalty to the state. We therefore call our invitation an appeal and not a request, for it would be shameful to have to ask for alms for men to whom we owe such gratitude. No, this article is not a request to the charitable, it is an appeal to duty. It will not be in vain; the many fine proofs of the public's sense of patriotism are attested by other collections for war relief to which the public has freely given. And surely in this case as well, all that is necessary is merely a hint as to the importance and patriotic nature of the goals toward which we strive, as well as the inevitable obligation of private generosity, in order to achieve complete success.

Millions are needed.

Donations to buy wreaths, dedications in honor of the fallen, contributions for celebrations of all kinds, and many other occasions—donation upon donation should flow in, until the collection is sufficient to be equal to the fullness of the task, that millions become available to care for disabled veterans, to provide work for all returning soldiers, and to see them through the roughest times during their period of unemployment. Millions are needed, in Bohemia alone, and only a few hundred thousand kronen are available at present. As considerable as this sum may sound, it is no more than a drop in the bucket, an insufficient, a tiny portion of the needed amount. The tasks that must be completed are many, and each calls for sizable amounts. The year-end accounts of the Public Crownland Agency for 1915 show K 886,000 in donations, to which the assets that were taken over by the Crownland Commission for Disabled Veterans, amounting to K 268,000, are added. The assets at the last year's end closing amounted to K 608,000. This is a tidy sum, but, as we have noted, it is far from enough.

The Tasks of the Public Crownland Agency

The Public Crownland Agency of the Kingdom of Bohemia for Returning Veterans covers a sizable group of equally important tasks involving war relief, such as health care for the disabled, specialized medical attention for veterans suffering from internal disorders, support for the manufacture of prostheses, employment arrangements, and, most recently, aid to those veterans who lost their sight in battle, the most unfortunate of disabled veterans. In addition, the disabled must be provided with education and training that offers them the possibility of earning their own living once more, pulling themselves up out of their helplessness and becoming valuable, even if not fully capable members of their trade. For this is above all the goal of the Public Crownland Agency: to return disabled veterans to civil employment wherever it is even halfway possible, to make them independent again, and not to abandon them to the bitter necessity of having to live on donations. A visit to the schools for disabled veterans, of which there are two in Prague, shows how successful these efforts are. In one of them—that of Regimental Medical Officer Prof. Jedlicka—721 disabled veterans were trained and 745 were thoroughly prepared for new careers by professionals in various adult-education courses; 190 students in these courses were then also provided with permanent jobs. In the second half of 1915 alone, the same institution produced 1,543 plaster casts, 910 provisional and 84 permanent prosthetic feet, 64 artificial hands, and 86 prostheses applicable to work. During its brief existence, the second major school for disabled veterans in Prague, led by Senior Medical Officer Dr. Kuh, has treated, trained, and employed in its workshops 1,197 patients and has produced 252 prostheses and orthopedic devices.

The German-Bohemian Welfare Organization for Disabled Veterans and Wounded Veterans in Reichenberg has demonstrated outstanding success: As of September 30, 1916, the home for disabled veterans cared for a total of 743 wounded veterans, administering 1,570 X-rays, carrying out 535 surgeries, and applying 1,310 plaster casts and 11,920 bandages. For the purposes of follow-up treatment at the home, 180,872 outpatient visitors received a further 545,765 therapeutic treatments (baths, sweat baths, electric treatments, massages, quartz lamp radiation, and diathermy sessions). The prosthesis workshop delivered 694 orthopedic supports, including artificial limbs. Under the care of the department for the training of the disabled of the Reichenberg Chamber of Commerce, 1,497 individuals were trained and counseled. The department's employment agency arranged for 176 jobs.

A permanent committee for the care of the disabled, headed by the wife of Lieutenant General Zanantoni, was established in Leitmeritz; as of early April, 560 disabled veterans who were trained in this institution were looked after and promptly provided with an occupation.

The Association for the Assistance of the Disabled in the city and district of Teplitz is developing a broad and ever-increasing scope of activity; it is headed by the industrialist Josef Max Mühlig, along with a number of coworkers willing to give of their time and energy, including General Director Dr. Bruno von Enderes; k. k. State Trade School Director Anton Willert, Engineer; and k. k. Principal Physician, Dr. Paul Glässner. In the short time since its establishment, the German Association for Assistance to the War Wounded in Pilsen has succeeded in creating an impressive home for housing Germans wounded in the war, who are using the opportunities offered by German training facilities in Pilsen; and connected with this home are a psychiatric hospital specializing in neuro-cardiac conditions and a model workshop for producing cardboard packaging, employing Germans wounded in the war.

Since, in the overwhelming majority of cases, even after the conclusion of medical treatment, disabled veterans remain limited in what they can perform, their training must be especially intensive in order to replace their diminished physical abilities with increased mental acuity and technical skills. Thus the intention is to keep the disabled in their former occupations and homelands, if at all possible, introducing them to new occupations only if their previous lines of work can no longer be carried out profitably in spite of medical-technical treatment and the skilled use of artificial limbs.

Here is where the transition to another extensive area of activity of the Public Crownland Agency lies: finding employment for those injured in war. Its k. k. Employment Agency for Disabled Veterans is the department specifically established for this effort; it facilitates direct contact between employers and those seeking work. This office will therefore act chiefly along two lines. The employers will learn to trust that the disabled are quite capable of doing the job, that they can be employed and can compete effectively once they have learned to increase their employability, and that they can provide valuable service to their employers in the occupations in which they had become skilled and experienced before the war or in the occupation for which their careful training has prepared them. The other workers will also have to accept their invalid handicapped comrades at work, for both ethical and economic reasons.

A very important line of work of the Public Crownland Agency—the chief prerequisite for its other activities—is the therapy provided the returning fighting men. Though the military administration is the first agency to administer therapeutic care of returning soldiers—even those whose fitness for continued military service cannot be guaranteed—much remains to be done by the Public Crownland Agency on the latter point. And much is indeed being done. In brief, special emphasis is given to: orthopedic cures (in which the German-Bohemian Welfare Organization for Disabled Veterans and Wounded Veterans in Reichenberg plays a special role), treatment for tuberculosis, nervous and cardiac conditions, and stomach and intestinal disorders. A vast amount of work has been done especially in this last area of activity by the Public Crownland Agency. Medical specialists direct the hospitals, volunteer nurses care for the sick, and assistants help in the administration free of charge. The system of combining a state authority with a council of private experts has proven to be excellent in this department of the Public Crownland Agency, as in other departments.

Now, however, state and private work should be combined in another aspect, and this brings us back to the starting point of our appeal. Private willingness to give must be united with state aid to bring the great work that has begun so successfully and beneficially to a successful conclusion.

The Collections

The Public Crownland Agency for Returning Veterans has already received significant sums through various events. However, these successes are far from enough. The contributions of the broad masses, and the donations from the rural areas and from several cities in Bohemia—areas that have been so willing to sacrifice themselves in promoting the war in other ways—are still outstanding. The Public Crownland Agency, whose achievements in the course of this long war are, by its very nature, increasing day by day, is confronted with a task of superhuman dimensions. In the early days of the war, it was forced to give its first priority to assist soldiers in the field. Now the Agency can no longer stand back under the flood of demands; it must call on the patronage of all those who are accustomed to doing their duty in the hinterlands, exhorting them to join in the great task of helping the innumerable wounded veterans. Let each give according to his ability! Send your donations to "Public Crownland Agency for Returning Veterans, Prag, Poříč 7" or to the Bohemian Eskompte-Bank in Prague, the Zivnostenská Banka Pragá, with an indication that the funds are intended for the Public Crownland Agency. Deposit slips will be sent on request.

The Public Crownland Agency's postal checking-account number is 119516.

Donations dedicated to special purposes: The Public Crownland Agency will also accept donations specified for a particular purpose—for example, to benefit one regiment, to help soldiers of a specific origin or nationality, or to support the blind or those with lung, nervous, or heart conditions. These special provisions are scrupulously noted and executed conscientiously as far as possible. Certain departments, such as the section for blinded soldiers, have kept their special applications and a separate fund within the framework of the Public Crownland Agency, in which the amount intended for them can be used fully only for this special purpose.

B. "Help Disabled Veterans!"
(*Deutsche Zeitung Bohemia*, May 10, 1917)

The goal of state-organized aid to wounded veterans is to provide occupational counseling and training to soldiers who return from the war maimed or ill, so that they can find an appropriate civilian occupation. In handling many such cases every day, the Public Crownland Agency for Returning Veterans has come to realize that many of the disabled veterans injured in the war find themselves in dire straits before they succeed in beginning their new occupation and getting back on their feet. They lack the necessary clothing, underclothing, shoes, and often the cash to cover their most basic needs. Until a final legal regulation is made for these provisions, anyone with a charitable soul will find that these cases offer a rich and rewarding opportunity. The stated purpose of the Public Crownland Agency as set out by statute permits the agency to use its own resources only for immediate therapy, training, or negotiating employment.

Only with the fund created by the Crownland War Aid Office and augmented by Countess Coudenhove-Taaffe, wife of the governor, did it become possible to rush to the assistance of disabled veterans in such urgent cases of temporary need. But the fund is gradually being depleted, and there is serious danger that this temporary assistance, so urgently needed, can no longer be granted if the fund is not strengthened and augmented by a substantial influx.

We thus urgently appeal to the public to make cash contributions to this fund for the emergency support of those wounded in war.

Every donation, even the smallest, is accepted with heartfelt thanks in the interest of these maimed and ill soldiers; material donations, such as used clothing, underclothing, and shoes are especially welcome.

We give our heartfelt thanks to all who have eased the lives of wounded veterans and have alleviated their temporary need with their donations!

All contributions and gifts should be sent to Dr. Robert Marschner, Head of the Public Crownland Agency for Returning Veterans, Prague II., Pořitsch 7.

Commentary 18

೭

In his October 30, 1916, letter to Felice Bauer, Kafka points to "much more" he had written for the Public Crownland Agency for Returning Veterans. The two newspaper articles, "Help Disabled Veterans!," fit precisely into Kafka's sphere of responsibility within that authority (see "Kafka's Office Writings," supra p. 42ff.). They are closely related to the two previous articles recommending the establishment of a psychiatric hospital in German Bohemia, and they pursue the very same strategy: to make use of the catchwords of the discourse of mass suicide for the sole purpose of inverting their meaning.

Kafka's strategy is to reconceive the core concepts of "fatherland," "state," "duty," "sacrifice," and "life." These key words allow us to trace a network of significant correspondences between, on the one hand, Kafka's literary scenario of national defense in his two stories "Building the Great Wall of China" and "A Page from an Old Document" and, on the other hand, Werner Sombart's influential 1915 war pamphlet *Händler und Helden* (Traders and Heroes). To give meaning to industrialized mass killing on World War I battlefronts, Sombart contrasts the German "type" of the "hero" with the English "type" of the "trader." While the latter strives to turn his life into a "profitable deal," the former prepares to sacrifice his life "without a reciprocal gift. [. . .]. The trader is concerned exclusively with his rights, the hero exclusively with his duties."[1] Since the heroic worldview disdains individual life, whose sole meaning is its obligation to sacrifice itself for a higher, spiritual life, this view requires the "idea of the fatherland" as the people's collective calling. Connected to this view is the (typically German) "organic idea of the state," which is opposed to the (typically English) "mechanical idea of the state." According to the latter, the state is the result of a contractual agreement between individuals and could be conceived of as a "mutual insurance institute"; in the framework of the former idea—the German idea—the state "is neither constituted by individuals, [. . .] nor has it the purpose of fostering individual interests. Rather, the state is [. . .] the conscious organization of a superindividual entity, to which individuals belong as its parts."[2] Individual life, then, is entirely subsumed under the "life" of the state. Individual abilities and achievements exist in order to contribute to the general profit of the superindividual.

Like Kafka's Chinese scenario–which begins with a heroic vision of national defense and ends with a conquered fatherland of helpless traders and merchants—the article in the *Prager Tagblatt* (doc. 18A) echoes and inverts Sombart's public appeal for collective suicide. Whereas Sombart's pamphlet addresses an ideal "people," Kafka's appeals to an empirical "population." And if the first section of his piece employs the key formulas of war propaganda (such as "fate," "sacrifice," "duty"), these terms are used specifically to discuss individual fates. "Our sacred duty" refers, not to a redemptive death for the fatherland, but to a "bearable existence" for wounded veterans. In the same vein, while the opposition between "love of fatherland" and "selfishness" seems to confirm Sombart's dichotomy, Kafka in fact calls on the "fatherland" to bring together the two models of the "organic" and the "mechanical" state. In the latter model, the state is assigned a "duty with regard to disabled veterans"; in the former, nothing distinguishes the state from the people—"all of us are the state." Kafka's subsumes the individual under the state and even praises military success, not in the name of collective death, but in the name of individual life: "Each of us has our victorious armies to thank for the safe enjoyment of his property, his personal security, and the guarantee of a happy future under a freely elected leadership." Apart from Kafka's official responsibility in the field of veterans' welfare, it is his remarkable pacifism—something more than unexamined antimilitarism—that connects these two articles to his campaign for a psychiatric hospital in German Bohemia (doc. 17A,B).

FROM KAFKA TO KAFKAESQUE

JACK GREENBERG

❧

Franz Kafka worked as a highly ranked lawyer and high official at the Prague Workmen's Accident Insurance Institute, a quasigovernmental agency that insured some 33,000 businesses in Bohemia, the industrial heartland of Europe. He was one of only two Jews employed in the large organization, hired through the efforts of its chairman, a schoolmate's father. His career advanced slowly because he was Jewish, but he nevertheless moved up to major responsibilities. Daily, he returned home in mid-afternoon and, until early hours of the morning, wrote stories that have given rise to the concept of Kafkaesque. The principal sources among his writings for this adjective are *The Judgment*, *The Trial*, "Before the Law" (which appears also within *The Trial*), and *In the Penal Colony*.

The term has become familiar, not only in common discourse, but indeed, in judicial opinions. Recently, a United States District Judge criticized the Federal Emergency Management Administration (FEMA) for cutting housing funding and subjecting victims of Hurricane Katrina to a convoluted application process. FEMA had sent these victims notification letters with "reason codes" instead of actual reasons, gave different information each time they called the agency help line, and erroneously determined that houses had "insufficient damage" or that someone else in the households (often a roommate) had already applied for assistance. The judge called the process "Kafkaesque."[1] He is far from alone. Another recent district-court opinion observed: "The government's use of the Kafkaesque term 'no longer enemy combatants' deliberately begs the question of whether these petitioners ever were enemy combatants." Abroad, opponents of a new voting system in France called it "Kafkaesque."[2]

A Lexis search of state and federal courts turns up 245 opinions in state and federal courts that employ "Kafkaesque," including five in the Supreme Court of the United States.

Outside the courtroom, encounters of everyday life with the law, and the bureaucracies of state and society, evoke "Kafkaesque" with even greater frequency. Between 2002 and 2006, Westlaw's *All News* reported between 455 and 669 references per year. Not all are highbrow. The *New York Post* had a half-dozen references, including a description of a baseball player's stream of consciousness before he hit a home run, as "Kafkaesque."

Outside the legal context, "Kafkaesque" is sometimes a synonym for "weird," "bizarre," "phantasmagoric," "strange," "mad," "confusing," "bewildering," "nightmarish," "absurd," and "bureaucratic." It may criticize a type of bureaucracy (for example, "in the best of times, covering Guantanamo means wrangling with a Kafkaesque bureaucracy"); a type of government culture/management style (such as "Kafkaesque culture of denial" or "no one has yet written a book about the scandalous administration of the public sphere, and the Kafkaesque logic of its operation"); and/or very difficult experience with government (as in "Kafkaesque obfuscation and stonewalling").

In thinking about the connections between Kafka's job, his stories, and the characterization "Kafkaesque"—the task of this concluding essay—three sets of questions emerge. First, do the people, places, and events Kafka encountered in his daily work at the Workmen's Accident Insurance Institute appear in some form in the stories?

The second question, harder to answer, yet perhaps deeper, and more interesting, is whether his day job shaped the weltanschauung of the creative writing.

Most important, but perhaps harder to identify: do the feelings and attitudes that his job generated, as expressed in the writing, offer a clue as to why his readers (and many who have never read his writings) today often describe encounters with law and government as "Kafkaesque"?

First, as to the obvious. Some job-fiction connections are apparent. Kafka's workaday writing was lawyers' and bureaucrats' stuff, conducting administrative proceedings or adjudicating them; he tried cases in court and advocated for and against legislation. In this, he represented the Institute and, indirectly, the workers to whom it paid workmen's compensation benefits when they were injured and for whom it promoted safety in the workplace. Much of the work arose because premiums for insurance and safety promotion were an unwelcome expense. Businesses and their advocates often lied about danger and the cost of safety measures and otherwise improperly tried to get out of paying what was due. I shall suggest only a few of numerous examples, and argue that Kafka's reaction to this obfuscation, misrepresentation, and other attempts at evasion very well may have produced or reinforced attitudes expressed in his stories.

That same resistance to paying premiums has persisted over time and across continents. A 2007 New York study estimated that employers cheat the New York State's workers' compensation system by neglecting to pay $500 million to $1 billion a year that they owe in premiums. An official said that "New York's honest businesses who are playing by the rules have had to subsidize those who don't even cover their employees or those who seriously underpay for the coverage they do have."[3] Kafka had the same complaint. In a similar formulation, he referred to employers "who had borne unending costs [on one side] and on the other, employers who had contributed a disproportionately small amount and who went unpunished and without fear of future additional payments" (doc. 8).

Workplaces in the Stories

Quarries

In Kafka's professional writing about insuring quarries, we find what may be a one-to-one correspondence with the location of the ultimate scene in *The Trial*. Kafka devoted major attention to quarries, dangerous places to work, which the Institute insured. The Institute paid benefits to injured quarry workers, a procedure that incurred substantial losses. In a 1914 report on quarry safety, Kafka displayed intimate knowledge of different kinds of quarries—for example, those where sand, pebble, gravel, or stone was mined—and of quarrying techniques, such as excavating and blasting. Blasting by workers unfamiliar with the proper use of explosives was dangerous. Kafka described a (tobacco) pipe found next to a cache of dynamite. He criticized the custom of paying workers in kind with brandy and of locating taverns near quarries, and he was critical of the fact that some quarry owners owned the taverns. Labor contracts provided for the custom of furnishing brandy and deducting the cost from wages. Alcohol consumption reached as high as 30 percent of total wages for individual workers. Kafka deplored the fact that eye injuries were commonplace, and he noted that, although goggles were required on the job, workers rarely wore them, ascribing part of the blame to insufficient supervision. His report included a meticulously detailed ordinance to promote worker safety.

One visit to a quarry site may have imprinted itself on his memory and found its way into *The Trial*. The 1914 report on quarry safety described a quarry in which there was "a loose stone block 1m³" and accompanied the text with a photograph. That year, Kafka began writing *The Trial*, which ends in a chilling execution scene in a quarry. We do not know whether Kafka visited the site before or after he wrote *The Trial* or visited it more than once. As the executioners lead K to his execution, the author relates that "the other man searched for some suitable spot in the quarry. When he had found it, he waved, and the other gentleman led K over to it. It was near the quarry wall, where *a loose block of stone* was lying" (T 230, italics JG). It is not difficult to surmise that the loose 1m³ block of stone of the quarry report prompted Kafka's imagination of the loose block of stone of *The Trial*. At that spot, they executed K with a knife to the heart. He died "like a dog."

Planing Machines

Not as congruent as the quarry of the insurance report and the quarry of the execution site, but suggestive nevertheless, is the relationship between wood planing machines insured by Kafka's Institute and the torture machine of *In the Penal Colony*. Planing machines caused many injuries that required workmen's compensation. In a report directed at technical experts, mechanical engineers, and business owners, Kafka wrote of finger joints and entire fingers cut off by square-shaft planing machines, presenting a lengthy argument, illustrated with drawings, that advocated replacing them with much safer cylindrical-shaft planing machines. With the level of detail of a technical manual, he described blades directly fastened with screws to shafts' naked cutting edges that spun at 3,800 to 4,000 revolutions per minute; the gap between blade shaft and table surface; the risk of a worker's hand slipping into a blade slot; using safety plates or reducing the size of blade slots; workers' loss of finger joints or entire fingers when blades fell out of alignment. He knew which shafts had been manufactured by which machine tool maker and the patents of different shafts.

Because planing-machine owners would be reluctant to incur the expense of switching to cylindrical-shaft machines, Kafka supplemented his engineering analysis with a cost breakdown. He demonstrated that cylindrical-shaft machines would be more economical, taking into account ease of sharpening, air resistance, noise levels, and effectiveness in planing thin and thick shavings, ease of replacement, and the economic benefit of working without worry about danger.

Commentators have likened planing machines to the torture apparatus in *In the Penal Colony*. That device is vastly more complex and, happily, resembles nothing in use in the real world. It consists of a bed to which a prisoner is strapped, over which is suspended a harrow designed to inscribe on his back the commandment that he has violated. The torture machine is more elaborate than ordinary square or cylindrical planing devices. For example, it includes means to carry away the blood that would flow from the prisoner's wounds, and a device for feeding the prisoner. Nonetheless, the level of engineering detail suggests an author who understood the minutiae of that kind of machinery.

Small Farms

The third example is the correspondence between measuring acreage for insuring small farms at the Institute and surveying a site in *The Castle*. (The link is more tenuous than that for the quarries or planing machines, but once we assume that Kafka's real-world experience insinuated itself into his fiction, imagination readily constructs a relationship). There had been difficulty in setting premiums for small farms. Their wage base was unlike that of modern enterprises: workers' status as employees or self-employed contractors was problematic. Often farm laborers were paid in kind, or they may have been members of the farm family, and pay varied seasonally. For these sorts of reasons, the Institute proposed and Kafka defended the simple technique of setting small farm premiums at a flat rate according to acreage and machinery on the premises. Calculating acreage required surveys, suggesting the surveyor who appears in *The Castle*.

Kafka's Approach to Enforcement

Miscreant businesses and trade associations resisted paying premiums and maintaining a safe workplace. As a lawyer and a bureaucrat, Kafka deployed a range of means to achieve compliance, none of them Kafkaesque—a term obviously not in use at the time, although adversaries accused an Institute staff member of believing himself to be "detective, prosecutor, defense attorney, and judge all in one" (doc. 12). In fact, Kafka as principal compliance officer, went about his job moderately. He employed persuasion to promote the use of safer machinery, like cylindrical planing machines as an economy measure; in newspaper articles and official reports, he excoriated employers who faked records and maintained unsafe workplaces; he adjudicated administrative proceedings; he lodged criminal prosecution against really bad actors.

He was conservative in interpreting the statutes governing his work. For example, over time, insurance coverage of the workplace had shifted under changing interpretations. The 1887 Austrian accident insurance law had left open whether workshop labor was covered by insurance. In 1906, the Administrative Court decided that it was. But, in 1908, industrialist lobbies persuaded the Court to revoke that decision. Later that year, a special committee of experts submitted to the Reichsrat (parliament) a proposal that would have overturned the 1908 decision and would once more provide complete coverage. According to Kafka's linguistic analysis of the 1887 law, the 1908 decision was wrong: he contended that the authors of the law had intended to include all workshop labor. But he argued that the Court should not abandon its 1908 decision because a repeated modification of the interpretation would have "highly negative consequences, if for no other reason than that it would have introduced a new and dangerous confusion into the legal situation" (doc. 2). Contrary to a popular myth that he was a spokesman for the working classes, he saw vacillation in the law as more harmful to society than its possible misinterpretation.

Adhering to the interpretation that maintained stability of legal interpretation, he took a different route to achieving comprehensive coverage. The Institute conducted an opinion poll to ascertain employers' and workers' preferences. It established that they favored including workshop labor. The Institute then entered into individual contracts with employers, which, by November 1908, effectively bypassed the May 1908 Administrative Court decision. The value Kafka accorded to stability of interpretation resembles that which common law (and constitutional law) place on precedent, although that doctrine played no part in Kafka's approach to the problem within the framework of Roman law (so-called paragraph law).

Kafka confronted a second commonplace jurisprudential issue: should a law be read literally or according to the intention of the legislature when a literal interpretation appears to run contrary to that intent? A good example concerns the premiums for loom operators. The Institute charged operators of wool looms lower premiums than those demanded of cotton- and silk-loom operators because wool looms were slower and safer. The issue was complicated in setting premiums for looms that wove wool and cotton or silk, or all three. Kafka's institute claimed that cotton is cotton, silk is silk, and operators should pay the going (and higher) rate for those threads, whether or not they are combined with low-premium wool. The businesses disagreed, arguing that looming a low percentage of cotton and silk mixed with the wool operated at the same slow speed of wool-only looms. Since these looms were less dangerous than higher-speed cotton and silk ones, the owners should therefore pay the wool rate. The purpose of the law, the operators argued, was to charge more for the more dangerous process. The court accepted the business argument. Kafka's institute lost.

In deciding to continue a preexisting course of regulation and to accept plain language rather than interpret according to purpose, Kafka and his institute continued doing what they had been doing—the reaction of most bureaucrats, which is how Kafka self-identified. Similarly, some of his most memorable characters do not advocate changing path or transgressing beyond the obvious, although a few are proactive. *The Judgment* focuses on Georg Bendemann. As Georg first appears to the reader, he is not particularly distinctive. He is planning his wedding. He frets over whether his friend, who lives a solitary life in Russia with no prospect of change, would be upset by the news. Georg's happiness might cause his friend to deplore his own situation in comparison. Georg has an overbearing father who excoriates and humiliates him. The father's cruel remarks, culminating in his uttering a death sentence to Georg, cause Georg to break emotionally and hurl himself to his death into the river. The range of possible reactions could have been great, from defiance to dejection or beyond. Kafka chose the most passive—acquiescence.

In *The Metamorphosis,* Gregor Samsa's transformation into a gigantic insect is utterly unexpected, unexplained, unexplainable. His reaction is hopelessness. He offers feeble resistance: reads his affliction as a bad cold, scares his mother away when she attempts to clear out the furniture, attempts to protect and possess his sister after hearing her play the violin. None of these gestures amounts to fighting his condition. Given the enormity of what has befallen him, vigorous resistance would be futile. No one, other than Kafka himself, could fathom how Gregor could fight back, but fighting back, assuming some mode of opposition were conceivable, is not discussed as an option, although Kafka could have, in a work of fiction, examined any possibilities.

None of these figures is shown to have deserved his fate. None fights back, although Josef K goes slightly through the motions of defending himself. Richard Posner has referred to most of Kafka's protagonists as "schlemiels": "[. . .] Joseph K. is colorless and mediocre, very much an Everyman—or less. Most of Kafka's protagonists have something of the *schlemiel* about them."[4] One dictionary defines the term as "a dolt who is a habitual bungler." But that is wide of the mark for not taking into account such characters as Amalia in *The Castle,* who reacts indignantly against sexual harassment and rejects her assailant's advances, or the fierce, entrepreneurial hero of *The Burrow.* But the principal tendency among Kafka's leading characters seems to be just letting things be.

Influence of Work on World Outlook

Did Kafka's experience at the Institute influence his weltanschauung, if at all, by shaping a personality that already had been formed as he grew up? Work experience did not inscribe on a blank slate. He wrote to his father: "My writing was all about you; all I did there, after all, was to bemoan what I could not bemoan upon your breast" (DF 177). Of course, one can only guess how influential the job experience could have been in affecting this existing condition. Probably, as a conscientious civil servant, he despised the fact that employers concealed, confused, conspired and lied about the danger their workers faced; they strained to "make the worse case appear the better," as it might have been characterized since the days of the Sophists. Yet, confounding speculation about whether his job shaped his outlook may be that his adversaries were not unlike his father: callous and ruthless. His reaction to them may have merely echoed his reaction as a son. But, maybe not, maybe not as distinctly, maybe not as mordantly. We can only speculate.

In any event, the struggle at work was about whether and how much businesses had to pay for insurance. For many years, they had succeeded in keeping their premiums down through political influence, misreporting the facts, hiding the facts, misinterpreting the law, and other means. As a result, when Robert Marschner, Kafka's boss, took over the direction of the Institute, it was running a large deficit. Marschner, and Kafka, who often wrote for Marschner's signature, embarked on a successful campaign to require that employers pay the premiums required by the law. They, indeed, turned the Institute around so that it no longer paid out more than it received. In the course of this effort, they addressed the tactics that had been used to avoid paying requisite amounts.

The Renelt Case

The case of Josef Franz Renelt, which Kafka litigated, could have driven to despair anyone concerned with even-handed administration of the law. Josef Franz Renelt, an orchard and quarry owner in the northern Bohemian village of Pömmerle, had not reported the wages he paid and, consequently, how much he owed for insurance premiums, which were set proportionately. The amount was confounded because he owned an orchard and a quarry. While he was obliged to insure workers at the quarry, the orchard workers were exempt. Employing a single group of workers for both, he claimed that they worked at the orchard even when, in winter, there would have been little or no work for them there. The Institute sued Renelt repeatedly. Evidence was difficult to gather, witnesses recanted, memories failed, and Renelt's side used physical force to wrest records from investigators.

The Renelt chronicles left traces in all three of Kafka's major novels. In *The Man Who Disappeared,* or *Amerika*, written at the time the Renelt chronicles began, Karl Rossmann loses his job and runs into a policeman. After a short interrogation, he attempts escape and runs away again. He sums up this episode (as well as Renelt's nine years of legal dispute with the Institute): "From time to time racing with the police is a useful exercise." "Renelt" is a variant of the German *Rennen* or "to race."

Shortly afterward, Kafka started writing *The Trial*. As "Renelt" encounters insurance law and criminal law, the accused Josef K—who, like Renelt before the Aussig district court, "is not in custody"—tries to identify the jurisdiction he is dealing with. His later reflections on his strange trial could be regarded as a copy of Renelt's successful shift of focus from the factual to the procedural aspects of the legal dispute, and its ensuing transformation into an out-of-court settlement: in a deleted passage of Kafka's last novel, *The Castle*, we find a comment on the vain struggle for the physical possession of written evidence that occurred in yet another phase of the Renelt matters.

Political Influence

Kafka encountered the kinds of misfeasance that emerged in the Renelt case in his other work as well. Employers, using political influence, enlisted lawmakers and bureaucrats to work out advantageous rates. In one report, Kafka singled out an Assemblyman Glöckner, who had intervened to reclassify a business. Where such reclassification could not be accomplished, there was incentive to hide or misreport facts about numbers of employees and employees' pay as well as the dangers that employees faced, all as a way to pay less.

False Reporting

Businesses were supposed to report to the Institute on payroll, danger, and other factors. But many of them falsified information in order to pay less. Kafka noted wryly that whenever a business's risk classification went up, its reported wages went down as a means of compensating for the extent to which premiums would have risen. To combat cheating, an insurance company ordinarily would want to inspect the insured premises. But that step was forbidden by a law that created what were known as trade inspectorates. The inspectorates were established during the trades reform law (*Gewerbereform*) of 1883. The first draft of the accident law, of that same year, had granted the right to inspect to the insurance institutes. After industrialist lobbying, the legislation of December 1887 transferred this right exclusively to the inspectorates.

Trade Inspectorates

Instead of serving as a means of law enforcement, their ostensible purpose, the trade inspectorates became a formidable obstacle to enforcing the insurance laws. The Accident Insurance Law of 1887 facilitated obfuscation. Enacted at the behest of industrial lobbyists, nominally to preserve "trade secrets," it prohibited insurance institutes from inspecting the businesses they insured, restricting inspection of individual businesses to employer-friendly trade or industrial inspectorates. For observers of United States business-government interaction, this brings to mind litigation over entities authorized to inspect factories to enforce environmental-protection legislation. Making similar arguments centering on trade secrets, businesses have succeeded in maintaining some control over access for inspection. Uninspected by the Institute, and pseudoinspected by the inspectorates, businesses filed false reports with impunity, becoming black boxes. This practice impaired the accident-insurance system, which depended on reliable data. In a massively documented 1911 report, Kafka lambasts the inspectorates. He accuses them, not merely of concealment and falsification, but also of becoming advocates of the employers. They went beyond misreporting, he claims, to interpreting accident-insurance law in ways to promote the employers' goal of paying lower premiums and spending less on workplace safety.

He denounces the fact that after almost 25 years of workmen's accident insurance, the institutes still have no right to visit the businesses they insure. He writes that the trade inspectors, who did visit, acting as "advocates of the employers," use weasel words like "approximately," "almost without exception," and "possibly" in describing factors that determined premiums. The inspectorates do not merely deliberately side with employers. They employ terminology concisely or weakly, hesitantly or aggressively, according to the individuality of the trade inspector, for example, using the term "normal operations" in different ways in the same report, sometimes with a double meaning within the same sentence.

Many trade inspectorates go even further and contradict information that employers provided in response to questionnaires. But employer-furnished information was "so defective and inadequate that it did not represent the actuality and resulted in a completely unjustified distribution of the charges among the individual commercial groups," leading to "ever-increasing annual losses" at the Institute (doc. 8). Moreover, where there was no deliberate falsification, Kafka found substantial ignorance of basic statistical data that the inspectorates might have consulted but did not. This affected not only rates but also worker life and safety. In one case, misled by the apparent objectivity of an inspectorate report on quarries, the Institute was prepared to reduce a classification of risk level. But before it could do so, a massive accident occurred; a falling boulder killed a quarry worker. Several others suffered life-threatening injuries caused by unreported conditions. Kafka found this incident to be particularly galling because the Institute contributed substantially toward the expenses of the trade inspectorates.

Individual Industries' Efforts to Avoid Coverage

Wherever there was a legal ambiguity, businesses and their counsel tried to twist the situation in their favor. Spa operators in Marienbad attempted to avoid insurance coverage by claiming that commercial lodging space was part of their homes and that employees were domestic servants. The Institute's rejection of the claim was upheld by the Administrative Court in Vienna.

The Institute required that businesses with machinery on their premises take out insurance. Extending this regulation, in 1905, Austrian law subjected all commercially operated hotels equipped with electric elevators to comprehensive compulsory accident insurance. At the behest of the hotel trade association, the law later was limited to elevator staff. In April 1910, the hotel trade association opened a campaign against competition from the increasing number of rooming houses and boarding houses that had installed elevators but were still getting away without insurance. With support from the hotels, Kafka's institute happily required insurance of these smaller, family-run accommodations.

But most of these smaller accommodations were outraged when they received their insurance payment notices from Prague. Their lawyer based his appeal on a linguistic argument: He claimed that compulsory insurance was restricted to businesses run on a commercial basis (German: *gewerbsmäßig*); since they were not members of any trade association (German: *gewerbemäßig*), he declared that they were not run on a commercial basis. Indeed, "there is no such thing as a rooming house business; the term was invented by the Institute merely so that the law governing workmen's accident insurance could be applied willy nilly to the persons in my employment." Making an argument that today might be called Kafkaesque, Hochsieder—the rooming-house owner in question—argues further that a rooming house that has an elevator should be exempt, as it is "not using a motor" in the house. "The power that activates my elevator is generated in the local electrical plant, and in the house there is only a changeover switch that is locked by the electricity plant and accessible only to its representatives. The control (a knob) is so simple that it can be operated by any of our guests at no risk whatever" (doc. 10). This line of argument was carried so far as to claim that coverage was limited to sites where a staff member was actually in touch with the engines that gave rise to coverage. This argument led to employers' defining the applicable premises and shifting workers around to place them out of the range of machinery.

The Institute, through Kafka, had to link employees to particular sites, a daunting task involving numerous businesses that had been broken up into compartments—some with machinery, some without. Kafka had to deal with appeal letters about closets, side rooms, and storerooms where engines were locked away, accessible only to qualified personnel. Perhaps not inadvertently, long passages in *The Man Who Disappeared* discourse upon the activities of "lift boys," whom we would call "elevator operators."

Kafka would have none of this nonsense: The facts were the facts. The employers had to pay. Fictions got the employers nowhere. But sometimes fictions could be useful in aligning the laws with the needs of the times. The liability law of August 9, 1908, created a legal framework that forced insurance institutes all over Austria to treat car owners as entrepreneurs, cars as firms, and drivers as workers. Kafka complained about this system and that the institutes had not been allowed to participate in the process of lawmaking. He described the Institute's efforts to cope with this situation. He was among regulators worldwide who, confronted by the fact that automobiles were beginning to play a major role in society, sought to twist long-time rules to accommodate a new exigency. As discussed above (com. 4), an American fiction, created to deal with negligent drivers from distant states, declared that they had consented to submit to the jurisdiction of courts where an accident occurred, even though they might live elsewhere, a circumstance that would ordinarily have placed them outside the jurisdiction. Justice Felix Frankfurter wrote: "The defendant may protest to high heaven his unwillingness to be sued and it avails him not. . . . The liability rests on the inroad which the automobile has made on . . . so many aspects of our social scene. . . . We have held that this is a fair rule of law as between a resident injured party . . . and a non-resident motorist. . . . But to conclude from this holding that the motorist, who never consented to anything and whose consent is altogether immaterial, has actually agreed to be sued . . . is surely to move in the world of Alice in Wonderland."[5]

Grappling with such obfuscation, manipulation, lying, and mischaracterization, Kafka could not have had, in his day job, a sunny view of the governmental process and of lawyers who manipulated it. This attitude is reflected in his creative writing. In *The Trial,* he characterizes the lawyer Huld as someone who deals less with law than with influence. K, having been arrested, goes to Huld to represent him. It is not clear that Huld has any influence, although he tries to create the impression that he has. He communicates nothing of substance, and it is not certain that he has anything to communicate. True, lawyers always have adversaries; tactics, like those Kafka faced, are not rare. But Kafka worked in a context that could give emotional charge to his experience. The Institute was protecting workers' lives against death and maiming injuries. His reports wrote of amputated fingers and joints, of falling boulders, workers drunk under the influence of employer-provided alcohol, eye injuries that might have been prevented by the use of protective goggles. Lies translated, not only into lower premiums, but also into danger to lives and limbs. Kafka would have been immune to ordinary human reaction if he had not deeply resented those who manipulated for profit the system he administered.

The Alchemy of Insurance Regulation into the Kafkaesque World View

In an article that, in style, reads like one of his stories, very different from his Institute reports or decisions, Kafka advocates creating a psychiatric hospital for World War I veterans. The article conveys a feeling rarely seen in the detached way he treats his fictional protagonists—K, for example, in *The Trial*. He begins by describing a likely patient: "He was a soldier returned from the front. He could move only on crutches or had to be pushed along in a wheelchair. His body shook without cease, as if he were overcome by a mighty chill, or he was standing stock-still in the middle of the tranquil street, in the thrall of his experiences at the front. We see others, too, men who could move ahead only by taking jerky steps; poor, pale, and gaunt, they leaped as though a merciless hand held them by the neck, tossing them back and forth in their tortured movements" (doc. 17). This plea addresses empathy, which might transcend the particular veteran described, beyond the need for creating a hospital. Generalized, it might have been part of forming a dour view of how law, government, and bureaucracy affect mankind. It could have provided a cathexis that shaped childhood (perhaps also innate) disposition into a wider world view. The eloquence with which Kafka captured and expressed that reaction perhaps explains the embrace expressed in the term or concept "Kafkaesque."

From Kafka to Kafkaesque

Kafka's daily encounters over the years with cheating on insurance premiums by evasion, concealment, and distortion probably contributed to the Kafkaesque tone of his stories. His frustration, anger, and resentment insinuated their way into his characters and the situations he described. Modern readers of Kafka's stories, who encounter analogous frustration or bafflement in everyday life, recognize their reaction in his writing. One of his biographers, Ernst Pawel, referred to Kafka's "experience in handling disability and death claims on behalf of workers maimed or killed on the job, [which] served to reinforce his manifest instinctive identification with the underdog."[6] So penetrating was his focus, and so widely has it resonated, that today his readers (and, indeed, those who have never read his works but to whom it has been described) now have the same reaction that Kafka had then. "Kafkaesque" could apply to countless daily events, among them:

- political denial of manmade global warming;
- upholding the sentence of a death-row defendant after a trial at which his lawyer slept;
- appointing as head of family planning at the Department of Health and Human Services a person opposed to contraception.

One of America's most important social and, consequently, legal issues—racial discrimination—illustrates how some fundamental problems have been addressed by dissembling. Race comes particularly to mind when we wonder about connecting Kafka with American life today. Enigmatically, Karl Rossmann, Kafka's protagonist in *The Man Who Disappeared,* travels west in search of a job. At the employment office of the Nature Theater of Oklahoma, where he registers as an engineer (contrary to fact), he gives his name as "Negro." He is hired and then referred to as "Negro, a secondary schoolboy from Europe," or "Negro Technical Worker." Nothing explicit is made of the name (the incomplete or partially lost text is fragmentary), but for someone in search of connections, Karl Rossmann's unhappy travels raise the image of American racial experience, which in many ways is Kafkaesque. It is likely, of course, that Kafka, personally affected by anti-Semitism and deeply interested in Zionism, readily equated the two groups.

The United States Supreme Court embedded racial segregation in constitutional law in 1896 in *Plessy v. Ferguson.* One part of its justification was based either in falsehood or in ignorance: "We consider the underlying fallacy of the plaintiff's argument to consist in the assumption that the enforced separation of the two races stamps the colored race with a badge of inferiority. If this be so, it is not by reason of anything found in the act [that required segregation], but solely because the colored race chooses to put that construction upon it."[7] There is a perverse truth in this defense of segregation: of course, the "colored race" assumed that segregation stamps it with "a badge of inferiority," because that is what it was intended to do. But that was not the *sole* reason why segregation was objectionable.

That was the Supreme Court at its worst. But circumlocution has characterized much of the Court's treatment of racial issues even in its finest hours. When the time arrived for the Court to hold racial segregation unconstitutional, it walked a fine line between upholding basic principles of equality and setting off a near-revolutionary opposition, or worse, in the racist-dominated South. As a consequence, decisions that prohibited discrimination at the same time left in their wake victims of the racism the Court at last set out to destroy.

A single example taken from the Supreme Court's most famous decision, *Brown v. Board of Education*,[8] suffices to illustrate. In 1948, the parents, mostly farmers, in the first of the cases that became *Brown*, sued the Clarendon County, South Carolina, school board because their children's education was grossly inferior to that provided for whites. They did not attack segregation. Constitutional law had not yet developed that far; they had not dreamed of it. Their school combined many classes in a single room, it had no indoor plumbing: a hand pump brought water from a well; toilets were outhouses. Library, equipment, budget were vastly inferior to those of white schools. Black children's books were handed down from whites. Their lawyer bungled. He filed in the wrong district. There was only one black lawyer in this part of South Carolina. White lawyers would not help. Filing the case anew took until 1950.

By then, the Supreme Court effectively had held unconstitutional segregated graduate and professional education. Its reasoning was based on the intangible, psychological, and social value of an integrated education. The NAACP Legal Defense Fund decided then to file at the elementary and high-school level only suits that sought an end to segregation.

With Thurgood Marshall, the Clarendon County parents in 1950 sued to put an end to segregated schools. Between 1950 and 1955, the case went through trial; appeal to the Supreme Court; return to the trial court; further appeal to the Supreme Court; oral arguments in the Supreme Court in 1952, 1953, and 1954; ending in the celebrated Earl Warren opinion that held school segregation unconstitutional.

Whites retaliated against the plaintiffs, cutting off credit, seizing their cattle, firing them or family members from jobs, threatening violence, allowing their church to burn to the ground while withholding firefighting. Some of the plaintiffs fled to other states.

The 1954 opinion decided that segregation was unconstitutional under the equal-protection clause of the Fourteenth Amendment to the Constitution. But it did not order any white school district to admit black children. It postponed for yet another argument the question of how and when to desegregate. In 1955, the Court required only a "prompt and reasonable start,"[9] allowed time only for administrative changes, like teacher reassignment or creating new transportation routes, and prohibited delay because of opposition to the decision. It then wrapped all the standards within the oxymoron "all deliberate speed." "Deliberate" can mean slow. "Speed" connotes fast. A Kafka aficionado would find the impenetrable contradiction delicious. The ambiguity masked a complex maneuver to obtain a unanimous decision and the hope of fending off destructive Southern resistance. But the Kafkaesque quality was not then exhausted.

Baffled by "deliberate speed," the plaintiffs were blindsided by eruptions never seen since the Civil War. One hundred and one Southern congressmen and senators signed the Congressional Manifesto that denounced the Supreme Court. Southern states adopted comic (but not to them) manifestos of Nullification and Interposition; they funded State Sovereignty Commissions dedicated to fighting desegregation; they passed laws that would close white schools if a black student were admitted; they made it illegal to belong to civil rights organizations; they attempted to disbar civil-rights lawyers; and they launched state legislative inquiries into civil-rights activities.

Whatever "deliberate speed" might have meant, this climate caused courts to cower and give it the most dilatory application possible. In politically advanced areas—Delaware, Kansas and the District of Columbia—white schools had admitted some black students right after 1954. But not until 1969, in *Alexander v. Holmes County Board of Education*,[10] did the Supreme Court overrule "all deliberate speed." This was after the civil-rights movement brought about the civil-rights acts of the mid-1960s, in a more benign political climate.

Five- and six-year-olds began attending integrated schools where blacks had been barred earlier. But, by 1969, plaintiffs who first sued in Clarendon County in 1948 were at least twenty-six years of age, long out of school. For them and for thousands like them, the decision had no effect on schools, even though its principle radiated throughout the rest of society. For the country, new pathways opened. Nevertheless, in 1969, for the first courageous youngsters who had applied in 1948, the victory of 1954 and the end of "all deliberate speed" in the deep South in 1969 were Kafkaesque.

One of Kafka's most famous passages in "Before the Law" captures the moment: "Before the law stands a doorkeeper. A man from the country comes to the doorkeeper and asks for admittance to the law. But the doorkeeper says that he cannot grant him admittance now. The man reflects and then asks whether he will be allowed to enter later. 'It is possible,' says the doorkeeper 'but not now'" (KSS 68).

Acknowledgments

I have, of course, depended on Stanley Corngold and Benno Wagner, as should anyone who seeks to understand Kafka's writings and life. To work with them doubled the pleasure of rereading the stories and, for the first time, reading Kafka's lawyerly writings. I liberally cribbed from their writings, but since it was in a good cause, I hope they will forgive. I am grateful also to the Columbia Law students, particularly Tony O'Rourke, who enrolled in Stanley's and my seminar, "Kafka and the Law," which was great fun to teach together. We read and discussed, profitably, Kafka's legal writings, translated for the first time into English, along with his stories and criticism to get ideas for this book. By practicing law, some of them will forego careers as outstanding literary critics. I am grateful too, to Columbia colleagues who discussed my manuscript at a faculty lunch workshop, particularly John Witt, who knows all about United States workers' compensation and spoke to our seminar, and Carol Sanger, who made many useful comments on my manuscript.

CHRONOLOGY

1883

July 3   K. born in Prague, the first child of the fairly affluent businessman Hermann Kafka and his wife Julie (née Löwy). Hermann Kafka's father was a butcher in a provincial town; among Julie Löwy's forebears were several learned rabbis.

1889–1901

K. attends elementary school (German Boy's School) at the Fleisch-markt in Prague.

1893   K. attends the Altstädter Deutsches Gymnasium, together with a majority of middle-class Jewish boys.

1901–1906

K. attends Charles University, where he studies chemistry, German literature, and history of art; in 1902, he decides to study law.

June 1906   K. receives his JD in Law.

1906–1907

Internship at the Provincial Court and the Criminal Court.

1907

Oct. 1   K. is hired as deputy clerk by the Assicurazioni Generali, an Italian insurance company with worldwide operations.

1908

Feb.–May   K. attends a vocational-training course at the Prague Commercial College; he passes the final exam "with distinction."

June 30   K. submits a job application to the Workmen's Accident Insurance Institute for the Kingdom of Bohemia in Prague.

July 2   The Institute grants K. an interview, and the following week he receives a job offer.

July 15   K. submits his resignation to the Assicurazioni Generali, allegedly for health reasons.

July 30   K. joins the Workmen's Accident Insurance Institute as deputy clerk. He is assigned to the actuarial department, which is headed by Eugen Pfohl.

K.s first long legal essay is published in the Institute's annual report for 1907 (doc. 2).

1909

April 4   As part of his on-the-job training, K. is transferred to the accident department.

Sept. 4–14   K. goes on special leave to Lake Garda, Italy.

Sept. 17   K. returns to the actuarial department.

Oct. 1   K. is promoted to trainee.

Oct.–Dec.   In preparation for the risk classification of firms for the period 1910–1914, K. is sent to visit northern Bohemian industrial towns and Pilsen.

K. attends winter-term courses in machine technology at Prague's Institute of Technology.

K. composes a speech on the occasion of the installation of the Institute's new director (doc. 1).

K. writes two long chapters for the annual report for 1908—one on the introduction of fixed-rate insurance premiums for small farms (doc. 3) and the other on the inclusion of private automobiles in compulsory accident insurance (doc. 4).

1910

May 1   K. is promoted to the rank of *Concipist* (law clerk); he is now a "tenured" official of the Institute and head of the appeals department, a subunit of the newly-created business department. He must address 3,100 appeals against the recent risk classification of firms.

Sept. 29   K. is sent to Gablonz (Jablonec), where he explains the Institute's program to a critical audience of small-business owners.

Oct. 8–17   K. on a vacation trip to Paris.

For the Institute's annual report for 1909, K. writes a long chapter on accident prevention in the use of wood-planing machines and a shorter chapter on risk classification. He publishes a review of Robert Marschner's book *Maternity Insurance* in the monthly *Die Deutsche Arbeit*.

1911

Feb. 10   The Institute authorizes K. to act as its accredited representative.

Sept. 14–20   K. writes a second long chapter on accident prevention for wood-planing machines (annual report for 1910).

K. writes two long articles on the state of workmen's insurance for the *Tetschen-Bodenbacher Zeitung* (doc. 8A,B).

1912

Jan. 9   The "Club of German Officials" of the Prague Workmen's Accident Insurance Institute is constituted, with K. as treasurer.

Sept. 22–23 *The Judgment.*

Oct.–Nov. K. writes most of his America novel, *The Man Who Disappeared.*

Nov. 25–26 K. goes to a liquidation court at Kratzau, northern Bohemia, where he unexpectedly succeeds in securing K 4,500 of unpaid insurance fees for his institute.

Nov.–Dec. *The Metamorphosis.*

Dec. 11   K. writes a long letter to the Institute's Board of Directors, asking for a raise in salary for officials of his group (law clerks) (doc. 11).

1913

March 1   K. is promoted to the rank of Vice-Secretary.

March 27 K. goes to Aussig for pretrial hearings in the Institute's criminal proceedings against Josef Renelt on the grounds of insurance fraud (doc. 12).

April 22 K. goes to Aussig to represent the Institute in the criminal trial against Josef Renelt.

May 15   K. goes to Aussig to hear the verdict in the trial against Renelt; the Institute loses the case.

June 22   In a letter to his fiancée, K. considers leaving his job at the Institute, feeling that office work is an unbearable obstacle to his literary ambitions.

Sept. 9–13 K. joins the Institute's delegation to the Second International Congress for Rescue Service and Accident Prevention in Vienna. He attends the two sessions at which his bosses, Marschner and Pfohl, deliver the speeches on Bohemian and Austrian accident prevention that K. had written for them.

1914

Feb. 28–
March 1   K. visits Felice Bauer in Berlin; subsequently, he mentions his "resolution" to live in Berlin and become "a journalist or something of the sort" (LF 386).

April 12–13 K. goes to Berlin to become engaged to Felice Bauer.

July–Dec. *The Trial.*

July 11–13 K. goes to Berlin to break off his engagement to Felice Bauer.

August   K. is exempted from military service.

Oct. 5–18   K. takes a two-week vacation to concentrate on his writing and composes *In the Penal Colony.*

Nov.–Dec.   "Before the Law."

1915

March   The Institute's appeals department, headed by K., must deal with more than 2,000 appeals against various firms' recent risk classification.

May 25   The Bohemian Crownland Agency for Returning Veterans is established under the auspices of the Workmen's Accident Insurance Institute and managed by its officials. Kafka is assigned to the Committee on Therapy.

June 3   K. is given a medical exam and found fit for military service.

June 23   In response to the Institute's claim that K. is an indispensable employee, his exemption from military service is renewed.

Aug. 8–
July 20   K. stays at the sanitarium Frankenstein, near Rumburg (northern Bohemia). In 1916, he propels the transformation of the sanitarium into a psychiatric hospital for war veterans.

Dec 24   In a confidential conversation with Pfohl, K. discusses three options for leaving the Institute: unpaid leave; lifting of his exemption from military service; and submitting his resignation.

K. writes more than eighty pages for the annual report for 1914, among them a long essay on accident prevention in quarries (doc. 14).

K. contributes extensively to the Institute's voluminous anniversary report (doc. 15).

1916

May 8   K. asks Marschner for a long unpaid leave; instead, he is granted a three-week special leave.

June 21   K. is again found suitable for military service, but his exemption for reasons of indispensability is upheld.

July 2–14   K. spends his special leave at the Marienbad spa, part of the time in the company of Felice Bauer.

Oct. 8   K. writes an article calling for the establishment of a psychiatric hospital for war veterans in the German part of Bohemia; it is published in the *Rumburger Zeitung* under the name of Eugen Pfohl (doc. 17A).

Oct. 14   The German Society for the Establishment and Maintenance of a Public Veterans' Psychiatric Hospital for German Bohemia is constituted in Prague; K. participates in the meeting and becomes involved in this project as a key figure on the levels of organization and promotion (doc. 17B).

In the annual report for 1915, K. discusses the impact of war on risk classification and accident prevention (doc. 16).

Winter   "A Country Doctor."

1917

Jan.–Feb.	"The New Lawyer."
Jan. & May	"The Hunter Gracchus."
March–Apr.	"Building the Great Wall of China"; "An Imperial Message"; "A Page from an Old Document."
May 4	The Board of Directors rejects K.'s application for promotion to the rank of Secretary.
May–June	"A Report to an Academy."
July 11–19	K. and Felice Bauer visit Budapest.
Aug. 12–13	K. suffers two pulmonary hemorrhages.
Sep. 3	K.'s doctor finds "apical tuberculosis."
Sept. 7	In a discussion of the possible consequences of K.'s diagnosis, Robert Marschner rejects K.'s suggestion of retiring and grants him a three-month sick leave instead.
Sept. 9	K. goes to Zürau near Saaz (northwestern Bohemia), where his sister Ottla runs a small farm.

1918

May 2	After his sick leave has been repeatedly extended for medical reasons, K. returns to the office.
Sept. 8–28	K. is on convalescent leave in Turnau.
Oct. 9	The Public Crownland Agency for Returning Veterans nominates Kafka for an award "for merit in the area of veterans' welfare."
Oct. 14	K. contracts a severe case of the Spanish flu.
Nov. 19	K. returns to the office.
Nov. 20	The Institute's physician, Dr. Kodym, recommends that K. take another four or five weeks' sick leave and go to the countryside.
Nov. 23–29	K. falls ill with a high fever.
Nov. 30–Dec. 22	K. is on sick leave in Schelesen, on the Elbe River.

1919

Jan. 12	After another check-up by the Institute's doctor, K. applies for another three months of convalescent leave.
Jan. 22	K. returns to Schelesen.
April 1	K. returns to the office.
Nov. 4–20	K. goes back to Schelesen.
Dec. 19	K. is promoted to the rank of Secretary.

1920

Feb. 25	Dr. Kodym diagnoses advanced infiltration of the lungs with tuberculosis and recommends a three-month stay in a sanitarium.
April 2	K. goes to Meran for a cure.
July 5	K. returns to the office.

Oct. 14   Dr. Kodym recommends another three-month cure. However, K. remains at his job.
Fall   "On the Question of the Laws."
Dec. 18   K. goes to Tatranské Matliary for another cure.

1921

March   K.'s doctor in Matliary recommends a further six months of treatment in his sanitarium. The Institute's Board of Directors agrees.
Aug. 29   K. returns to the office.
Sept. 13   Dr. Kodym recommends that K. extend the cure.
Oct. 22   Dr. Kodym recommends that K. retire from his job.
Nov.   K. undergoes systematic treatment in Prague, supervised by his general practitioner, Dr. Hermann.

1922

Jan.   K. has a nervous breakdown.
Jan.–Sept.   *The Castle.*
Jan. 27   K. goes to Spindlermühle in the Riesengebirge, accompanied by Dr. Hermann.
Feb. 14   The Institute informs K. of his promotion to the rank of Chief Secretary.
Feb. 17   K. returns to Prague.
Spring   "A Starvation Artist."
April 27   K. asks for convalescent leave, to be followed by his annual vacation.
June 7   K. submits his request for provisional retirement.
Summer   "Researches of a Dog."
June 30   K.'s request for retirement is granted, beginning on July 1, with a pension of K 10,608 a year.

1923

Sept.   K. moves to Berlin to live with Dora Diamant, whom he had met that summer at Müritz on the Baltic Sea.
Winter   "The Burrow."

1924

March   K.'s health deteriorates seriously, and he returns to Prague. "Josefine, the Singer or the Mouse People."
April   K. visits the sanitarium Wiener Wald, in Lower Austria; from there he is transferred to the Vienna clinic of Prof. Hajek; from April 19, he visits the sanitarium of Dr. Hofmann in Kierling, near Klosterneuburg.
June 3   K. dies in Kierling.

NOTES

PREFACE

1. Italo Svevo was a mere correspondence clerk from 1880 to ca. 1900 at the Triestine branch of the Viennese Union Bank. Fernando Pessoa was a mere bookkeeper and correspondent for a Lisbon company from ca. 1910 to 1935. T.S. Eliot, as well, was a mere currency trader in the Foreign and Colonial Department of Lloyds Bank, London, from 1917 to 1925. Comparisons of Kafka with the clerks Svevo, Pessoa, and Eliot are malapropos.

2. See Stanley Corngold, *Lambent Traces: Franz Kafka* (Princeton: Princeton University Press, 2004), xii.

3. Stevens' rank of vice-president exceeded that of Kafka's rank as chief legal secretary, but there are interesting parallels to be made. Stevens dealt in "surety bonds—a form of insurance whereby a party contracting to have work undertaken (for example, a public authority) would be protected and compensated should the work fail to be completed or to be satisfactory." (Tony Sharpe, *Wallace Stevens, A Literary Life*, Macmillan: London, 2000, 3–4). To provide compensation for a "damaged" public authority resonates to some extent with Kafka's job description. A scholar writing in the *Daily Kos* under the nom de plume "acreosote" enlivens the matter: "Stevens [was a] lawyer who set up first paperwork needed to bond tradesmen performing construction of roads, buildings, and such. He seemed particularly good at interviewing prospective companies; fewer defaults on his contracts. Seemed to have an ear for honesty." http://www.dailykos.com/story/2006/3/20/151249/ 242. This point strengthens the analogy. Ruth Hein, who had a years-long friendship with Stevens's daughter, recalls that Stevens "always walked to and from the office and was in the habit of composing his poems as he walked. [Score one for the analogy—Eds.]. He never had a problem reconciling his two occupations (rather than making a schizoid separation). [Score another for the analogy, as this book will show—Eds.]. In temperament he could not have been more different from Franz Kafka: a solid, patriarchal, deeply self-satisfied man, who allowed no doubts or demons in his life. [In these respects the analogy is inappropriate—Eds.]." (Private communication, February 23, 2007).

4. Reiner Stach, *Kafka: The Decisive Years*, trans. Shelley Frisch (New York: Harcourt, 2005).

5. Corngold, *Lambent Traces*, xii.

6. We were reminded of this passage after consulting Richard Heinemann's excellent "Kafka's Oath of Service: 'Der Bau' and the Dialectic of Bureaucratic Mind," *PMLA*, vol. 111, no. 2. (March, 1996), 256–70. http://links.jstor.org/sici

?sici=0030-8129%28199603%29111%3A2%3C256%3AKOOS%22B%3E2.0
.CO%3B2-5.

7. Derrida, Jacques, "Before the Law," *Acts of Literature*, ed. Derek At-
tridge (New York: Routledge, 1992), 181–220.

8. Recent research by Wolf Kittler shows that Kafka's knowledge of trench
warfare, as it might shape the preoccupations of the master builder of *The Burrow*, is owed to Bernhard Kellermann, "Der Krieg unter der Erde," in *Das
große Jahr 1914–15*, a book about World War I that Kafka owned.

9. Anthony Northey, "Myths and Realities in Kafka Biography," in *The
Cambridge Companion to Kafka*, ed. Julian Preece (Cambridge: Cambridge
UP, 2002), 200.

10. "heißt nicht an unserem Gewissen, sondern was viel ärger ist an unsern
Beinen rütteln" (KKAF 1, 356).

11. *Unfashionable Observations*, trans. Richard Gray, *The Complete Works
of Nietzsche*, ed. Ernst Behler, (Stanford: Stanford UP, 1995), 2:167.

12. Franz Kafka, *Amtliche Schriften*, eds. Klaus Hermsdorf and Benno Wagner (Frankfurt a.M.: Fischer, 2004).

KAFKA AND THE MINISTRY OF WRITING

Parts of this introductory essay were previously published in "Kafkas Schloß:
Das Amt des Schreibens," *Odradeks Lachen: Fremdheit bei Kafka*, eds. Hans-
jörg Bay and Christof Hamann (Freiburg i. Br.: Rombach, 2006), 205–229.

1. "Das Wort 'sein' bedeutet im Deutschen beides: Da-sein und Ihm-gehören."
KKAN1, 123.

2. The passage continues: "How did you get on these lofty, useless pathways? Does that deserve a serious question, a serious answer? Perhaps, but not
yours, that is a matter for loftier rulers. Quick, retreat!" I leave these potent
words undiscussed for now.

3. Cf. Nietzsche: "Every artist knows how far from any feeling of letting
himself go his 'most natural' state is—the free ordering, placing, disposing, giving form in the moment of 'inspiration'—and how strictly and subtly he obeys
thousandfold laws precisely then, laws that precisely on account of their hard-
ness and determination defy all formulation through concepts (even the firmest
concept is, compared with them, not free of fluctuation, multiplicity, and ambiguity)." *Beyond Good and Evil*, Section 5, aphorism 188, in *Basic Writings of
Nietzsche*, ed. and trans. Walter Kaufmann (New York: The Modern Library,
1968), 290–91.

4. As Heidegger's concept of *Dasein* is articulated in *Being and Time* in
"Existentialien," so the world of K in *The Castle* is articulated in elements of
Schriftstellersein that one could call "Scriptorialien." Martin Heidegger, *Being
and Time*, trans. John Macquarrie and Edward Robinson (New York: Harper
& Row, 1962).

5. "Bureaucrats make it a point of pride to defeat the intelligent, even when
they are supposed to be on the same side." Frank Kermode, "Disgusting," a review of vol. 2: *Against the Christians* by John Haffenden, *London Review of*

Books, vol. 28, no. 22, November 16, 2006. http://www.lrb.co.uk/v28/n22/kerm01_.html.

6. Stanley Corngold, *Lambent Traces: Franz Kafka* (Princeton: Princeton University Press, 2004), xii.

7. This thesis was, to my knowledge, first put forward, in apodictic form, by Peter Mailloux, in his biography of Kafka, *A Hesitation before Birth*: "A [. . .] plausible interpretation of the castle, and of K's reasons for wanting to get there, one that takes into account its negative associations as well as its separation from the village and its inaccessibility, might therefore be that it represents the world of writing, something that always concerned Kafka and that particularly preoccupied him during the writing of *The Castle*. His definition of writing—as a 'descent to the dark powers,' a kind of death in life—parallels exactly his descriptions of the castle. K's inexplicable but irresistible attraction to it corresponds exactly to Kafka's impulse to write. His failure to get there reproduces Kafka's own condition that he had not yet succeeded in writing the kind of work he wanted. Most striking of all, the irony that Kafka developed throughout the winter of 1922, that he intimated whenever he talked about his writing—that writing, while the most important thing to him, was also the reason he had not yet managed to be part of life—is clearly present in K's relation to the castle. For him, the castle may be the place he most wants to get to, to the point that his very existence seems to be at stake if he cannot establish contact with it." *A Hesitation before Birth: The Life of Franz Kafka* (Newark, DE: University of Delaware Press, 1989), 524.

8. *Being and Time*, 205. Heidegger is writing about the "aim" of " 'poetical' discourse."

9. By alluding to bureaucratic organization, I refer to the necessary and inescapable condition of the functioning of higher social-political institutions in capitalist modernity—a condition I will elaborate.

10. Whereupon the time of the narrative of *The Castle* might be termed an *Organisationszeit*. This phrase was a slur on the lips of reactionary German agitators, aimed at the rule of the Weimar Republic (1919–33).

11. Some of this is caught up in Arnold Gehlen's comment: "When we reflect on the notion of personality in the strong sense as truly admirable productivity, we find it nowadays not so much in detached cultural—in literary or artistic—activity as there where one undertakes to realize the major tendencies of the spirit in the apparatus itself. . . . The personality is in this instance an institution." Arnold Gehlen, *Die Seele im technischen Zeitalter* (Hamburg: Rowohlt, 1957), 118.

12. Max Weber, *Wirtschaft und Gesellschaft. Grundriss der verstehenden Soziologie*, 5th rev. edition (Tübingen: Mohr, 1985), 552.

13. R.J. Kilcullen, On *Bureaucracy*, http://www.humanities.mq.edu.au/Ockham/y64l09.html.

14. Cornelius Castoriadis, *Political and Social Writings*, vol. 2, trans. and ed. David Ames Curtis (Minneapolis: University of Minnesota Press, 1988), 272. Cited in John Guillory, *Cultural Capital: The Problem of Literary Canon*

Formation (Chicago: University of Chicago Press, 1993), 248. This and the next few pages have greatly profited from Guillory's discussion, along with his mention of authorities. Thanks to Jeff Nunokawa for encouraging me to reread this remarkable book.

15. *Max Weber: On Charisma and Institution Building; Selected Papers*, ed. S.N. Eisenstadt (Chicago: University of Chicago Press, 1968), 69.

16. Guillory, 249.

17. Kafka's letter to Milena is dated "Saturday evening, July 31, 1920."

18. *Der Prozeß, Gesammelte Werke*, ed. Max Brod (Frankfurt a. M.: Fischer, 1965), 316.

19. Guillory, 250.

20. Claude Lefort, *The Political Forms of Modern Society: Bureaucracy, Democracy, Totalitarianism*, ed. John B. Thompson (Cambridge, MA: MIT Press, 1986), 109. Cited in Guillory, 250.

21. Hartmut Binder, *Kafka in neuer Sicht. Mimik, Gestik und Personengefüge als Darstellungsformen des Autobiographischen* (Stuttgart: J.B. Metzler, 1976), 409.

22. Binder, 411.

23. Joseph Vogl, "Kafka's Political Comedy," Course Book, "Kafka and the Law" (L8250), Columbia University Law School, Spring 2006, 3.

24. Weber, *Wirtschaft and Gesellschaft*, 552.

25. The cardinal piece of family language exchanged between father and son in *The Judgment* is the son's allusion to his father's pajama top as a "shirt without pockets"—that is, a shroud. The implication is parricidal, horrible, and so goes a long way toward explaining the father's retaliation in issuing a death sentence to his son. "Pockets" then becomes a sort of mnemonic for the Kafkan supermemory of a maximum of violence aimed at the father by his son. Wouldn't the day of reckoning, "When Gregor Samsa woke up," call for retribution along the trace line of "the pocket"? Wouldn't it be exactly right for the father to turn "the pocket" to his advantage, the "pocket" that marks the peak moment of filial hubris, by packing it with "small, hard apples"—a rhetorical ballistic reservoir? The text reads: "It was an apple; a second one came flying right after it; Gregor stopped dead with fear; further running was useless, for his father was determined to bombard him. He had filled his pockets from the fruit bowl on the buffet and was now pitching one apple after another, for the time being without taking good aim" (M 28f). Why, otherwise, "fill his *pockets*"? And so "the last shirt" is, contrary to all childish expectations, "the uniform." And what has Daddy got in his uniform coat? Pockets full of murderous family tropes.

26. Cf. Alan Bennett in *Kafka's Dick* (perish the title!): "Daily at his office in the Workers Accident Insurance Institute Kafka was confronted by those unfortunates who had been maimed and injured at work. Kafka was not crippled at work but at home. It's hardly surprising. If a family is a factory for turning out children then it is lacking in the most elementary safety precautions. There are no guard rails round that dangerous engine, the father. There are no safeguards against being scalded by the burning affection of the

mother. No mask is proof against its suffocating atmosphere. One should not be surprised that so many lose their balance and are mangled in the machinery of love. Take the Wittgensteins, etc." (London: Faber and Faber, 1987), xiii–xiv.

27. It cannot be supposed that Kafka knew Wordsworth, though Kafka was well read and knew something of Wordsworth's sources. Kafka's diaries and letters mention *As You Like It, The Comedy of Errors, Hamlet, King Lear, Othello, Richard III; Robinson Crusoe* (1719); and *Gulliver's Travels* (1726). He read Byron's diaries. A Romantic tradition celebrating a life of exorbitant feeling was hardly unknown to the author of *The Castle*, who writes of Frieda's craving to lie in a common grave with her beloved K.

28. William Wordsworth, *The Prelude*, ll. 470ff.

29. Joseph Vogl, 3.

30. Charles Bernheimer, *Flaubert and Kafka: Studies in Psychopoetic Structure* (New Haven: Yale University Press, 1982).

31. Ibid., 208–09, 193.

32. *Prozeß*, 316.

33. When his writing is going well, Kafka refers to himself as "inside" writing: when it is not, he feels, typically, that he has "dragged [himself] . . . out of writing by [his] . . . feet and must now bore [his] . . . way back in with [his] . . . head" (LF 166).

34. Some of the preceding paragraphs are abstracted from my *Franz Kafka: The Necessity of Form* (Ithaca: Cornell University Press, 1988), 162, but here the context is different.

35. Walter Benjamin, *Ursprung des deutschen Trauerspiels*, in *Gesammelte Schriften* 1/i, ed. Rolf Tiedemann and Hermann Schweppenhäuser (Frankfurt: Suhrkamp, 1974), 404.

36. See Stanley Corngold, "Von wegen der Wahrheit: Kafkas spätere Erzählungen und Aphorismen," trans. May Mergenthaler with the author, *Franz Kafka. Eine ethische und ästhetische Rechtfertigung*, ed. Beatrice Sandberg and Jakob Lothe (Freiburg: Rombach, 2002), 17–31.

37. Elizabeth Boa, "The Castle," *The Cambridge Companion to Kafka*, ed. Julian Preece (Cambridge: Cambridge University Press, 2002), 61–79.

38. Anne Jamison, "Form as Transgression: Structuring a Modern Poetics," PhD diss., Princeton University, 2001.

39. Binder, 265–507.

40. Kafka read *Gulliver's Travels*; if he had also read Swift's *A Tale of A Tub*, he would have encountered the figure of Momus in "A Digression Concerning Criticks" [sic], viz., "The Third and Noblest sort, is that of the TRUE CRITICK whose Original is the most Antient of all. Every True Critick is a Hero born, descending in a direct Line from a Celestial Stem, by Momus and Hybris, who begat Zoilus, who begat Tigellius, who begat Etcetera."

41. Apropos these passages, Richard Heinemann asks cogently, "What is the relation between Kafka's 'bureaucratic' nature and his literary being or 'Schriftstellersein' (Corngold, *Franz Kafka: The Necessity of Form* [Ithaca: Cornell University Press, 1988], 295) [. . .]? The boundary between Kafka's professional

and private lives, between his bureaucratic work and his writing, may be more permeable than critics have assumed." "Kafka's Oath of Service: 'Der Bau' and the Dialectic of Bureaucratic Mind," *PMLA*, vol. 111, no. 2. (March, 1996), 257.

42. Jeremy Adler, "In the Quiet Corners," *The Times Literary Supplement*, no. 5140 (October 5, 2001), 7.

43. "My development is now complete and, so far as I can see, there is nothing left to sacrifice; I need only throw my work in the office out of this complex in order to begin my real life" (D1 211).

44. Compare these *Steigerungen* with the ability to produce a *Zuspitzung*, or critical heightening, in the organization of the narrator's "powers," which the narrator of "'You,' I said . . ." specifically attributes to a higher society (*Gesellschaft*).

45. Benjamin, *Ursprung*, 353.

KAFKA'S OFFICE WRITINGS: HISTORICAL BACKGROUND AND INSTITUTIONAL SETTING

1. The files of this recruitment campaign are preserved in the Austrian State Archive, holdings of the Ministry of the Interior, Section V (Insurance), fascicle 60. According to the plans of the Ministry of Education, vocational courses to attract new staff were to be established in all Bohemian towns with a commercial college. As competent teaching staff was scarce, teachers were expected to travel from town to town. Although admission to service in public social insurance was formally controlled by a final exam at the end of each course, literally everyone was welcome: fifty-two out of fifty-two candidates of the Prague course Kafka attended successfully passed the exam. Nonetheless, in the following year, the enrollment at the Bohemian commercial college in Prague was so low that the course was not offered again. Interested readers will find further "blueprints" for almost any other organizational detail of Kafka's Nature Theater in the files specified above.

2. "I haven't seen it myself yet," Fanny, Karl's old acquaintance among the theater staff, has to "admit" at one point in their preliminary job talk (A 205–6).

3. Kafka to Hedwig Weiler, early October 1907.

4. "Any act whatever of man which causes damage to another obliges him by whose fault it occurred to make reparation" (Article 1382, Civil Code).

5. François Ewald, *Der Vorsorgestaat* (Frankfurt/M.: Suhrkamp, 1993), 21.

6. Ewald, 377.

7. Michel Foucault, *"Society Must be Defended": Lectures at the Collège de France, 1975–1976*, ed. Mauro Bertani and Alessandro Fontana, trans. David Macey (New York: Picador, 2003), 223.

8. Israel Zangwill, *The Principle of Nations* (New York: Macmillan 1917), 46–48.

9. Robert A. Kann, *A History of the Hapsburg Empire 1526–1918* (Berkeley/Los Angeles/London: University of California Press, 1974), 358.

10. Herbert Hofmeister, "Austria," in *The Evolution of Social Insurance 1881–1981. Studies of Germany, France, Great Britain, Austria and Switzerland*, ed. Peter A. Köhler and Hans F. Zacher in collaboration with Martin Partington (London: Frances Pinter, 1982), 277f.; 289.

11. See Hofmeister, 289f. (for Austria) and 292f. (for Germany).

12. Hofmeister, 265.

13. Moriz Ertl, *Das österreichische Unfallversicherungsgesetz. Die Genesis und die wesentlichen Bestimmungen desselben im Vergleiche mit der Unfallgesetzgebung anderer Staaten, insbesondere Deutschlands* (Leipzig/Vienna: Toeplitz & Deuticke, 1887), 28f.

14. Joseph Redlich, *Austrian War Government* (New Haven: Yale University Press, 1929), 1; 16f.

15. Redlich, 11.

16. Ferdinand Kürnberger, *Der Amerikamüde. Amerikanisches Kulturbild* (Frankfurt/M.: Insel, 1986). Kürnberger's 1855 novel was a major sourcebook for Kafka's America novel (*The Man who Disappeared*). For Plato, see Benno Wagner, "Der Bewerber und der Prätendent. Zur Selektivität der Idee bei Platon und Kafka," *Hofmannsthal Jahrbuch für Europäische Moderne* (Rombach: Freiburg, 2000), 8, 287.

17. For an original scene of this double occupation, see the confession of Kürnberger's bogus land surveyor: "humbug and business have nothing to do with one another. In business I am the most reliable man shone upon by the New York sun; humbug is my recreation, my private affair outside of business. . . . In humbug I tax human foolishness;—but in the shop the individual looks to me for his needs, the necessities of body and soul—to betray his trust on these grounds would undermine the existence of all states and peoples" (*Der Amerikamüde*, 86). It would take some time to find a more precise description of Kafka's personal division of labor—it being understood that the humbug/business distinction must be applied to both sides of the clerk/poet distinction.

18. Ertl, 15.

19. Stöger, "Art. 'Arbeiterunfallversicherung,'" in *Österreichisches Staatswörterbuch. Handbuch des gesamten österreichischen öffentlichen Rechtes*, ed. Dr. Ernst Mischler and Dr. Josef Ulbrich, vol. 1, A–E (Vienna: Hölder, 1905), cited in Hofmeister, 316.

20. *Fünfundzwanzig Jahre Arbeiter-Unfall-Versicherung. Bericht über die Entwicklung der Arbeiter-Unfall-Versicherungs-Anstalt für das Königreich Böhmen in der Zeit vom 1. November 1889 bis 31. Oktober 1914*, ed. Dr. Robert Marschner (Prague: Selbstverlag, 1915), 155.

21. Erich Graf Kielmannsegg, *Geschäftsvereinfachung und Kanzleireform bei öffentlichen Ämtern und Behörden. Ein Informationskurs in sechs Vorträgen* (Vienna: Manz, 1906), 31.

22. Kielmannsegg, 20.

23. Kielmannsegg, 6.

24. Kielmannsegg, 40ff. We find a grandiose parody of such a raid in chapter 5 of *The Castle*, in the superintendent's vain search for the file regarding the issue of K's employment as a land surveyor.

25. *Gutachten über das Regierungsprogramm für die Reform und den Ausbau der Arbeiter-Versicherung* (Report by the Committee of the Chambers of Commerce and the Association of Industrialists in Austria), (Vienna, 1906), 57.

26. "These workers care only about a fair allocation of pensions," the employers argued, in order to exclude the workers from the organization of accident insurance (*Gutachten*, 64). While this allegation was mocked by Social Democrats and unionists, it returned as an implicit quote in Kafka's 1917 story "Building the Great Wall of China," where the architect distinguishes his professional class from the rankings of the workers by the former's commitment to the higher purpose of the defensive construction: "such men were driven, of course, not only by a passion to perform the most thorough work but also by impatience to see the construction finally rise up in its perfection. The day laborer knows nothing of this impatience, he is driven only by pay" (KSS 114).

27. Leo Verkauf, *Die Sozialversicherung als Organisationsproblem. Ein Votum zur österreichischen Regierungsvorlage* (Vienna: Verlag des Arbeiterschutz, 1911), 106. Kafka's "Chinese" transcription of this diagnosis reads: "Now, the result of such opinions is, to a certain extent, a free, ungoverned life. By no means immoral; on my travels I have hardly ever encountered such purity of morals as in my homeland. But still, a life that is subject to no current law and follows only directives and warnings that extend to us from ancient times" (KSS 122).

28. Verkauf, 101f.

29. Verkauf, 186.

30. *Gutachten der territorialen Arbeiter-Unfallversicherungsanstalten über das Regierungsprogramm für die Reform und den Ausbau der Arbeiterversicherung* (Report by the Association of the Crownland Workmen's Accident Insurance Institutes), (Vienna: Jasper, 1907), 3.

31. *Gutachten*, 5.

32. Kann, 439.

33. Redlich, 25.

34. See the programmatic writings by Karl Renner (pseud. Rudolf Springer), *Der Kampf der österreichischen Nationen um den Staat* (Leipzig: Deuticke, 1902); Bruno Bauer, *Die Nationalitätenfrage und die Sozialdemokratie* (Vienna: Brand, 1907); and the Social Democratic monthly *Der Kampf*, published by Renner, Bauer, and Friedrich Adler, starting in 1908.

35. Foucault, "Society Must be Defended," 223.

36. See Kafka's letter to Max Brod of November 13, 1917: "The Institute is closed to Jews. . . . It's inexplicable how the two Jews on the staff . . . got in, and there will not be any more." The other Jew was Siegmund Fleischmann, whose failure to handle the critical situation of the legal department when Marschner undertook to clean up that Augean stable of insurance fraud and nepotism led to the establishment of a special "claims department," with Kafka as head. Fleischmann and Kafka cooperated closely; Fleischmann, who regularly wrote for insurance journals, even asked Kafka to coauthor some articles with him, but Kafka declined.

37. For a detailed account of this highly embarrassing scene, see Kafka's letter to Felice Bauer of January 9, 1913 (LF 146–148).

38. See *Amtliche Schriften*, Materialien, doc. 19 (b).

39. In doc. 1, Kafka carefully hints at that opposition. In his letter to Felice Bauer of May 14, 1916, Kafka quotes Marschner speaking frankly about his "enemies" of that time (LF 468.).

40. In March 1908, the Munich bimonthly *Hyperion* had published eight pieces of Kafka's short prose under the title "Betrachtung" (Observation).

41. Foucault, 253.

42. Alois Gütling, "Beiträge zu den Themen Unfallverhütung und Unfallstatistik," *Österreichische Zeitschrift für öffentliche und private Versicherung,* 1916, 189.

43. "A slap by the master protects the apprentice better than the best safety devices," he quoted an industrial factory foreman skeptical of safety technology (doc. 13).

44. *Kafka's Other Trial: The Letters to Felice*, trans. by Christopher Middleton (New York, Schocken, 1974), 80.

45. On Kafka's comparison of writing *The Judgment* to a "birth," see Stanley Corngold, *Lambent Traces: Franz Kafka* (Princeton: Princeton University Press, 2004), 13f.

46. LF 277; 373. The fear of his inaptitude for office work may have been increased by his failure in the Renelt case, which had gained some prominence earlier on in his correspondence with Felice Bauer (see commentary to doc. 12).

47. See *Amtliche Schriften*, Materialien, doc. 50c.

48. Giorgio Agamben, *Homo Sacer: Sovereign Power and Bare Life*, trans. Daniel Heller-Roazen (Stanford: Stanford University Press, 1998), 122.

49. See the Institute's Annual Report for 1915, *Amtliche Schriften*, Materialien, doc. 40.

50. See *Amtliche Schriften*, Materialien, doc. 50d.

51. *Národní Listy*, October 26, 1919. For a documentation of this debate in Czech and German newspapers, see *Amtliche Schriften,* Materialien, doc. 46.

52. See Marek Nekula, *Franz Kafkas Sprachen, "... in einem Stockwerk des innern babylonischen Turmes ..."* (Tübingen: Niemeyer, 2003), chap. 9.

COMMENTARY 1

1. "Eine Festrede," in *Hochzeitsvorbereitungen auf dem Lande und andere Prosa aus dem Nachlaß*, ed. Max Brod (New York/Frankfurt a.M.: Fischer, 1953), 426–429.

DOCUMENT 2. THE SCOPE OF COMPULSORY INSURANCE FOR THE BUILDING TRADES (1908)

1. All phrases in brackets are supplied by the editors.

2. As Kafka's essay undertakes an in-depth interpretation of § 1 of the accident law of December 28, 1887, we render the law's full text here in translation to support this and further references:

§. 1. All workers and managers employed in factories, iron works, mines for nonreserved minerals, shipyards, ship stocks, and quarries, as well as in all facilities belonging to these firms, are insured against the consequences of workplace accidents according to the provisions of this law.

The same applies to workers and managers employed in commercial firms whose business includes performing construction work or who are otherwise employed in construction. This provision shall not apply to workers whose sole task is the execution of occasional repairs in construction but who are not employed in a commercial firm of the designated kind. For the construction of residential and commercial buildings of one story on level ground, and for other agricultural buildings, there is no compulsory insurance insofar as only the builder, members of his household, or other residents of the same site who do not execute such construction commercially are employed.

The following are the same as the businesses listed in the first paragraph according to this law:

1. Businesses in which explosive materials are made or used;
2. Commercial agricultural or forestry businesses that use boilers or other driving mechanisms powered by elementary forces (wind, water, steam, coal gas, hot air, electricity, etc.) or by animals. This provision does not apply to businesses for which a powered machine that is not owned by the business facilities is used only temporarily.

If a powered machine belonging to the facilities in an agricultural or forestry business is used in such a way that only a certain number of workers and managers are exposed to the danger of the entire machine operation, the insurance obligation is limited to those persons who are exposed to this danger.

There will be a separate law for the insurance of workers and managers employed in mines for reserved minerals and their facilities against the consequences of workplace accidents.

According to this law, workers and managers also include apprentices, volunteers, interns, and other persons who receive no or low payment because they have not yet completed their education.

3. Law of July 20, 1894, regarding the extension of accident insurance (Extension Law):

With the agreement of both houses of the Reich Council I hereby decree as follows:
Article I. In so far as they are not already subject to compulsory insurance according to the law of December 28, 1887 [. . .] regarding workers' accident insurance, the following businesses shall be subject to compulsory insurance according to the provisions of that law:

1. The entire railroad industry, regardless of what motorized power is used for operation.

2. The work of all other firms concerned with commercially transporting people or goods by land or on rivers and inland waters, save the exceptions set down in § 2 of the cited law regarding the shipping companies subject to maritime law.

3. Excavations.

4. Businesses involving the commercial cleaning of streets and buildings [. . .].

5. Commercially operated warehousing businesses, including the warehouses and large-scale wood and coal storage.

6. Permanent theaters, even if they are not operated year round, with regard to all workers and managers employed therein as well as the actors.

7. The professional fire department.

8. Commercial canal cleaners.

9. Commercial chimney- sweeps.

10. Commercial stonemasons, well-diggers and ironworkers, with regard to all business categories that are not yet included under compulsory insurance.

COMMENTARY 3

1. Note here the figure of stating, then revoking, then restating the conditions of security; we will encounter this figure again in Kafka's great fragmentary novella of 1917, "Building the Great Wall of China."

2. In Kafka's scrapbook there is a postscript to these reflections, entitled "A Page from an Old Document." Here, the Chinese narrator confronts us with the fragment of a damaged old manuscript, which consists of an eyewitness report. A cobbler describes the horrors of a siege of the imperial city from the days of the nomad occupation of China (the temporal and spatial logic of Kafka's two narratives follows precisely the real course of events in Chinese history between the thirteenth and seventeenth centuries). This report underlines the importance of a strong central power, of strong leadership for the defense of the country against foreign enemies, and thus revokes the conclusion of the main narrator of "Building the Great Wall of China." We see no further attempt in the file to reconcile these two conflicting views on political organization.

3. As Kafka's papers show, in the decades following these messages, anything even resembling a reliable system of legal security for Austrian workmen, like the Emperor's message to the Chinese people, would remain "a dream."

4. See note 2.

COMMENTARY 6

1. Leo Verkauf, *Die Sozialversicherung als Organisationsproblem. Ein Votum zur österreichischen Regierungsvorlage* (Vienna: Verlag des "Arbeiterschutz," 1911), 176.

2. *Gutachten über das Regierungsprogramm für die Reform und den Ausbau der Arbeiter-Versicherung. Bericht des Präsidial-Ausschusses der vereinigten Handels- und Gewerbekammern und des Zentralverbandes der Industriellen Österreichs* (Vienna 1906), 57.

COMMENTARY 7

1. Ludwig Wokurek, *Die Österreichische Unfallversicherung. Eine kritische Studie* (Leipzig/Vienna: Franz Deuticke,1898), 42. The picture of Sais refers to the veiled figure in a well-known Romantic novel of this name by Friedrich von Hardenberg. "The Veiled Figure of Sais" is also the title of a 1795 ballad by Friedrich Schiller. Like Hardenberg, he refers to Egyptian mythology to illustrate the impossibility of a direct contact with truth.

2. A formal or official statement of a transaction or proceeding; specifically, the detailed record of the procedure and results in a scientific experiment; hence, experimental procedure.

COMMENTARY 8

1. "Hinter Tetschen-Bodenbach wird kein Mensch Kafka verstehen." Max Brod, *Über Franz Kafka* (Frankfurt a.M.: S. Fischer, 1974), 278.

2. Hartmut Binder, "Bauformen" in *Kafka-Handbuch*, vol. 2, *Das Werk und seine Wirkung*, ed. Hartmut Binder (Stuttgart: Kröner, 1979), 63.

3. See "Die Arbeiterversicherung und die Unternehmer" (Workmen's Insurance and Employers) in *Die Arbeit. Politische Zeitschrift. Zentralorgan der österreichischen Arbeitgeber* (Work. Political Magazine. Official publication of Austrian employers), 18. Jg., 17. September 1911, no. 1196, 2: "An essay in the *Tetschen-Bodenbacher Zeitung* of September 13 offers a remarkable commentary on the development of workmen's accident insurance in Austria. Although the author of the article in question takes great pains to view matters from an objective standpoint, one would not be far wrong to assume that he is close to the executives at the Prague Institute. In any case, his remarks on the topic deserve great attention, nor can we allow some passages to go uncontested from the standpoint of employers."

COMMENTARY 9

1. Cf. Ludwig Wokurek, *Die Österreichische Unfallversicherung* (Leipzig/Vienna: Franz Deuticke, 1898), 8.

2. *Denkschrift der territorialen Arbeiter-Unfallversicherungsanstalten zu dem Entwurf eines Gesetzes, betreffend die Sozialversicherung,* (Brünn: R.M. Rohrer, [1909]), 22; 20.

3. Arthur Schnitzler, *Professor Bernhardi* (Berlin: S. Fischer, 1913), 223.

4. "Herr Dr. Kafka? Mit mir sprechen!"

COMMENTARY 10

1. Gilles Deleuze and Félix Guattari, *Kafka. Toward a Minor Literature*, trans. Dana Polan, foreword by Réda Bensmaia (Minneapolis: University of Minnesota Press, 1986), 50.

COMMENTARY 11

1. See Klaus Hermsdorf, "Arbeit and Amt als Erfahrung und Gestaltung," in *Franz Kafka, "Hochlöblicher Verwaltungsausschuß!" Amtliche Schriften*, ed. Klaus Hermsdorf (Frankfurt a.M.: Luchterhand, 1991), 52f.

COMMENTARY 13

1. Friedrich Nietzsche, *Beyond Good and Evil*, trans. Walter Kaufmann (New York: Random House, 2000), 287f.

2. "Sozialversicherung und Wehrkraft," in *Zeitschrift für die gesamte Versicherungswissenschaft*, vol. 16 (1916), 367.

3. Theodor Herzl, *The Jewish State* (New York: Scopus Publishing Company, 1943), 45. A fuller treatment is found in Benno Wagner, " 'No One Indicates the Direction': The Question of Leadership in Kafka's Later Stories" (KSS 316ff.).

COMMENTARY 16

1. Paul Kaufmann, *Soziale Fürsorge und deutscher Siegeswille* (Berlin: Vahlen, 1915), 19.

2. Kafka began to write his story on or shortly after October 5, 1914—a few days after Kaufmann's speech in Prague. For a detailed analysis of this connection, see Benno Wagner, " 'Die Majuskel-Schrift unsres Erden-Daseins.' Kafkas Kulturversicherung," *Hofmannsthal Jahrbuch zur europäischen Moderne*, vol. 12, 2004, 358f.

DOCUMENT 17. A PUBLIC PSYCHIATRIC HOSPITAL
FOR GERMAN-BOHEMIA (1916)

1. The term "Cisleithania" refers to the Austrian part of the Empire.

COMMENTARY 17

1. See Sigmund Freud, "Einleitung," *Zur Psychoanalyse der Kriegsneurosen* (Internationaler Psychoanalytischer Verlag: Vienna, 1919), 5.

2. *Amtliche Schriften*, CD Materialien, no. 39.

3. Heinrich Rauchberg, *Kriegerheimstätten* (Vienna: Manz, 1916).

COMMENTARY 18

1. Werner Sombart, *Händler und Helden. Patriotische Besinnungen* (Munich, Leipzig: Duncker & Humblot, 1915), 64.

2. Sombart, 76f.

FROM KAFKA TO KAFKAESQUE

1. *Ass'n of Cmty. Orgs. for Reform Now v. FEMA*, 463 F. Supp. 2d 26, 35 (2006).

2. *New York Times*, April 4, 2007, A 3.

3. *New York Times*, January 25, 2007, B1.

4. Richard A. Posner, *Law and Literature* (revised and enlarged edition) (Cambridge: Harvard University Press, 1998), 135.

5. *Olberding v. Illinois Central Ry. Co.*, 346 U.S. 338.

6. Ernst Pawel, *The Nightmare of Reason: A Life of Franz Kafka.* (New York: Farrar, Straus & Giroux, 1984), 187.

7. 163 U. S. 537 (1896).

8. 347 U. S. 483 (1954).

9. 349 U. S. 294 (1955).

10. 396 U. S. 1218 (1969).

ABOUT THE EDITORS

Stanley Corngold graduated from Columbia and Cornell universities and has been professor of German and Comparative Literature at Princeton since 1981. He is well known as a translator and commentator of the works of Franz Kafka (his two editions of *The Metamorphosis* published with Bantam and Norton have sold nearly two million copies), and he has completed a Norton Critical Edition of *Kafka's Selected Stories* (2007), which includes his new translations of thirty of Kafka's stories, along with notes, essays, and commentaries. He is past President and Honorary Member of the Board of the Kafka Society of America. His latest critical work on Franz Kafka is *Lambent Traces: Franz Kafka* (Princeton University Press, 2004). Corngold is also the author of *Complex Pleasure: Forms of Feeling in German Literature* (Stanford University Press, 1998); *The Fate of the Self: German Writers and French Theory* (Columbia and Duke University Press, 1986, 1994); *Borrowed Lives* (a novel; State University of New York Press, 1991); *Franz Kafka: The Necessity of Form* (Cornell University Press, 1988); *The Commentators' Despair: The Interpretation of Kafka's "Metamorphosis"* (Associated Faculty Press, 1973); and many articles and edited books dealing with German literature and philosophy, literary theory, and media studies.

Jack Greenberg is Professor of Law at the Columbia University Law School. Along with Thurgood Marshall, he argued a number of historic civil rights cases before the U.S. Supreme Court, including *Brown v. Board of Education*. From 1961–1984 Greenberg was director-counsel of the NAACP Legal Defense Fund and thereafter joined the faculty at Columbia University Law School, where he also served as Dean of Columbia College from 1989 to 1993. Throughout his career, Greenberg has remained active in civil-rights and human-rights causes.

In 2001 Greenberg was among twenty-eight distinguished Americans honored by President Bill Clinton with Presidential Citizens Medals at a White House ceremony. President Clinton said of Greenberg, "In the courtroom and the classroom, Jack Greenberg has been a crusader for freedom and equality for more than half a century." Greenberg has been the recipient of many other awards, including the American Bar Association Thurgood Marshall Award in 1996 and an Honorary Doctor of Laws from Howard University in 2004.

Among Greenberg's publications are *Crusaders in the Courts: How a Dedicated Band of Lawyers Fought for the Civil Rights Revolution* (Basic Books, 1994), a history of the NAACP LDF (the book received the ABA's Silver Gavel Award), and, most recently, *Brown v. Board of Education: Witness to a Landmark Decision* (Twelve Tables Press, 2004).

Benno Wagner is Associate Professor of Literary Theory and Modern German Literature at the University of Siegen (Germany). He received his Ph.D. in 1990, *summa cum laude,* for a dissertation on the semiotics of political dissidence in postwar Germany. In 1999, he completed a major work on Franz Kafka entitled *Der Unversicherbare: Kafkas Protokolle* (The uninsurable: Kafka's records), which established his teaching career in Germany. Together with the late Klaus Hermsdorf of Humboldt University, Berlin, he published a comprehensive, very favorably reviewed two-volume edition of Franz Kafka's *Amtliche Schriften* (Office writings) for the Frankfurt critical edition of Kafka's works (Frankfurt, a.M.: S. Fischer, 2004).

Wagner's other books include *Im Dickicht der politischen Kultur* (In the thickets of political culture), a study of the party system, media symbolism, and so-called alternative groups in Germany in the early 1990s (Fink, Munich, 1992). Together with Friedrich Balke, he edited *Zeit des Ereignisses—Ende der Geschichte?* (Does this age of "great events" imply the end of history?) (Fink, Munich, 1992), and *Vom Nutzen und Nachteil historischer Vergleiche. Der Fall Bonn—Weimar* (On the uses and disadvantages of historical analogies: the case of Bonn and Weimar) (Campus, Frankfurt a.M., 1997). With Ernst Müller and Karl Ludwig Pfeiffer, he edited *Geisteswissen* (Knowledge of the human spirit) (Verlag für Akademische Schriften, Frankfurt a.M., 1991). Benno Wagner has published widely on modern German literature and is currently preparing a trilogy that will reconstruct Kafka's literary use of such specialized professional categories as risk, accident, insurance, compensation, and file keeping as the basis of a general model of modern culture. The trilogy is entitled *Kafkas Akten* (Kafka's files); volume 1, *Eine Poetik des Unfalls* (A poetics of accidents), is due out in 2009.

INDEX

Page references followed by *fig* indicate a figure or photograph.